The Revolutionary Career
of Maximilien Robespierre

PLATE I
(Private collection)

The Revolutionary Career
of Maximilien Robespierre

David P. Jordan

THE FREE PRESS
A Division of Macmillan, Inc.
NEW YORK

Collier Macmillan Publishers
LONDON

The Free Press
A Division of Macmillan, Inc.
866 Third Avenue, New York, N.Y. 10022

Collier Macmillan Canada, Inc.

Printed in the United States of America

printing number

1 2 3 4 5 6 7 8 9 10

Jordan, David P.
  The revolutionary career of Maximilien Robespierre.

  Bibliography: p.
  Includes index.
  1. Robespierre, Maximilien, 1758–1794. 2. France—
History—Revolution, 1789–1794. I. Title.
DC146.R6J67 1985   944.04   85–1871
ISBN 0-02-916530-X

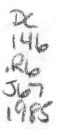

For
Peter R. McKeon
1938–1979

Contents

List of
Illustrations

Acknowledgments

"THIS STORY WILL WRITE ITSELF" was a favorite expression of the Night City Editor who taught me how to be a reporter. The stories he assigned no more wrote themselves than has this book; but while it was not writing itself I had much help which gave direction to my gropings.

I shamelessly exploited the intelligence, taste, and kindness (not to mention patience) of Richard S. Levy and Jonathan L. Marwil. Both read the manuscript in its several versions, improved it immeasurably, and tolerated the addition of Robespierre's company to our friendship. Their labors are everywhere evident to me, and as I was the beneficiary of their work so too will be the reader. The title and its implications I owe to Jonathan Marwil.

Burton Bledstein helped sharpen the argument of the book. Stanley Mellon, who first taught me French history and continues to do so, made several radiant suggestions which I have silently incorporated.

Dr. Colin Lucas, of Balliol College, whose academic obligations exploded my assumptions about the leisurely life of an Oxford don, found time to read the manuscript in an earlier (longer) version and made suggestions both numerous and shrewd. These too I have gratefully incorporated.

My editor, Joyce Seltzer, is a worthy representative of an endangered species, an editor who edits. Her deft skill has enhanced my prose and the book.

With the exception of the Humanities Institute of the University of Illinois at Chicago, whose fellowship gave me the leisure to rethink and rewrite, no fund or foundation, agency or institution, whether public or private local or national, thought a book on Robespierre worthy of support.

The Notes at the end of the text will, I hope, make abundantly clear my debt to those who have already written about Robespierre. The references in parentheses in the text are to the volume and page of Robespierre's *Oeuvres complètes* (1903–1967).

Those who knew and those who loved Peter McKeon, to whom this book is dedicated, will understand the void left by his death and my desire to offer this memorial.

D. P. J.

Prologue

PLATE II
(Carnavalet Museum)

ROBESPIERRE has no Paris monument. Only a fairly recent Métro station, on an obscure line that predominantly serves working-class Paris, carries his name. There was no monument in his natal Arras until the 1930s, when the left-wing Popular Front government was able to place a small plaque on the last house he inhabited before departing for the Revolution and his destiny. The project for an accompanying statue was never realized. Most recently, in 1949, on the 160th anniversary of the Fall of the Bastille, a statue was dedicated in the city of Saint-Denis, a poor, working-class town hugging the Paris periphery. The work was executed by a certain Séraphin and erected in the Place du Théâtre. It is the only such memorial in France. Saint-Denis was a provocative choice: it is the site of the first great Gothic cathedral whose crypt has for centuries been the traditional burial place for French kings. The remains of Louis XVI, whom Robespierre helped send to the guillotine, were ostentatiously interred here in 1816. The inscription on Robespierre's statue reads: "A Maximilien Robespierre l'Incorruptible."

Almost as if he knew his memory would not be preserved in stone or metal, Robespierre created his own monument in words. The French Revolution divided the nation, its people and its politics, so deeply that, with very few exceptions—perhaps General LeClerc, the hero of the liberation from German occupation—France does not have national heroes, only partisan ones. The old wounds are closed but unhealed, and national crisis often starts the bleeding. Robespierre was one of the creators of this division. He saw and fought the Revolution as a struggle to the death between the Revolution and the counterrevolution, "them and us," virtue and vice. He offered no compromises or accommodations and prided himself on his rectitude. A national monument, especially one in Paris, was (and remains) an unthinkable compromise. Other revolutionaries have their streets and statutes; but Robespierre, posthumously as during his life, remains beyond national generosity.

But if France cannot remember her revolutionary hero unequivocally, the Bolsheviks had no such difficulties. In the garden of Alexander, under the walls of the Kremlin, a monument to Robespierre was erected several months after the October Revolution. The decree was signed by Lenin, who describes Robespierre as a Bolshevik *avant la lettre*, the inspiration and leader of the Jacobins, "one of the highest summits attained by the working class in struggling for its emancipation."[1] The statue itself was hastily made and has fallen to dust, but there remains a Quai Robespierre in Moscow.

This Bolshevik determination to memorialize Robespierre as a pre-

cursor, a great figure in an ongoing revolutionary history, is an appropriate remembrance. In the last five years of a short life, the years that hold his revolutionary career, Robespierre spoke frequently of the continuity of revolutionary aspirations and predicted an eternal future for revolutions and revolutionaries. At the same time he saw himself as the first of what might be thought a new race of men: a man wholly and absolutely devoted to revolution. It is this new man that he revealed and analyzed in his speeches, pamphlets, and journalism, which constitute an extraordinary testament.

He thought his career unique (as did many of his contemporaries) and set himself the task of being its chronicler. Among the Greeks and Romans, whom he deeply admired, he recalled regularly a few figures, none of them rebels or revolutionaries. Cato the Elder he invoked as a model of republican virtue to be emulated. The patrician popular rebels Tiberius and Gaius Gracchus, who led a movement for land reform, he mentioned only once. Algernon Sidney, the English republican executed in 1677 for a plot against Charles II, he invoked with Cato as an exemplar of personal and civic virtue. William Tell, the almost legendary Swiss hero, whose prestige was enormous in the eighteenth century, goes unnoted. There are no French rebels in Robespierre's pantheon, and he was unimpressed by any of the American rebels. He loathed Lafayette and thought Tom Paine, who participated in the French Revolution as an elected deputy to the Convention Assembly as well as a pamphleteer, a lackey of the moderates. Cromwell he detested as a military dictator who had used the English Revolution for personal gain. The Corsican rebel, Pasquali Paoli, who had led the fight to free his island from Genoa when Robespierre was a boy, is neglected. If the revolutionary is a figure of pregnant significance, Robespierre thought himself the first of the species. His revolutionary self was as original as the Revolution he served.

Robespierre is one of those rare figures in history who are perceived by their contemporaries as well as posterity as embodying the essence of the passions and contradictions of their historical moment, who seem to personify an age or a movement; whose lives represent general propositions about significant human experience. Robespierre is as central to any history of the French Revolution and republican France as Louis XIV is to the age of monarchy. His revolutionary career has become a reference point for judgments of the French Revolution, a metaphor for all revolutions and revolutionaries. He himself did a good deal to encourage and even suggest this perception. He was self-conscious about his political role, and this awareness shaped all his utterances. He spoke much, and often, and always in public, about himself, but not in a familiar biographical or autobiographical mode. Rather it is the career he describes and analyzes: the private man is overwhelmed by the public revolutionary.

And he spoke of himself in a language usually reserved to express states of mind or feelings not associated with revolution. The complex of instincts and thoughts, emotions and perceptions, actions and feelings, the elaborate and intricate relationships between muscles and brains and heart that we sum up as the self, had no existence apart from the Revolution. His health, his physical well-being, was a topic of public revelation. He spoke of being consumed by the Revolution as by a slow fever; and this was more than a simile. His physical self was bound to the Revolution in a vague yet intimate way. His body as well as his soul were possessed by the great historical forces he simultaneously personified and analyzed. He spoke of himself as a living martyr, a phrase that echoed what was said of those thrown into the horrendous prisons of the monarchy. He revealed his emotional life by describing his passion for liberty, equating this heartfelt inspiration with those less exalted but imperious urges that drove most men. And in all this revelation and analysis of self, this introspection made public and central to his political thinking, Robespierre sought to convey the uniqueness of his revolutionary self while simultaneously revealing a revolutionary Everyman.

Contemporaries noticed and remarked this powerful synthesis of the ego and the Revolution in Robespierre, and several correctly attributed his hold over them to these qualities. This total politicization of the inner and outer man—impossible under the *ancien régime*—is what made him a revolutionary. Robespierre's identity merged with that of his historical moment. His was a totally political self, and he had the capacity not only to see that he was unique (enemies would say odd) but to analyze and reveal this unexpected self.

Robespierre was a literary intellectual, as were most of the leaders of the French Revolution. He bent his skills to creating not an unforgettable personality, but a political type, the revolutionary. A generation before the Romantics enshrined the revolutionary (along with the artist) as hero, Robespierre had presented himself to his contemporaries as such. The nineteenth-century fascination with the rebel, the revolutionary as creator, almost a force of nature essential for the renovation of mankind, helped preserve Robespierre's memory and gave his self-revelations a new and complementary context. For some of the French Romantics especially, Robespierre was no figment of the literary imagination, no Byronic creation. He was an authentic revolutionary hero. Perhaps he was a bit too reserved and rational for the Romantics— certainly too radical for many—and too rarely a man of action, yet he benefited from the new sensibility as did revolutionaries generally. To this day in French political culture there are those anxious to declare themselves descendants of Robespierre: the list of self-proclaimed *robespierristes* in the nineteenth century is more extensive. France's revolutionary tradition, which Robespierre had an important part in forming and describing, was often exported and carried his fame and example throughout the world. Even the career of such professional revolutionaries as the Russian nobleman Alexander Herzen are beholden to Robespierre, although Herzen thought his predecessor a repellent man. The novelists and playwrights who chose the Revolution as a subject— Victor Hugo, Charles Dickens, Georg Büchner—all imagined a Robespierre larger than life. Thomas Carlyle, whose history of the French Revolution (along with Dickens's novel *A Tale of Two Cities*) profoundly influenced English views, was fascinated by Robespierre, whose memory depended as much on those who saw in him all the demonic energy of the Revolution as well as on those who adored him. Robespierre the revolutionary troubled the consciences of future generations and filled their imaginations. The Bolshevik apotheosis is the culmination of a century of mixed and sometimes bitter remembrance, but enduring attention.

It is the persona Robespierre himself created that formed the basis for all this posthumous attention. He left no confessions of a private self in the manner of Rousseau's celebrated book, although he was deeply influenced by that remarkable work. His creation of a political self has proved as durable and perhaps as influential. Robespierre was and has described the prototype of the modern revolutionary. Long after the specific events to which he responded have been forgotten by all but the specialist, the revolutionary lives on, a cerebral, almost abstract being without a satisfying mundane dimension.

His remarkable dominance over contemporaries and hence his importance in the Revolution seems independent of those special powers of attraction that are sometimes called charisma. Robespierre himself attributed his success to the rightness of his principles and the sincerity with which they were expressed. But many of these same principles, on the sincere lips of others, were less compelling. It is the connection between principles and self that he recognized yet could not fully analyze. He was his ideas rather than their conduit. Made to flow through another self, Robespierre's ideology became transformed, maybe diluted.

He had a gift for analysis, argument, and abstraction, and possessed rhetorical and political skills of a very high order. But it was the self that infused these talents with a unique intensity and purpose. Just as he insisted on binding himself physically and spiritually to the Revolution, so were he and his ideas inseparably bound.

Purpose and technique were perfectly harmonized in Robespierre. The style and the man, a favorite juxtaposition of the eighteenth century, were one. Revealing himself to contemporaries from the speaker's rostrum, Robespierre said almost nothing about his life as a private man. His childhood, boyhood, youth, and early manhood, the first thirty years of a life that ended when he was thirty-six, are unilluminated. He considered his biography insignificant, a sentiment he shared with most contemporaries. Whether they had been successful or not, in easy circumstances or in want, there was little that could be recalled about the years before 1789 that were not embarrassing or humiliating. Robespierre did not want to be reminded that he had, as a schoolboy, recited a Latin panegyric before Louis XVI and Marie Antoinette. Others were equally eager to forget the past. A man's life began with the Revolution. He made of his wonderful rebirth what he could and was held accountable only for his postrevolutionary actions. When the revolutionaries began purging one another and a man's life was held up to scrutiny and censure, it was understood that responsibility began in 1789. Louis XVI went to the guillotine only for what he had done subsequent to 1789, fifteen years after he ascended the throne.

Robespierre's style was the ideal instrument for conveying what needed expression. In his formal, oratorical periods he revealed his revolutionary self. The details he suppressed or slighted are now beyond recapture. Only intermittently did this obscure provincial attract any notice other than those fleeting official snapshots when the administrative apparatus recorded some public deed—birth, schooling, admittance to the bar. These few authentic facts are supplemented by an equally few snapshots of recognition for achievement—a celebrated law case pleaded, a philosophical essay awarded a prize. Otherwise all is darkness. There are so few early letters, no diaries, only a handful of useful recollections (and many of these tainted), and some light verse that is wholly unrevealing. What we know about Robespierre the man is, in large part, only what he chose to tell; and his attention was on his political mission. But because Robespierre was a celebrated and controversial man, these enormous biographical gaps were filled by others, especially after his death. Almost all this testimony is tainted by its provenance or purpose, or both.

The genuine historical record is sparse. Robespierre's was an uneventful life, although lived amid (and often at the center of) extraordinary events. If one were to set, side by side, a chronology of Robespierre's revolutionary career and a chronology of the Revolution, the former would be a list of speeches given, pamphlets published, newspapers edited, meetings attended. On only two great revolutionary occasions would he participate directly in events, become a historical actor in the familiar sense of the word: at the festival of the Supreme Being (June 8, 1794; 20 Prairial) and on 9 Thermidor (July 26, 1794). On the former occasion he delivered two remarkable speeches; on the latter he fell from power. At no time was he able to present the kind of revolutionary credentials—attacked the Bastille, marched with the women to Versailles, petitioned in the Champ de Mars, attacked the Tuileries, purged the Convention—that many a street radical offered and demanded as a certificate of patriotism. This absence of militancy was not held against him, any more than were his old-fashioned dress and manners and speech.

In revolution a man of words is a historical actor, and Robespierre is the first example of the exceptional importance of verbal acts. He created the model others would imitate or acknowledge. He was, arguably, the most significant historical actor of the Revolution. Some rivals sought to undermine his authority by harping on his absence from all the important battles of the Revolution, but these smears had no apparent effect. As Robespierre lived and articulated it, the Revolution was a transcendent spiritual experience. All his considerable skills as a tactician and strategist were bent to realizing the vision of what the world could be, a vision that he made and that then held him in thrall and exercised over his auditors a similar fascination. The record of Robespierre the revolutionary is to be found not in the usual sources of political history, the documents, both official and private, but in his collected works. This self-conscious and extensive repository is the best source for his revolutionary career. The annals of the Revolution record where he was and what he did. His utterances express the spiritual revolution. They are a chronicle of the Revolution itself, reflecting and refracting the extraordinary events that he saw and shaped. No previous rebel had created and left behind such a record as this.

Robespierre carefully selected the materials for his future biographers. Everything not pertaining to the revolutionary is excluded. This does not mean that a biography of Robespierre cannot be written, despite the omissions. His life has been often written, and several times with distinction.[2] But a successful biography of Robespierre demands not only mastery of the complex history of the Revolution, but considerable powers of imagination. It is no easy matter to penetrate into the personal darkness that a man so intelligent and purposeful as Robespierre had no desire to light.

His purposefulness is striking, whether we consider the career as a whole, some particular episode, or even the structure of a specific argument. More than any previous rebel, more than any of his contemporaries, Robespierre was acutely aware of what he was doing and the novelty of his actions. He had the unique ability to see himself as a historical actor and to describe himself and his deeds as manifestations of *the* revolutionary. In obliterating his private self in the Revolution and presenting only a new political revolutionary self, Robespierre made himself an ideal type, a representative figure. The paradox of this creation, which has troubled all students of Robespierre, is that the man, although we see him but dimly, appears too insignificant for his historical role. What we forget is that Robespierre was a man transformed, purified in the heat of the Revolution, which melted away the old flesh to expose the new spirit. His was a destiny rather than a life. This transformation from provincial lawyer to universal revolutionary is the most important of his career. When he found himself on a world stage in the spring of 1789, standing for election to the Third Estate of the recently summoned Estates-General, he did not even pause to look back and discredit a past that was not notable. He threw himself into the politics of the Revolution, and shortly into the more turbulent radical politics of Paris, in the name of the nation and its people. The old Robespierre had ceased to exist, although much, obviously, was incorporated in the new self. Robespierre's authentic revolutionary voice is clearly recognizable in his first political pronouncements of early 1789. This voice is not earlier heard except in a passing phrase or sentence.

What is distinctive about Robespierre's ongoing analysis of self and Revolution simultaneously is not merely the degree of intellectual or rational intensity, but the distance he is able to maintain when depicting or discussing himself. The personal pronouns are prevalent in his utterances, and not a few contemporaries thought his incessant invocation of self tasteless; yet Robespierre's ego is oddly disengaged. The purpose of these self-conscious postures is not personal aggrandizement. Robespierre talks about himself in an abstract, dispassionate manner. He is able to objectify himself, personify himself. He never refers to himself by name (which was Rousseau's habit), but always by epithet—"the representative of the people" or "the defender of the constitution." His auditors are asked to contemplate him from a distance, to observe his behavior as one would observe that of any historical actor. When he speaks of himself, eschewing all details that might make him a distinct personality deserving of the interest of others, he is not puffing Maximilien Robespierre the man, but Robespierre the revolutionary.

This analytical distance, whether directed toward the self or the Revolution, is Robespierre's highly original application of the epistemology and critical reason of the Enlightenment to the subject of revolution and revolutionaries. There had been rebels and rebellions, revolutions and revolutionaries before Robespierre; but none had been so self-aware of what these activities meant, what they themselves were doing, and how it all fit into a general scheme of human history and aspiration. The vehicle for this singular achievement was autobiography, a genre that, with the novel, flourished in the eighteenth century. By extending the autobiographical interests of his age to a hitherto neglected but significant type, the revolutionary, Robespierre enriched the Enlightenment tradition. He adapted a vigorous literary genre to the purposes of the Revolution: the autobiographical form was available, young and capable of experiment, and Robespierre needed new bottles for new wine.

Not until the eighteenth century could so secular a revolutionary appear. And only with the possibility of secular rebellion could the primacy of the self appear. Robespierre would speak at significant moments in his career about some providential scheme of which he was a part, but his providence is so politically conceived, so deliberately tailored to the immediate needs of the French Revolution, that it would be wrong to think of these appeals in traditional religious terms. Robespierre's providence was a special providence guiding and informing the virtuous and revolutionary struggle for freedom. His self-consciousness of historical task and cultural moment as well as his own place in these great movements derives not so much from the religious traditions of Europe as from the newer traditions of the Enlightenment, and specifically those qualities of the new culture analyzed by the philosopher Immanuel Kant in his essay "What Is Enlightenment?" ("Was ist Aufklärung?").

The philosophers and critics of the eighteenth century knew what they were doing in their critiques of religion, education, political theory, and culture, and they saw their work as a historical mission. These rational assaults on received opinion were undertaken deliberately. Robespierre understood his own mission to be similar: his subject was revolution. Reason and revolution would be henceforth intimately related. Revolutionaries would be expected to analyze and explain what they were doing and why. Their followers would expect, as they expected of Robespierre, a comprehensive and philosophically convincing critique of the Revolution as well as the *ancien régime*. Here is Robespierre's originality as a thinker and revolutionary theorist. His words are not only the record of his participation in the Revolution as one of its central figures, but an extended self-conscious analysis of the Revolution as a phenomenon conforming to rational, natural laws, and a simultaneous and equally self-conscious analysis of himself as a special human type, the revolutionary, in whose mind and heart work the same fundamental laws of history.

———————

I have not here attempted a biography of Robespierre but have written perhaps a species of biography, intellectual biography. I have laid heavy stress on his words. The reader is asked to see the Revolution and revolutionaries through the mind of a man who was witness and creator, participant and philosopher, chronicler and autobiographer. His appraisal of himself and the Revolution is not the only possible one, not even (as he would have had it) the only correct one: it is unique. Yet because he was the first to attempt to describe the unconditional giving of self to the revolution, his words and views have a powerful claim on our attention.

I have, as one must when dealing with evidence of a literary kind, taken Robespierre at his word. This is the way contemporaries took him. The political actor is here presented strutting on the stage of the Revolution and projecting his lines. The script, however, is of his own authorship and the stage he trods is a world stage. I have lingered over some lines and scenes rather than others because I consider them more revealing and because his career, although obviously lived in a linear chronology, sometimes defies rigidity of presentation. I have taken the liberty of presenting some tableaux out of chronological order, and ask the reader to imagine a multilevel stage. I have tried, when possible, to expose the dressing room and the backstage apparatus to the audience. Robespierre and his contemporaries abhorred the contrived illusions of the *ancien régime*. They demanded that all be open to public gaze.

The argument sketched here asserts that Robespierre's importance lies in the voice that speaks from the collected works. Here emerges the prototypical revolutionary whose moral integrity would enflame the Revolution and ensure its success. He believed revolutionary politics was morality in action, the polar opposite of the wretched machinations of tyrants and oppressors. Revolutionaries, consequently, must have the moral advantage of their opponents. The cause itself, and its champions, must be virtuous, or both will fail. He did not shrink from using force—as no revolutionary can—but he insisted that necessary force emanate from virtue (about which he said a great deal) lest it be as criminal as the violence of the oppressor, the *ancien régime*.

He prided himself not only on his virtue but on his consistency and perseverance, and demanded these qualities of all who would make revolution. Not only did he present in the course of the Revolution a remarkably consistent view of what was happening—a homogeneity he often pointed to as a way of stigmatizing the opportunism of his rivals—but even in his last speech he insisted, with much redundancy, that when so many had succumbed to temptation, he, almost alone, had fought on. He had derived no personal advantage from the Revolution and had given himself, to the detriment of his health and at the risk of his life, to the tasks of the Revolution, to the people, as he preferred to put it. This single-mindedness and sacrifice were the result of an early embraced article of faith: the Revolution would not be over, would not be won, until the counterrevolution had been destroyed or reduced to unconditional surrender.

Robespierre demanded of revolutionaries, as he demanded of himself, the profane virtues of probity, austerity, sincerity, sacrifice, dignity, and industriousness. His example held a strong appeal for a sizable part of the French people: professionals, tradesmen, small shopkeepers, numerous artisans (journeymen, apprentices, and masters alike). All found in Robespierre a living exemplar of their social and moral values. In him they saw the ideal political citizen, personally selfless and publicly one with the nation. He had accumulated for contemporaries as well as for posterity an enormous catalogue of opinions and arguments on the tactics, strategy, and purpose of democratic revolution. This, too, enhanced his reputation and attracted followers. He had spoken on the relationship between war and revolution, on the place of the army and its generals, on the old religion and the new one he envisioned, on the nature of parliamentary government in crisis and the need for emergency government, on whether radicals ought to join with conservative coalitions, on the relative rights of the individual and the collectivity. He had proposed educational and military reforms along with constitutional amendments and general declarations of principle. He had argued for regicide and theorized about violence, terror, and urban insurrection. He had defined revolutionary justice and revolutionary government and had himself built the Jacobin Society, the first such revolutionary instrument. Here was the most compelling and extensive and coherent collection of opinion and analysis on revolution yet assembled. Here was the fruit of an intense revolutionary life, made accessible not only to contemporaries but to posterity because it was presented in personal terms, presented as a form of revolutionary autobiography.

Robespierre's career set the pattern for the modern revolutionary. It revealed not only the dynamics of the Revolution unfolding before his eyes, but the dynamics of self-politicization and radicalization. Napoleon's career may be more spectacular or romantic, but the metamorphosis of Robespierre—from the serious orphan concerned about supporting his siblings, the brilliant and lonely student, the provincial lawyer of enlightened and liberal opinions, the small-town *académicien* aspiring to literary recognition, the fluent but uninspired versifier, the prudently gregarious clubman, into the self-conscious revolutionary—is remarkable. That self may be his greatest and most enduring creation.

CHAPTER 1

The Memory of a Tyrant

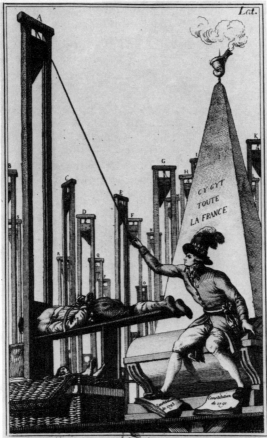

ROBESPIERRE, guillotinant le bourreau après avoir fait guillot. tous les Francais
A *le Bourreau*, B *le comité de Salut Public*, C *le comité de Sureté générale*, D *le Tribunal Revolution.*
F. *les Jacobins*, F *les Cordeliers*, G *les Brissotins*, H *Girondins*, I *Philipotins*, K *Chabotins*, L *Hébertistes*,
M *les Nobles et les Prétres*, N *les Gens à talens*, O *les Vieillardes*, *Femmes et Enfants*, P *les Soldats et
les Genéraux*, Q *les Autorités Constitués*, R *la Convention Nationale*, S *les Sociétés Populaires*.

PLATE III
(Phot. Bibl. nat. Paris)

A S ROBESPIERRE LAY on a table in the antechamber of the Committee of Public Safety, drifting in and out of consciousness, his ball-shattered jaw bound up with a bandage, his triumphant enemies, in another room of the Tuileries palace, were creating the monster who would soon pass into historical legend.[1] This Robespierre, created by using materials scavenged from old calumny, damaging anecdote, and sometimes sheer malicious invention, was one of the founding acts of a new revolutionary government. The Thermidorians—thus have Robespierre's conquerors and successors been dubbed—sought not only to justify their *coup d'état* of July 1794 (the month of Thermidor in the revolutionary calendar) but to evade the opprobrium they shared with Robespierre and his comrades for deeds done during the agonizing crisis of the previous year, during the Terror. The vengeful malice of the Thermidorians was partly successful: their caricature of Robespierre has proved durable.

The Thermidorian Robespierre was given official shape and sanction on January 5, 1795 (16 Nivôse, Year III), when E. B. Courtois, in the name of the Committee of Twelve that had been appointed to examine Robespierre's papers, presented his report to the National Assembly. Published shortly afterward by the government, Courtois's *Rapport* is a record of the motives and fears of its makers, which necessitated much manipulation and some destruction of the evidence.[2] It is a political and ideological statement in which Robespierre is depicted as a betrayer of his class, of the *honnêtes gens*, who had now reclaimed their rightful place in society. He is accused of having sought "the *leveling* [of society] by the extinction of wealth and the ruin of commerce."[3] He is presented as the embodiment of all the brutalities of Year II, the year when the common people, the *sans-culottes*, led, encouraged, and instigated by him, had tried to rule over their social betters.

Order, hierarchy, propriety, authority—these constituted for the Thermidorians what they liked to call *une saine harmonie sociale*, a healthy (and natural) social harmony.[4] The Thermidorians were determined to ruin the man who had threatened it, using the whole arsenal of weapons accumulated in years of denunciation. The victim is presented full-length, his most despised acts springing from a soul depraved and corrupted. Robespierre is permitted no remnant of decency, no talent, no humanity. He is a monstser whose impact on contemporaries and the Revolution is not explained but cursed. He is seen as a man of small talent and enormous vanity. His lack of natural gifts he masked through tenacity and hard work, while he expressed his vanity by surrounding himself with flattering self-images. The hours spent alone by this solitary are imagined consumed with schemes for destroying his enemies, who included all men of talent as well as those who had slighted him, however casually or inadvertently. At the podium, the portrait continues, he was stiff, pedantic, hampered by a weak voice, a provincial accent, artificial gestures, and an inflated style, all of which expressed and revealed a shallow spirit and deep meanness. His oratorical success they attributed to his ability to inspire fear. All his political maneuverings the Thermodorians thought devious yet clumsy, and directed to the end of dictatorial rule that they presumed to be his ruling passion. His manner they described as cold: he was indifferent, envious, arrogant, unapproachable. He avoided the company of women, perhaps through distaste or excessive timidity (although there was a competing view that his sexual tastes were unusual and he was cruel toward women). He was bilious, gloomy, irascible, and uncontrollably jealous of the success of others.[5]

Courtois's Robespierre even exceeds Julius Caesar in vileness, the historical figure regularly invoked by the revolutionaries to express their contempt for personal ambition and as the ideal of a tyrant. The Roman at least had an "elevation of soul" that put him above the depths of depravity inhabited by Robespierre. Caesar had not put his foe Cicero to death, despite the latter's attacks, whereas Robespierre had murdered all those who criticized him: "it is much easier to kill a man than to kill the truth."[6] On a more mundane level Courtois's *Rapport* twisted innocent details of daily life to signify bad ends. Stanislas-Louis-Marie Fréron, who knew Robespierre personally, recalled his love of oranges, which were thought to aid a bilious digestion. One could always tell where Robespierre had sat at the table: the place was littered by a pile of orange peels. Fréron glosses this anecdote to suggest that Robespierre had an excessive, even unnatural appetite for oranges and that the Duplays, from whom he rented rooms, suffered hardship in providing "this sacred fruit during every season of the year."[7] A man who craved exotic foods, or ate excessively (or even heartily and regularly) when much of France went hungry, was a stock figure for righteous indignation. La Reveillière-Lépeaux, another Thermidorian who conveyed his recollections of Robespierre to Courtois, also sneered at the private man. At the Duplays', he reports, Robespierre received the homage "one renders a god." In a special small alcove was displayed "his bust . . . amidst diverse ornaments, verses and decorations . . ." while in his room there were additional smaller busts in terra-cotta, as well as portraits of the "great man" done in pencil, in water colors, and engraved. The table behind which Robespierre sat to receive his visitors groaned with gorgeous fruits, fresh butter, and pure milk, and from it rose the perfume of fresh-brewed coffee. "The god deigned to smile at me and offered me his hand," the deputy continues, while the entire Duplay family hovered on the other side of the glass doors watching for the slightest motion of hand or head that would signal that they might enter the sanctuary.[8]

Robespierre, for his Thermidorian biographers, was born blemished; he was demonic from his earliest years. Even as a schoolboy, Fréron reports, his face was contorted by "convulsive grimaces" and he was never seen to laugh, not even once.[9] He was a boy who could "dissimulate his resentments."[10] Courtois's official character assassination took some of its authority from the testimony of former acquaintances of the dead man who had deserted his cause. For the first time in years these men could publish their resentments, share their bitter recollections. But the most frightful portrait of Robespierre as a boy and young man came not from former colleagues but from his first biographer, abbé Proyart, an official at Louis-le-Grand, Robespierre's school in Paris.

Proyart first published his malicious *Life and Crimes of Maximilien Robespierre* in 1795.[11] A biography whose richness of detail appear to spring from long intimacy, it has remained the source for many of the most repulsive details concerning Robespierre. Proyart's Robespierre, who complemented and seemed to corroborate the official Thermidorian view, was consumed by intellectual pride, addicted to forbidden literature (doubtless that of the *philosophes*), and unpopular with other boys. He kept excessively to himself during these formative school years, working diligently at his studies. "He never laughed and hardly ever smiled." "He was incapable of friendship, and had not a single friend." "His character and the kind of life he led kept him completely apart from women." These characteristics he carried into adulthood. As a lawyer "he would have been furious if he had prevented a lawsuit by reconciliation."[12] Mme. de Staël, who had met Robespierre only a few times, was as bitter and slanderous as Proyart. She describes his appearance as "common" and his complexion as pale, and states (remarkably) that he had veins of a "greenish color." This particular detail would later be taken up by Michelet and Carlyle. This oddly tinted man, Mme. de Staël continues, "supported the most absurd theories with a coolness that had the air of conviction," and he held these outlandish opinions merely because "his jealous and evil disposition make it a pleasure for him to adopt" them.[13] He reminded Fréron of a cat, his handwriting seeming to have been done with a claw.[14] Pierre Villiers made him cruel and unfeeling toward the mistress he gave him,[15] while Galart de

Montjoye reports the arrangements Robespierre made for his regular sexual orgies.[16]

All these details were fitted into a mosaic of a demonic and fanatical revolutionary whose depravities led him to pervert the Revolution. There is almost nothing new about the pieces cut and cemented in place. Robespierre's numerous enemies had been at work assassinating his character since the first months of the Revolution. What the Thermidorians did was replace former royalist slander with their own republican brand, an easy enough task in 1795 when there were none to protest or question. Cannibalism and ghoulishness were attributed to the dead man in place of the former royalist accusation that he was descended from Robert Damiens, the man who had tried to assassinate Louis XV. And even Montjoye's reports of sexual orgies pale before Proyart's visions of the eater "of the roasted flesh of priests" and creator of "a tannery for human skin" out of which to make shoes for the *sans-culottes*.[17]

Such vehement malice and exaggeration sprang from fear posing as self-righteousness. Pierre-René Choudieu, no friend of Robespierre's, saw this. "Two powerful motives provoked them," he wrote of Robespierre's conquerors: "the fear of perishing themselves on the scaffold and the desire to revenge their friends."[18] Robespierre's enemies were many, reminded Filippo Buonarotti, a comrade who would continue his revolutionary life in France after his friend's death, and then in Italy, as the theoretician of conspiratorial revolutionary struggle. He "fought equally royalists, the aristocracy, both noble and bourgeois, the atheists and dissolute men lusting after power and money." These various foes "saw in him an enemy, a tyrant, and although they had for each other profound hatreds that would shortly manifest themselves, they joined together . . . to revenge themselves and to escape from the justice with which they felt themselves threatened."[19] The Revolutionary Government had made them tremble for their lives, and Robespierre was the man of the Revolutionary Government. His posthumous punishment was to be a ritualistic revenge on Year II, on that part of the Revolution most closely identified with Robespierre's views and leadership. Yet in making Robespierre the monstrous symbol of the Terror, of all fanaticism and excess, they not only created a vile legend, which was politically useful at the moment, they also recognized, in their frantic efforts to exorcise Robespierre's disturbing shade, his significance. In a sense Thermidorian vituperation kept Robespierre alive. The very intensity of their malice tended to mythologize the man they sought to obliterate. The next generation, with different purposes and sensibilities, would take up the memory of Robespierre, still warm from the passion of Thermidorian hatred, and create a heroic figure, a savior of France and a champion of humankind. Monster and hero have remained the poles of Robespierre's changing reputation.

Vilification was not uncommon or infrequent in the Revolution. In the murderous struggles of Year II, those who lost went to their deaths only after having been anathematized, cast out of the new society by having their hypocrisy and treasons (real and confected) exposed and cursed before the entire nation. The victim's political and personal biography was presented as a series of increasingly brazen acts of counterrevolution that were now unmasked and exposed for all to see: a warning to others, a ritual of purification. What set Robespierre's destruction somewhat apart from all the others was the scale and frequency of the slanders, which continued long after he had been killed. The destruction of the man and his legacy became an obsession.

In the entire Revolution there are only two individuals who fared as badly as Robespierre, and in both cases slander, once spewed, soon stopped, and ceased entirely after death. Ironically enough, they are Louis XVI and Marie Antoinette. When the nation in revolution brought the King to trial as the only adequate means of settling the long and profound struggle with the monarchy, it was clear to all—republicans and royalists alike—that the monarchy, more than the person of Louis XVI, was on trial. Louis personally inspired little hatred. The attractive aspects of his life and character were many, and his personality, his dignity, his humanness, proved a strong defense. It was the monarchy that was judged by the nation, found guilty and sentenced to death. During the long weeks and months of the trial,[20] which generated more than four hundred speeches or pamphlets from the deputies, it was clear that not only did men have to argue and posture, persuade and cajole to justify their unprecedented thoughts and acts, but they did so compulsively. After his head fell, on January 21, 1793, Louis was scarcely again mentioned by the revolutionaries.

The attack on Marie Antoinette was accomplished differently, in two separate but related assaults. Before the Revolution the Queen's foolish behavior had focused resentment and frustration on her extravagance and insensitivity, synthesizing feelings of impotence into a character assassination of the Queen. Her pride, her vanity, her sexual immorality, her tyranny, these were the categories of the accusation, bandied about in the streets of Paris and even whispered at Court. The second assault against Marie Antoinette began in the first years of the Revolution when she became identified with the more reactionary elements at Court, and culminated in October 1793 when she was brought to trial. In addition to the old accusations, a particularly repugnant series of sexual perversities was added, pathetically testified to by her young son, who was forced to be witness to his own supposed victimization.

But slander did not permanently deform. Biographers have succeeded in restoring a mundane humanity to the royal couple. Historians have proved generally less hostile to royalty than to revolutionaries, especially if they can be shown to have been well-meaning if inept bunglers. Louis and his queen have shed the slander of their contemporaries as Robespierre has not. Remnants of Thermidorian loathing cling to him, in some cases reinforced by the imprimatur (and immortality) only literary genius can bestow. Mme. de Staël's "veins of a greenish color" became in a relatively short time Carlyle's "sea-green incorruptible" and Michelet's "reptile." Michelet also took up Pierre Villier's nasty (and dubious) circumstantial anecdotes, and these slanders even turn up in a modern, erudite biography.[21] Circumstance and personality seem to have conspired against Robespierre's memory.

The legend of a monstrous Robespierre not only grew unchecked, for when it was being made none dared challenge the new masters of the Revolution, but was reiterated and embellished by government apologists and men who found the legend useful for propaganda, a reminder of the revolutionary excesses from which they insisted they had saved France. Napoleon, whose *coup d'état* in 1799 ended the reign of the Thermidorians, as First Consul or later as Emperor, had no desire to remind the people of his brief but real *robespierriste* past. He had no intention of rehabilitating Robespierre's reputation, let alone connecting himself with the Terror. The Restoration that followed Napoleon's defeat, presided over by Louis XVI's two younger brothers, Louis XVIII and Charles X, found the Thermidorian monster a ready-made villain. Their only modification was to make regicide the most heinous of Robespierre's many crimes, something the republican Thermidorians and the upstart Emperor chose to ignore.

Not until 1832 was a significant collection of Robespierre's speeches published, by the Romantic socialist Albert Laponneraye, who devoted his life to rehabilitating Robespierre and making him a revolutionary hero.[22] With Laponneraye begins not only the rehabilitation (and eventual revolutionary apotheosis) of Robespierre, but the emphasis on his words. He became again what he had been during the Revolution, the ideologue, the man whose deeds were verbal, whose ideas explained and enflamed. For Laponneraye, and those who followed him, Robespierre's life was made worthy of his destiny: his biography became the unfolding of a revolutionary hero. The chief bit of evidence used to create this heroic life was the *Mémoires* of Robespierre's sister, Charlotte. Laponneraye tracked down his hero's sister, by then an old and frightened woman leading an obscure life and carrying a despised name. He encouraged her and inspired her to write about her brother, and he published these recollections after the old maid's death (in 1834).[23]

Here was the belated and necessary antidote for Thermidorian poison. Charlotte remembered her brother as "naturally gay," his character as "gentle and fair, which made him loved by all," while his "friendliness toward women won him their affection."[24] For all its filial piety Charlotte's *Mémoires* is a touching work. We learn that Robespierre loved to make lace with his mother when a small boy; kept and loved birds; was distraught at having to sign a death warrant when a young judge in Arras.[25] And we get one of the rare physical descriptions of the man:

> He was of medium height and had a delicate complexion. His face exuded kindness and benevolence, but was not as conventionally handsome as his brother's. He was almost always smiling. A great number of portraits of my older brother have been published. That most resembling him is the one painted by Delpech.[26]

Even Charlotte's desire to save her brother from slander, to leave to posterity the portrait of a good, decent, kind, and eminently bourgeois man, admirable alike for character and convictions, could not erase the monstrous Robespierre. The Thermidorians were closer to an essential truth about Robespierre than was his devoted but simple sister. Charlotte's Robespierre is too ordinary, too bland, too conventional for his destiny. The Thermidorian monster is at least larger than life; a man of such proportions is capable of dominating the Revolution. The Thermidorians remembered Robespierre savagely, demonically, but they remembered him as a revolutionary. Charlotte recalled only the lovable brother.

It is for the historian to approximate the actual man, neither monster nor beloved sibling. But this is no easy matter. Revolutionary and counterrevolutionary myths have a long life in our age, when revolution is not only the most extreme and audacious form of social and historical change, but also the most familiar. Robespierre was the first to be made into a revolutionary hero, and our own restless and revolutionary world has made him, so to speak, a contemporary figure. His self-analysis was, in this sense, prophetic. He wanted to be seen as a revolutionary, and he has had his wish fulfilled. He was what the French aptly called *un homme dur*, a hard man. Yet he never aspired to be loved for his personality (as Charlotte loved him). He demanded, and received, respect, devotion, even love—for he had several close friends who resembled an extended family[27]—for what he insisted he was, a revolutionary.

Robespierre depended far less on personal charm than did any of his contemporaries. Almost as if he thought such manipulation of others reprehensible, he remained what he had always been: a reserved, fastidious and obviously provincial man. It is not only his advanced opinions that made him unwelcome at the more brilliant salons and dinner parties of the Revolution, but his inability to scintillate. He was not a good talker, he was not a wit, and he had enjoyed no adventures worth recounting. But those who sought his company regularly did not mind these shortcomings, and those who had occasion to consult him, even at the height of his prestige and authority, found him affable, charmingly polite, and attentive. They commented that although he was accessible to all, he insisted on a prearranged interview, preferably in writing. It was unthinkable to this proper and fastidious man to receive guests without preparation, let alone at odd hours and wrapped in a towel, which was often Marat's costume when he was at home. It was equally unthinkable that he would indulge in the coarse bonhomie and unbuttoned familiarity that Danton favored.

The curious juxtaposition of social propriety and advanced revolutionary ideas did not elicit much comment from contemporaries. His probity, his clinging to old-fashioned styles of speech and dress and manners, were thought to certify his sincerity. The rectitude of his personal life complemented the stances he struck in public: his personal and public lives are scarcely distinguishable. It is the richness and brilliance of his political life that magnetized contemporaries, and it continues to hold us. This is also the most extensively documented part of his life. While the biographer bemoans the obscurity of the first thirty years of Robespierre's life, the historian of his revolutionary career equally bemoans the loss of so many early speeches, preserved only in fragments or conflicting versions,[28] and the haphazard way in which his early political utterances were treated.[29] What we do have are, aside from the speeches and pamphlets printed during his lifetime or recorded in the minutes of the Constituent and Convention or Jacobins, the surviving items from the deliberate destructions of his papers by Simon

Duplay, the son of Robespierre's Paris host, as well as those of the Courtois Committee.[30]

Yet enough remains to watch the unfolding of the revolutionary career, the self-conscious revelation of self and purpose publicly conducted
by Robespierre. And in examining the career, we can understand how
and why memory has extruded from the surviving materials what history has needed.

CHAPTER 2

The Revolutionary
Revealed

PLATE IV

ROBESPIERRE was born on May 6, 1758, in Arras, the small capital of the province of Artois, four months after his parents were married. His father, Maximilien-Barthélemy-François, a lawyer, the son and grandson of local lawyers, had been admitted to the Arras bar in 1756. His mother, Jacqueline-Marguerite Carraut, was the daughter of a successful brewer and innkeeper of the town. Maximilien-François-Marie-Isidore was born into comfortable bourgeois surroundings. Fortune and his father's temperament soon changed all that. The Robespierre family grew quickly. There were five children by 1764, although the last of these died at birth and caused the death of Robespierre's mother shortly afterward.[1] His father allowed his law practice to deteriorate after his wife's death. Two years later, in 1766, he abandoned his young family to the care of relatives. Although the father reappeared in Arras on occasion, Robespierre was in fact orphaned at the age of eight. Their childhood, says Charlotte, was "filled with tears, and each of our early years was marked by the death of some cherished object. This fate influenced, more than one can imagine, Maximilien's character; it made him sad and melancholy."[2] A plausible diagnosis, although these particular characteristics were not noticed or stressed by those who knew him as an adult.

The children were dispersed among relatives: Robespierre was taken in by two aunts. He early showed intellectual aptitude and was able to win support from charitable foundations when he entered the *collège* in Arras. A former Jesuit institution, the *collège* was, in 1765, governed by a local committee appointed by the bishop, and the teachers were secular clergy (the Jesuits having been expelled from France in 1763). Here Robespierre remained for four years. At the age of eleven he won a much-coveted scholarship to Louis-le-Grand, in Paris, one of the finest schools in the country, where he continued as a scholarship boy for twelve years. He was a model student and a brilliantly successful one; between 1769 and 1776 his name appeared on the annual prize list for achievement in Latin and Greek verse and translation. His teachers at Louis-le-Grand were the Oratorians, a distinguished teaching order that had long vied with the Jesuits for prestige and pupils. Robespierre's mind was formed, as were those of the majority of his educated contemporaries, in an old-fashioned, narrow, rigorous yet rich tradition. The Oratorians had no desire to achieve the individual liberation of their pupils. They strove, rather, to form subjects for a monarchy, as Robespierre would later strive to form citizens of a republic. There is no evidence that he was unhappy with the formality or authority of the school. He was a docile pupil, assimilating the materials taught and the social values inculcated.³ Yet despite their conservatism, the schools of the *ancien régime* proved to be a training ground for a generation of revolution-aries.

Robespierre was not so much precocious as he was industrious. But even as a schoolboy he displayed the characteristic that was not only to enhance and inspire his intelligence, but also to render it unique and broadly compelling. He could, like an actor, assume another self and personify it. His gift was not an ability to enter another being and live as if he were that being, but a sort of spiritual mimicry. He had no interest in imitating idiosyncrasies of personality, and his purpose was not to amuse others or to satirize. Robespierre seized some spiritual es-sence of a time or a circumstance or even an individual or group of individuals, and made it a part of his own character. He could emulate, and thus become, the qualities he admired. He always generalized these enhancements of self, never attaching them to a specific person. He sought to be an ideal type, the personification of an abstraction, and spoke of himself in this way, often insisting on his persona as the "rep-resentative of the people." The first recorded instance of his capacity occurred while he was at Louis-le-Grand. Robespierre was considered the best Latinist in the school. He was referred to as The Roman, the first of several epithets that would be attached to him or that he would attach to himself. So thoroughly had he learned Latin that he appeared to contemporaries a native speaker. In 1775 he was chosen, not because he embodied the moral posture of a Roman from the time of the Re-public, but because he was so accomplished in the language, to deliver a Latin address (written by a faculty member) welcoming Louis XVI and Marie Antoinette, who briefly visited the school on their return from coronation ceremonies at Rheims Cathedral.⁴

Otherwise there are few anecdotes or reliable recollections of Ro-bespierre at Louis-le-Grand.⁵ He was thought diligent, studious, not es-pecially popular with the other boys, a bit withdrawn. He was a poor boy at a prestigious school. When the Bishop of Arras, his patron, vis-ited Louis-le-Grand, the young man wrote to the prefect of the school asking him to apprise the Bishop of "my situation, in order to obtain from him those things I need to appear in his presence." Lacking were "a proper suit and . . . several things without which I cannot appear in public."⁶

His academic successes at Louis-le-Grand, where he also received his law training, earned him an extraordinary graduation prize. For "good conduct during twelve years, and his success in his classes, both in gain-ing the prizes of the University and in his examination in philosophy and law, the Board has unanimously granted to Sieur de Robespierre a gratification in the sum of 600 livres."[7] It was not a fortune, but when the average worker in Paris earned twenty sous or one livre for a day's work, this was a significant sum, enough to launch a law practice. In addition, he was exceptionally allowed to pass his scholarship on to his brother, Augustin, then nineteen.

In 1781, the year following his graduation, Robespierre was admitted an advocate before the *Parlement* of Paris, the most important law court in France. He decided, however, to return to Arras, to his siblings, to a provincial life and law practice. He was a prudent young man. By returning home he spared himself those painful episodes of despair and frustration brought on by wretched circumstances and prospects, the familiar experience of many contemporaries similarly without well-placed patrons in the capital who sought to make their way in Paris only on talent.[8]

Robespierre was admitted to the Arras bar on November 8, 1781, and pleaded his first case on February 27, 1782. Within a month of this maiden litigation he was made a judge, one of five, of the tribunal of the episcopal court of Arras, which was the seat of the ecclesiastical jurisdiction of the province as well as its civil jurisdiction. So precocious an advancement suggests influence, perhaps with the Bishop, but the records are silent. Otherwise Robespierre's first years at the bar were unexceptional. His practice was successful enough to render him materially comfortable, his abilities won him professional respect. He had enough leisure to pursue literary interests, which took the form of competitions in essay contests sponsored by provincial academies. On one occasion he won a prize from the Academy of Metz. These competitions were essential to France's intellectual life during the *ancien régime*, and if little of enduring value was thus produced, there was the example of Rousseau, whose literary career had been brilliantly launched when he won a prize from the Dijon Academy for an essay on the progress of the arts and sciences. Robespierre had no such success. His prize essay, on whether the crimes of parents ought to taint their children, is competent rather than brilliant. It did attract some national attention when favorably reviewed by Pierre-Louis Lacretelle, an intellectual of some reputation. Later, under the Restoration, when Lacretelle published his complete works, he recalled this review and added to it a trite but accurate comment:

> Nothing in this [literary] debut hinted at the man of seven years later. It is easy to believe that he himself was unaware of it. One must see a whole

revolution in order to know at what point it can transform a man, or rather develop in him the hidden and still unfermented poisons.[9]

There is little on the surface of Robespierre's prerevolutionary life that prefigures his greatness. Neither he nor his generation was overtly disaffected from society. In Robespierre's case there is no recorded crisis of alienation, no outward rebellion, before 1788.[10] Later, in revolutionary oratory and journalism, he would talk much about himself, but he never revealed details of his life before that time.

Life in Arras was tranquil and uneventful for Robespierre. His habits were frugal and austere, his dedication to work and discipline a bit excessive, his self-absorbtion complete. He rose early and worked for an hour before taking his coffee, which, along with a passion for fruit, was his only expressed alimentary interest. Charlotte, on her own testimony, took pains to see her brother well and pleasantly fed: he seems not to have cared what he ate. He never did the marketing himself and always found a meal waiting for him. But this was an expectation common to men at the time, especially those of his circumstances and station. He drank little wine, confining himself at dinner to a single glass, heavily cut with water. He regularly took a constitutional after dinner, then returned to do some work before retiring. In the style of the day he was dramatically courteous to women and did not shun their company but avoided intimacy or informality. He apparently had no serious encounters or affairs. As a child he had kept pigeons, of which he was fond, and liked animals generally. He was careful and even finicky about his dress, especially his hair, on which he spent a good deal of time, contemplating himself and his appearance while he was worked on with comb, curling iron, and powder. Robespierre was concerned with all aspects of his presentation of self. His dress, his manners, his comportment, as well as his prose and oratory, all express deliberation and self-consciousness.[11]

In the first years of his law practice a sufficient number of cases came along. The most famous of these, the so-called lightning-rod case of 1783, would have been the delight of any young, enlightened, ambitious lawyer. A local man, M. de Vissery, had installed one of the first lightning rods in the province. His neighbors pressured the authorities to have the device removed because they thought it would divert the lightning to their houses. Vissery went to court. Robespierre's friend and patron, A.-J. Buissart, a dabbler in scientific matters as well as a lawyer, prepared a comprehensive brief and took elaborate notes, then generously turned the opportunity to plead the case over to Robespierre.[12]

Here was a chance to castigate superstition with the latest scientific truth, to preach the usefulness of discovery, to parade one's enlightenment and sophistication not only regionally but nationally and internationally, for the educated could be counted on to take an interest in this provincial confrontation between science and superstition. Robespierre neglected none of these opportunities. His successful defense kept Vissery's rods atop his house and brought Robespierre attention. "A man called Robespierre," writes a certain Ansart from Arras to a Paris friend,

> a recent arrival from your part of the world, has just made his first appearance here, in an important case, which he pleaded throughout three hearings here so well as to discourage anyone who intends to follow him in the same career. . . . One can see nobody among the younger generation capable of putting this brilliant light into the shade.[13]

It was as an orator, not an essayist, that Robespierre possessed genius.

His other cases brought less notoreity. His views were moderately advanced and liberal by the standards of the day, perhaps especially so in so stuffy a town as Arras, but were by no means radical. Except for one lapse into impatience with the delays of the Arras courts—he was reprimanded from the bench for uttering some "insulting" remarks[14]— he experienced no difficulties with the legal establishment. But his professional advancement did not continue. The number of his cases gradually fell off, for no apparent reason. The explanations later offered that he was too radical, took only cases of poor clients, and had offended the courts are unsupported by convincing evidence.[15] It may simply have been that in a small provincial town, tightly controlled by a handful of powerful nobles and the Bishop, who supported and protected a legal oligarchy, Robespierre had risen as high as he might hope to rise on talent alone. He himself expressed no bitterness on this subject, either at the time or later; and his Arras friends and acquaintances continued unchanged and sought his company. He regularly joined in the doings of the Rosati, a local society of men who read essays to each other and indulged in light verse, conviviality, and a contrived but charming chivalric conceit involving the rose and its relationship to wine and women.[16]

Robespierre's thirtieth birthday fell in 1788, a time of prerevolutionary excitement and agitation. From the materials available to all men of his class and generation, Robespierre would make a unique and compelling revolutionary personality in which the self served to synthesize passions, principles, and ideas. Although the revolutionary and prerevolutionary careers of Robespierre the man and historical actor seem almost unrelated, he was not noticeably different from his contemporaries. The disproportion between the man we see before 1788 and the revolutionary who emerged afterward is striking. But if his is the most remarkable revolutionary career, it is not the only such. The coming of the French Revolution released new political possibilities, a new political discourse unimaginable under the *ancien régime*. Just as the English Revolution discovered in Oliver Cromwell, an otherwise obscure and undistinguished landowner and parliamentary back-bencher, a political and military genius equal to the great events of his century, so too did the Revolution reveal Robespierre. The rapid emergence of his revolutionary self presumes the presence of the necessary raw materials. Had there been no French Revolution, it goes without saying, there would have been no other Robespierre but the small-town lawyer in Arras.

The representative body of France, the Estates-General, had not met since 1614. For 175 years the kings had governed without having to consult thier subjects. In 1788 Louis XVI called for elections to a new Estates-General, a move forced upon him by a nobility that refused to make the bankrupt monarchy solvent by taxing itself unless it received substantial concessions. Robespierre would throw himself into these elections. But before becoming completely absorbed in the political ferment, he pleaded his most remarkable case, and the only one to foreshadow Robespierre the revolutionary, on behalf of Louis-Marie-Hyacinthe Dupond. Years before Robespierre took the case, his client had left Artois and served as a soldier in first a French and then a Swedish and finally a Danish regiment. When he returned to France, after an absence of twenty-six years, he claimed his portion of a family inheritance. His relatives had him imprisoned under a *lettre de cachet*—one of those detested royal warrants that could incarcerate, without trial, during the King's pleasure—obtained by his family on the false pretext that Dupond was a deserter. This original assertion was reinforced over the years by a series of perjuries made or bought by the greedy family. Dupond remained in prison from 1774 until his release in 1786. The law case was then further complicated by suits and countersuits for restitution and damages. Robespierre became involved only in this final phase, and when he departed for Versailles to assume his duties as a deputy for the Third Estate, the Commons of the Estates-General, elected from and by all those who were neither clergy nor nobles, the case was assumed by his brother.

Robespierre's long brief on behalf of Dupond (ninety-three pages in its printed version) is exceptional for both its manner and matter. Here

are all the themes that will concern and obsess Robespierre for the rest
of his life, gathered together for the first time and presented in his mature and authentic revolutionary voice. His emotional description of the
horrors of incarceration, only intensified by the institutionalized cruelty
of jailers, who conduct a "war of armed tyranny against shackled and
defenseless innocence,"[17] is smoldering, its empathy for the victim rising
well above fashionable pathos. His musings on death, which "is not the
greatest evil for oppressed innocence,"[18] signal a preoccupation with his
own mortality in a political context and a connection, not yet fully
worked out, between virtue, its public expression, and a violent end.
The brief is punctuated with oaths of the kind soon to seal all revolutionary undertakings, and speculations on his own destiny: "perhaps I
will not die without having done something useful for some poor unfortunate."[19] He insists on bearing personal witness to injustice[20] and
savagely berates the provincial bourgeoisie for their greed, their cruelty,
their lack of morality, their hypocrisy.[21] He makes no distinction between public and private morality, and declares that he who uses the
law to take advantage of the weak "is an enemy of *la patrie* . . . clearly
guilty of high treason,"[22] a startling accusation in peacetime. He concludes his *plaidoyer*, for this is 1788, with a paean in the form of a peroration addressed to Louis XVI and more especially to Jacques Necker,
the first minister—for first ministers traditionally received the petitions
of subjects—to end injustice by "leading men to happiness and to virtue
by laws founded on the immutable principles of universal morality."[23]

This goes well beyond the enlightened hostility to superstition found
in his earlier briefs. Here is the voice of a revolutionary Robespierre.
Defending Dupond, he has declared himself and sketched his politics.
It is not that his sentiments are uncommonly radical, for they are not.
Arbitrary imprisonment without trial, legal chicanery, vile and barbarous prisons were regularly attacked. Even Robespierre's sentiments
about universal morality and virtue and a society of laws were, by 1788,
commonplace. What is revolutionary is the combination of concerns
with the intense personal involvement of Robespierre, the insistence
that specific episodes of injustice descend, inevitably, from the abuse of
social position, encouraged by a society whose laws are a jumble of privilege, that he feels these injustices as deeply as the victim, and that any
man who lends himself or his office, however slightly, to injustice is
"guilty of high treason." And the presentation of these views in a rhetoric that is both ornate and direct, personal and general, and deeply
impassioned, makes the work unmistakably Robespierre's. There is still
in the *plaidoyer* for Dupond a measure of circumspection that will soon

vanish from his utterances—he does not, for example insist that rich and poor are natural enemies—but one can extract from the brief an outline of Robespierre's ideology. He considers politics an act of the will that has morality as its goal. He insists there is a providential scheme assuring success to just causes. He wants to free the poor from a harsh life that degrades them into pining for wealth. Equally significant is the crystallization of his incomparable rhetoric and his need to put all human and divine virtues in one camp, all tyranny and oppression in another.[24]

It is conventional when writing about Robespierre, indeed when writing about any revolutionary, to see the rebel foreshadowed in childhood or created by some traumatic adult experience. For Robespierre this is not the most fruitful approach or assumption. The seeds of revolt were deeply planted and long nurtured, but there is little evidence before the mature growth of 1788–89. If he experienced a dramatic moment of conversion, he neither then nor later said anything about it. The revolutionary persona he would become in the Revolution had no overt existence before 1788. His infatuation with Rousseau, which is much stressed and indeed is important for the revolutionary, was not in itself abnormal, although the peculiarly personal aspects of this attachment might be considered unusual, and another aspect of Robespierre's capacity for spiritual mimicry first revealed in "The Roman" of Louis-le-Grand.

Robespierre's intellectual and emotional debt to Rousseau is complex and profound. Yet his devotion, his loyalty and faithfulness as a disciple, owed more to felt similarities of personality and character than to identity of philosophical interests. Robespierre's utterances are punctuated by echoes of Rousseau, paraphrases of Rousseau, quotations from Rousseau, imitations of Rousseau, all of which reveal his familiarity with the entire range of his mentor's writings, including the little-read *Contrat social*. But it is Rousseau's inner life, as set forth in the autobiographical *Confessions*, that most shaped Robespierre and influenced his historical mission. By "the elevation of his soul and the grandeur of his character" Rousseau had shown himself to be the "teacher of the human race." He "attacked tyranny with freedom, he spoke with enthusiasm of the divinity." The "purity of his doctrine" as well as "his invincible scorn for the intriguing sophists who usurped the name of philosophers" earned him the hatred and persecution of his rivals and false friends. "Ah!" Robespierre exclaims, "If only he had been witness to this Revolution of which he was the precursor, and which has carried him to the Pantheon, who can doubt that his generous soul would have embraced with transport the cause of justice and equality" (X, 455). Robespierre identified completely with Rousseau the moral man. He disregarded the many divergences of opinion between himself and his mentor, and even took Rousseau's philosophical opponents, all long dead, as his own enemies. The Encyclopedists, that group of intellectuals whose only formal bond was having contributed articles to the great *Encyclopédie* (as did Rousseau himself) edited by Denis Diderot, Robespierre repulsed. Robespierre's Rousseau is the champion of the people, the man of lofty ideals who was persecuted by his more pliable and compromising rivals who aspired to worldly fame and rewards. Those of his own contemporaries who expressed ideas he associated with the Encyclopedists, or who disparaged Rousseau, Robespierre banished from his affection.[25] "This sect," says Robespierre, "in political matters, always remained below the rights of the people; in moral matters it went well beyond the destruction of religious prejudices" (X, 454). As their revolutionary disciples, the Encyclopedists "were bold in their writings and servile in the reception rooms" (X, 455).

Thus, it was not the Encyclopedists who led Robespierre to revolution. He disliked their ideas, which he thought overly materialistic and mechanical, and associated such ideas with shallowness of character, opportunism, and eventually counterrevolution. He discovered his revolutionary self, as he later explained, through Rousseau, specifically in the pages of the *Confessions*. In his first newspaper, *Le Défenseur de la Constitution*, Robespierre recalls a promenade he made, while still a student, in the forest of Montmorency, in the course of which he was able "to contemplate the august character" of Rousseau. The walk supposedly took place in 1778, the year of Rousseau's death. It is unclear whether Robespierre actually talked to the great man or saw him only at a distance, or perhaps only in his mind's eye. Charlotte Robespierre has added to our befuddlement: "I do not know on what occasion my older brother encountered [*se rencontre*] Jean-Jacques Rousseau, but what is certain is that he had an interview with him."[26] She adds she would have been ignorant of this extraordinary meeting were it not for a "dedication that he addressed to the spirit of the philosopher of Geneva." This *Dedication to Rousseau* (*Dédicace à Rousseau*) is authentic and has survived.[27] But despite its rhapsodic tone, its exultation, the *Dedication* does not prove there was an encounter. "It is you, O spirit of the citizen of Geneva," Robespierre writes, "that I dedicate this work! [which is unknown or lost]. And should it see the light of day it will be thus under the protection of the most eloquent and the most virtuous of men. Today, more than ever, we have need of eloquence and virtue"

(I, 211). Robespierre then goes on to credit Rousseau with teaching self-awareness and political principles: "Divine man, you have taught me to know myself. As a young man you showed me how to appreciate the dignity of my nature and to reflect upon the great principles of the social order" (I, 211). From self-awareness and principles comes the essence of a revolutionary: "The old edifice has collapsed; the portico of a new edifice has been built on its ruins and, thanks to you, I have been able to contribute my block of stone" (I, 211). Called to play a role "in the midst of the greatest events that have ever agitated the world, present at the death-throes of despotism and at the dawn of a true sovereignty," the example of Rousseau inspires as no other. He ardently hopes to leave a name and reputation for virtue by remaining "constantly faithful to the inspiration that I have derived from your writings" (I, 212). The *Confessions* (and only the *Confessions*) are mentioned.

This is as close as we can come to a conversion experience, and if the *Dedication to Rousseau* records a fundamental alteration in Robespierre's life, then his was a conversion unlike those most frequently recorded in the lives of exceptional individuals. Still, there was arguably such a transformation. The *Dedication* expresses sentiments that harmonize with what we know about Robespierre's relationship with Rousseau. The discovery of an authentic self, the connection of eloquence and virtue, the revolutionary experience as essentially spiritual and moral, and hence a worthy subject for autobiography, these are the very qualities that distinguish Robespierre from so many of his contemporaries in the Revolution. That he was led to such self-awareness through Rousseau's *Confessions* is believable. His may have been a bookish conversion, but Robespierre was a bookish man. His pronouncements on the *Confessions* are heartfelt: "Your admirable *Confessions*, that unequivocal and courageous emanation of the purest soul, will pass to posterity less as a model of art than a prodigy of virtue" (I, 212). Robespierre would have appreciated such an assay of his own writing, indeed of his revolutionary career.

Even in the history of Rousseau's reputation and influence, Robespierre's preference for the *Confessions* is a bit unusual. The two most significant texts for the Rousseau cult that attracted numerous devotees were his sentimental and didactic novel *La Nouvelle Héloïse* (1761) and his treatise on education, *Emile* (1762), whose core contains a long and remarkable digression on deism. Robespierre never specifically mentions either work. It is the *Confessions*, "with their author's self-regard, his consciousness of moral superiority and his suffering at the hands of wicked men who had pretended to be his friends," that seduces.[28] Rousseau's *Confessions* were posthumously published in 1782. In that year Robespierre was twenty-four, newly established in Arras. Sometime between 1782 and 1788–89, when he wrote the *Dedication*, he read the *Confessions*.

Intellectual influence cannot usually be rendered in cause-and-effect terms. Rousseau was a powerful, inescapable presence in the eighteenth century, and his impact varied radically from reader to reader. In the *Confessions* Robespierre saw himself, his moral fervor, his self-awareness of his own powers and will and virtue, and he identified closely with the persecutions one had to endure for such moral intensity.[29] Chaste, sober, taciturn, given to melancholy, finding his few pleasures in the modest and quiet security of a family augmented by a small circle of loyal friends, but often alone, Robespierre might have been reading his own autobiography in Rousseau's remarkable book.[30] Even the mode of personal revelation appealed strongly: Robespierre, too, tended to see the world through the distorting lens of his own ego and thought or assumed others would be interested in his innermost self. Rousseau insisted he was a virtuous man, worthy of admiration, perhaps even emulation: Robespierre thought the same of himself. "What placed Jean-Jacques Rousseau above all other writers of his century," argues Sébastien Mercier, "was the fact that his eloquence had a moral character, a real and necessary object of public utility."[31] The belief that politics is a moral science whose undertaking is fit only for the pure, a conviction that gave Rousseau's political writings an appeal and a power beyond those of reason alone, also made Robespierre potent.

More than 250 years after Machiavelli had sundered morality and politics, Robespierre, following Rousseau, rejoined them. The politics of expedience and opportunity may have come eventually to dominate the Revolution, but Robespierre owed much of his authority to his refusal to indulge in such politics. He saw politics and political association as a means of creating happiness, a true human community. Without this goal, political activity had no redeeming characteristics. He considered the practice of politics a moral act permitted only to those above reproach, those who sought no personal gain, who made no compromises. He further thought democracy the only just government because the only natural one: "Every man has, by his very nature, the ability to govern himself by his own will" (VI, 86). Force and fraud, the traditional means of ruling, were with the Revolution to be replaced by virtue and truth: "Man is born for happiness and liberty," he announced, echoing the opening of the *Contrat social*, "and everywhere he is enslaved and unhappy. Society has for its goal the conservation of his rights and the perfection of his being; and everywhere society degrades and oppresses him" (IX, 495).

The goal of all political activity, Rousseau declares in the *Confessions*, is to "form a people [who are] the most virtuous, the most enlightened, the wisest, in a word the best, taking this in its broadest sense."[32] "Those who would treat politics and morality separately," he warns, "will never understand anything about either one."[33] Politics is not arbitrating some compromise: it is "a question of choosing between the general interest and sectional privilege."[34] Those who failed to distinguish, Robespierre believed with his mentor, betrayed the majority for their own advantage. Robespierre, when he came to present his own life and values, did so as a struggle for the realization of virtue in a depraved world, closely following the *Confessions*, although he offered no intimate details about his daily life. But unlike Rousseau, he was an actor. He knew himself to be virtuous, and knew that he could not long remain so in the world as it was. But he did not devote his energies to fleeing society, as did Rousseau, in order to realize his virtue and lead a good life. Robespierre dedicated himself to changing the world.

These profound affinities with Rousseau are complemented in Robespierre's utterances by the frequent citation of his mentor. Rousseau is used as a scriptural authority on education (VIII, 179), the dangers of military dictatorship (IV, 142), human nature (V, 58), and representative government (IX, 504–5), as well as a number of other issues. He found his authentic self in Rousseau in the years immediately preceding the Revolution. As soon as he could, he enlisted in the Revolution.

In 1788, it is estimated, Arras had a population of 20,000.[35] It was the capital of a province that was one of the few remaining *pays d'état*, that is, one that had retained its own representative body, or Estates, when most had been leveled by the monarchy over the years. The Estates of Artois were dominated by the high aristocracy, who, with the assistance of the Bishop of Arras, chose the municipal officers. This oligarchy had struggled successfully for years against the encroachments of the royal government. The summons for elections to a national Estates gave the local version its last chance to assert its privileges. The Estates of Artois met on December 29, 1788. Their first task would be to collect and edit the grievances of the region, the *cahiers de doléances* solicited by the monarchy when it sent out writs calling for elections. Robespierre became involved in this process. He had been asked by the Cordonniers Mineurs, a shoemakers' guild, to draw up their grievances. So well did he accomplish his work that the shoemakers did not even bother to recopy his draft; they signed and submitted it as is.[36] These purely local grievances bear Robespierre's imprint. He rendered the complaints of the shoemakers national in scope by arguing that their economic troubles were caused by the commercial treaty with England, which had raised the price of leather. He also announced, in a purely political context, one of his enduring themes: the duty of the magistrates and the privileged was to protect the poor.[37]

The elections to the national Estates were scheduled for April. Because we cannot precisely date Robespierre's pamphlet *To the Province of Artois* (*A la nation artésienne*), we do not know when he determined to stand for election. Such precision, were it possible, might fix the moment of his conversion. Early 1789 is a good guess because the pamphlet was reissued in an augmented version and was, additionally, followed by another pamphlet, issued just before the elections.[38]

Neither pamphlet displays striking philosophical originality or political radicalism. Robespierre's theoretical contributions to the revolutionary tradition would come later. But both pamphlets might have been written months, or even years, afterward. Here is Robespierre speaking in his familiar revolutionary voice on the issues that would consume his life. "Let us seize this unique moment, chosen from all the centuries by Providence," he says, "to recover the imprescriptible and sacred rights whose loss is both a matter for shame and a source of calamities."[39] Such a moment might never come again. The regeneration of France "depends absolutely on the character and principles of the representatives to whom we are going to give the responsibility of fixing our destiny."[40] An elected deputy, "to be worthy of serving his country must be pure, above all reproach."[41] The elimination of evil "depends on the virtue, on the courage and on the sentiments" of those elected.[42] Robespierre had no doubt that he qualified: "While the enemies of the People have the audacity to play with humanity, could I lack the necessary courage to reclaim its rights?"[43] In his second pamphlet, much more aggressive and devoted to "unmasking" the enemies of the country, by which he apparently means the privileged of Artois— who never forgave him these charges or his election—he announces another characteristic theme, martyrdom: "What does it matter if they try someday to punish the zeal with which I will act to support the public welfare!" The enemies of the country "are already considering making martyrs of all the defenders of the people!"[44] This personification, defender of the people, will soon become his favorite revolutionary personification, representative of the people.

Here is the language of a new, revolutionary political discourse. The "enemies of the country," the "defenders of the people," the "public welfare," the necessity of "virtue" in politics, and the need to "unmask" traitors. In such terms will the Revolution be fought. Robespierre coined none of these words or ideas, but he infused them with a special moral intensity, that of a self-committed and aware revolutionary. At this historic moment, on the very eve of the Revolution, Robespierre revealed himself as he would remain for the rest of his life.

On April 26 Robespierre was elected as the fifth deputy of the Third Estate. He had successfully challenged the regional oligarchs by addressing himself to those outside the narrow circles of political and social power. This tactic, too, would remain essential with him. Not only did he emerge from the election campaign, which was sharply and bitterly contested, a revolutionary speaking a new language, but he also emerged as a man with considerable, hitherto unrecognized and unused political gifts. He was not a man, as his revolutionary career would demonstrate, to leave things to chance.[45] His first election was as carefully prepared as would be all the subsequent elections in which he had a part. So, too, would he orchestrate parliamentary business.[46] Robespierre was that exceedingly rare creature, an ideologue with political skill.

Soon after his triumph, Robespierre packed his few possessions, which included a worn black suit, another (also worn) of the same color but redyed, three pairs of *culottes*, all much used, six shirts in fairly good condition, a new pair of shoes, a box with silk and wool thread and needles to make repairs, and a pile of printed copies of his published briefs and pamphlets, and set off for Versailles.[47]

These are the few actual details of a largely obscure, uneventful prerevolutionary life. These are the unexceptional, ordinary materials out of which Robespierre and history will make a revolutionary career. This career, or at least its spiritual and emotional components, will be carefully recorded by Robespierre himself, and presented regularly to his contemporaries. He will continue the work begun at Arras before the Revolution: writing his political autobiography. He adds nothing to the few biographical details of his life that have survived. His subject is the revolutionary he has become.

In addressing his contemporaries on the subject of himself, Robespierre assumed not only that he was a representative figure, but that many wanted to hear him. French history has had several such figures, self-conscious embodiments of an ideal. However radically different are Jeanne d'Arc, Napoleon, Charles de Gaulle, they all share the belief (or illusion) that they are the saviors of the nation. Robespierre presented himself to contemporaries not only as savior but as revolutionary. He demanded the allegiance of his auditors because of what he was and represented, and knew himself to be. And lest there be any doubt, he incessantly revealed himself in public.

Robespierre was aware that his hold over contemporaries emanated from the imposition of his person on revolutionary politics. His words were a vehicle for expressing the identity of himself and his will with the nation's. Eloquence and virtue, in Rousseau's formula, were inseparable. "You have no idea of the power of truth or the energy of innocence," he writes with revealing naiveté, "when sustained by an imperturbable courage." The great Mirabeau, his words worn smooth from citation, agreed: "He will go far, he believes everything he says."[48]

The unexpected ease with which the society, politics, ideology, assumptions, and self-confidence of the *ancien régime* collapsed at the first blows heartened the revolutionaries. It also put everything up for grabs. The representatives who gathered at Versailles in May 1789 were obsessively concerned with declaring their principles and intentions to fill this cultural void. Robespierre was not alone in providing examples of the new and necessary language of revolution, nor was he much listened to in the first months of the Revolution. But a large part of the politics of the Revolution turned on words and the flow of ideas, on ideology, and Robespierre would eventually win the keen competition to give the Revolution voice, to provide its ideology.[49] His edge in the struggle to lead would be his unique combination of self, principles, and virtue. Marat, the most verbally bloodthirsty of the revolutionaries, was closest to Robespierre in political style. He attributed his success to "the frightful public scandal" he created by "the effusions of my soul, the outbursts of my heart, my violent denunciations of oppression, my violent attacks on the oppressors, my accents of grief, my cries of indignation, fury and despair."[50] The two men were political innovators.

Robespierre's enemies complained that he talked incessantly about himself, which most attributed to a revolting vanity. "A citizen," says Marat in defense, "who is constantly accused by the enemies of the Revolution who hide behind a civic mask, is often reduced to the sad necessity of justifying himself."[51] Neither vanity nor self-defense explain fully. Robespierre's conversion was his recognition of self. Henceforth he could not talk about the Revolution without talking about himself. The self he revealed to his comrades and colleagues was attractive and compelling not because his was a scintillating personality. It was the qualities of his rich and highly politicized inner life that he offered. His asceticism, his righteousness, his total devotion to the Revolution, his virtue, all presented as the stuff from which his political principles arose and all essential to the Revolution, these qualities were more universally appealing than the brilliant personalities surrounding him.

For those who found Robespierre too conventional, Marat and his imitators were more appealing. But what Robespierre lacked in personality and audacity and extravagance, he made up for in intellectual intensity and the disciplined regularity of his personal life. He seemed to have some control over the bewildering succession of events, a profound communion with the logic of the Revolution, which he revealed not only as a great historical occurrence but as his own personal drama as well. In him the particular reveals the universal, the self becomes Everyman. Robespierre had no life apart from the Revolution. He was absolutely absorbed in it. In 1789 the single-mindedness that had expressed itself in eccentricity—as when he left his sister stranded in the street to rush home and resume his reading, oblivious of what he had done when she arrived—became fixed on the Revolution.

So, too, were his moral preoccupations given scope by the Revolution. "The Roman" of Louis-le-Grand prefigured "the representative of the people" just as his exclusive identification with certain causes is already evident in his defense of Dupond. Discussing the long imprisonment of his client, Robespierre suddenly assumes the role of the victim, enumerating *his* sufferings, *his* mistreatment, *his* humiliations.[52] This exceptional capacity for empathy and embodiment would be extended in the Revolution to encompass the longings of the many in his own personal vision. Incongruously the Revolution was mirrored in the mind and sensibility of a provincial lawyer, and the reflection was familiar to an exceptionally large number of his contemporaries.

"Little by little," Nietzsche remarks, "it has become clear to me that every great philosophy has been the confession of its maker, as it were his voluntary and unconscious autobiography."[53] The autobiographical mode came easily to Robespierre and is evident in all his political utterances, from his first pamphlet to his final speech. His revelations of self were presented in the abstract "language of equality"[54] that had supplanted the despised rhetoric of the Court. One now spoke of the rule of laws, of constitutions, declarations of the rights of man, a harmony between men's laws and those of nature, of imprescriptible principles, inalienable rights, of the equality of all men. Robespierre used this language with the ease of a native speaker, and enriched it with the addition of his self. What may now appear stylized verbal formulas were then heard as effusions of the heart that revealed the innermost self of the man at the podium, Robespierre. "Jacobin rhetoric," writes a critic, "is not mere verbiage. It attempts to bridge the gap between theory and practice, to set against the abstract universalism of the *philosophes*, the practicality of morality in action."[55] This is an apposite description of Robespierre's role in the Revolution: he bridged the gap between theory and practice.

The self he revealed was of his own making. He is no longer The Roman personifying some stoic ideal. He is a revolutionary, the representative of the people. In the speeches from the time of the Constituent Assembly he unfolds the characteristics of this self. The representative of the people must be absolutely truthful (IX, 537) and remember that he represents all of France and not merely the region that elected him (VIII, 169). The true representative will "sometimes struggle alone, with [his] conscience, against the torrent of prejudices and factions" (VIII, 64), and the test of his worthiness will be to offend all factions, all corporations (VIII, 309). Absolute personal integrity is essential. "Never has a single person accused me of having practiced a base *métier*," he declares in a bit of social and class snobbery, "or of stigmatizing my name by dishonorable connections or scandalous proceedings" (VIII, 307). Contemporaries agreed in valuing his rectitude. "If you ask me," writes Billaud-Varenne, an enemy and rival, "how he was able to have so much ascendance over public opinion, I would answer that it is because he ostentatiously showed the most austere virtues, the most absolute dedication and the purest principles."[56]

He considered the position of deputy superior to all others in the Revolution, and reminded that he had resigned a "tranquil post" on the High Court of Versailles "in order to seek a painful and dangerous post" as deputy (VIII, 362). He later refused a nomination for mayor of Paris because "he knows of no human force that could make him agree to exchange the position of representative of the people for any other, no matter how important it might appear."[57] When offered a ministry, he spurned it: "A representative of the people who has only loyalty and freedom is infinitely above a minister . . . with the enormous treasures the Revolution has put into his hands" (IX, 215). It is ironic that a man who so consistently avoided office and the influence it carried should have been charged with seeking the dictatorship.

Robespierre's ideal representative, which he considered himself, has no private life. Although he never discusses intimacies, he does talk about his health. Even these patches of revelation are curiously political and public, for he always speaks of his health in terms of the Revolution. What in another might be thought hypochondria or the annoying habit of taking his pulse in public, is in Robespierre tracking the Revolution. His recurrent complaints of fatigue, exhaustion, vague, undiagnosed illness, seem synchronized with times of crisis.[58] There is a temptation, which Robespierre encouraged, to take these fluctuations of health as a barometer of the Revolution. He speaks of himself as "exhausted by four years of revolution and by the intolerable spectacle of the triumph of everything that is most corrupt." He describes himself, in the midst of his career (IX, 537–38), as "consumed by a slow fever, and even more by a fever of patriotism." "I no longer have the necessary vigor to fight the intrigues of the aristocracy," he laments. He is "exhausted by four years of painful and fruitless work." His physical and moral powers are no longer "up to the level of a great revolution" (IX, 553).

"Had it pleased God," he remarks after a serious bout of incapacitating illness, "that my physical powers were equal to my moral powers I would today have confounded all the traitors and called down on all guilty heads the national vengeance" (X, 374). He often worried aloud that the Revolution had chosen a weak instrument. His mission was compromised by his frail physique. Near the end of his career he appeared to function on sheer willpower. Would he live long enough to finish his work? Had he the force of will to endure all that his destiny, all that the Revolution demanded? Who, he asks, would carry on if his health collapsed? (X, 373). These are late fears, but the extension of his early and complete identification of self and Revolution. Robespierre had no life of his own, no hobbies, no relaxations, no diversions for the mind, the spirit, the body: he was unable to replenish his diminishing forces. If he ceased to struggle, he would die.

Indeed he saw himself as doomed. In a sense he saw all revolutionaries as doomed. If the Revolution didn't kill him, an assassin would. Assassination was part of the stoic baggage many of the revolutionaries carried. Tombs and suicides and frightful oaths of personal sacrifice, an almost hysterical defiance of death, are frequent in the oratory of the Revolution. Robespierre often struck these familiar poses: "They compare me to the Gracchi. They have good reason to compare me to them; what there will, perhaps, be in common between us will be a tragic end" (VIII, 326). At the end as at the beginning of his career he spoke of a "final debt" that he had contracted when he entered the Revolution. "The founders of the Republic can only find peace in the tomb" (X, 399), he cries, and later invites tyrants and conspirators to do their worst: "There will always remain to me my position as representative of the people and I will wage a war to the death" (X, 516). This was not posturing. The Revolution was dangerous. His earliest presentations of self were largely literary, his imagined violent end presented in stylized and even tragic form. But soon enough these literary conceits became real. He felt himself at risk: "My life belongs to my country; my heart is free of fear. If I should die it will be without reproach and without ignominy" (X, 414).

This morbid theme he linked to a concern for posterity, both for himself and for the Revolution. In his most self-indulgent moments he saw "in the tomb" the "only sure and precious asylum reserved by Providence for virtue" (IX, 623). Rejected, literally as well as metaphorically, by his contemporaries, he hoped for posthumous acceptance. His murder, as he persuaded himself of its reality, would be his reward for his virtue and would simultaneously certify it. He did not seek martyrdom, although he talked often about it. This was the unavoidable price to be paid by a revolutionary: "If the virtuous men despair of the Assembly, if they can no longer struggle against the current of intrigue and prejudices, they can at least die at the tribune, defending the rights of humanity" (VIII, 183). His violent death had been foretold: "I have been called to a tumultuous destiny. I must follow its course until I have made the final sacrifice that I can offer my country."[59] This was the preordained end to a revolutionary life. "I sometimes tremble of being soiled in the eyes of posterity," he laments, "by the impure proximity of these perverse men who insinuate themselves into the midst of the sincere defenders of humanity" (X, 574).

Robespierre reserved nothing from the insatiable demands of the Revolution. And his fears were realized: the Revolution devoured him. But in preaching the new politics of moral regeneration, and attaching himself to all his actions, when he fell his death took on the proportions of a morality play, one that still has the power to move. The epithet he most consistently applied to himself, the representative of the people, did not outlive its creator. In its place was put another epithet, also created at the time of the Revolution, The Incorruptible. This stuck. The authentic revolutionary is incorruptible.

CHAPTER 3

Representative of the People

PLATE V
(Phot. Bibl. nat. Paris)

ROBESPIERRE arrived at Versailles to represent the Third Estate of Artois just before his thirty-first birthday. He had had, like hundreds of his colleagues, no political experience, certainly no parliamentary experience. His reputation as a forceful and enlightened lawyer, a people's lawyer, even a poor man's lawyer, hardly reached outside of Arras. His two first political pamphlets had not circulated beyond the province. France had been inundated with pamphlets for more than a year, since the King lifted the censorship, and several of these were more radical and important than what Robespierre had written: Abbé Sieyès had become a celebrity upon publication of *What Is the Third Estate?* Not only did Robespierre bring with him no reputation, but his quiet life in Arras had not even been disturbed by any participation in the lively national debates on reform in which the court had been embroiled in the last years of the *ancien régime*.[1] Indeed, there is no evidence he had much interest in such matters. But, if he was only another obscure provincial at Versailles, undistinguished from the hundreds like him, he had announced his views and declared himself before he left Arras. He arrived ambitious to realize the ideas and the self he had proclaimed.

The first meetings of the Estates-General, once the formalities of the opening of the sessions with a *Te Deum* in the Church of Saint Louis and a formal procession of the three orders of representatives—Clergy, Nobility, Commons—were held separately and were mostly taken up with administrative matters. In the Commons there were tedious days of verification of credentials and a growing feeling, voiced by many, that they, although they represented the overwhelming majority of Frenchmen—Abbé Sieyès had estimated the Third Estate composed 97 percent of the population—were being snubbed, and there was considerable sentiment that the three orders should meet as one, that the nation should no longer be divided politically according to the traditional but now artificial divisions inherited from the medieval past.

By the third week of May 1789, when Robespierre sent his Arras friend Buissart a remarkable letter analyzing politics and personalities, nothing to match the subsequent revolutionary legislation had been achieved. The Commons were bogged down in internal wrangles, they had yet to declare themselves the National Assembly, they had yet to swear they would not disperse until they had given France a constitution (as they would do in the Tennis Court Oath of June 17), and they had yet to hear the proposals of the King. The "bourgeois revolution," as one historian designates the seizing of the initiative by the Commons, had hardly begun, and all its heroic deeds lay in the future. The great urban and rural upheavals of the summer that would establish the Revolution beyond the reach of dispersal by an armed Court, had not occurred. Yet Robespierre was able to see what others missed. Nearly fifty years later, this penetrating letter was shown to King Louis Philippe, who had himself actively participated in the Revolution and well remembered the circumstances being analyzed: "It is perfectly exact," the King said.[2] It was Robespierre's first essay as an analyst of the Revolution and shows at the outset of his career his instinct for such work. He disregards details and goes right to the essence: revolution and not reform is the issue:

> The power of the clergy has been thrown down by the decree that declares ecclesiastical goods at the disposal of the nation. The parlements [law courts considered a bastion of the aristocracy] received the following day a guarantee of their destruction. . . . The feudal aristocracy is almost annihilated. The greatest abuses seem to have disappeared at the voice of the representatives of the nation. Will we be free? I believe I can still put this question.

It was a question Robespierre would put for the next five years. One of the qualities of conviction and mind that gave him prestige and attracted followers was his belief that the Revolution must be fought to its conclusion, which he saw as the complete destruction of the counterrevolution, in its various forms. From the first weeks of the Estates-General this article of faith was among his tenets. Once begun, the Revolution must be fought to its end. Compromise or expediency was out of the question. Shortly they would be considered by him yet another form of counterrevolution.

In June, when the Commons won their first revolutionary victories and were able to sweep aside the old Estates-General with its three orders and constitute themselves as a single legislative body, shortly to be called the Constituent Assembly, the bourgeois revolution, largley judicial and legal in character, had taken its first steps. The successful attack on the Bastille in Paris (July 14) would solidify these first victories and convey Paris into the hands of the Revolution. The massive rural riots of the late summer, the so-called Great Fear, would not only reveal the profound weaknesses of the crumbling *ancien régime*, its inability to police the nation, let alone reform it, but would provoke, during the dramatic night of August 4, when the nobility voluntarily divested themselves of feudal privilege, the destruction of the feudal regime of encumbrances on the land and on persons. By early fall the Constituent Assembly ruled. The dismantling of the church, the official proscription of nobility, the legal curbs on the King's authority, and the writing of France's first constitution remained to be accomplished. But the first months of revolution had made France a parliamentary nation. All looked to the Constituent for regeneration.

Robespierre had participated in all these parliamentary struggles, and in Jacques-Louis David's unfinished painting commemorating the Tennis Court Oath he was given a prominent place among the oath-takers. But if he had partially emerged from the shadows of obscurity, his politics of virtue, of moral intensity and even messianic fervor, had found few adherents. The Constituent was a school of adversity for Robespierre. Nearly all his proposals were rejected by the deputies. Even his most reformist suggestions were thought ominously radical. He defended positions that had little popularity in the Constituent, and although his advocacy of democratic procedures (one man, one vote) and the elimination of all privilege surviving from the *ancien régime* seem essential to any liberal society, and not especially radical, he was distrusted and unheeded. Part of the reason, aside from the fear that the democratization of France was premature and would lead to some kind of mob rule, was Robespierre's manner of confronting his colleagues. He consistently supported his proposals, and provided his auditors (even when not asked) with moral views and moral definitions of the Revolution. The deputies wanted no such guidance. They understood regeneration as the excision of the most obvious and hateful corruptions of the *ancien régime*, accomplished with as little basic disruption as possible. Thus would health be restored to the nation. Robespierre went further. His moral stridency was received, and rightly so, as a rebuke to those who disagreed with him. In addition, his insistence on the mission of the Revolution and its deputies made him appear a demagogue.

By regeneration Robespierre envisioned not so much a world cleansed of old refuse, intransigence, privilege, and obscurantism; he saw a world remade, a world filled with men rededicated to the common good. He viewed basic, revolutionary change as a moral matter. The task of the Revolution was to change human nature itself. This obsession had textual justification in a famous passage from Rousseau's *Contrat social:* "he who would undertake to create a people should see himself as involved, so to speak, in changing human nature."[3] Robespierre had no hesitations or reservations about so immense an undertaking.

The Constituent, like all the assemblies of the Revolution, was bourgeois in social composition, and consisted overwhelmingly of lawyers. Nearly half its members were, like Robespierre, provincial lawyers. Such professional training may have induced caution and circumspection and much respect for procedures as well as a taste for purely judicial distinctions. But in addition, most of Robespierre's colleagues thought him far too daring in his proposals. As a body they had more willingness to compromise and negotiate; they considered politics a series of acts that could be principled yet accommodating to the demands both of personality and circumstance. They certainly had no desire to alter human nature, and doubtless many thought this beyond possibility. In principle they did not object to legal equality, to the various civil freedoms of speech and press and assembly and worship, but each of these principles had to be realized and expressed within an inherited context of self and corporate interest, traditions and expediency. Freedom needed careful definition, careful hedges against license, careful legal qualifications and restrictions. Robespierre's moral imperative, which cut through all this prudence, was threatening. With it, the Constituent thought, came disorder and an encouragement to social agitation. Robespierre did not, in the Constituent or in the Convention in which he later sat, call for an attack on property, a destruction of all social distinctions, or a general leveling of society, although he was frequently charged with such advocacy. But those to whom he appealed, from the beginning of his career, were outside the assemblies. This cultivated popular following was another of the reasons he was feared by his colleagues. Transcending the procedures of the Constituent, looking to the streets, so to speak, as the basis of political authority, was abhorrent.

These fears were exaggerated. Robespierre never went so far to the Left as his enemies averred; that they thought him a dangerous radical, only slightly less unsavory than Marat, is instructive. Robespierre would not be called by his colleagues, either in the Constituent or the Convention, to assume some official post of authority at their disposal until the summer of 1793. He was estranged from the majority in the Constituent by his radicalism, as he would be subsequently, although in the intervening years both he and the Revolution had moved to the left. Here is but another of the remarkable consistencies about his career.

In the Constituent he incessantly went to the podium to propose and to dissent. He first spoke on May 18 (almost two weeks after the meetings began), making a proposal concerning the clergy (VI, 251). In the first eight months of the Revolution he went to the tribune, as the speaker's dias was called, twenty-five times. In 1790 Robespierre was at the tribune more than eighty times; and from January to September 1791, more than sixty times. From the beginning those who found his politics and his personality uncongenial were outspoken. He was accused of talking too much about himself. He was accused of intransigence. He was accused of pomposity and an annoying posture of moral superiority, of arrogance and outlandish opinions stridently maintained. This early-compiled list of grievances, with only a few additions—most notably a supposed lust for dictatorship—would be often quoted against him. This catalogue of calumny and shortcomings is as revealing of its victim as of its compilers. It is a list, not necessarily realistic, of what his colleagues feared about him. One of the central ironies of Robespierre's revolutionary career, which is a parliamentary career, is that he was quite unsuccessful as a parliamentary politician or leader. In the Constituent only one of his legislative proposals was accepted; and even in the Convention—he served only in these two assemblies—he was not irresistible in debate or argument and did not overcome the continuing resistence to his person and ideas by commanding a tight parliamentary organization that could produce the needed majorities. Quite the contrary.

What authority Robespierre had in the Constituent and the Convention he brought into the sessions from outside its precincts. This popularity beyond the walls of the National Assembly Robespierre's colleagues both despised and feared. It added to dislike and distrust of the man, who appeared to represent a massive, potentially riotous, and faceless constituency. He was not, like so many of his rivals, a man of the Assembly, wholly dependent upon it, wholly devoted to its interests and prerogatives. He was not elected president, he never sat at the secretaries' table, he neither served on nor headed any important (or unimportant) committee. Only in the midst of the grim summer of 1793, with civil war convulsing the west of the country, with Lyons, the second city in France, in open revolt, with the southeast equally rebellious, with the foreign war stagnating and vast sections of the nation beyond the control of the government, only then, after more than four years of revolution, on July 27, did his colleagues choose him to sit on the Committee of Public Safety. And even this choice was made with enormous reluctance: it came after a purge of the Convention and some months after that famous Committee had been first established. Robespierre had had to wait an exceptionally long time for power, and the only power he received, the only power the Revolution would tolerate, was collegial: he shared the Committee's dictatorship of the Revolution with eleven colleagues.

That this enormously popular man was kept so long from power is instructive. Whatever the specific reservations about his personality or politics, he was feared. The false accusation that he aspired to the dictatorship is ample evidence. And he was feared by the majority of his deputy colleagues, at both the outset and the end of his career. It is important to remember that most of the elected representatives were back-benchers. They took no active, conspicuous part in the debates or deliberations. They had no desire to call attention to themselves, leading the terrorist Carrier to quip that most were known only to the paymaster. These back-benchers, in the crisis of revolution, could be drawn from their obscurity—as they were in some of the agonizing roll-call votes of the Revolution—but as a group they sought accommodation rather than confrontation and were most comfortable with those parliamentary leaders who not only catered to them, but offered easy, safe choices. They were referred to, sneeringly, as the Marais, the swamp that lay between the benches of the right and the left. But not only did the Marais hold the balance of voting power between the contending factions; it was the majority of the National Assembly. No parliamentary business could be done without these reluctant votes. Robespierre, like other orators, addressed his arguments to the Marais, but he was singularly uncompromising in his relationship with them and more often than not gave the impression that he was more interested in impressing those outside the Assembly—the Paris militants or the Jacobins, both Parisian and provincial—than in winning over the uncommitted deputies. He was not a smooth seducer.

For most of his career the Marais remained not only deaf to his pleas and arguments, but hostile. They had refused to take a seat with either the Right or Left, an expression of pusillanimity Robespierre detested, and they were not about to throw themselves into the politics Robespierre advocated. It is difficult to persuade those one despises. His moral imperatives, his depictions of self as more worthy than others, his dangerous proposals for more democracy, his concern for the poor, and his sinister support in the Paris streets, often from the most feared militants, all drove the Marais to seek other options. He was frequently linked with Marat, for his opponents shrewdly guessed that this would deepen suspicion of Robespierre, and the two men inspired social fears in the Marais, indeed throughout the Constituent.

Even among those who later adhered to his leadership, who followed a *robespierriste* line, there were several who did so reluctantly. In the middle ranks of the Jacobins, those who did not formally make policy but who were trusted with various missions outside Paris because of their political reliability and personal energy, there were misgivings about Robespierre. These men were the backbone of the Jacobins, and when they were eventually proscribed and forced into exile, they accepted their fate without abandoning their beliefs. In the imposed leisure of defeat, some explained their adherence to Robespierre, for whom they had little personal affection. René Levasseur and Jean Dyzèz, to name but two such reluctant *robespierristes*, said they followed him because he offered the only acceptable line, the only ideology that led to the great goals of liberty, equality, and fraternity for which they had first joined the Revolution. Robespierre was not loved because he was not lovable. But as his adherents overcame their reservations, so even the Marais had eventually to overcome its fears. When Robespierre was at last called to power in the Convention—and he never exercised an exclusively personal power even at the apogee of his career—his authority had become necessary and irresistible.

At the outset of his career tenacity was his most important quality. He was often heckled by spectators hired by his enemies. Undaunted, he continued to mount the tribune. Soon he was recognized as the spokesman for the Artois deputation, both by his fellow *artésiens* and the Constituent. Notoriety, even when occasioned by paid hecklers, was useful. By June 6 the unknown provincial was being listened to, or at least there was a diminuendo in the general level of noise that greeted most speakers, so wrote a witness to his correspondent in Arras.[4] And although his views were shared by so few of his colleagues, he gradually came to be listened to, not as an eccentric or a crank but as a man who had something to say. Indicative of his emerging stature, and there is no dramatic confrontation, no single brilliant speech we can point to as the turning point, is the space gradually given to his speeches in the newspapers, which begin to report them with accuracy and thoroughness: they even learn to spell his odd name.[5]

Robespierre spoke on virtually all the issues that came before the Constituent, although he hadn't a great deal to say on economic or administrative matters. He was especially interested in questions of social equality, political democracy, and the constitution. These questions would continue to engage his attention. Throughout the Constituent he tacitly supported the *laissez-faire* policies voted and condoned the vast confiscations of church property carried out under the complicated legislation referred to as the Civil Constitution of the Clergy (1790), one of the fundamental pieces of revolutionary legislation, which stripped the church of its worldly wealth while subjecting its clergy to the discipline of the state. "The clergy," Robespierre insists (here in complete agreement with the majority), "is not a landlord; indeed it is not good for religion, for the state, nor for itself that it be a landlord."[6] His willingness to see the church expropriated and regulated by the state did not dull his concern for those in holy orders whose lives would be permanently disrupted. He appealed to "the humanity of the Assembly" to provide for "old ecclesiastics" who had only "poverty and their infirmities" to show for a lifetime of duty and devotion (VI, 437). His hatred of privilege is apparent in his attack on the generous provisions made for bishops forcibly retired because they refused to support the Revolution, while the lesser clergy were shown no such consideration (VI, 408). But when the most important piece of legislation dealing with the rights and obligations of labor and business, the Le Chapelier law, was debated and passed, Robespierre was silent. He thus allowed all labor organizations and workmen's combinations—as well as those of manufacturers, but this was less socially threatening—to be prohibited. The champion of the *sans-culottes* did not see their interests to be best served by their own organizations. It is this assumption that all the interests of the poor, of the working class, would best be served by broad-based revolutionary organizations rather than by separate agitational groups, that determined Robespierre's stance. He was not, as has sometimes been argued, indifferent to economic matters. He considered them less important than ideololgy (as did virtually everyone at the time). Nor was he hostile to the workers, a man of the bourgeoisie incapable of budging on basic class issues, which has also been argued. He deeply distrusted all organizations capable of developing an *esprit de corps*, particular interests that might conflict with the general interest. He sincerely believed the interests of the working class would be best served by the triumph of the Revolution, which during the Constituent meant the success of his democratic proposals and the curbing of all old privileges and preventing new ones from emerging. On these issues he was an isolated voice, without faction or following, regularly supported only by his comrade, Jérôme Pétion. But the majority successfully opposed the kind of egalitarian democracy Robespierre advocated and articulated.

France was to be regenerated, Robespierre believed, through good laws. The creation of a political democracy resting on political equality guaranteed by a constitution was fundamental. The legal authority of the nation was to be used to create liberty, by force if need be. Following Rousseau, he considered the law an instrument for social change and was as authoritarian as his mentor in his willingness to compel citizens to do what he thought right. On the question of civil liberties, which he considered less important than using the law to transform the nation, he had sound liberal views. He fought for freedom of speech (VII, 140), freedom of the press (VII, 321), freedom from arbitrary search (VII, 540), freedom from censorship (VII, 459), and freedom from tamperings with private correspondence (VII, 85). He insisted that judges be elected (VII, 26) and that there be citizen juries (VII, 65) and equal punishment for crimes in the armed forces (VI, 507). He shared the faith of his age in the need for a constitution but strenuously opposed the successful attempt to exclude vast numbers of poor from all the rights of citizenship, making them "passive and useless members of the public body."[7] He called for frequent elections (VI, 78), democratic access to the new militia, the National Guard (VI, 622)—both of which causes he lost—unrestrained right of petition (VI, 451), and, his most significant legislative success in the Constituent, the decree that deputies could not be reelected (VII, 408; VIII, 419–20). The *esprit de corps* he feared among labor or manufacturing combinations he feared equally among his colleagues. He wanted deputies paid lest the people be delivered "up to the aristocracy of the rich" (VII, 36), and he argued that "each deputy belongs to the people and not to his colleagues" (V, 169). He himself had no other source of income save his salary, and diligently sent some of it home to Charlotte (X, 111).[8] Much more radically he demanded an armed citizenry as the only sure defense against state intrusion (VII, 288), a position he would incessantly defend.

On a number of minor matters, especially those dealing with the rights of small and despised groups, he was equally attentive. He thought the prejudice against actors "absurd" in itself and harmful in a society where the theater should become one of the "public schools of sound morals and patriotism" (VI, 168). With striking modernity he insisted that Jews by citizens since they had been made an alien element by their oppressors. It was the task of the Revolution to expiate the "national crimes" committed against Jews: the vices attributed to them are "our own injustices." If the Jews were excluded from the new society, it would rest "on the violation of the eternal principles of justice and reason which are the basis of all human society." He similarly loathed slavery and demanded citizenship for *les hommes de couleur,* as nonwhites were called in the colonies. They were now represented by white men, which, he argued, was like asking an assembly "half composed of ecclesiastics and half of nobles" whether or not the Third Estate ought to be consulted (VII, 349). "Let the colonies perish," he cried, rather than slavery continue (VII, 362). Slaves were not property. "Ask this merchant of human flesh what is property. He will tell you, pointing to this long coffin that he calls a ship, in which are locked and chained men who appear to be alive, 'Here is my property. I bought them at so much per head.' " "Ask this gentleman who has lands and ships," he provocatively continues, "or who believes that the universe should be overturned so that he can acquire more, and he will give you almost identical ideas about property" (IX, 460). He prudently deleted the offensive equation of slave ownership with private property from the published version of the speech. The slavers never forgave.

He opposed, unsuccessfully, all attempts to limit the franchise by imposing a property qualification. The Constituent tied voting to taxes paid, creating two classes of citizens; "active" and "passive" were the euphemisms of the day. Robespierre's democratic faith rested on the poor being able to defend themselves from the rich, for goodwill was not wholly reliable (VI, 131). It was the government's responsibility to ensure universal participation,[9] and he spoke passionately of a duty to protect "the weak from the strong" (V, 18). All who failed to do so were "tyrants, oppressors, slaves, the national enemies of equality" (VII, 472).

In harmony with this democratic bias, Robespierre wanted severe limitations on the King's power. The King ought to be no more than a mere magistrate. With his scrupulousness for the conformity of words and things, he demanded that the King "be called the first public functionary, the chief of the executive power, but never the representative of the nation" (VII, 614). The new constitution, which restricted the kingship to the Bourbon family and otherwise created numerous privileges denied all other citizens, made them "a family distinguished from other citizens . . . what absurdity!" (VII, 664–65). And the absurd was politically dangerous, leaving in the midst of the Revolution "the indestructible root of the nobility" (VII, 669). To grant this absurd remnant a veto over legislation, he continues the argument, even a suspensive veto that could only delay laws for two legislative sessions but not destroy them, was "to annihilate the first principles of the constitution" (VII, 612–13).[10] Leaving the King with considerable constitutional power while preserving some of his unique privileges—a peculiar kind of legal immunity from most crimes, with the hypothetical exceptions of withdrawing his constitutional oath, fleeing the country, or fighting against the citizenry—only delayed what Robespierre thought the inevitable reckoning between monarchy and Revolution. The King *was* the counterrevolution for Robespierre.

Another of the concerns, or obsessions, that runs through Robespierre's utterances during the Constituent is a fear of government itself. A commonplace for eighteenth-century liberals was the need to protect the individual from the state. One proposal was to have all administrators, ministers, and appointees answerable to the elected deputies (VII, 105–6) rather than the King. And lest the deputies themselves become oppressors, he wanted to increase their numbers: "The more numerous they are, the more difficult it will be for intrigue to appear" ((VI, 140). The law courts, to which the abused appealed, were to be "totally renewed and as often as possible" (VI, 583).

He shared as well the humanitarian sensibilities of his age and pursued them logically. He opposed the death penalty as barbaric, while the majority made capital punishment part of a renewed France. All these views commanded grudging attention, for although only a minority adhered to Robespierre, he did represent a respectable part of society, and his views had deep roots in the writings of the *philosophes.* In general, those of moderate opinions in the Constituent, although they did not vote to support Robespierre, were loath to attack him for defending such causes. At best they would insist that one must move slowly and cautiously toward democracy and egalitarianism, that Robespierre was both too idealistic and too rash. The royalists had no such reservations: they lavished upon him a vile and scurrilous attention, one that his more moderate or temperate critics did nothing to stop. He was the most verbally abused man in the Constituent, indeed in the Revolution, both while alive and after his death. This verbal mauling in the royalist press was a certificate of radicalism, a purple heart to be proudly worn,[11] but Robespierre would doubtless have done without the wounds. He was able to defend himself, to give as good as he got (and often better), yet the attacks had their impact. Calumny came, increasingly, to obsess him. It gradually assumed enormous proportions in his mind as one of the chief weapons of the counterrevolution. For a man of words these symbols are of unquestioned importance. Schemes for destroying calumny became a part of many of his proposals, and in the privacy of his notebooks he often recorded his impotent rage at those who insulted him and went unpunished. In a sense his assumption that the counterrevolution turned on vilification of the Revolution is the logical antithesis of his assumption that the Revolution was largely, maybe exclusively, a spiritual phenomenon. But the long years of vituperation he endured, first from the royalists and later from republicans in opposition, cemented this belief and set up in his mind a reflex: calumny was counterrevolutionary, a dangerous synapse in a bitterly fought revolution where personalities as well as ideology were daily attacked in debate and in the press.

Robespierre's words in the Constituent, taken together, set forth his first attempt at an ideology for the Revolution. Much that he said would be retained for the rest of his career, taking its place in an ever-enlarging mosaic as the Revolution evolved. The same can be said of his personal life, which complemented his thought. He appeared to live what he taught. He had long insisted that public and private morality could not be separated, and one of the purposes of the Revolution was to make a world in which virtue would be rewarded, be demanded, and have scope. In the new society Robespierre envisioned, virtue would not be confined to hearth and home.

As his reputation spread from the Constituent to the provinces, he began attracting unsought supporters who wanted to emulate not only what he said but what he was. The most famous example of his emergence as an exemplary model is Saint-Just's oft-quoted letter of August 19, 1789. Young, enthusiastic provincials wrote seeking advice (or offering it), lavishing praise, conveying information. Robespierre was assiduous in responding.[12]

> You who sustain the vacillating country [writes Saint-Just] against the torrent of despotism and intrigue, you whom I know as I know God, by your miracles, I address myself to you, monsieur, to beg you to join with me in saving my poor region.
>
> I don't know you, but you are a great man. You are not merely the deputy of a province, you are the representative of humanity and of the republic.[13]

It was this kind of support, from outside the assemblies of the Revolution, that formed the basis of Robespierre's eventual power, and the enthusiasm for his public person as worthy—and most knew him only through his words reprinted or reported—is significant.

There are some glimpses of his purely private life in the early months of the Constituent meetings, after the Assembly had moved from Versailles in October. Indeed it is almost exclusively from his Paris years that the little domestic information we have comes.

His first rooms in Paris, at 30, rue Saintonge, were respectable, if a bit austere, complementing his frugal life and declaring his political situation, lying between the popular quarter of the faubourg Saint-Antoine, from whence were recruited most of the attackers of the Bastille, and the more bourgeois and aristocratic quarters of the western parts of Paris.[14] Although he had far less leisure time on his hands than he had had in Arras, his life was not significantly changed. He continued to rise early and gave considerable time to his appearance, especially his hair, which received careful combing, curling, and powdering even now that this style was becoming outmoded and even thought "aristocratic," and his coat, which was always well brushed despite the clear signs of wear inevitable in a wardrobe that contained only two coats. He would continue to dress in a style of the *ancien régime* while most around him ostentatiously abandoned the manners and fashion of a rejected past. Robespierre's coiffure and dress, as well as his invariably correct comportment, were a declaration of a self he thought appropriate to a representative of the people. He never considered changing.[15] He had no need to dress in the manner of a street radical. He looked always like the provincial lawyer he was. Later, when he was the acknowledged spokesman for the radicals and the Left and the *sans-culottes*, he declined to wear the symbolic Phyrigian cap or red bonnet, one of the symbols of popular street politics, thought originally to have been the cap given to a freed slave in the Roman Empire.

Robespierre insisted upon distinguishing himself from those he represented and said he loved, those he would be willing to die for but not join in the streets. He found it unthinkable to dress in any manner other than one that befit his place in society, although the society in which he was jealous of his status was in full revolution: the distinctions he was anxious to maintain were fast vanishing. Nevertheless, a representative of the people need not dress like his constituents. His neatness of appearance was frequently noticed, and there were few critical remarks of his style of dress.

Concerning that other material declaration of self, a man's physical surroundings at home, we have some information. Charlotte Robespierre is unconcerned with describing how she and her brother lived in Arras from 1787 until 1789. All the details about the rooms in the rue Saintonge come from Pierre Villiers, a tainted source. But when Robespierre moved—as a matter of personal safety during the panic that seized radicals when repression set in after the King's attempted flight abroad and Lafayette's massacre of unarmed petitioners in the old military exercise grounds of the Champ de Mars where they were calling for Louis's abdication, in the summer of 1791—he emerged from these domestic shadows.

Robespierre was offered a temporary refuge from possible arrest (or even assassination) during the reactionary period by a Jacobin supporter, Monsieur Duplay, at 366, rue Saint-Honoré. Duplay was a master carpenter who employed as many as a dozen journeymen and apprentices in his shop, which was attached to his house. In addition to this property in the rue Saint-Honoré, he owned two other pieces of real estate in Paris. He was a devoted *robespierriste* and would eventually suffer the fate of his leader. He was also a typical Jacobin: relatively comfortable, politically dedicated and active, a self-made man who was hard-working, attached to the cause of the artisanate, and a patriot. His entire family shared his political enthusiasms and were delighted to have

Robespierre as a temporary guest—more than delighted, for in their circles it would have been an honor, a subject of neighborhood gossip. Robespierre, it is conventionally said, was engaged to Eléanor Duplay, the eldest daughter, but this is only on her testimony. Another daughter did marry the young *robespierriste* Le Bas, who was guillotined with Robespierre, and the Duplay home became a regular meeting place for Robespierre's friends and intimates, for the inner circle of his comrades.

At the Duplays', Robespierre's life and surroundings were comfortable, respectable, eminently bourgeois; and he was pampered by his adoring hosts. He did not, when fleeing rumored reprisals, seek shelter in the faubourg Saint-Antoine; he did not seek out a hovel in the bowels of Paris, where lay much of his popular support. The Duplay home was suitable to one of his position, with its respectable neighborhood, vine-covered walls, quiet courtyard, and proper owners. He stayed on until his death. These surroundings declare the man. By the summer of 1791 he was established as a leading figure on the left, one of the major attractions at the Jacobin Society. He was ready to abandon the solitude of the rue Saintonge for the unique domestic comforts offered by the Duplays. He found here not only the tranquillity he needed, discreetly arranged and maintained by Mme. Duplay and her daughters—and Robespierre seems to have loved all this female attention—but he found that he could also fulfill a satisfying role as elder brother, one he had played all his life but now, for the first time, could enjoy without the many attendant responsibilities and worries of supporting Charlotte and Augustin. At the Duplays' he enjoyed being the most respected member of the family, whose moral and intellectual ascendancy was unquestioned. Briefly he tried to gather his own little family into the comfortable Duplay nest, but Charlotte proved so jealous of his attention, so hostile to Mme. Duplay, that he and Augustin reluctantly decided to send her back to Arras, after some worry that such a move would cause them to be ill thought of.

Although Robespierre was most at his ease in the midst of bourgeois domesticity, he depended upon others to create such an environment for him. Left to himself, he would have perpetuated his solitude in bleak rented rooms. It is worth noting that he fought the Revolution from the comfort of a bourgeois home.[16] His passivity, his willingness to have others look after him, bespeaks an indifference to the mundane. He knew nothing of the marketplace; in Paris, as it had been in Arras, food awaited him at table, including the fruit he adored. Similarly, he knew nothing of the conditions of the desperately poor, with whom he never fraternized extensively. And there is no record that he ever went next door at the Duplays' to talk to the carpenters in the shop: the employees were forbidden to enter the house.[17]

The contrast between Robespierre *en famille* and at the tribune of the National Assembly or the Jacobins is as striking as that between his politics and his dress, manners, and comportment. Often, after an evening promenade, when there was no meeting at the Jacobins, Robespierre would read aloud Corneille, Voltaire, or Rousseau to the assembled family and frequently his intimate friends as well. Gathered in the sedate house of the Duplays were some of the most advanced and audacious radicals of the day, listening to Robespierre read the French classics or Filippo Buonarotti play the piano and sing. Buonarotti would shortly become one of the first theorists (and practitioners) of conspiratorial politics conducted by clandestine cadres. The sophisticated culture of the *ancien régime*, the salon culture, thrived in the Revolution, certainly among its leaders. Unlike Rousseau, Robespierre did not abandon his society. He disliked the unconventional in life, although he almost daily denounced the conventional from the tribune. He was a virtuous man, and virtue need fear no unease in these matters. Virtue, for Robespierre, was not a matter of class or circumstance: it was an emanation of the will. He did consider the aristocracy incapable of virtue, while the poor he thought virtuous in an abstract sense. Still, these social and personal habits brought from Arras enhanced his reputation rather than tarnished it. His life was seen, by him as by others, as modest, industrious, absolutely above scandal or suspicion.

Because Robespierre was willing and eager to have others order his life for him, he left little room for personal expression. His own room at the Duplays' was simply furnished, with a bed, a writing table, a small bookcase. Only a terra-cotta bust in a niche, his portrait on the wall, declared the place his. Otherwise he was content with the simple yet bourgeois surroundings in which he lived. His probity, application to work, revulsion against great wealth and destructive poverty, his modest habits, all received adequate expression at the Duplays'. He was able to appeal as a representative figure not only to the Jacobins, who much resembled him and held many of his values, but also to the *sans-culottes*, who were not bourgeois but nevertheless shared several of these values.[18] He similarly appealed to those who owned a small shop, made their living by the pen, were in business, or held minor positions as functionaries. These disparate social groups not only saw a lack of posturing or pretense in Robespierre, but "loved him for his bourgeois politeness, his well-combed and powdered head, the richness of his vests, the whiteness of his linen, the elegant cut of his coat, his short *culottes*, his well-fitting silk stockings, the buckles on his shoes and his sash; in a word the *Monsieur* in him as opposed to the *sans-culottism* of Marat."[19] And just as those a bit below his station were attracted, so too were those a bit above. The bourgeoisie inclined toward Robespierre because it thought him less a champion of the masses, whom it feared and hated and who, it was thought, supported the vile and fearsome Marat. Robespierre did not periodically call for heads to roll, the necessary numbers being constantly increased. He appeared a man who might be assumed to desire equality not absolutely and not at the risk of social war, but a man who by his dreams and style of life might be thought to desire equality in the same degree as did the bourgeoisie: not enough to share it indiscriminately with the lower classes. The bourgeoisie understood democracy in the narrow sense that permitted invidious distinctions between those who worked with their hands and those who did not, and they understood equality as strictly legal, with no admixture of social democracy. This view of democracy and equality, they persuaded themselves, was at least partly shared by Robespierre.

The contrast with Marat was made much of at the time. In Marat the revolutionary bourgeoisie denounced a heretical and dangerous prophet of social war. Popular violence, always directed from above, was Marat's constant cry, his only answer to the hypocrisy and guile and corruption of government.[20] Robespierre's appeal as a political leader was much broader. Like Marat, Robespierre offered himself as exemplary, as a living representative of the politics of virtue. But the two, so similar in the personal appeals they made, stood for different views, offered different paths to fallen man's painful redemption. Robespierre, unlike numberless of his contemporaries, refused to sacrifice Marat to the vengeance of the moderates and the right, although he did not much like the man. Perhaps he felt some curious affinity with a man whose politics were also those of virtue and emulation and embodiment and self.

Although largely ineffectual in the legislative work of the Constituent Assembly, Robespierre gradually became a significant force in the Revolution. He had precociously discovered his voice and his issues before he came to Versailles and Paris. By the spring of 1791 he was one of the best-known and respected politicians in France. He had been dubbed The Incorruptible, and he had become the representative of the people he had envisioned. He had a following at the Jacobins and in the provinces, and he had the makings of an unlikely but potentially powerful coalition between the politically radical bourgeoisie and the politically excluded *sans-culottes*, with important fragments drawn from the fringes of these two groups. He still had a good deal of competition as a popular champion and was himself far from being convinced that the way to salvation for the Revolution lay through the streets. He tended to assume, with very little concrete evidence, that his values were those of most, that his countrymen were very much like him. Those who were not he thought of as actually or potentially counterrevolutionary. Still, Robespierre's popularity in Paris was slow in coming, his ascendancy long incomplete; there remained a disjunction between respect and attachment and political action.

The *sans-culottes* were "sincerely attached to the men who incarnate the Revolution, to Robespierre in particular,"[21] but it was not easy for a man of his temperament to appeal directly to those he avoided socially. Robespierre considered himself poor, but poverty was a relative conception. He did not mean by poverty the misery that prematurely wastes a man's powers and degrades him.[22] He understood poverty as an honorable, hard-working self-reliance. He sought to represent this social ideal, which he made from his imagination and from generalizing from his own limited experience.[23]

It is one thing to insist that a representative of the people concern himself "with the most numerous and the most unfortunate class" and to demand generosity for "the numberless multitude of our fellow citizens despoiled by so many abuses; for the fathers of families who cannot feed the numerous citizens they have given to the country" (VI, 421), and to have, like both Danton and Marat, the common touch, which included a strong streak of vulgarity, a liking for low company, along with mastery of the language of the streets. All this Robespierre lacked. Yet his rather literary and cerebral picture of the Paris poor and the abstractions with which he addressed them proved adequate. Robespierre became a great popular leader by default and because he was able to bridge the class distinctions inherited from the *ancien régime*. His greatest support during the Constituent came from the provinces, where his adherents "were probably wealthier and better educated"[24] than were his adherents in Paris.

By the time of Mirabeau's death, when the revolutionary post of tribune of the Revolution was vacant and many aspired to it, Robespierre was recognized as a potential successor and an orator worthy of comparison. As early as April 1791 the influential left-wing newspaper, *Les Révolutions de Paris*, could write: "Let the French people not despair for the public welfare so long as there remains a representative of the stamp of M. Robespierre."[25] It is also around this time that Robespierre's portrait became readily available throughout Paris, and a few of those early portraits already carry the epithet The Incorruptible. The makings of a personality cult in search of an icon were discernible. The book-sellers merely catered to this market.

The reactionary Lacretelle, who had earlier noticed Robespierre's talent, recalls that in the Constituent Robespierre was one of the few orators to receive applause that was not bought.[26] In July 1791, in the midst of the convulsions that threatened to lead to the crushing of the Left, the *Gazette Universelle* reports that "his bust was carried in triumph in several parts of the capital. . . ."[27] In August he published his first political pamphlet since leaving Arras, *Adresse aux Français* (Address to the French),[28] in which he summed up his work as a deputy and surveyed his speeches, actions, and voting record. He found them coherent, logical unfoldings of fundamental ideas, of his principles. In contrast, he bitterly exposed the politics of compromise and accommodation and self-interest pursued by the majority of his colleagues. He explained their actions as egoism. His was the triumph of truth over falsehood, consistency over opportunity, virtue over vice, morality over convenience: his ego is unimportant. Thus will he always see himself. The insistence that one's opponents are driven by the lowest motives and oneself by altruism is a familiar assertion for a political figure. There is no doubt that Robespierre believed this assessment. What is significant is that many others also believed it. His constant presentations of self as uncompromising and devoted exclusively to the Revolution were received as accurate. He had, since the outset of his career, appealed to an authority and to values above those of his colleagues or parliamentary politics. He appealed to the people, and he accepted full responsibility for championing the popular cause. In a sense he cared very little what his colleages thought of him, so long as he was in harmony with the abstract values of the Revolution as he saw them.

Even the violent aspects of the popular revolution he accepted as an inevitable or at least necessary part of the Revolution. The rioting, the looting, the ghastly lynchings and murders that followed the Fall of the Bastille—and it may be useful to add that he was not present at any of these bloody events—when the heads of the governor of the prison and of the *prévôt des marchands* or mayor, among others, was paraded on the ends of pikes, he considered a kind of popular justice. He was not a bloodthirsty man. He argued that these grim killings were regrettable but necessary, and were caused not only by the intransigence of the counterrevolution but by the savagery of the *ancien régime*, whose brutal penal code had coarsened the populace and degraded justice itself. The Revolution was violent, but vengeance, too, was violent, and the counterrevolutionaries had to be punished. The people in arms were never criminals for Robespierre; they were moral revolutionaries.

He was an extremist of a very peculiar kind. His political views, his assumptions about human capacity and behavior, his habits, his tastes, even his few amusements, were categorical. The politics of virtue engenders such rigidities. His personality was efficiently organized, his character integrated, so the self he presents and reveals has a power that comes from organic unity and concentration of means. He did not need, as did the young Saint-Just when he threw himself into the Revolution, to shed an earlier, frivolous self and a life of indulgence and indirection. There was no ostentation about Robespierre's assumption of the role of revolutionary. This was his true self. Once his revolutionary transformation occurred, he never looked back.

On the dissolution of the Constituent (September 30, 1791) Robespierre had the delicious experience of popularity. He and his friend and comrade Pétion, arms linked, emerged from the Assembly to walk through the deep rows of cheering Parisians, accompanied by a popular ovation remarkable even for that unruly city. Amid the cheers, an excited partisan even thrust an infant into his arms, and he accomplished part of his triumphal march carrying this burden. In October and November he allowed himself a small vacation by visiting his natal province, a visit that became a triumphal procession. Everywhere he was received as a hero. In Arras he had to descend from the coach in which he was riding in order to prevent his admirers from unhitching the horses and pulling the vehicle themselves. He loved this outpouring of affection. It solidified his conviction that the course he had followed in the Constituent, that had earned him only frustration and rebuke, was correct. Here was confirmed his belief that he was serving the people. Like Lenin after him, Robespierre "did not think of himself as a person looking for personal advantage or personal power, but as the selfless embodiment of a political line which was the only conceivably correct one."[29] After he had recovered from this extended apotheosis—at one provincial reception the host theatrically blew out a lamp, announcing that in Robespierre Diogenes' honest man had at long last been found— he returned to Paris and the Revolution.

CHAPTER 4

Robespierre the Orator

PLATE VI
(Phot. Bibl. nat. Paris)

ROBESPIERRE emerged from parliamentary obscurity, established his preponderance, and would eventually govern France through his oratory. From the beginning to the end of his career, words were paramount. He spoke of himself as having been made for revolution, and he fought the Revolution almost exclusively with his words. "The love of justice, of humanity, of liberty," he says, defining his natural revolutionary bent, "is a passion like any other. When it dominates one sacrifices everything" (VIII, 89). His oratorical skills were already apparent before the Revolution, as was his characteristic use of oratory as an instrument of popular agitation. During the months of prerevolutionary excitement and activity in Arras, there has been complaints that Robespierre deliberately affronted the local oligarchy by addressing himself to those outside its sphere. His electioneering would draw the same charge. Once a deputy, he would be pursued by the accusation of demagogery.

All political oratory has at least a dash of demagoguery, and in revolution more than a dash. Robespierre would carry into the Revolution his early refusal to limit himself to the arbitrary expectations of a privileged group, whether it was the Arras oligarchy or the panel of judges he apparently offended by expressing to them his impatience. In the emergence of Robespierre the orator, more clearly than in most other aspects of his career, the continuities with his prerevolutionary self are apparent. The same habits and propensities that had annoyed or impressed Arras would continue in the Revolution. He easily and quickly adjusted his oratorical skills to the needs and circumstances of rebellion and to the unprecedented demands of persuading a nation. As one right-center deputy in the Constituent complained in his journal:

> But I must say that I thought the speech of Mr. Robespierre was made for the habitants of the faubourg Saint-Antoine in order to please them and put himself under their protection, and not at all addressed to the Assembly.[1]

The Revolution was a great age of oratory, and Robespierre shared with his contemporaries an inordinate faith in words. He enjoyed reading aloud from the French classics, an amusement and taste that reveal a love of the music of words as well as an oratorical cast of mind. He occasionally complained that the formal oratory dear to the deputies, made self-consciously in imitation of Roman models, especially those of Cicero, was less valuable than what came sincerely from the spontaneous effusions of a simple heart (X, 413), but he himself was a maker of such elaborate speeches. He spoke almost always from a prepared text. The few surviving manuscripts in his hand show dozens of emendations that certify his concern. His ideas were dressed, combed, and powdered as carefully as his person before being presented to the world. In both cases much of the taste of the *ancien régime* lingered.

Revolutionary oratory in France was the offspring of classical models, which had once been modified to accommodate the needs of pulpit, law court, or lecture room, and now were further modified for the Revolution. Demosthenes and Cicero, the greatest orators of antiquity, were closely studied, as were the critics and grammarians who had rationalized and analyzed what was essential for oratory. Aside from these purely technical concerns, both Demosthenes and Cicero had been the opponents of tyrants—the former of Philip of Macedon, the latter of Julius Caesar—and their republican sentiments and passion were much appreciated by the revolutionary orators. Now for the first time in French history the subjects of citizenship, patriotism, and the duty to resist a king were openly preached. When the revolutionaries went to the font of ancient oratory for inspiration and instruction, they did so in a new spirit: the substance was at least as important as the style.

The revolutionaries loved oratory as one might love the opera or the theater. The newspapers of the Revolution are filled with critical appreciations of oratorical performances, and most of the great revolutionary careers rest on oratory. Mirabeau, the first of the tribunes of the Revolution, owed much of his authority, says Michelet with some chauvinism, to "the power of eloquence over this nation, sensitive above all to the genius of the word."[2] Robespierre's career was equally indebted to oratory, and although he was not thought one of the greatest orators of the age—for contemporaries Danton and Vergniaud, very different temperaments with very different styles and ideas, had that honor—he was much admired by colleagues, and he was arguably the most effective.

Form and substance are inseparable. Here I stress the form since Robespierre's substance is the basis of all that follows. When Robespierre qualified for the bar, critics of legal oratory distinguished between two types of speaking: the *avocats*, who sacrificed style to the desire to win a case, and the *gens de lettres*, who used style to reveal rational underlying principles. The latter aspired to literary excellence as the means not only of realizing their philosophical interests but, equally, of arriving at the truth. Robespierre was among these.[3] His law cases, as he pleaded them, became specific instances of general propositions. The Pagès case, involving loaned money, became a discussion of usury; the Mary Somerville case, involving a disputed inheritance, became a discussion of women's rights; the Déteuf case, involving a false accusation of theft made by a monk desirous of revenging himself on the family of a woman who had resisted his attempted seduction, became a discussion of the place of the clergy in society. We have already seen that the lightning-rod case and the Dupond case became, respectively, the confrontation between science and superstition and a diatribe against arbitrary justice and imprisonment. This habit of abstraction freed Robespierre's oratory, even that before the Revolution, of much of the legal jargon and professional narrow-mindedness that blemished that of so many of his contemporaries who also came to revolution from a legal career. Robespierre rarely pronounced dicta on oratory, and when he did they were never fixed on the technical aspects of that art. He considered the inspiration of the Revolution, for himself and for anyone who would speak purposefully and significantly, as central:

> Collot d'Herbois then spoke [Robespierre reports], and in order to know to what level liberty elevates the soul and genius of men it should suffice to compare the improvised discourse he addressed to General Dumouriez with those which our academicians, for example, would formerly have pronounced on a similar occasion. (V, 34)

As an orator Robespierre began the Revolution with some technical disadvantages. He spoke with a marked regional (*artésien*) accent. His voice, too high-pitched to be naturally pleasant, was also feeble in volume and lacked tonal variation.[4] His physical stature was unimpressive. He was short and slight, with a large head. His weak eyes required glasses, which he sometimes pushed up onto his forehead while speaking, so he could rub his eyes. His gestures at the podium were small and a bit fussy and cramped. In a word, he lacked the presence of a great and commanding orator, and this shortcoming was accentuated by his habit of reading his speeches from a pile of manuscript, often with his head buried in his text.

Robespierre was well aware of these liabilities, and he worked diligently to overcome them or make his auditors forget them. His potency, however, lay not in his technical perfection but in what he had to say. What could not be learned was what mattered most, "an eloquence that springs from the heart, without which one cannot persuade."[5] This he had as a gift that found scope only in the Revolution. He could even improvise brilliantly, although he seldom did,[6] preferring not to trust himself to the passions of the moment and anxious to achieve a kind of precision that can come only with the pen. His few surviving manuscripts are littered with clots of crossings-out and networks of hatch marks.[7] There are two types of corrections. Sometimes "with a passion for destruction," he struke out whole passages "with an untidy network of dark lines." At other times he substituted a word here, a word there, carefully erasing in his quest for the right word.[8]

Robespierre's manuscripts also show a careful concern for impact. He thoughtfully inserted pauses "designed to strike his auditors with horror or make them break out in enthusiastic applause."[9] And because he spoke always to those beyond the walls of the Asembly who would have to read or hear accounts of his speeches, he had to assure that his words were correctly recorded. He perfected a manner of pausing frequently, in a sense dictating his speeches. "Since the eloquent Robespierre often pauses to wet his lips," writes a journalist, "one has time to write."[10]

These carefully made speeches, deliberately delivered, with appropriate quotations looked up in Bacon and Leibniz and Condillac and Montesquieu and Rousseau, among the moderns, peppered with the classical allusions so dear to the age, with pauses for drama or emphasis or applause, were the means by which Robespierre revealed himself, dictated his revolutionary autobiography, while simultaneously revealing the Revolution. He had a further habit of appearing to think aloud before his auditors. This he accomplished by using rhetorical questions, which he often left unanswered, serving not only to plant an idea but to provide a rhetorical flourish. This mannerism both annoyed and intrigued. What should we do next? How can we best ensure the survival of the Revolution? Will my death strengthen the foundation of virtue? These, and other such, are the means by which he engaged his auditors in a public moral dialogue, sharing with them his doubts and fears.[11]

He did have more private fears that he did not incorporate into his oratory, for his appearance at the podium was one of self-assurance and control and authority. He found it "extremely difficult . . . to speak, although he often took the rostrum, especially during the evening sessions."[12] Fréron goes on to compromise this observation by exaggeration, insisting that Robespierre was often forced into silence while speaking, by shouts and insults. It was not the heckling that made him feel trepidation. He himself confessed to Etienne Dumont, Danton's friend, "that he was as timid as a child, that he always trembled in approaching the tribune," but that "once he began to speak" he was released from anguish, "he no longer felt himself."[13]

Certainly part of this stage fright came from his use of oratory to reveal himself. Most autobiographers do not have to look into the eyes of their audience. Consequently he was always more comfortable at the

Jacobin Club than standing before the National Assembly. Not only had the Jacobins been formed in his own image, but he was assured of a sympathetic hearing before his friends. Robespierre had been a member of the Jacobins from its earliest Versailles days when it began inconspicuously as a gathering of deputies from the province of Brittany, along with some other interested adherents, who called themselves the "friends of the constitution" and met informally to discuss political matters. The group did not acquire its famous nickname, the Jacobins, until it rented an abandoned Dominican monastery, in the rue Saint-Honoré in Paris, whose monks had been known as Jacobins and whose building also shared the name. The Paris club, the most important of a significant provincial network of affiliated clubs, was within easy walking distance of the epicenter of the Revolution. The Tuileries, where the King resided; the Manège, the abandoned riding academy in the Tuileries gardens where the National Assembly sat; the Palais Royal (now renamed Equality Palace), where the Duc d'Orléans (also renamed Philippe Egalité) lived and plotted; and the Hôtel de Ville, from whence the city was governed—all were within a few minutes' walk. The Duplay house was on the same street as the Jacobins.

The premises, like all those inherited or expropriated by the Revolution from the *ancien régime*, had not been made for debate or democracy. Most of the business of the court or the cloister had been conducted in whispers; when courtiers or clergy gathered publicly, it was usually for ritual or entertainment, not to govern. The Revolution improvised. The old refectory of the monastery proved inadequate for meetings. The new Jacobin tenants decided to turn the second-floor library into their public place. Untroubled by or indifferent to the iconography left by the monks, the Jacobins changed little. The bookcases lining the walls and broken into sections by niches bearing the portraits of important Dominicans were left in place. The books themselves were carefully protected by attaching a lattice to the cases so that volumes could not be removed. The fresco of Saint Thomas Aquinas was left undisturbed, as was the altar at the end of the oblong room. Benches were built along the walls, and a small raised area, with two elevations— one for the president and a slightly lower one for the secretaries—was set up in the middle of this improvised amphitheater. A narrow tribune for the speakers was erected, facing the raised area. The entire hall, since public meetings were held at night, was lamp-lit, and there were incessant complaints about the lack of light: the irony of fighting a revolution of enlightenment in the shadows was not thought worthy of comment.

Virtually every curious visitor up from the provinces or from abroad, as well as Parisians, came to the Jacobins. It was one of the significant sights of revolutionary Paris, and was consequently much described. The German Halem, who visited in October 1790, noted "the dim light in this vaulted room," which gave the place "a somber aspect."[14] In these obscure surroundings Robespierre often spoke. As of October 14, 1791, the meetings were open to the public, and the Club deliberated before a considerable audience. Those who shared the increasingly left-wing politics preached at the Jacobins, and who could afford the entrance fee, purposely high to assure bourgeois membership, joined or attended.[15] Robespierre was not the first to see and exploit the unique revolutionary potential of the Paris Jacobins and especially their extensive provincial affiliations, but his is the first revolutionary career so deeply beholden to the Society.

Unlike many who came only occasionally to the Jacobins because they wanted something specific, had some proposal to make, Robespierre was assiduous in attendance. Here he was at home. He felt proprietary rights and he was recognized as the master of the place:

> Entering the club [notes a contemporary visitor] he would throw himself on a solitary chair near the door, cross his legs, lean back his carefully curled head, and, without taking any part in the discussion, give the impression that he owned the club, and was waiting to see if anything turned up to interest him.[16]

At the Jacobins, as elsewhere, Robespierre was not a man to depend on the inspiration of the moment. He worked hard and constantly at politics, and despite his preoccupation with ideology, he was deeply concerned with mundane matters. Of all the leaders of the Revolution he had the broadest political interests; that is, all aspects of politics absorbed him. Most of his rivals either couldn't be bothered with the drudgery of daily politics, were too mercurial to be consistently effective, were too concerned with the feelings and thoughts of their friends to consider their constituents, or were so wholly absorbed in administrative matters that they avoided the high road of ideological persuasion tramped by Robespierre. At least part of the explanation of Robespierre's capture of the Jacobins was the long siege he conducted over months of regular attendance and complete allegiance. He did not so much inherit this politcal space, this arena that would become a weapon, as create it.

Despite its headquarters in Paris, the great strength of the Jacobins, something Robespierre early recognized, lay outside the capital. There were about one thousand affiliated clubs,[17] and the "movement had struck roots in virtually every significant town in France."[18] Even the "most visionary and militant" of the Jacobins could not have imagined, in 1791, what lay in the future, but the clubs were well organized, the only such organized political entity in France, and they attracted remarkable men.[19] Robespierre "always took great care to reply in flattering terms to epistles from the societies."[20] By early 1790 he was sending printed copies of his speeches to selected clubs, which wrote back with praise, honorary memberships, and local news: the Marseille club engraved his name on a monument to the "true friends of the people."[21] This cultivation made Robespierre a national figure among the Jacobins at the same time he appeared an outsider, a disquieting gadfly, to his colleagues in the Constituent.[22] He was no Lenin building up a revolutionary organization whose ultimate goal would be to seize power, but his wooing of the Jacobins would have profound impact on the course of the Revolution.

Those he wooed came from the same social background as he and would prove capable of moving much farther to the left then appeared possible or necessary before 1791. "The typical club member," according to the historian of the Jacobins, "was bourgeois in outlook as well as in social rank"[23] and had a paternalistic yet genuine regard for the people, who were thought of as "an amorphous entity comprised of manual laborers, poor artisans, and landless peasants."[24] This first generation of Jacobins was more similar to "present-day bourgeois special-interest groups" than to a revolutionary cadre.[25] Until the flight of the King to Varennes (June 1791), the Jacobins were moderate in politics and eminently respectable. They "took great pains to dissociate themselves from the tiny republican party which had begun to develop in Paris."[26] Yet there was inherent in the bourgeoisie who joined the Jacobins the seeds of considerably more daring and radicalism, as their capacity for transformation under Robespierre's guidance was to prove. The clubs were offspring of the Revolution and self-consciously devoted to its work of moral regeneration as well as reform. As we have seen, Robespierre's career in the National Assembly was limited to that of a gadfly. It is from his dominance of the Jacobins that would come his eventual dominance in the Revolution. The unquestioned authority attributed to Robespierre in the year of his preponderance (1793–1794) was enjoyed only at the Jacobins. Even on the Committee of Public Safety he had to share power, and his leadership was tempered and curbed by his colleagues. At the Jacobins he was supreme.

The Jacobins did not become unquestionably *robespierriste* until the late summer of 1792, and the club was not given daily space in the

Moniteur, the semi-official and most reliable newspaper of national politics, until November 5 of that year, but Robespierre's personal importance had long been recognized. And contrary to assumption and slander, Robespierre did not come to dominate at the club by purging his enemies. The Paris club had, indeed, been several times purged, which gave him his opportunity to mold the remnants, but these changes in membership were caused by events and circumstances that rearranged factions, realigned personalities, called forth men who aspired to lead. In a sense the Jacobins, from the beginning, policed and purged themselves, for the tendency was inherent in the organization, as it was in the Revolution. Exclusiveness was inescapable, and the Jacobin oaths, even from the early months of the Revolution, make this clear. Here is the oath required by the Moulins club, sworn by all members:

> I swear to maintain with all my might the unity and indivisibility of the republic; I swear moreover to recognize as my brother any just man, any true friend of humanity, whatever his color, his stature, and his land; I swear moreover that I shall never have any other temple than that of Reason, other altars than those of *la patrie*, other priests than our legislators, nor other cult than that of liberty, equality, fraternity.[27]

The moral and practical bases for the purges that accompanied the Terror are here: "1793 already exists in 1789."[28]

Robespierre's oratory flourished amid the most dramatic and dangerous events of the Revolution, not least of which was the attack on the Jacobins in early summer of 1791, caused by the belated vitality of the King. For nearly two years he had played a duplicitous game but to no definite purpose, for royal policy was nearly incoherent, a hodgepodge of delay and bribery and changing ministries, all led by a stubborn yet indecisive king who hated what was happening to his throne and his nation but knew not how to stop it. Finally he decided to flee France rather than accept the constitution that would have rendered his a paper throne. He would join the forces of the counterrevolution across the border and return to France at the head of this army.

On the morning of June 21, 1791, Lemoine, the King's valet, found his master's bed empty. By the end of the day the news of Louis's flight was all over Paris. The flight created possibilities, alternatives hitherto undreamed of. At the Jacobins there was a brief reconciliation between the two contending factions, the so-called "moderates" and the "democrats." Robespierre belonged to the latter group. With the King's capture at the border town of Varennes and his return to Paris as a prisoner, this delicate alliance collapsed. The "moderates" did not want Louis punished, let alone removed from the throne—which was the position of the "democrats" and the Paris populace also. This would mean a republic rather than a constitutional monarchy, and such was unthinkable. Those who desired to reestablish the King gathered around Lafayette. The lines were clearly drawn, yet Robespierre preached caution. He did not think the time ripe for a republic, and he feared counterrevolutionary backlash. His analysis was correct, although it led him to oppose a demand from the streets.

On July 15 a crowd of several thousand streamed into the Jacobins, demanding the Society draw up a petition calling for Louis's abdication. The next day the "moderates" formally left the Society to join Lafayette and his friends in forming a group that came to be known as the Feuillants (because they, too, rented a former monastery, this one near the Tuileries; the Cordeliers, too, the third of the important political clubs at the time, also rented ex-holy space, formerly belonging to the Franciscans, and all took their nicknames from their premises). Robespierre opposed the petitioning as provocative, playing into the hands of the reactionaries. He was sadly presceint. The petitioners gathered in the Champ de Mars on a Sunday (July 17) to sign their demands. Lafayette commanded the troops who sabered and shot the unarmed men and women caught on the exercise ground, under a flag of martial law. Robespierre was not present, but from this moment—and the massacre would be followed by weeks of reaction during which many radicals feared for their lives—may be dated his implacable hatred of Lafayette, who now began his quest for personal power.

Lafayette's secession from the Jacobins he explained to all the clubs as necessary since the society had fallen under the control of dangerous agitators who had "completely perverted the spirit which existed in its foundation."[29] The pamphlet bore the infamous date of the massacre, and by implication announced the proposed destruction of his enemies. Marat went underground; Danton ended up in England for a time. Robespierre, who was not directly implicated, merely changed his residence. He was thus the most important of the popular leaders to remain in Paris, and he saw the Club through its first major test and provided a continuity of leadership.

With its leaders scattered, the left was in disarray. The Jacobins had, in the exaggeration of the *Journal de la Révolution*, "only Pétion and Robespierre [who] have not abandoned the cradle of liberty."[30] They were to prove the "great trump cards of the Jacobins."[31] Robespierre's rectitude and his months of attendance and concern were about to pay

off. He immediately countered Lafayette's analysis with his own, an *Adresse aux Français*. The prestige of his name and reputation only enhanced his arguments; some wavering affiliates in the provinces returned to the fold.[32]

Enough returned so that the Society emerged even more cohesive than before the crisis. Struggle had made the Jacobins stronger, Robespierre's importance was reinforced. He and the left were seen as worthy and durable, and resilience in the face of crisis fertilized the soil for additional growth. Now the left, too, could offer myths to compete with those for so long monopolized by the counterrevolution. The nobility who had fled the Revolution asserted that they were the true France. Momentarily, the litany ran, the rebels had captured some of the traditional symbols of the country, including the monarch, but the genius of the country lived in exile: "Where the fleurs-de-lis are, there the country is." This magical shibboleth had its revolutionary counterpart now: "Where Robespierre and Pétion are, there is the true patriotism."[33]

One of the unexpected results of schism and repression, an advantage circumstance created and Robespierre exploited, was that the Society, now in the hands of the "democrats," had become a revolutionary instrument rather than the debating club *cum* pressure group it had previously been. Crisis had rid the Society of its more cautious, moderate members, and their desertion to the counterrevolution gave the remaining members a moral edge they had not previously enjoyed. It is this renewed Society that Robespierre rebuilt in his own image, shaping it to conform to his ideas and vision.

Robespierre's peculiar gifts as an ideologue were amply demonstrated during the Constituent, but it is only at the Jacobins that he enjoyed success. While explaining the Revolution to his comrades, he perfected his oratory, the essential tool with which he reformed the Jacobins. In the monastery's converted library he extended his growing hold over contemporaries through the elaboration of his own committed acts. At the Jacobins, more so than elsewhere, the charismatic qualities of the man are apparent. The Jacobin Loyseau describes Robespierre's ascendancy:

> To speak always, always of one's self, of one's virtues, of one's principles, of the sacrifices one has made for liberty, of the dangers by which one is surrounded, is to use means known to gather support.

This is what the Jacobins expected of Robespierre, and they came to watch their leader certify his right to lead with these oratorical performances. Loyseau is not entirely happy with Robespierre's monopoly of

moral enlightenment, but his authority is unquestioned: "You have
reached the point of being able to say anything, do anything, dare anything without fear because you have the multitude on your side."[34]

Of the great orators of the Revolution, only Robespierre preferred
the intimacy of a small hall and craved the comfort of being surrounded
by allies and comrades. Mirabeau disliked the Jacobins as a forum. He
had difficulty modulating his voice and gestures to the surroundings,
and he could not count on his extraordinary personality covering up
gaps in reasoning.[35] Robespierre loved the place, and his appearance at
the tribune always attracted a considerable crowd. At the beginning of
meetings, when the usual business of the club was transacted—reading
letters, expediting routine matters—only the three hundred or so reg-
ulars were present. But as the time of Robespierre's appearance approached, "the multitude became innumerable."[36] At the Jacobins, as
at the Duplays', Robespierre was at ease: his prestigious role was recognized and honored. There would be few surprises and no personal
assaults, nor the slightest hint of disrespect. Here he was among friends.
He even learned to import some of this reassuring support into the Constituent. By the time he attacked Lameth and Barnave, two of the leading orators in the National Assembly and among the most influential
deputies (on May 15, 1791), he had brought along his own claque to
cheer him on. He was bathed in applause and encouragment.[37] The
public galleries would continue to be filled with his supporters as his
popularity grew. He had created a partial illusion of being at the Jacobins even when he stood before hundreds of deputies who were not
his followers.

There were, of course, those who despised and feared Robespierre's
success and its external manifestations at the Jacobins. Loyseau's cautious reservations about his moral monopoly were inflated into a "despotism of opinion" by Jean-Baptiste Louvet, who hated Robespierre.[38]
After a speech lasting "hours on end," Louvet complained, Robespierre
was greeted not by applause but by "the convulsive stamping of feet, it
was a kind of religious enthusiasm, a holy elation."[39] In oratorical confrontation with Brissot and Guadet at the Club (April 27, 1792), "he
was interrupted at each sentence by the applause of his auditors" and
some of his words "excited delirium among his hearers."[40]

His presentation of his prepared speeches was calm, his tone imperturbable, his manner untheatrical. This plain delivery was in contrast
to the highly literary quality of the speeches.[41] His variations in rhythm
and voice and emphasis were subtle yet adequate to produce in his listeners that "long, sustained emotional trembling" singled out as the

essence of "the horrible eloquence of Robespierre."[42] Even enemies conceded Robespierre had that most admired quality in an orator, eloquence.

Eloquence, said Cicero, supposes a soul. An orator who had eloquence not only could reveal his own soul but could cause the souls of his auditors to vibrate with his own. Eloquence was composed of a complex of qualities and technical mastery, but it was generally thought that eloquence could not be learned: one's soul had a voice or it was mute. Eloquence was thus essentially an emotional quality, or a prerational one. When joined to the intellect, when the eloquent speaker had something to say, when he had principles, as contemporaries put it, he was irresistible. All the most admired speakers of the Revolution—Mirabeau, Danton, Barnave, Vergniaud, Robespierre, Saint-Just—were remarkably intelligent men. The modern-day reader is struck by the density of these speeches, their close argumentation, their complexity and deep seriousness of subject. Those who demanded they be moved to tears by a cunningly made peroration also demanded that it be on a subject of suitable gravity. Standards were exceptionally high, men exceptionally critical, for there was a good deal to admire, remarkable examples of oratory on which to form and refine one's taste. Robespierre was among those who met these standards. "One sees in his writings a truly virtuous and masculine soul, complemented by a series of truths that are irresistible," a contemporary noted in her diary, linking virtue and truth, principles and morality, which was Robespierre's unique strength as an orator. His was "a truly great, pure soul," she continued. "Our petty intriguers are incapable of such qualities, although they don't lack brains."[43] No contemporaries thought Robespierre's oratory infected by "mystical tendencies," which is a modern hypothesis for his potency.[44]

The spoken word is elusive, evanescent. The historian is left to imagine how a speech might have sounded. Because Robespierre's oratorical performances were public, there are numerous reports to draw upon. Some complain, as does Joseph Garat, a future Minister of Justice, about his "eternal repetitions" and self-revelations, but most found Robespierre eloquent, and oratory (along with music, the other aural art) often depends on repetition and can more easily tolerate it than the other arts. Desmoulins, unsatisfied with merely acknowledging Robespierre's eloquence, suggests that it derives from a unique ability to give voice to "the uncreated law that is engraved in every heart."[45] Of his June 21 speech to the Jacobins on the King's flight (VII, 518–23), Desmoulins writes: "I was moved to tears in more than one place, and when this excellent citizen in the middle of his speech spoke of the certainty of paying with his head for the truths that he had come to present, I found myself crying out: 'We will all die before you. . . .' " And it was not only the then passionately devoted Desmoulins who was pulled from his seat, forced to cry out: "more than 800 persons rose at the same time, compelled, like me, by an involuntary movement" who "swore to rally around Robespierre."[46] Others are less circumstantial and effusive (and perhaps hyperbolic). Etienne Dumont quotes his friend Reybaz, who was sitting next to him when Robespierre spoke against the clergy in the Constituent: "This young man is not yet experienced, he is too verbose and does not know when to stop; but he has a fund of eloquence and originality which will not be lost in the crowd."[47]

Interest commands attention. Robespierre's speech to the Constituent in favor of his proposal that deputies not be allowed to sit in the next Assembly lasted about two hours, but was "heard in a religious silence."[48] Now and again a contemporary used "sublime" to describe Robespierre's oratory, by which was meant an elevation of soul and sentiment and language. A monarchist deputy thought this same speech "sublime." The official (and partial) *Feuille du Salut Public* described his November 17, 1793, speech on foreign affairs as valuable for "the grandeur of its ideas, the depth of its political principles, and the sublimity of its republican eloquence."[49] In oratory, at least, right and left spoke the same language. Corneille and Rousseau, among Robespierre's favorite authors, those he sometimes read aloud to friends, fixed in his ear cadences and metaphors that when they appeared in his speeches sounded familiar overtones for contemporaries. He had absorbed the eloquence of his age and in his speeches gave back to his auditors, in revolutionary context and with a revolutionary purpose, the literary pleasures they had grown up with.

Virtue, along with eloquence, was thought essential. Robespierre himself had discovered the juxtaposition in Rousseau, especially in the *Confessions*, and noted the discovery in his *Dedication to Rousseau*. He was not alone in insisting on the necessary concurrence of virtue and eloquence. "I don't fear being contradicted by true patriots," writes the deputy Jacques-Vincent Delacroix, "when I say that he is the most eloquent man of the Revolution because he is the most virtuous. He is more eloquent than that charlatan, that comedian, Mirabeau, who envelopes the soul with grand words and grand gestures, without ever touching it." "Only virtue," he elucidates, "is truly eloquent because it takes its inspiration from nature, while intrigue uses alien and artificial means which seduce without persuading . . ." It is these artificial devices that are used by the charlatan "who never has these sublime movements of the soul that characterize so perfectly the virtuous man and separate him from the intriguer who coldly calculates his technique."[50] Robespierre himself knew that part of his power came from these depths: "I have followed the sentiment of my soul,"[51] he once explained. But if this ability to touch his own soul, to conduct one of those raids on the unconscious that T. S. Eliot thought was so essential to art, gave Robespierre power, it also put him in touch with a soul that was troubled, agitated, often chaotic and in angry motion. This complex, turbulent inner life, lovingly nurtured and contemplated by Robespierre and given voice in his oratory, became the voice of the Revolution. When Robespierre found the words for his deepest thought and feelings, he simultaneously found the words for the aspirations and contradictions of the Revolution.

Robespierre's literary ambitions, which he shared with so many men of his generation, had not been left behind in Arras. But with the Revolution his instinctively oratorical style and mode of expression were given a forum they would not otherwise have had. The few remarkable orators who made a reputation under the *ancien régime* have vanished to all but the specialist. Robespierre has achieved a posthumous reputation, something he long craved, in the Republic of Letters. Long before the sharp frustrations of Year II he was concerned with posterity's judgment, history's judgment. He did not seek only literary fame, but he certainly aimed his speeches not only beyond the walls of assembly and club, but beyond his present to an envisioned future. There is a good deal of prophetic and oracular apostrophe in Robespierre's speeches, reminders that the dual themes of a posthumous victory and a useful death were much on his mind,[52] and that the Revolution was the beginning of the future.

It is also significant to notice that Robespierre's oratory is old-fashioned. The themes are new but presented in a form and style that were familiar to his auditors. His was an academic rhetoric that resonated in the minds of his educated auditors. He lacked the verbal originality and virtuosity of Saint-Just, the street-corner vulgarity and vigor of Danton, the serene literary ease of Vergniaud, but his studied speeches were easy to listen to and absorb, for he spoke within a tradition.[53] Just as Robespierre retained the manners and comportment of the *ancien régime*, so he spoke in the form and accents of a now despised age. The privileges and prejudices of his class, especially in cultural matters, are everywhere evident. He worried aloud, as he did most of his worrying in the Revolution, that the voice of the Revolution was a schooled voice.

"Nothing is more contrary to the interest of the people and equality," he said, than a snobbish attitude toward language (X, 433). But he made no attempts to change, and rather than adapt he generally avoided street politics; he had no weapons that were efficacious there. His strengths were perfectly adjusted to the tasks he tackled. His revolution was fought in parliament and at the Jacobins, and eventually around the green table where the Committee of Public Safety deliberated France's fate. For this he was supremely qualified.

Robespierre's style and ideas crystallized simultaneously. Both proved uniquely fit for revolution. There was no need for pretense, only for polishing. His first literary manner, which manifests in his prize essays, was easily shed when he precociously sounded his political voice in 1788. The aphorism that style is the man fits Robespierre. In his utterances run most of the major sensibilities of the eighteenth century. He occasionally, if rarely, aped the wit and elegance of Voltaire, whose brittle irony and deft yet wavering skepticism seem grossly inappropriate to revolution.[54] The prize Latinist of Louis-le-Grand was also an adept, although less an addict than others, at the bandying of classical tags and allusions.[55] He could occasionally make an epigram, compressing and then fixing an idea in a form that lodged in the mind, but his efforts lacked the genius of Abbé Sieyès or Saint-Just.[56] About as infrequently he hit upon an aphorism,[57] and could show an occasional flash of purely verbal wit.[58] But these are minor aspects of his style, his voice, just as they are minor aspects of his character. His mind inclined strongly to paradox and antithesis as a means of expressing complexity and tension: "Europe doesn't know how to live without kings and nobles; we don't know how to live with them" (X, 445). Or later in the same speech: "All the combinations formed to make war on us rest on crime. They are, in the eyes of truth, nothing more than hordes of regimented savages, disciplined brigands" (X, 446).[59]

Robespierre's mind was given to a dialectical mode of thought and expression. He did not seek repose and serenity, although the form of his speeches expresses order and poise in a very high degree. He wanted vigor, thunder for anathemas, as when he denounced General Dumouriez (IX, 361–67) or apostrophized despotism as a sea without shore, inundating the world, making it "the patrimony of crime" (X, 180). There are dangers in such a style. Robespierre, like Rousseau before him, was often carried away by rhetorical excess, caught up in a rhapsody of his own making, enthralled by the sound of words rolling in waves over the subject, burying sense in sound. Robespierre, when he loses control over his verbiage, when it becomes detached from concreteness and drifts from detail, finds himself floating hopelessly, piling up images and abstractions.[60]

These few details of style are less important than their overall impact. Robespierre's speeches, for all their shortcomings, were richly satisfying and broad in appeal. Men listened and thought they heard not only a talented and powerful orator, but a voice larger than its possessor, a voice that somehow was a vehicle for transcendental truths. Robespierre seemed, even to those like Pierre-Louis Manuel, who was no friend, the voice of the Revolution. After hearing Robespierre speak to the Jacobins "On the Means of Saving the State and Liberty," Manuel insisted that the speech be printed and sent to all the affiliated clubs: it completely expressed the Society.[61]

So long isolated and feared in the Constituent, Robespierre's unique and powerful voice became first that of the Jacobins and then that of France in revolution.

CHAPTER 5

The War Debates

PLATE VII
(Phot. Bibl. nat. Paris)

THE WAR FIRST DECLARED against Austria (April 20, 1792), and eventually against most of monarchical Europe, revolutionized the Revolution. Whatever the separate circumstances and motives, war and revolution soon became what they have remained in most modern revolutions: inextricably linked, bound together in a pattern of cause and effect. French foreign and domestic affairs would not be divided for more than twenty years, and the fate and direction of the Revolution would often be decided on the battlefield, away from Paris.

It is doubtful that the monarchies surrounding France—and the King and Queen were related by blood to several, most importantly those of Spain and Austria—would or could have allowed France to conduct her Revolution without interference. Nor is it likely that revolutionary France, the declared enemy of the *ancien régime*, would have tolerated on her borders what she was crusading against at home. But if war was unavoidable, the timing and circumstances were determined by the domestic development of the Revolution.

The King, when he attempted to flee the country to join the counterrevolution, may be said to have made war inevitable and hastened its outbreak. His capture at Varennes only delayed the declaration of hostilities. The Court was the first to appeal to war to solve the Revolution's problems and dilemmas, but many others also saw war as the only way out of the doldrums into which the Revolution had sailed. By the time the new constitution was accepted by the King, in September 1791, and a new assembly, called the Legislative, had been elected as the first representative body to sit under the constitution, war was widely desired. The King's new Minister of War, the Count of Narbonne, wanted war, as did the general staff who had remained behind in France when many of their colleagues had fled. The *émigrés*, from the King's brothers down to lesser fry who had left the country, wanted war, and were agitating at the courts of Vienna, Turin, and even London.[1] Lafayette considered war essential to his own plans for mediating the nation's destiny. In the Legislative Assembly, hopelessly factionalized and hence paralyzed, the royalist sympathizers supported the bellicose Court. But there was also an articulate war party of radicals who saw war not only as a crusade against monarchical, reactionary Europe, for the war party attracted a large number of republicans, but also as the means of destroying the stalemate of the Revolution by forcing all, from the Court to the Commons, to choose between the Revolution and counterrevolution. Politics would be savagely simplified by war, and the nation would rally around the flag of patriotism, which the parliamentary war party, as well as the Court, hoped to control.

The risks were enormous, and all who agitated for war minimized them. War itself was risky, especially so for a fragile economy that was only now recovering from the wretched harvests of 1788 and 1789. In a society where the conquests of the Revolution were not yet secure, only recently subjected to a constitutional government, and with a King who despised that document, war could prove disastrous. The army and the generals were suspect, and rightly so. And the nation was unprepared to fight. War, whatever its outcome, would raise the stakes of the Revolution to all or nothing. War would demand the arming of the people, who would do the fighting, and this was potentially dangerous for all who feared additional social upheaval. These difficulties, and many others, became the subjects of a vast national debate whose most intense focus was at the Jacobins, where a fierce miniature drama of the nation's agonizing decision was enacted almost nightly, from the late autumn of 1791 to the spring of 1792. Robespierre was a regular participant in this drama,[2] and the *dramatis personae* included virtually all the revolutionaries on the Left.

Only Robespierre, it soon became clear, did not want war. And even he realized that it could not easily be avoided. "My greatest regret," he gloomily confessed to Fréron, "is not having embraced the *métier* of arms at the end of the Constituent Assembly, of not knowing the art of war."[3] Here was the intellectual's lament, for if those who sought to lead the Revolution were dependent upon the generals, they were at the mercy of the generals. Robespierre was especially suspicious of the generals, and one of his persistent arguments against the war party would be that they were conveying into unclean and treacherous hands the fate of the Revolution.

Not only was Robespierre without military experience or skills, he was also outside the government. All members of the Constituent had been excluded, on his initiative, from sitting in the Legislative. He had no choice but to don the unenviable and dangerous mantle of an unarmed prophet. He was heard at the Jacobins, but was unheeded, and he no longer could confront the deputies of the Marais or join in the debates. Shortly, as the nation drifted toward war, even those few left-wing newspapers that had sympathized with him and his views joined the clamor for war.[4] By the time hostilities were declared, he was isolated, a fact that became significant in his career.

The period occupied by the war debates was fruitful for Robespierre's development as a revolutionary theorist. He solved, to his satisfaction, several basic problems of the Revolution—the relationship of war to revolution, of the generals to the Revolution, of political faction to the Revolution, of the King to the Revolution—which became theorems in his ideology. It was also fruitful in his growth as a tactician. Left only with the Jacobin Society for a forum, Robespierre now looked upon it not as a supplement to his duties as a deputy, which were nonexistent, but as the sole base for his revolutionary activities. Soon enough there would be yet another desertion of the Jacobins, with the war sympathizers abandoning the Society to Robespierre and his few followers. "Robespierre sinks himself more and more," the student Gérard noted in his diary. "The number of his supporters diminishes every day. He is no longer this virtuous man, the cherished model for all friends of liberty."[5] In fact, his moral prestige remained unblemished and would be instantly reasserted by the end of the tumultuous summer of 1792. But he was left with little else once war was declared. The Jacobins, both during the debates and afterward, continued to publish his speeches and send them to provincial affiliates, where his reputation seems to have remained unimpaired. But the Society was not exclusively his, had lost much of its potency by the new desertions, and had, yet again, to be rebuilt.

Of all those who preached war, at the Jacobins and in the Legislative, none was so categorical, none more passionate, and none more persuasive than Jacques-Pierre Brissot. This extremely likable journalist, pamphleteer, man of letters, and deputy, whose naive enthusiasms were infectious, was also a man of the most unimpeachable personal integrity. He was poor as only a hack journalist with a growing family could be poor, and there was never a hint that he improved his circumstances out of the Revolution. Of Robespierre's many rivals, Brissot was the one most immune to moral comparison. But Brissot was a disastrous political leader. "War is actually a national benefit," he declared. "We need treachery on a grand scale; our salvation lies that way, for strong doses of poison remain in the body of France, and strong measures are necessary to expel them." Brissot imagined war rallying the country behind the Revolution and forcing the duplicitous King either to support the war and the Revolution or else reveal his counterrevolutionary intentions and provide reasons for his dethronement: "if he betrays us," Brissot threatened, "the people will be ready."[6] These were domestic benefits; Brissot's vision also included an element of crusading zeal. War would carry liberation to the oppressed peoples of Europe, groaning still under the despotism France had thrown off.

The Court despised the parliamentary war party but welcomed the war. "The fools!" wrote Marie Antoinette. "Don't they see they are serving our purposes." The King was a bit more circumspect in his analysis. "The physical and moral state of France," he assured the exiled Baron de Breteuil, the general he was going to join when he was captured at Varennes, "makes it impossible for her to mount even a demi-campaign." War would discredit the revolutionaries, and "the nation will see no other resource but to throw itself into my arms."[7] There was also a social dimension to the war policy, one that Clavière and Roland, future ministers and adherents of Brissot, candidly admitted in private, even exceeding the cynicism of the Court. Arming the *sans-culottes*, arming the very people who had stormed the Bastille, might prove dangerous. "We should keep ourselves in a state of war," Clavière wrote, since "the return of our soldiers would only augment our difficulties and destroy us." Roland was blunter: "We have to make the best men we have under arms march as far as their legs will carry them, or else they will return and cut our throats."[8]

In the midst of this belligerency it was not easy to formulate a policy, let alone articulate it. Robespierre at once grasped the breadth of the problem. War could only "lead to the death of the body politic." War was "the greatest disaster that can befall liberty." War was "the most dangerous course" (VIII, 37). He never deviated from this conviction throughout the months of the war debates, never modified it to accommodate what he thought trivial and dangerous concerns, whether of individuals or groups. In ideological struggle he was both creative and intractable. War and revolution were incompatible, antithetical. This was his text, which he elucidated and ornamented but never compromised.

He thought the war a mistake strategically as well as ideologically. The constitution had just been signed, the Legislative Assembly just elected. The enemies of the Revolution were at home, not abroad. Those who had already fled the country declared thereby their hostility to the Revolution. But those who remained behind, the protectors and sympathizers of the *émigrés*, were far more dangerous. They were "nothing more than the defenders of the French Court and the French nobility" (VIII, 40), and they were undeclared enemies only waiting their chance to destroy the Revolution. "Are the most numerous and dangerous of our enemies at Koblenz? No, they are in our midst." They were at the Court, and any declaration of war would return power to the Court. The pathetic *émigré* communities gathered at Koblenz or Tournay he thought more a nuisance to their hosts than a threat to France. Robespierre was willing to concede to the war party that something should be done about the *émigré* settlements on France's borders. They were "an insult to the nation," which demanded redress. "We must draw around Leopold the circle that Popilius drew around Mithradates" (VIII, 24). But "Koblenz is no second Carthage; the seat of danger is not in Koblenz, it is in our own midst, in our own breast" (VIII, 63).

"During a war," his analysis continued, "the people forget the issues that most essentially concern their civil and political rights and fix their attention only an external affairs." They tend to give "all their interest and all their hopes to their generals and their ministers, or rather to the generals and the ministers of the executive authority" (VIII, 48). This is precisely what the executive authority, the monarchy, wants. In the Roman Republic, "when the people, fed up with the tyranny and the pride of the patricians, reclaimed its rights through the voices of its Tribunes, the Senate would declare war." War, he went on, was "the familiar coffin of all free peoples" (VIII, 49). And if ancient history proved the folly of war, so too did modern history. In response to the argument that the proposed war would be like the American War of Independence, he said that if the Americans had triumphed "by fighting under English flags and under the orders of English generals," or if the Dutch and Swiss, respectively, "had entrusted to the Duke of Alba and the Austrian and Burgundian princes the responsibility of revenging their outrages and assuring their liberty," then there might be apposite historical precedents for France fighting under the aegis of the Bourbon monarchy.

The utopian dimension of the war party's presentation had considerable appeal, and this, too, Robespierre attacked. Brissot's vision of a world freed of kings and priests and aristocrats by the liberating armies of revolutionary France was warmly received. "The most extravagant idea that can be born in the head of a political thinker," Robespierre told the Jacobins, "is to believe that it suffices for a people to enter, weapons in hand, among a foreign people and expect to have its laws and constitution embraced." It is "in the nature of things that the progress of reason is slow," and "no one loves armed missionaries; the first lesson of nature and prudence is to repulse them as enemies" (VIII, 81). A year later he is still making this argument: "One can encourage freedom, never create it by an invading force" (V, 271).

The major difficulty for Robespierre, however, was not that his opponents were guilty of drawing false historical analogies or painting inspiring pictures of a world without kings. It was political simplicity he deplored. None of the war schemes, whether from Court or Commons, took account of the strength of the counterrevolution. The Revolution was not yet secured, and any policy that put a strain on the fragile compromises and alliances, on the still-unsettled new state, was not just ill-advised, it was fatal. The counterrevolution, Robespierre correctly saw, was not some despicable, contemptible remnant to be swept away with ease. The counterrevolution was momentarily stunned by the successes of the Revolution. It appeared docile but was, in fact, sulky, undefeated, and vengeful. The war, however useful it might be in solidifying the Revolution by a dramatic appeal to patriotism, would put the sword back into the hands of the enemy, the King and the generals. Robespierre became obsessed with a nightmare vision of military dictatorship, exercised by Lafayette, that would become a reality in war. His loathing of Lafayette—profound, intractable, blinding—was expressed in hysterical ejaculations, designed to wound rather than convince.

Ambitious generals had not disputed the sovereignty of France since the days of the civil and religious wars of the sixteenth century. For nearly two hundred years the French monarchy had been served by its generals rather than dominated by them. But the monarchy was now weak and desperate. It either could not or would not control the generals. For the Revolution irresolution and weakness came to the same thing. It mattered not whether military dictatorship had the blessings of the monarchy; the Revolution would be destroyed. A pusillanimous king "is nothing but the prey of the ambitious who divide the spoils among themselves," he argued. And when a king is as weak as Louis XVI, "your real kings are your generals . . ." (IV, 320).

Robespierre knew little of generals and war except what he had read, and his reading taught distrust. "In troubled times . . . the army commanders become the arbiters of their country. . . . If they are Caesars or Cromwells they themselves seize power. If they are courtiers without character . . . they lay their power at the feet of their master and help him to seize again his arbitrary power, asking only to be his first servants" (VIII, 49). He could just as well have cited Montesquieu on the dangers of military dictatorship, referring his auditors to Book X of the *Spirit of Laws*, for from that vast quarry could be mined appropriate materials. But contemporaries were more persuaded by Brissot's history lectures than Robespierre's.

Robespierre's bitter, obsessive sensitivity to the dangers of military dictatorship owed much to his hatred for Lafayette. What made Lafayette so loathsome (and dangerous) was his hypocrisy. He used his reputation earned in America as a military leader to mask his ambition and reactionary politics. Masks and unmasking are recurring themes in

Robespierre's utterances, and they first achieve prominence during the war debates and the attackes on Lafayette. The Revolution was, for Robespierre, a revelation of self, a restoration of virtue, a regeneration of fallen man. These wonders would be achieved, simultaneously, by individuals and society, by people and *the* people. All the crippling perversions of the *ancien régime* would be transcended. Men would discover their true selves, as Rousseau had chronicled in his *Confessions*, as Robespierre regularly described in his speeches. The masks worn, of necessity, during the *ancien régime*, would be discarded, and unmasked man would now stand in his dignity. But when Lafayette was unmasked, he revealed not man as he ought to be, but the Old Adam. One saw not virtue but the hideous face of ambition, greed, cruelty, arrogance. One saw the very vices against which the Revolution struggled. Lafayette's hypocrisy was his revolutionary activity. "You," Robespierre rhetorically accused, "only want a revolution measured to your aristocratic prejudices and for your personal interests" (IV, 170–71).

The struggle with Lafayette differs from almost all Robespierre's other political struggles, with the possible exception of his attack on the King, which would shortly follow the assault on Lafayette, and which in his mind represented a single attack on the counterrevolution in its several forms. With these two exceptions all Robespierre's factional struggles were with men who had been comrades but had gone into opposition or, as he saw it, joined the counterrevolution. Yet for all his notorious hardness of character and conviction, his reputed coldness and cruelty, Robespierre was reluctant to punish those who had fought with him, those he had once trusted and cherished. Danton and Desmoulins, among others, were defended long after they had any right to expect his tolerance, let alone support. He demanded that Desmoulins be kept a member of the Jacobins long after no one else would have dared make such a plea. He was reluctant to attack Danton, despite the pressure of his colleagues on the Committee of Public Safety. But the King and Lafayette had always been counterrevolutionaries. To sharp and irreconcilable political differences were added social and personal animosities and resentments that fueled envy and concentrated revulsion. Lafayette he considered the undeserving favorite of fortune, endowed from birth with freedom from all the struggles for success and survival that Robespierre had had to endure. Now Lafayette expected to use the Revolution for the realization of his private desires for glory and greatness. Robespierre thought it his duty to expose Lafayette for what he was. Spite complemented reason.

Although Robespierre's unmasking of Lafayette was informed by a special vituperativeness, he had never sought patronage from Lafayette, he had never adhered to the general's liberal politics at the outset of the Revolution, nor had he ever joined in the chorus of adulation heaped upon him at the height of his popularity. Socially, the two men obviously inhabited different worlds. Robespierre did not hate Lafayette as did the Court and some aristocrats, as a vile turncoat, a renegade to his class and cause. He hated Lafayette for what he was, what he had been born and continued to be and express, for Robespierre did not believe Lafayette was anything but an aristocrat who would betray the Revolution as soon as he could. In 1791–92 there was no need to get involved in such explanations: Lafayette was the butcher of the Champ de Mars, the man who sought to hunt down the Jacobins, and he had an army at his back. Yet even as Lafayette lay languishing in an Austrian jail, into which he had been cast when he fled France in July 1792 after his *coup d'état* failed, Robespierre continued to hate him. The animus was mutual.[9]

Robespierre's attacks were unrelenting and slanderous, and even some of his later speeches contain venomous asides directed at Lafayette. In a particularly bitter speech, he charged Lafayette with the murder of the baker Françoise in the fall of 1789, as a pretext for creating the Martial Law Act, the very act he would subsequently invoke at the Champ de Mars in 1791. He also accused Lafayette of arranging the murders of two men at the Champ de Mars to furnish him the needed episode to declare martial law. He then rounded off these preposterous charges by implying that Lafayette was capable of murdering the King so that he himself might seize the power he lusted for (VIII, 399). In Robespierre's private war against Lafayette, he often used wild exaggeration. He inflated the Champ de Mars casualties to 1,500 and repeated atrocity stories of children in Brabant being slaughtered in their mother's wombs by Lafayette's soldiers and carried on the ends of bayonets (IV, 225). That such a monster also desired Robespierre's murder was not difficult for the victim to imagine: and it may have been true. The theme of assassination, so long in Robespierre's utterances as a stoical literary device, now (April 11, 1792) becomes real: "I am surrounded by enemies, by assassins; but on the day when the daggers reach my breast, that will be the day on which I denounce him and hold him up to public scorn with all my powers" (VIII, 268)[10]

Robespierre's distrust of generals was drawn from literature but fixed first on Lafayette, in whom he saw all that was odious in Julius Caesar, Marius and Sulla, and even Cromwell, all of whom were invoked as examples of the dangers of military ambition. Throughout the Revolution he thought military dictatorship a real danger. The only generals he found tolerable were those he encountered in books. He was skeptical about the revolutionary sentiments later expressed by General Dumouriez, whom he saw, and rightly so, as another Lafayette. He wanted "a citizen like those Greek heroes, those models of republican virtues, that Timoleon who, after having saved Syracuse, went into retirement, not back to his lands" (VIII, 146). Loathing was one thing, controling the generals another.

The only imaginable way for Robespierre to prevent military dictatorship was to create an army that would serve the Revolution and not its destroyers. He conceived of a citizen army, organized on democratic principles, which would dilute the regular army, especially its officer corps, still littered with the dangerous debris of the *ancien régime*. So long as the army blindly obeyed its officers, it was potentially fatal to the Revolution. "The spirit of military discipline," he insisted, had to be broken (VI, 621). He had no quarrel with necessary discipline, the legitimate authority in all purely military matters, which "is anchored in the very nature of things and in reason" (IV, 57–58). But all authority beyond what is needed to command an army in the field "is based on prejudices and servitude." It is the generals who need disciplining, not the ranks: "You will much more easily find a hundred thousand perfidious and ambitious generals than a single army gratuitously guilty and rebellious" (IV, 54). The generals are the natural enemies of the Revolution. They are armed aristocrats, counterrevolutionaries with weapons. "You have destroyed aristocracy," he reminds, "and the aristocracy still lives at the head of the army; the aristocracy reigns in the army" (VII, 469).

These were commonplaces on the left.[11] Robespierre did not imagine dangers unseen by others, but he did show more tenacity than his comrades, and he never capitulated to the seductions of war. He watched and railed as he saw comrades convey "the responsibility of defending equality" (IV, 229) into the hands of their blood enemies. The war party itself—he called Brissot and Condorcet, Guadet and Vergniaud and Gensonné, "the most notorious chiefs"[12]—was drawn from the ranks of the Jacobins. He was powerless to stop this drain of patriots. All attempts at reconciliation (none inaugurated by Robespierre, however) failed. One major attempt at unity was made, and Robespierre and Brissot embraced publicly, before the Jacobins. Robespierre immediately and scrupulously wrote to Gorsas, the editor of the influential newspaper *Courrier des 83 Départements*, insisting that "cordial embrace" meant only that he did not regard "the debates on the destiny of the people as *personal quarrels,"* since his only passion was for "the public good."[13] The *rapprochement*, made with so many reservations on both sides, lasted but a short time.

The factional struggle for control of the Revolution, in both word and deed, began during the war debates. The Girondins—a contemporary designation for the group Robespierre preferred to call the Brissotins—had correctly seen that the Revolution was stalemated. They concluded that only drastic action could induce movement, and in their enthusiasm they assumed any movement would be, somehow, in a revolutionary direction. Their proposals of war were dangerously simple, risky, and extreme, but had the distinct advantage of being attractive, even seductive, because they were given energy, patriotism, enthusiasm, and clarity by Brissot and his friends. Robespierre's analysis of stalemate was not significantly different from that of his opponents. His solution was feeble in itself, especially so in comparison with the vitality of the war party. He called for, and himself assumed, a rigid, narrow legalistic stance. This he expressed in himself and in the title of his newspaper. He spoke of himself as "the defender of the constitution," which name he also gave to his first sustained attempt at journalism (*La Défenseur de la Constitution*). Robespierre's politics, approximately from the autumn of 1791 to the summer of 1792, from the dissolution of the Constituent through the declaration of war to the growing insurrectionary ferment in Paris, was to do nothing that might give the forces of reaction a pretext to act. He had been frightened by the King's flight to Varennes, appalled by the willingness of the Constituent to reinstate such a monarch, had opposed the petitioning in the Champ de Mars, and had been convinced that so long as the left was weak and divided, it could not defend itself against Lafayette's ambition. It was best to avoid all suspicion of radical vitality lest Lafayette decide to liquidate the left.

Throughout the period of reaction, although he remained in Paris to guide the Jacobins through the crisis, he sought to dissociate himself from the more extreme (and pathetically few) radicals, the so-called republicans. He refused to call himself a republican at this time—"a vague word that can be used in a thousand ways" (VII, 551)—for he declined to share the slanders that equated republicans and "anarchists." During the long reactionary interlude of the war debates, dominated by Lafayette, in whose shadow the debates were waged, Robespierre became circumspect:

Yes, gentlemen, I love the character of a republican. I know that it is in republics that great souls are nourished, that one finds all the noble and generous sentiments. But I believe that we should declare ourselves, at this time, openly, the confirmed friends of the constitution . . . [which was monarchical]. (VIII, 212)

Much of Robespierre's later politics and attitudes are foreshadowed in the war debates. For it was the only time in the revolutionary period he was not in government, and this enforced leisure gave him time to reflect. The debates provided the occasion for publicly presenting himself and his ideas. He arrived at a number of fundamental positions. Factions had always been dangerous: more so when they were composed of those on the left. The Brissotins, he was convinced, craved what courtiers had always craved: power and place. The new triumvirate against which he now thundered was "aristocracy, moderation, and ministeralism, [a] single monster under three aspects" (VIII, 178). His views on whether revolutionaries could enter coalition governments were subject neither to compromise nor negotiation. Under no circumstances could a revolutionary enter a government that was not revolutionary. Should the Court choose ministers from among the Jacobins, "I would have no more confidence in the patriotism of the Court" and little "in the virtue of those who were chosen." There can be nothing in common between the Court "and true patriots" (VIII, 171).

Until the appointment, in March 1792, of the so-called patriot ministers—Clavière, Dumouriez, Roland, and later Servan—all the King's ministers were of the upper nobility or from the Court.[14] He dryly said, when the King took on the patriots, "I prefer the declared champions of reaction to those hypocritical deserters of the people's cause" (VIII, 171). Anyone who aspires to the ministry "is worth no more" than those who have been or are now ministers (VIII, 77). The Court, in appointing Brissot's friends, had not suddenly become enlightened. The Court did not dismiss ministers to appoint better ones. It chose only "the most hypocritical and the most adroit" (VIII, 171). When the patriot ministers were removed by the King, on June 13, Robespierre was smug. It was a welcome event. "I say that the public good resides not in the character of ministers that the Court can dismiss as often as it wishes, but in the energy and patriotism of the National Assembly. As soon as the National Assembly learned of the dismissal of the patriot ministers, it assumed real character" and could now make sure that "the enemies of liberty respect the Declaration of Rights" (VIII, 372).

As a strategy, his insistence on defending the constitution was riddled with contradition, both practical and theoretical. The Court, the appointment of ministers, the composition and discipline of the army, all were assured by the constitution. Robespierre was thus advocating defense of the very forces of counterrevolution he accused his foes of supporting. Simultaneously he was insisting that the constitution not only legitimized significant aspects of the counterrevolution, but also made further revolution possible. For the moment he had to accept the King and Court in exchange for their acceptance of the Jacobins, a radical press and those deputies of the Legislative in whom he had not lost faith.

He seems to have found the war bewildering. He was angry that so many former or potential comrades wanted to fight Austria. He himself could not propose any means of reinvigorating the Revolution, but he was convinced the war would ruin it. For all his intelligence, for all the shrewdness inherent in his analysis of the disasters of war, in the short run these dire predictions did not come true. Instead, many of Brissot's extravagant predictions did, and ironically Robespierre was to be the beneficiary of the adventurist policies preached by the war party.

Marat had an interview with Robespierre in the spring of 1792. It is perhaps the only time the two met privately and alone. Here is Marat's oft-quoted analysis:

> This interview confirmed me in the opinion I had always had of him, that he joined to the insights of a sage senator the integrity of a truly good man and the zeal of a true patriot. But at the same time he lacks both the vision and the audacity of a statesman.[15]

There is much shrewdness here. Consumed with his hatred of Lafayette, helpless to prevent the fragmentation of the left, he had neither vision nor audacity. On the very day war was declared, he pleaded that the debates continue. It was his only choice. "Let no one come and say to us, the war is declared, we cannot discourage our generals, we must have confidence in the constituted authorities. No, it is now more than ever that one must watch the executive authority and the constituted authorities" (VIII, 291). He was ignored. It was the popularity of the war that baffled and disturbed Robespierre. When the Constituent Assembly had debated the constitutional question of which branch of government should have authority to declare war, Robespierre had vigorously opposed Mirabeau's support for the monarchy: "The King will always be tempted to declare war to augment his prerogative."[16] It was the Assembly that would keep the peace. Those who represented the people would always have "a direct and even personal interest in preventing war" (VI, 364–65). What had seemed sound political sense in 1790 had become nonsense in 1792. The Legislative was at least as eager for war as the Court. The Revolution seemed determined to destroy itself.

Robespierre had a mixed record as a prophet in the crisis of 1792. On November 9, 1792, the expansionist nature of the war was formally recognized by a decree that promised France's aid to all wanting to regain freedom, a euphemism for revolt, insurrection. This famous decree overturned an equally famous prior decree renouncing all wars of conquest and expansion, and launched France on her imperial career. The Revolution had been put on horseback. Brissot and his friends had changed the course of history and the Revolution far more directly and profoundly than had Robespierre. He himself, although he would subsequently fight the war with tenacity, was never reconciled to it. "This ought to furnish us with a useful lesson" (V, 272), he could not resist writing when the French armies were driven out of Brussels. His fear of military dictatorship, although not realized in Lafayette—who tried, as did Dumouriez later, but failed—was later realized.[17] From Lafayette to Napoleon, from the war of 1792 to the Italian campaigns, the Revolution was plagued by the generals. Robespierre's preternatural suspicions were generally correct, but his timing was off. It is Napoleon who finally fulfills the prophecy, and ironically enough this is the one general Robespierre had personally picked, on the recommendation of his brother. "The generals inflicted themselves on the Republic from its birth to its ruin."[18]

If the generals failed to seize power when Robespierre predicted, it was not through lack of trying. Nor was it a question of discipline, as Robespierre had argued. The armies of Lafayette and Dumouriez continued to fight under the same crue discipline as had the armies of Condé in the previous century. Yet these armies resisted the treason of both generals, whose failed *coups d'état* drove them from France, accompanied only by their staffs. The armies developed a revolutionary perspective that alienated them from their counterrevolutionary officers, and it was only when the army was commanded by a man of the Revolution, Napoleon, that the soldiers followed their leader into rebellion.

Robespierre may have lost the war debates, but only in the narrowest sense. As in the Constituent, he had not swayed enough men to do what he proposed. He had yet to experience the causal relationship between his words and revolutionary deeds that he would soon enjoy at the height of his influence and authority. But in the war debates, as in the Constituent, he had patiently created the foundations on which his preponderance would rest. For months he had stood on principle when it was extremely unpopular to do so. In the Jacobins he had regularly mounted to the tribune to argue his case, engaging in oratorical contest with some of the best speakers and most respected minds of the left. In the Revolution, and especially at the Jacobins, a man who aspired to lead had to prove his worthiness by just such displays of oratory and analysis. To argue, to debate, to orate, were essential to revolutionary leadership. Robespierre's splendid series of speeches had proved his capacity, even his virtuosity, to his followers. These oratorical confrontations, because they were between men on the left, were even more significant in his emergence as a leader than his principled stances throughout the Constituent. There he had countered men whose politics had little appeal to the left. It was worthy and necessary to struggle against the moderates and the reactionaries, but less significant in building a reputation for leadership than the dubious triumphs of internecine battle.

Brissot and his friends, potential rivals at the Jacobins and on the left, now abandoned the Society, creating a second schism. Robespierre was left in undisputed control. He would never lose the friendly forum of the Jacobins, even on the very eve of his fall. He had established his integrity, his prophetic voice, his principles, and his persona. He had displayed his incorruptibility, for he was untainted by any proximity to the Court. He was rapidly becoming, or being seen as, an indispensible man of virtue. It would not be long before he came into his inheritance.

With the Society shrunken but secure, on May 19 he began publishing his newspaper. After almost three years of revolutionary struggle, Robespierre returned, with a faith yet strong, to explaining and analyzing himself and the Revolution. This time the Defender of the Constitution addressed himself to the nation.

CHAPTER 6

Conversion to
Insurrection

PLATE VIII
(Phot. Bibl. nat. Paris)

THE DISTANCE TRAVELED by Robespierre from April to August 1792, from the declaration of war to the attack against the monarchy, is enormous. He began as an isolated prophet preaching the defense of the constitution of 1791; he ended as the apologist and partisan of urban insurrection against the King and as the theorist of revolutionary insurrection. This significant change of perception and position he personified, revealed and chronicled in his first newspaper, *La Défenseur de la Constitution*.[1]

Journalism, as it has remained, first became the vocation for revolutionaries with the French Revolution. Robespierre was not the first or the most successful radical journalist, but in the complex emerging character of this self-conscious revolutionary, the journalist had a place. Deprived of a governmental forum, Robespierre addressed his contemporaries, announced to them his ongoing analysis of the Revolution, in his newspaper. Several contemporaries and rivals—Marat and Desmoulins and Brissot—had made their names first as journalists before standing for election, and they continued to get out their papers long after they had become deputies. Others—Hébert is the best example—sought to govern, so to speak, through their newspapers, looking upon their readers as a political faction whose chief weapons were the petition and, ultimately, the riot. Still others—Prudhomme and Loustalot, who were the two editors of *Les Révolutions de Paris*—remained exclusively journalists, having no personal political ambitions, although anxious to influence men and events.

Virtually no one with political ambitions could hope to succeed without his own newspaper or at least some friendly, regular, and ready presentation of his political line in a newspaper and access to its editor. With pamphlets and posters, newspapers were the media. They were not conceived, in the French Revolution, as conduits of information, chronicles of events, newspapers of record whose prestige and reliability depended on their detachment. Newspapers were political weapons. One did not read this or that newspaper to get the news, but to learn Robespierre's or Brissot's or Lafayette's politics. There were at times several dozen newspapers circulating in Paris, not to mention provincial publications. Their appearance and disappearance followed closely the contours of revolutionary change. The suppression of a faction meant, automatically, the suppression of its newspaper, the stilling of its voice. Newspapers as well as those who wrote and edited them were part of the revolutionary struggle.

Robespierre, shortly after his arrival in Paris, had established some contacts with newspapers and contributed articles to a couple of them,

L'Union and the *Journal de la Liberté*, but these first efforts had no immediate sequel.[2] He concentrated his energy on oratory, and as his reputation grew he could count on relatively accurate reports of his speeches in the Constituent Assembly, although it was not for some time that similar coverage was given to his utterances at the Jacobins. Desmoulins and his future colleague on the Committee of Public Safety, Bertrand Barère, were journalists early interested in Robespierre, the former out of affection, the latter out of political curiosity.

During the Constituent and the Legislative, at least, the newspapers focused on the Assembly. When Robespierre ceased to be a deputy, he no longer had automatic access to the public; his speeches were no longer automatically news. During the war debates at the Jacobins he was dependent on those few left-wing newspapers sympathetic to the Society; and when these joined the war cause, he was confined almost exclusively to the walls of the Jacobins' library. He continued to send his speeches to provincial affiliates, and some found their way into provincial papers, but this was not enough. Robespierre's decision to turn journalist coincided with his ascendancy at the Jacobins and the political isolation he suffered as a result of the war debates.[3] The definitive break with the Brissotins came in June when an attempted reconciliation failed.[4] Robespierre was now in sole possession of what remained of the Jacobins. In self-defense he started his newspaper, the semi-official organ of the Society.

"You know," Robespierre told the Constituent, "that publicity is at one and the same time a right of the people and the safeguard of liberty" (VII, 110). *La Défenseur de la Constitution* was begun with this ideal; it was wholly written by Robespierre and appeared on Thursdays. Unfortunately, he did not date his issues, and sometimes the precise time of publication has to be deduced from the contents. A subscription cost thirty-six livres per year, twenty-one livres for six months, twelve livres for three months. This was expensive. A deputy, for example, would pay three days' wages for a subscription, and the deputies were decently paid. These subscription rates automatically limited Robespierre's readership, for although a café might subscribe and thus make the papers available to a wider audience, only the more comfortable citizens could afford *La Défensuer de la Constitution*. Robespierre did not envision mass circulation.[5] The new newspaper was on sale at the bookshop of Pierre-Jacques Duplain, in the rue Saint-Honoré, near Robespierre's rooms and the Jacobin Club, and, as the paper proudly if inaccurately announced, "at all the major bookshops of Europe" (IV, ix). We have no idea how many copies of each issue were printed. Robespierre's printer, a certain Léopold Nicolas, later served on his local Revolutionary Tribunal and would be guillotined ultimately for his adherence and loyalty to Robespierre.[6]

Fellow journalists variously greeted the new paper and its publisher. Louis Prudhomme of *Les Révolutions de Paris* devoted a long article to his rival's prospectus, expressing astonishment at Robespierre's desire to become a "hack journalist" (*folliculaire*).[7] Brissot flippantly referred to the enterprise as "some obscurely published sheet." Both men had successful papers, Brissot especially so, and they showed little enthusiasm for a newcomer to the field.

The line declared by the newspaper's title and explained in the first issue was prudent and legalistic. The extreme democrat of the Constituent, the "representative of the people," had become the defender of a constitution he had himself sharply attacked when its clauses were being debated. But he now saw defense of this flaws document as the only means of repulsing "the attacks of ambition and despotism" (IV, 6). In the midst of storms "stirred up by all the factions," an atmosphere poisoned by internecine feuds and "wickedly confused with the war, fomented by intrigue and corruption, encouraged by ignorance and egoism and credulity," what is needed is some point of rally and support: "I know of no other besides the Constitution" (IV, 7). These were reactionary times, as Robespierre saw it, and in issue after issue he advised his followers to do nothing that might give the forces of reaction an excuse to attack the exposed fragments of the left.

The conflicting claims of political consistency and changing circumstance clashed. Robespierre had declared the Constitution (in August 1791) a settlement favoring the rich (VII, 622). Not only did it exclude from the franchise all those who could not afford the money qualification for "active" citizenship, but it left considerable power in the hands of the King and thus made any legislation impossible unless Louis cooperated. This in turn made revolutionary politics intimately dependent on the Court. Robespierre now rather lamely excused these provisions as "the work of men," while the Constitution's principles were "the work of heaven."[8] This distinction and sophistry may have been lost on many, especially since he argued that the entire Constitution, both its celestial and mundane parts, should be accepted.

Robespierre was right about the declaration of war reinvigorating the Court and giving reaction new vitality, but he retreated too readily. Doubtless he thought the declaration of war a personal as well as political catastrophe, and he seems to have made his stand on defending the Constitution as the only possible way to keep the Jacobins intact and thus prevent the total triumph of counterrevolution. He wanted to minimize the damage the Court might do by holding it to constitutional limits. The defense of the Constitution was a desperate policy. In his isolation Robespierre may have panicked, or at least allowed his pessimism to dominate. The fears he had expressed throughout the war debates now seemed about to be realized. Either the resurgent Court would overwhelm the Revolution, or Lafayette would destroy the left and impose his own settlement, or the unprepared French armies would be defeated and the victorious Austrians would impose a Carthaginian peace. Almost anything was preferable to these alternatives. "Frenchmen," he exhorted his readers, "representatives, rally around the Constitution. Defend it against the executive power. Defend it against all the factions" (IV, 13).

Robespierre felt no need to go into hiding, and never had he been attracted to conspiratorial or clandestine activity. But neither did he much heed the growing rumblings in the Paris streets. Although he had no taste for what Georges Lefebvre has aptly called "the tumultuous agitation of the streets,"[9] he did not fear Paris. But his activities were confined to the Jacobins and to watching the Legislative and the Court and Lafayette. The insurrectionary developments unfolding before him were unnoticed at first. He did not, for some time, conceive of urban insurrection as the solution to the crisis of the Revolution. Wavering between unacceptable alternatives, Robespierre stood aloof. He maintained his reputation for incorruptibility, and while others—Brissot and his friends, for example—were suspiciously intimate with the Court, he had no taint of ambition, yet he was unable to fix on an active course. Once he realized what was happening in the streets of Paris, he was able to fit the spontaneous movement toward insurrection into the framework of the Revolution and realize its significance, but his isolation seems to have slowed his political reflexes.

More than any other, the French Revolution was made by insurrections. Popular convulsions, some planned, some spontaneous, beginning with the Fall of the Bastille, had thrust the Revolution forward. Robespierre had taken part in none of the earliest insurrections, but he had welcomed them retrospectively and made some tentative attempts at analysis. He was not the only revolutionary to see the fundamental place of insurrection in the Revolution, nor to see that insurrection was inescapable. But he was the first to give his observations, impressions, and experience a coherence and structure. He forged a compelling general theory of revolution from them, and, a necessary corollary, his ideas of the "people" as the makers of insurrection underwent extensive revision.

In his quest to understand the role of insurrection in revolution, Robespierre had no reliable guides. His views on war had flowed from reading and thinking, both in ancient and modern literature. His dislike of war, his fear of generals, his detestation of military dictatorship, these were commonplaces of the enlightened age, and to apply them in a revolutionary situation he had only to shift his angle of vision. But in working out his ideas on insurrection, he had no such foundations to build upon, no such historical fund to draw upon. The French revolutionary experience itself was the great and sole teacher.

Robespierre had instantly recognized, as had almost everyone in France—with the possible exceptions of the King, the Queen, and the more myopic courtiers—the significance of the Fall of the Bastille. The people of Paris had stormed a worthless royal fortress that the monarchy itself had considered demolishing rather than continue the expense of keeping the Bastille as a prison. There were only seven prisoners in the place when it fell, and none of these was being punished for having written against the monarchy. But the successful assault was far more important than its prize. The Bastille represented all the arbitrariness of the *ancien régime*; its medieval bulk dominated the eastern quarter of Paris, the sinister legends of dark deeds clinging to its stones. But most important, the Fall of the Bastille, the culminating act in days of urban uprising, not only put Paris in the hands of the Revolution, but marked the last moment when the Court might have destroyed the Revolution by force.

From that time Robespierre had seen insurrection—which meant to him, as to most contemporaries, only urban uprising, for he disregarded rural riot—as the motor of the Revolution. He also considered it a Parisian phenomenon. But he had an exalted idea of insurrection: only those uprisings that were political in inspiration and direction, or capable of being channeled to political ends, were creative, necessary, and worthy. Food riots, the risings of despair and alienation, which had riddled the *ancien régime* with violence and would similarly afflict the Revolution, he thought contemptible. Men, for Robespierre, acted with purpose, not because driven by the blind imperatives of need. That the price of bread on July 14, 1789, was the highest in almost a century would have been a fact of far less significance to Robespierre than his belief that men, on that day, set out to destroy tyranny and arbitrary justice in the name of humanity. Revolution and insurrection were inseparable, and both were rational activities undertaken by men, self-consciously, for their own improvement. His conception of politics left no room for the irrational. In his theorizing about insurrection, Robespierre would make several rigid distinctions between kinds of uprisings, and his sympathies would be strictly limited to the purposeful, political, deliberate insurrection aimed against the counterrevolution.

But even before he enriched his theory of insurrection in 1792, he had written Buissart (July 23, 1789) that those who vanquished the Bastille are "this national army."[10] Here was the germ of seeing the insurrectionaries as the representatives of the entire nation, even if they came only from Paris, or even a particular neighborhood of Paris. Those who stormed the Bastille, he insisted, saved the Revolution. It was the people of Paris and not the deputies at Versailles who triumphed. He dryly remarked, in the same letter (with a strategically placed emphasis), that "the despotism of the aristocracy" was disconcerted when the Third Estate showed a *"perhaps* unexpected firmness in supporting July 14.[11] The revolutionary alliance between the people of Paris and the deputies, an alliance Robespierre would provide with theoretical justification, was the essence of the Revolution. This alliance had its clearest expression in Paris.

Neither Robespierre nor his colleagues needed Tocqueville's brilliant analysis of the centralizing patterns of the monarchy throughout much of the *ancien régime* to know that Paris was a factor in the Revolution disproportionate to its size, although it was far and away the largest city in the kingdom.[12] Similarly, they needed no reminders that Paris' population was unruly because it was unique, with special needs and means for asserting them. Robespierre gave this fact eloquent expression. "The people is sublime," he told his listeners at the 1793 celebration of July 14, "but individuals are weak. In the midst of a revolutionary tempest, we need a rallying point. The people *en masse* cannot govern itself; this rallying point must be Paris . . . it is here that must be placed the center of the Revolution . . ." (IX, 559). Paris was, in fact and deed, the Revolution: "In losing Valenciennes we would lose a frontier; in losing Paris we would lose liberty" (IX, 601). These juxtapositions are crucial in Robespierre's thought. "Paris is only a kind of general gathering place, only a continual and natural federation that renews itself without cease with citizens of this enormous state. This is not a city of 600,000 citizens . . . it is the French people, it is the human species, it is public opinion and the invincible ascendance of universal reason" (V, 197). In this rich revolutionary soil his ideas on insurrection germinated. Robespierre was one of those provincials who adored the capital and made it both his spiritual and physical home. His celebration of the Parisians as a revolutionary people, Paris as the capital of revolution, would become a part of the myth that dominated revolutionary thinking throughout the next century, indeed into our own century.

Robespierre's revolutionary Paris was peopled by the *menu peuple*, the inhabitants of the popular, as opposed to aristocratic or bourgeois, sections of the city. Their unit of political activity was the neighborhood, which was represented in the forty-eight sections that composed the capital, equivalents to our wards. "During a time of crisis when each day seems to be pregnant with tomorrow's crimes and plots," he declared, "only the constant vigilance of the sections can save us" (VIII, 162). The history of the Revolution, he insisted long before it became one of the most tenacious conventions of revolutionary historiography, should be written in terms of the great days when Paris rose in rebellion and thus created "the glorious days of the Revolution." Yet although virtually all the elements necessary for his theory of insurrection are available before July 1792, Robespierre did not put them together into a coherent explanation. Throughout May and June and most of July he preached the defense of the constitution and patience as "the virtue of republicans" (IX, 296).

The lessons of July 1791, the massacre in the Champ de Mars and its aftermath, when the radicals went into hiding and their organizations and newspapers nearly disappeared, were not soon forgotten. Now, groping his way toward a theory of insurrection, he considered the Champ de Mars episode the ideal type of a "partial" insurrection, one doomed to failure and prone to backlash because misconceived, misdirected, mismanaged, or all three. Partial insurrections are "considered an act of revolt" and punished by laws still "in the hands of the conspirators [thus does he refer to those in power]" (VIII, 91). So stringent were his criteria for insurrection that only the attack on the Bastille qualified as a success.

Between July 14, 1789, and June 1792, he insisted, there had not been, nor could there have been, a successful insurrection. He had in mind particularly the demonstration at the Tuileries on June 20, 1792, which he had opposed. This massive demonstration had been called and orchestrated by Brissot and his followers, angry and humiliated by the royal dismissal of the "patriot" ministers. It was planned as a demonstration to intimidate the King into recalling Roland and Clavière and the others to their portfolios, and also to force him to withdraw the vetoes he had cast against recent legislative acts. The June demonstration sent thousands of men, women, and children (whose presence indicates that the confrontation was conceived as nonviolent) to the Tuileries to present the King with their demands. Robespierre abhorred this manipulation of the Paris crowd and warned that it would play into the hands of Lafayette (VIII, 386–87). But the Brissotins were not to be deterred, and they were lucky. They had summoned the people to insurrection, "the most holy of duties," for their own ends. The enormous crowd was unchecked by any authority, had easily penetrated the royal apartments, and had subjected Louis and his family to a harrowing couple of hours. Yet Louis refused to yield. His personal courage and stubborness, his gift for gesture and public dignity, diffused the crowd's anger. When the local authorities finally arrived, having deliberately let the scene run its course, in the late afternoon, the crowd dispersed. Lafayette had been given sufficient pretext to declare martial law, but he failed to act. His ineptitude, said Robespierre, was equal to that of the Brissotins (IV, 298), who had been willing to risk the people of Paris to get a few men reinstated as ministers.

The invasion of the Tuileries, however, was not followed by repression. The Court, stunned at the inadequacy of the security at the Tuileries, at once began to prepare some defense. Louis gathered reliable troops at the Tuileries, evicted those in houses attached to the grounds of the Château so that soldiers could be stationed, appointed a commander of his now-formidable defenses, the Marquis de Mandat, and transformed the Château, in a matter of weeks, into an armed camp in the center of Paris. These precautions, carried out in broad daylight in the center of the capital, convinced the populace and their leaders that Louis was preparing a *coup d'état*: he would strike Paris as he had failed to do in 1789. Everywhere it was believed that Louis was preparing to destroy the Revolution by force.

June 20 is significant not for what it accomplished, which was nil, but for what it portended. Gouverneur Morris, the American ambassador, realized, as he noted in his diary, that the blow had missed the King, but not the crown: "The constitution has this day I think given its last groan."[13] The King had nearly been toppled by a Paris crowd. Robespierre was less prescient than Morris. He was angry at the unnecessary risk taken by Brissot and his friends; he saw the Court arming. He wrapped himself even tighter in the rent mantle of legalism and rigid constitutionalism. He had no intention of taking another such risk, of goading the now-armed Court into using its weapons.

But circumstances, *la force des choses*, were changing. From all over France volunteer soldiers from the provinces, Federals, as they were called, were on their way to the war front, stopping off in Paris to mark the annual celebration of July 14 before marching on. As they arrived there was a heady, palpable patriotism in the capital. The neighborhood and street radicals, the sections and the Jacobins, were quick to appreciate what was happening and to cultivate these arriving allies. Two of the Federal contingents, from opposite ends of the country, Marseilles and Brest, the south and the west, were especially radical. They were determined to remain in Paris until the King was dethroned, or do it themselves.

The Federals gravitated naturally to the popular and patriotic neighborhoods of Paris. They were welcomed, taken in by their hosts, and quickly joined in the local political life of the sections. The Municipal Acts, which dated back to the first year of revolution and regulated the activity of the sections, and maintained the constitutional distinction between "active" and "passive" citizens (the latter were excluded from political activity on a local as on a national level), were ostentatiously ignored. All were admitted to meetings and participation. Even more important, "passive" citizens were admitted, for the first time, to the National Guard. In June and July Paris democratized itself. The lines of battle, between Paris and the Court, were being drawn. Neither of the protagonists had much interest (or would derive much advantage) from enforcing the Constitution. Indeed, both city and Court blatantly ignored that document. Even the Legislative Assembly abdicated its responsibility. Increasingly preoccupied with its own factional struggles, unable to decide which cause to join, the Legislative stood aloof. It could not have done much else, for the initiative in the Revolution had passed to the streets of Paris. The long-unresolved problem of the place of the monarchy in a regenerated France was about to be solved by force. The complex chain of command and decision making that controlled the mobilization of the sections, another part of the Municipal Acts of 1790 designed to make it exceptionally difficult for Paris to act, was snapped. By the middle of July this bloodless *coup d'état* had been carried out. Paris was, *de facto*, in the hands of its populace, the sections stood facing the Court.

Robespierre saw and was conquered. With the July 14 issue of *La Défenseur de la Constitution* he began to explain and exhort and analyze the new situation, quickly integrating the shifts of power into his synthesis of the Revolution. He was stuck with the title of his newspaper, but he began extricating himself from the now burdensome encumbrances of strict constitutionalism. Now and then he refers to himself as the "defender of liberty," discreetly dropping the defunct "defender of the constitution." "Brave and generous citizens," he apostrophized the

Federals, "your presence itself in Paris will give enormous advantage to the cause. Your union with the patriots that this city holds in its bosom . . . will render impotent this army of satellites and assassins that despotism and the foreign courts collect." The Federals were part of a vast network of patriotism, the armed representatives—his political vocabulary was becoming more military and aggressive—which presented "a common and simultaneous resistance" to oppression (IV, 297–98). "As for us," he assured his readers on behalf of the Jacobins, "we are not members of any party, we don't serve any faction, you know it, friends and brothers, our will is the general will" (IV, 309).

On July 11 he had proposed to the Paris Jacobins, an *Adresse aux Fédérés des 83 départements* (Address to the Federals of the 83 Departments), which was ordered printed and distributed as the Society's view of what was to be done. The Federals, Robespierre proposed, were to be integrated into the people of Paris, to mingle with the most politically advanced sections of the city and avoid contact with those neighborhoods where the more moderate and socially elevated citizens lived (IV, 297). In fact, the address does little more than to encourage the Federals to continue doing what they were doing. But it signals the alignment of the Jacobins, for the first time, with the politics of the street, and because of the prestige of the Paris club throughout the nation, it similarly attaches many provincial clubs to the growing agitation. And the agitation was not aimless or designed for mere intimidation. Nothing short of dethronement and the destruction of the monarchy was contemplated. Robespierre himself did not explicitly call for dethronement, preferring to remain cautious, for the specter of "partial" insurrection still haunted his imagination. Certainly he never contemplated descending into the streets to share the camaraderie or risks. But he insisted that the initiative seized by Paris and the Federals run its course.

He was slow to give insurrection his formal blessing, although he was considered a friend by those planning the uprising. Only on July 29, when the insurrection was probably irresistible, when the ultimatum, signed by forty-seven of the forty-eight sections, demanding the King's removal, had been sent to the Legislative, did he publicly commit himself. Yet even at this relatively late date he was careful, even circumspect, in his choice of words:

Serious ills call for drastic remedies [he told the Jacobins]. Palliatives only make them incurable. France's ills are extreme. Does anyone know the cause? No one, it seems to me, has tried to diagnose them completely. (VIII, 408)

The speech is a masterpiece of suggestion and innuendo: nowhere does he preach insurrection. His auditors in those feverish days needed no incitement: they heard Robespierre's diagnosis as a call to arms. But he spoke as much to the Court and the moderates as to his adherents. Should the insurrection fail, he would survive (and so would the Jacobins) to continue the fight. He did not underestimate the crisis, nor did he abandon his grip on reality, on what was possible. Robespierre was always gloomy, a bit febrile and fatalistic on the eve of great events. "The *dénouement* of the constitutional drama" was at hand, he pessimistically wrote his friend and comrade Georges Couthon. "What can give us hope is the strength of public spirit in Paris and in a number of departments; there is the justice of our cause."[14] But he himself, as always, would not participate.

Robespierre's analysis of the crisis is as forthright as his conclusions are veiled. It is not only the King who is to blame, but the Legislative as well. The former "wants to destroy the state"; the latter "cannot or will not save it." The state "must be saved by whatever means it can. The only means that is unconstitutional is that which leads to the ruin of the state" (VIII, 409–10). He now abandons his feeble policy of defending the constitution and does so by a clever paradox: destroying the constitution will actually fulfill it; he comes not to overturn the law but to realize it. "There is not," he elaborates, "a necessary measure for health which is not prescribed by the very text of the constitution. All that is necessary is the desire to interpret it and to uphold it in good faith" (VIII, 410).[15] Insurrection has thus become "a necessary measure" that is "prescribed" by the constitution. He had begun his defense of the constitution as a conservative means of holding the counterrevolution momentarily at bay. Now his constitutionalism has become insurrectionary. After the insurrection he wants a Convention Assembly to reorder France (VIII, 413). The specific elimination of monarchy and Legislative and constitution he does not mention, let alone demand through insurrection. But he is determined that deputies in the Legislative be forbidden a seat in the Convention. A few "zealous defenders of the people's rights" may be thus sacrificed, but this loss will "be more than compensated by the necessity of smashing the cabals of the party chiefs" (VIII, 419). Thus will the Brissotins be eliminated.

Once the state is saved, the primary assemblies, the more than forty thousand local units that composed the political nation throughout France, could be summoned, the national representation "regenerated," and public safety assured (VIII, 415). He wonders out loud "by what coincidence has it happened that the only faithful friends of the Constitution [he means here the constitution as he interprets it to be an insurrectionary imperative], the veritable pillars of liberty, are precisely this laborious and magnanimous class that the first assembly despoiled of citizenship?" (VIII, 415). France is to be saved by her "passive" citizens. But insurrection is never mentioned. Typically the speech is punctuated with menacing asides directed at the counterrevolution: "Such is the degree of illness to which we have come . . . that the cure has become necessarily difficult and perilous" (VIII, 417). "We have only two alternatives, to perish and bury with us the freedom of the human race, or to develop to the fullest great virtues and prepare ourselves for great sacrifices" (VIII, 418). "Let us purify these places [all the offices of government]," he exhorts his auditors, "with a new generation of magistrates worthy of the French people. What is more sacred to us than the happiness and liberty of our country?" (VIII, 420). The rhetorical question serves, throughout, as the instrument for inciting to insurrection. It carries the burden of moral imperative, and in the context in which Robespierre is speaking, there is no need to be more specific about the task at hand. His auditors understood that he was talking about insurrection, despite his penchant for abstract language. What to the modern reader may appear a hazy series of abstractions with a moral tinge, was taken by contemporaries as clear and eloquent expression. There are very few contemporary complaints about what Robespierre meant, and these few come almost exclusively from those who despised him.

After months of temporizing, Robespierre declared himself, explaining his decision, as was his habit, as the only possible conclusion to be drawn from analysis of the situation, while simultaneously providing a moral purpose for the proposed action. It was not so much the attack on the monarchy that had restrained him, for nowhere had he ever suggested that the kingship be preserved as essential to a new France. Nor was he especially reticent about unleashing the forces of urban uprising. He had never recoiled from the Paris masses as had many a contemporary. Quite the contrary. And with the collapse of Lafayette's schemes and his flight, there was no danger of a military *coup d'état*. What restrained him, I think, was the necessity of overthrowing the Legislative Assembly along with the monarchy. It was a body for which he had no respect, but it was the only revolutionary organ of the government. It and the flawed constitution of 1791 were all that stood between regenerated France and the counterrevolution. If the Legislative and the consitution were destroyed, all that would remain would be the organs of the *ancien régime*, battered and curbed but still existent, or chaos issuing in civil war. But once persuaded of the necessity of insurrection as the only conceivable line, he was ready to take the risk.

The deciding event was the abdication of the Legislative. The Assembly, now shrunk to fewer than one hundred sitting members—all those sympathetic to the Court, to Lafayette, or to moderation generally had stopped attending—received the sectional ultimatum demanding Louis's dethronement, submitted it to a committee, and on August 4 announced, with an accompanying reprimand to the forty-seven sections that had signed the ultimatum, that it would take no action. The Legislative thus declared its nullity: it was time to act. Nothing now stood between an armed Court and an armed city. Robespierre's speech of July 29 had been a species of blessing on the insurrection whose planning had been under way since July 26.

The two spontaneously organized bodies who planned the attack on the monarchy, the Central Committee of Federals (Comité Central des Fédérés) and the Central Bureau of the Sections (Bureau Central des Sections), were known to Robespierre, but he did not participate in their deliberations.[16] Nor were the Jacobins, as a group, involved. The rue Saint-Honoré monastery was deserted on the night of August 9–10, and the members who fought at the Tuileries did so as private citizens, not representatives of the Society. Even the small armed contingent that gathered at the Jacobins on the night of the ninth had no official sanction. Robespierre's Jacobins were not Lenin's Bolsheviks.

During the night of August 9 and on into the early morning of August 10, as the contingents for the attack gathered in the quarters of Saint-Antoine (on the right bank) and Saint-Marcel (on the left bank), the two most radical, working-class neighborhoods in Paris, Robespierre was absent, presumably at home with the Duplays. Virtually all the important leaders of the time—with the exception of Danton, who led the *coup d'état* at the Hôtel de Ville that deprived the Court of any possible aid from the city and its armed forces, and Barbaroux, who fought with his Marseillais Federals at the Château—were similarly absent. The civilian leaders of the Revolution were not expected to fight.[17]

The plan of attack was simple. Once the two contingents were up to strength, which did not happen until between six and seven in the morning, several hours later than planned, they would march simultaneously to the Tuileries. The forces from Saint-Marcel would have to cross the Seine, and if the Pont-Saint-Michel and the Pont-Neuf, the bridges they would use, were defended, there would be fighting before they reached their destination. The troops from Saint-Antoine did not foresee any fighting along their route. Before the insurgents from the left bank reached the bridges, there would be an attack on the Municipal Government at the Hôtel de Ville. The Commune would be replaced by a new insurrectionary Commune; all those unsympathetic to the insurrection would be removed. If the strike was successful, all the artillery guarding the bridges, and the National Guard contingents as well, both under the command of the city government, would be recalled.

This is precisely what happened. When the Saint-Marcel insurgents reached the bridges, they crossed without a fight. The two contingents joined up, about ten thousand strong, at the Tuileries. And while the insurgents were gathering, the Marquis de Mandat, Louis's commander at the Tuileries, was summoned to the Hôtel de Ville by the new insurrectionary Commune. After some delay he answered the summons, was browbeaten by Danton, and while being taken to prison was murdered. The Tuileries itself, prepared for the impending attack, was now without its commander. During the night a number of the National Guardsmen manning the artillery in the courtyard of the royal Château had deserted rather than have to fire upon their fellow citizens. The Tuileries were thus commanded by an indecisive King, and although the number of defenders was formidable, only the Swiss mercenaries and the professional soldiers and courtiers loyal to the King could be relied upon. When the King was persuaded to take refuge in the Manège, just across the garden from the Tuileries, where the remnants of the Legislative Assembly were sitting, there was no commander at the Tuileries. His departing orders, to oppose force with force, left the decision to resist or surrender in the hands of the Swiss generals. The fighting was bloody, the massacre that followed even bloodier. The King, walking across the garden with his family to seek asylum with the Assembly, remarked absently that the leaves were falling early that year. It would become a prophetic comment only a few hours later when the Tuileries fell to the insurrectionists and with it the monarchy itself.

Immediately after the victory at the Tuileries, Robespierre was ready to explain and analyze what had happened, to make it coherent by placing the insurrection in the larger context of the Revolution, while simultaneously giving action a moral base.[18] He immediately emerged to do what he did best, become the interpreter of action. On August 11 he was articulating the demands of the victors, and he devoted the entire last issue of *La Défenseur de la Constitution* to the events and issues of the insurrection. This is a farewell to the long and difficult, and politically ambiguous, summer of 1792. It is, as well, a hopeful, enthusiastic greeting of a new stage of revolution. As a piece of journalism, an example of Robespierre's abilities in that medium, his account of August 10 is excellent, especially well informed, indeed among the best contemporary accounts. As a political testament to revolution it is unique.

Virtually anyone in Paris in the days immediately after August 10 could have known a good deal about the insurrection. Nothing else was talked about. The Tuileries Palace, still smoldering from a fire that broke out after the Château had fallen, became the most significant attraction in Paris, visited by crowds of residents and tourists. Robespierre could easily have collected the available gossip, varnished it over with his impressive rhetorical style, and passed it off as adequate. Most contemporary newspapers did precisely this. Instead, he sought out the best eyewitnesses he could find, interrogated them, and from those several impressions and accounts constructed a synthetic view. His account is divided into three parts: "The Events of August 10, 1792" is an interpretive narrative more or less organized along chronological lines; "Interesting Details on the Events of August 10 and the Days Following" includes a number of anecdotes, probably garnered from François-Joseph Westermann, one of the organizers of the insurrection, a hero of the fighting, and Robespierre's principal informant;[19] and "Petition Presented to the National Assembly in the Name of the Place Vendôme Section," which is Robespierre's harangue delivered before the rump of the Legislative Assembly on behalf of his own section. The remainder of the issue is filled out with letters on August 10 and some documents that had been seized by the insurgents during the attack on the Tuileries.

The arbitrary separation of anecdote from chronicle reveals an attitude toward history. Well read in history, especially that of ancient Rome and Greece, Robespierre as historian was very much in the classical mold. With his law briefs and his oratory, he wanted to discover pattern and significance behind the manifest detail. He studied the past not for its own sake but rather as a vast repository of exempla that would illuminate the present, a shorthand of symbols and metaphors. When he himself came to write history—and the account of August 10 is his only attempt—he scrupulously separated anecdote from philosophy. Unlike the great historians of his century—Voltaire, Hume, Gibbon, Robertson, Montesquieu—he was unable to integrate details into a philosophic whole, and his single historical essay had contemporary history as its subject and political illumination as its purpose.

From his long opening dithyrambic sentence, it is clear that Robespierre saw the Revolution of August 10 as necessary for the survival of the Revolution and legitimated by "the eternal treasons of the govern-

ment" (IV, 350–51). In such assumptions of a just response to tyranny
did he hold, however tenuously, to the legality he had long preached.
The duplicity of the Court, the ambitions of a few—Lafayette, Louis
XVI, Marie Antoinette, and Pierre-Louis Roederer (a major official in
the *département* of Paris who was at the Tuileries during the attack) are
the only individuals mentioned by name—left the people no choice.
They provoked Paris and the Revolution and were thus the architects
of their own fall. Paris saw daily at the Tuileries "the formidable preparations for a new Saint Bartholomew's Day" massacre, that ghastly
sixteenth-century Catholic butchery of Protestants, inspired by the
Court and joined by the King. August 10, Robespierre repeated the
widely held contemporary view, was an act of self-defense. "The French
people, completely dishonored, oppressed for a long time, felt that the
moment had come to fulfill the sacred duty imposed by nature on all
living beings, and with even more reason on all nations, of being able
to take care of their own preservation by a generous resistance to
oppression" (IV, 351). Insisting on the natural right of insurrection, a
familiar tenet of eighteenth-century social-contract theory, Robespierre
swept away the legal restraints that had so long held him in thrall. This
meshed nicely with his July 29 argument that the constitution, rightly
read, not only permitted but demanded insurrection in certain cases.

The insurrection itself he could only compare in significance to the
Fall of the Bastille, which paled in comparison. In 1789 liberty "remained confused, the principles unknown," and the people had been
aided by "a large number of those we call 'great,' " the upper classes of
Paris. The year 1792 was something wonderfully different and far greater.
It was not the work of all the classes of society, but the work of the
people of Paris and the Federals, who discovered "all their resources in
themselves." "Against all their enemies" they made the necessary revolution (IV, 352). Robespierre does not lament the loss of social unity;
he celebrates the triumph of the "passive" citizens who have now
avenged their exclusion from the politics of the Revolution. The solemn
manner in which this great act was prepared was as sublime "as its motives and its object" and its social exclusiveness. August 10 was no
"spontaneous riot without object, fueled by some confusion," nor a conspiracy shamefully "entombed in the shadows." It was planned in broad
daylight, under the eyes of the people. The planners hadn't "deigned
to hide their designs" (IV, 353). Revolutionaries did their business in
the open, for their business was legitimate. He infused the insurrectionists with his own enthusiasm. "This army, equally imposing by the number and the diversity of its arms, and above all by the sublime sentiment

of liberty that animated every face, presented a spectacle that no tongue can describe and of which those who had not seen the events of July 14, 1789, can form only an imperfect idea" (IV, 354).[20] The heroes of August 10 are anonymous, they are the people, and Robespierre manages to give his account an atmosphere of grandeur. In revolution, he is becoming increasingly aware, it is the many and not the few who count and who act. And the many are becoming increasingly identified in his mind with the people of Paris.

There are, to be sure, some inaccuracies in Robespierre's account. Some are the result of incomplete information, others of deliberate emphasis or shading imposed by the demands of conviction and ideology. He says that "100 Marseillais" fell at the Tuileries. Not only is the number inflated, but Robespierre incorrectly attributes these deaths to the first penetration of the Château by the insurgents, that interlude of phony comradeship rudely shattered when the Swiss guards, the King's bodyguard, opened fire and picked off the defenseless attackers as they tried to run to safety across the open, cobbled courtyard. Robespierre apparently confounded the two assaults on the Château, of which the second and victorious charge was maniacal, irresistible, and bloody.[21] So, too, does he deflate the number of victims of the massacre that followed seizure of the Tuileries. The appalling butchery that began after Louis sent word that the defenders, and especially the Swiss, were to surrender, becomes in his account the execution of a few guilty aristocrats. The awful facts vanish behind his abstract language: "the people's justice punished, through the chastisement of several counterrevolutionary aristocrats, who dishonored the name of Frenchmen, the eternal impunity of all the oppressors of humanity." Even in their justified fury, he insists, the victors "observed all the forms necessary to protect the innocent" (IV, 354–55). In truth the massacre was frenzied and indiscriminate, even claiming two Brestois insurrectionists who had the misfortune to be wearing red uniforms that resembled those of the hated Swiss. But Robespierre refused to sully the people's victory he was celebrating. The conventions of writing of any war are to insist on its ultimate justice and necessity and to point out the magnanimity of the victors. Robespierre made no effort to be unconventional. Magnanimity and popular virtue are the qualities most conspicuous among the insurgents, and he reports, as evidence, that several thieves who tried to loot the captured Château were put to death on the spot" (IV, 365).[22]

Individual feats of arms or conscience are not much mentioned by Robespierre, with the conspicuous exception of the deeds of Westermann, which are somewhat exaggerated. The courageous street fighter is almost a hero out of romance.[23] And a useful hero he is. A new man, a man of the people, a man who rose to prominence in his section and carried no taint of national politics or suspicion of complicity, Westermann became in Robespierre's account a symbol for the people in arms.

The particular and complicated series of events that preceded the fighting is accurately reconstructed by Robespierre. Here it is not Westermann who was his informant, but perhaps someone who was in the Château throughout the long night of uneasiness, distractions, and panic before the King was persuaded to take refuge with the Legislative Assembly and the fighting broke out. He may have gotten some information from Roederer, a man he never much liked, since they had served together in the Constituent, but who did spend the night with the royal family. His account of the King's surrender is accurate, and his scorn for the supine Legislative, so anxious after the insurrection to avoid any significant condemnation of the King, is bitter. "It is detestable to hear such phrases as the *suspicions directed against the executive power*," he writes of the timid formulas of the Legislative, "when the nation and the National Assembly see nothing all around them but the proven crimes of Louis, of his family, and of his agents" (IV, 357).

In the section entitled "Interesting Details . . ." Robespierre puts an accurate and detailed account of the murder of the military commander of the Tuileries, the Marquis de Mandat. It would appear that he got his information from someone who was at the Hôtel de Ville, the City Hall, in the early hours of August 10 when Mandat was murdered. Both Desmoulins and Danton were present and may have been the source. Similarly, his account of the reactionary Henri IV battalion, which refused to join the insurrection and threatened to hold the Pont-Neuf, the most strategic bridge in Paris, against the rebels, is precise and accurate. The only missing detail is the removal of the cannon deployed there shortly before the insurgents made their crossing. Robespierre also has some interesting and accurate details about the artillerymen of the National Guard who were stationed in the courtyard of the Tuileries and who abandoned their guns during the night rather than have to fire on the gathering crowd. This was a strategic desertion, depriving the King of the firepower needed to repel attack. And he minimizes the role of Roederer, a slight which that vain man made up for some forty years later when he set down his recollections.[24]

Robespierre's is one of the best, most substantial and original accounts of August 10. He was a reliable and diligent journalist. In addition, this remarkable issue of *La Défenseur de la Constitution* carries, as his readers had come to expect, an analytical and critical explanation of the insurrection. Robespierre had his paper out within ten days of the events, perhaps earlier, despite the numerous distractions and feverish politics following August 10.[25] With the insurrection itself, which he studied so closely, he had discovered the law of insurrection and its place in the French Revolution. The presentation of so important a discovery and confirmation demanded a solemnity of style, an austerity of manner, and also the suppression of any details that might mar the pristine clarity of the historical logic at work under the clutter of detail. It is the movement of historical forces—the people, the court, the aristocracy, Paris—that matter, that reveal the truth. Small matters are sacrificed, individuals are minimized, a somber yet intense manner prevails.

August 10 marks the beginning of "the most glorious revolution that has ever honored humanity; let us say, even better, it is the only revolution that has had an object worthy of man, that of founding, at last, political societies on the immortal principles of equality, justice, and reason" (IV, 358). Before such significance the *métier* of journalist is overwhelmed, the "defender of the constitution" is laid to rest. "The partisan of all necessary and well-directed insurrections against despotism and intrigue" is revealed.

CHAPTER 7

The King's Trial

PLATE IX
(Phot. Bibl. nat. Paris)

A S SOON AS THE FIGHTING was over at the Tuileries, Robespierre was busy formulating the desires and demands of the victorious Commune, the city government now renewed and radicalized through insurrection. He was delighted with the first steps taken to institutionalize the triumph: the sections smoothly elected new delegates to replace those ousted from the Commune in the early morning *coup d'état* at the Hôtel de Ville. Robespierre thought this a "great and sublime conception, without which the insurrection would have flowed haphazardly, like a torrent, without leaving any trace, and the people would have fallen again into the hands of intriguers . . ." (VII, 499). He was relieved that authority was once again made regular, orderly, and rational, and that the insurrectionists were not themselves determined to seize power, but only to exercise it temporarily until a new assembly could be elected.[1] Robespierre never suggested restoring power to the despised Legislative and its newly elected executive council. He specifically told section Piques, which asked his advice, not to disarm.

Defending the insurrectionary Commune was a political declaration, at least partly encouraged by the victory of August 10 as well as the presence of old enemies in the Legislative. Brissot's faction, who were the most important group not to desert their duties in the Legislative, now sought to govern until the new assembly could take its seats. That contemptible body, in Robespierre's view, was to be commanded, not cajoled. He drew up a list of specific demands to be made to the Legislative. Lafayette, who had fled the country only to be captured by the Austrians, "must be declared a traitor to the country. The Commune should send representatives into the departments to explain the insurrection. All citizens must henceforth be admitted to the sections without distinction. The Commune should form popular societies and remain in permanent contact with those that already exist. Thus it will be possible to know the wishes of the people. . . ."[2] The unarmed Legislative, having stood aloof from the insurrection, was incapable of resistance.

Making durable the victory of August 10 was more complicated than merely articulating goals and intimidating the Legislative. The new assembly had to be composed of men sympathetic to August 10, and Robespierre gave a good deal of thought to who should sit, and did a good deal of manipulating to ensure that his choices were elected. The new deputies must be "pure, incorruptible, composed above all of citizens . . . whom despotism has proscribed" (IV, 333). He wanted the *conventionnels*, as members of the Convention came to be called, elected directly by the primary assemblies rather than having to submit to several stages of election, which tended to favor more moderate (and socially elevated) candidates. His proposal to prohibit "those who had been in the Constituent or Legislative" (VIII, 424) won Marat's support—he would have been eligible for the Convention, while Robespierre would not—but otherwise had little appeal. Robespierre prided himself on his consistency, and his self-conscious rectitude demanded that there be no suspicion of personal gain or advancement in any of his actions. The self-denying ordinance he now again proposed would also exclude Brissot and his followers from the Convention. He would rather take a chance on new men—and he assumed August 10 would call forth the republicans of France hitherto in the minority—than give his enemies an opportunity to dominate the Convention.

If he seems here to have expressed optimism about how the electors would respond to the insurrection of August 10, in Paris itself he took no chances. He managed the elections of the Paris delegation with attention and skill. No royalism, whether constitutional or cavalier, open or discreet, was tolerated in the press, and no royalist candidate, indeed no candidate who had not supported August 10, stood for election. All fiscal qualifications for voting were abolished, but because whole categories of suspected royalists were excluded, fewer Parisians voted in 1792 than had voted for the Legislative deputies. There was little expressed regret at these exclusions. Those who remained eligible to vote, of course, were susceptible to Robespierre's suggestions. The Paris delegation of twenty-four had a preponderance of radicals, was devoted to insurrection as the foundation act of a regenerated France, and was to prove the most politically formidable of all the deputations to the Convention.[3] It had not been hand-picked by Robespierre, although he did see to it that friends as well as his brother got elected, and he had been able to blackball those he thought undesirable.

For the first time since the Constituent, Robespierre was again the representative of the people, although what he meant by "the people" was undergoing some modification, as we shall see. The epithet is once more in his utterances. He speaks incessantly of the people, who remain abstract and even mythical, but are increasingly Parisian and predominantly *sans-culottes*. August 10 has necessitated some modification in his views of whom he represents. He now thinks of the politically active part of Paris as a representative population, expressing the will of all France, much as he thinks of himself and the other deputies as representing the people's sovereignty. He will draw important inferences from this view, and he refuses to tolerate any criticism of the insurrection or its participants: August 10 must be taken *en bloc*. The reason for this categorical stance is the September Massacres, the horrid and grotseque murder of prisoners—men, women, and children, without distinction. They began on September 2 at the Abbaye prison in the center of Paris, when some clerical prisoners were pulled from their cart and butchered. The massacres continued, with diminishing fury, until September 7, and the populace, from which *ad hoc* tribunals and volunteer executioners were drawn, went methodically from prison to prison, interrogating the prisoners and either killing them on the spot or setting them free.

The butchery sprang from fear. Those captured on August 10 at the Tuileries, especially the hated Swiss, had remained in prison for nearly a month without coming to trial. The cumbersome machinery of justice lagged far behind a widely felt desire for vengeance. And with the Austrian and Prussian troops advancing on Paris, commanded by the Duke of Brunswick, the city panicked. When his army was less than one hundred miles from the capital, the Duke published a fierce manifesto, threatening the city with fire and sword if it did not capitulate and reinstate Louis XVI. The Brunswick Manifesto reached Paris on August 30. The men on their way to the crumbling front, encouraged by the rabid journalists, believed a plot was afoot: the prisoners would be released or would escape to butcher the defenseless Parisians who would be trapped between the invaders and their domestic accomplices. Killing the prisoners became, in the popular imagination, a necessary ritual purge. The authorities in Paris were unable or unwilling to stop the massacres. None of the important leaders took part in the killing, but none tried to stop it. It is doubtful that the killings were the result of a conspiracy, as many argued, and it is equally doubtful that any individual or any group could have stopped them. The massacres were a force of nature that swept through Paris. When the fury had ceased and the recriminations began, there was hardly a man of importance who did not share in the guilt, whether from hesitancy to act, timidity, or a secret desire for the killings to continue, either because he judged them useful to the Revolution or because he desired the murder of an enemy.

Robespierre had neither instigated nor encouraged the massacres, but the task of defending them fell largely to him as the Jacobin ideologue and, most recently, the apologist for insurrectionary Paris. His insistence that August 10 and the September Massacres were of a piece, a single insurrection, would become the Jacobin line as well as that of the insurrectionary Commune. Robespierre and his followers would defend this view in the Convention. The most he was willing to concede was that a few innocents may have died, hacked to death in the streets, but on the whole the massacres were justifiable popular justice, necessitated by the failure of the government to punish those royalist traitors who had survived August 10 and were awaiting trial. About twelve hundred prisoners died, and Robespierre and the left insisted that a veil be drawn over the episode. Others were more vehement. Danton, Minister of Justice during the massacres, is reported to have said, "I don't give a damn about the prisoners." Later he made the case for the political usefulness of the massacres, a position Robespierre would never have taken: "I wanted to put a river of blood between the Paris crowd and the *émigrés*."[4] Robespierre would stick to his explanation of necessary violence.

The new role of voice of insurrection thrust upon Robespierre by August 10 would be additionally clarified in the opening days of the Convention. By choice and circumstance he was identified with Paris. His enemies, many of them dating from the war debates, now forced him to defend the unruly city, its unpredictable inhabitants, and its socially mongrel and politically aggressive Commune.[5] From the opening days of the Convention, the Girondins, whom Robespierre continued to refer to as Brissotins, launched an attack on Paris. The accusation against the city, comprehensive and flexible, formed the core of their political tactics throughout 1792 and into 1793. Every issue that came before the Convention was contaminated by this ongoing assault against Paris, and often the success of any piece of legislative business was made contingent upon Girondin proposals for punishing Paris, most often for the September Massacres or out of fear of a renewal of the butchery.

The task of defending Paris and its insurrectionary Commune fell, largely without competition, to Robespierre, the head of the Paris deputation and the first to have been elected. Through the summer and August 10 and the massacres and elections, Robespierre had assumed the role. He had become the acknowledged ideological leader of the left both inside and outside the assembly. Others might have prestige and a following among this or that group—Barbaroux with the heroes from Marseilles, Marat with the *sans-culottes,* Danton at the Cordeliers Club— but no other man had such broad support as Robespierre. All the apparent defeats in the Constituent and in the course of the war debates were forgotten. Robespierre's was the most authoritative voice in radical Paris, perhaps in all France. He would not hold any office nor sit on any committee for months to come, but his ascendancy in the Revolution was well under way and unquestioned. He assumed the role he had long prepared and would henceforth play: he was the voice and the embodiment of the Revolution as reinvigorated, redefined, regenerated, on August 10. That Revolution was increasingly seen as Parisian.

August 10, of course, was an attack on the monarchy. There remained the crucial question of the King, dethroned on August 10, imprisoned by the victorious Commune on August 13. The radicals were determined to try him, the Commune was impatient that he be punished, and even men who hoped to avoid the agony of a trial were uneasy about what to do with the fallen Louis. He and his fate hovered over the first months of the Convention and became quickly tied to the desperate and deadly fight between Jacobins and Girondins. The issues in the trial were many and complex. Much of the struggle for dominance of the Convention was fought over the King, caught between the warring factions. The Jacobins wanted to kill Louis; the Girondins wanted to spare him.

There is no clear social distinction between these factions, nor does a collective profile reveal significant differences of age, wealth, education, or place of origin. The antagonism between Jacobins and Girondins is a split in the ranks of the bourgeois republicans, which tiny group had once been united as Jacobins, before the war debates dispersed the original Society. The main issue on which they differed, and this leaves aside the poisonous personal animosities that intensified all struggle, was the social question. The Girondins did not see themselves as representing Paris. Not only had the capital rejected them in the recent Convention elections, but Paris was the home of the unruly *sans-culottes*, with whom the Girondins desired no alliance. Indeed, they had several times contemplated deserting the capital for the calm of a provincial town in which the Convention might deliberate without fear of intimidation. The lovely, sleepy town of Tours had been proposed as a refuge.[6] This fear of Paris led, during the trial, to a series of anti-Paris policies that, they were convinced, had to be realized before any of the pressing business before the Convention could be done. The Girondins blamed the September Massacres on Robespierre, insisting they were part of an enormous conspiracy to murder his political rivals under cover of these grim distractions.[7] The Girondins wanted the *septembriseurs* punished—and their list of the guilty corresponded with a list of their political foes—as well as an armed guard, drawn from the provinces, to protect the Convention from Paris. They demanded that the preponderance of the capital be checked.

Throughout the debates the Girondins vilified Paris in the persons of Marat and Robespierre, whom they consistently linked as representing all that was most frightful and irresponsible. Robespierre, for his part, looked upon his Girondin opponents across the aisle (for the antagonists sat daily facing one another in the stuffy and uncomfortable precincts of the Manège) as the men who had gotten France prematurely into war, had abandoned the Jacobin Society, and pursued their own careers. Now, he argued, they who had opposed August 10 (which was not entirely true) sought to exploit the victory for themselves.

Persistently attacked and slandered, Robespierre counterattacked. First on September 25 (the Convention began sitting on September 21) and thenceforth with energy and frequency, he went to the tribune. Self and cause became one: "Occupying this tribune to respond to the accusation against me, it is not my own cause I want to defend, but the public cause" (IX, 16). Increasingly it was Paris he defended, elaborating a vocabulary of metaphors for the city. Paris was "the rendezvous of all Frenchmen" (IX, 58), "the center of the Revolution" (IX, 481). It was this "citadel of liberty" (IX, 488) or, his most reiterated image, "the eternal boulevard of liberty" (IX, 354, 590, 601). Paris "has given the tone to the entire Republic" (IX, 601). The city had been politically precocious, toppling the Bastille, detesting Lafayette "when he was adored everywhere else" (IX, 51). It was against Paris that the counterrevolution aimed its blows: "The army of the Vendée, the army of Brittany, and the army of Koblenz are directed against Paris. . . . People of Paris, . . . you are the most estimable part of humanity" (IX, 488). If there had been any earlier hesitations or reservations, Robespierre the provincial lawyer was completely a Parisian by the first month of the Convention. He who had so carefully cultivated the provinces at the start of his career now left his opponents to find support outside the capital.

He shared the slanders flung at Paris, but became increasingly intolerant of insult. "The progress of calumny, since the beginning of the Revolution," he insisted, had caused "all the disastrous events that have disturbed or bloodied its course." It was calumny alone "which opposes itself to the reign of liberty and public peace" (IX, 45). Only a literary intellectual fighting a revolution obsessed with words and ideology could be so hyperbolic. "Arms against the tyrants, books against the intriguers; force to repel the foreign brigands, light to make visible the domestic sneak-thieves [*filous*]; there is the secret for triumph over all your enemies" (IX, 60). But the slanders were unabating. The day after this denunciation, Robespierre endured the most sustained attack to date. All the criticisms that had been made against him from the time of the Estates-General were gathered together in a clever speech long prepared by Louvet, the verbally agile author of frivolous romances and a spokesman for the Girondin faction. This speech, the *Robespierride*, as it came to be called, was answered by its victim on November 5. Neither the most decisive nor equal oratorical struggle of the Revolution,[8] the Louvet-Robespierre confrontation was notable and significant. Both men spoke, tacitly at least, as representatives of a faction, and Paris itself turned out to support Robespierre, who had asked for a delay in order to prepare his defense. His supporters spent the night of November 4 at the doors of the Manège, hoping to get a seat to hear their champion. The *Chronique de Paris* estimated that seven to eight hundred, mostly women (for whom he had a peculiar appeal), jammed the gallery to hear Robespierre. The *Thermomètre du Jour*, another newspaper, added the colorful detail that a couple of men "held a piece of tripe in their hands, waving it about and saying the morsel had been dipped in acid and was for the enemies of Robespierre and Marat to eat."

November 5 is a convenient date to indicate the beginning of Robespierre's extraordinary, if gradual, ascendancy over the Convention. It is from this date that the *Moniteur*, the semi-official newspaper whose coverage of assembly debates is the most careful and comprehensive of all contemporary newspapers, began to include a regular column devoted to the Jacobin Club. Henceforth Robespierre's popularity and predominance at the Jacobins would be regularly chronicled by an independent and influential source. The successful insurrection had restored his access to the public through newspapers, which he had lost during the war debates, and at the same time had enhanced his reputation.

Louvet raked together all the rancors, past and present, and forged them into an oration that imitated and echoed Cicero's *Cataline*, the most famous accusation of Roman oratory. The conceit was much appreciated. Louvet attacked Robespierre's vanity as intolerable in itself and one of the weapons used in the destruction of the Jacobins, where he encouraged the growth and ritualization of a personality cult, which destroyed equality and undermined rational debate, thus driving Louvet, and his friends, from the Club. Robespierre, says Louvet, set himself above the Revolution by encouraging adulation, and this Louvet uses as evidence that Robespierre aspired to the dictatorship.

At the same time of the schism at the Jacobins, Louvet argues, Robespierre exercised a "despotism of opinion" that destroyed all freedom of expression at the Club. Robespierre's preposterous ideas went unchallenged. Louvet concluded by blaming Robespierre for the September Massacres, connecting him to Marat, and by calling for Marat's impeachment and an inquiry into Robespierre's behavior. Connecting

Marat and Robespierre was a favorite opposition tactic. It was well known, and Marat regularly reminded, that the Friend of the People (which name he also gave his newspaper) was above faction, independent of all such obligations. But Marat was the most detested and feared member of the Convention, the very incarnation of the bloodthirsty men of the September Massacres. To link Robespierre to the hated Marat was to insinuate that he, too, had blood on his hands, that the victory of the radicals would be accomplished by a purge of all who stood in their way. Marat was everyone's bogey. Robespierre, having no intimate or political relations with him, was one of the very few deputies willing, nevertheless, to defend Marat. It was a decent and politically unrewarding undertaking when so many would gladly have sacrificed Marat to the impeachment demanded by the Girondins.

"To begin with," Robespierre responded to Louvet's accusation, "I don't know what this despotism of opinion is, above all in a society of free men . . . , unless it is the natural dominance of principles." Such an "empire is not personal," not the possession of him who enunciates the principle "It belongs to universal reason and to all men who heed its voice." It belongs "to all citizens who will defend the cause of liberty" (IX, 83–84). With his gift for paradox, he argues that there is a despotism of truth in the Revolution. Truth drives out falsehood, and he who speaks truth has influence. Truth, he insists, is not something an individual possesses but a quality he expresses. Truth is, so to speak, found in the realm of nature, to be discovered by all who seek.

He assumes a similar stance in defending August 10 and even the September Massacres. The insurrectionary victory and its aftermath are not due to any master plan. Both belong to the people, to liberty, to principles, to the Revolution.[9] He presents himself as nothing more than the voice that expresses eternal truths. He is no more than a vehicle of historical forces. It is not his person that is worthy, it is his message. His vanity is not simple self-adulation. Rather, he is vain because he has discovered the truth and because that truth speaks through his lips. This posture is not self-effacing, but it is one that disregards personal advantage, a disregard Robespierre prided himself on. The importance of his person should not be taken for vanity of the common sort.

While skillfully parrying Louvet's thrusts, Robespierre develops a theme he will extensively elaborate. Neither the Revolution nor its votaries are to be judged by standards created by and tailored to nonrevolutionary society. The moral world created by the Revolution is radically different from that it replaced. There may have been some excesses on August 10, he concedes to Louvet, but in battle public safety—this is one of his earliest uses of this famous formula—takes precedence over "the criminal code." Louvet accused the Commune of acting illegally. So, too, did those who stormed the Bastille, Robespierre counters. Revolutionary acts are "as illegal as liberty itself." Revolutions, like wars, are violent. Such upheavals are both necessary and bloody. "Citizens," he implores, "do you want a Revolution without a revolution?" (IX, 89).

It was generally conceded that Robespierre had triumphed over Louvet. There would be other confrontations during the months of the King's trial, but for the moment Robespierre's defense of himself and his followers was a success and stilled the voice of calumny. His victory served to deflect the attacks onto others: Marat and the Duc d'Orléans, who had legally changed his name to Philippe Egalité, proved more vulnerable. Character assassination and attacks on Paris were never absent from the trial.

When Louis had fled the Tuileries on the morning of August 10, before the assault began, and sought refuge with the Legislative, he had technically surrendered to the nation's elected representatives. At the time, there had been some subtle verbal refinements about his precise status. But these deep quibbles were settled, along with many others, on August 13. The victorious Commune, armed and irresistible, took the king from the Manège, over the protests of the Legislative, and carried him across Paris to be imprisoned in the old home of the Templar knights, the tower of the Temple. Henceforth his destiny lay in the hands of the Commune, whose council regularly debated every issue concerning their prisoner, from his diet to his requests for books and razors. The Commune was determined that Louis would pay for his crimes. As much as any man, Robespierre carried the desires of the Commune into the trial. He also found time to consider other matters.

Economic questions had never much interested Robespierre. He assumed France's ills would be cured through political decisions based on correct principles. But he was troubled, as were many, by the contradiction between private property concentrated in a few hands and the republic's commitment to equality. In early December he tried to square this vicious circle. The constitution of 1791 had enshrined the axiom that property is a natural right, prior to society and immune to governmental interference save in instances of national emergency. Robespierre rejected this axiom and groped his way toward a social rather than natural definition of property. "The first social law," he tells his colleagues, "is therefore that which guarantees to all members of society the means of existence; all other laws are subordinated to this one" (IX,

112). He had neither the time nor the inclination (nor perhaps the skill) to work out the inferences of this conviction. He would not again return to the tensions between property and equality until May–June 1793, when yet another Parisian uprising riveted his attention on the needs of the *sans-culottes*. In December, in the midst of the trial, it was too easy to assume that all problems were attached to the monarchy: that once Louis had paid for his crimes, the republic would be firmly established and the difficulties that plagued monarchical France would wonderfully vanish. Robespierre's faith was not greater than that of many others.

It is sovereignty much more than economics that consumed Robespierre's ideological energies during the trial as throughout his career. Part of his influence over colleagues was this single-mindedness. In the French Revolution, who governed and by what authority were the most enduring issue and arguably the most significant. Questions of authority had obsessed political thinkers in the eighteenth century and continued to obsess the Revolution. It is doubtless a truism that a leader cannot be great unless he confronts the central issues and anxieties of his age. Robespierre's obsession with sovereignty was that of his time. The King's trial, naturally, thrust the question of sovereignty forward. The people's sovereignty, first preached in the most influential pamphlet of the Revolution, Sieyès's *What Is the Third Estate?*, had remained unrealized under the constitutional monarchy destroyed on August 10. It was time to fulfill those long-delayed prophecies. But first the King had to be killed, and Robespierre did as much as any man to send Louis to the guillotine.

The debates on the King's trial officially opened on November 13. Saint-Just, a young provincial (he had just turned twenty-six), the obscure author of an obscene poem, who had ostentatiously abandoned his frivolous and lascivious preoccupations to give himself to the Revolution, retaining, however, a flamboyant sense of self coupled to a severe sense of duty and sacrifice, announced himself to the nation in a brilliant maiden speech. He presented what would remain the most radical position, one that Robespierre would elaborate, defend, and champion. Louis, said Saint-Just, had been judged on August 10 when the people in arms conquered the Tuileries. There could be no appeal from this judgment. There was no higher authority. Louis must not now be tried, for that presupposed the possibility of reversing the insurrectionary judgment, but must be summarily executed. He saw nothing but an enemy alien, the king of the privileged few rather than the nation. He was a foreign element in the body politic. The nation had no obligations toward him such as it had toward citizens, for Louis was not a citizen. The Convention's task was simple: it had only to carry out the death sentence passed by the insurrectionists on August 10. The kingship itself was, for Saint-Just, a capital crime. "One cannot reign innocently," he declared.

The speech caused a sensation. It was brilliant, highly original, and studded with epigrams not easily forgotten. The radical regicide view had been given extraordinary presentation. Robespierre would add nothing theoretically. He devoted his energies to endowing these abstract and rigorous propositions of Saint-Just with flesh and blood. Robespierre furnished the strategic and moral considerations largely neglected by Saint-Just. The King could not remain indefinitely in jail. So long as he lived, he served as the focus and pretext for counterrevolution. Nor could Louis be sent into exile, where he would only furnish the belligerents of Europe and their émigré guests with justification for continuing the war. And the definitive solution of the problem of the King was the founding act of the republic. To give Louis a trial would presume the possibility not only that August 10 had been in vain and illegal, but that Louis was innocent, a preposterous thesis. To contemplate any penalty less than death was to accept the despised royalist axiom that the King could do no wrong, the King was immune from the law.

The personality of the King was merely a detail for Robespierre, as it was for virtually all the advanced radicals who now provocatively sat high up on the benches of the left and proudly called themselves Montagnards. Robespierre had no personal animosity toward Louis. He was far less vituperative than he had earlier been to Lafayette. At issue was the principle of popular sovereignty, adequately represented in the elected deputies of the Convention.[10] Besides, Louis was personally attractive, and his two appearances before his judges proved his best defense. The Mountain prefered to put monarchy on trial. But Louis had many supporters, and Robespierre many enemies, some of whom gleefully reminded him that in the Constituent he had argued against the death penalty. He sought to transcend the contradiction by insisting, as he would throughout the republic, on the distinction between war and peace. "You are confusing the situation of a people in revolution with that of a people whose government is established," he lectured. "You are confounding a nation that punishes a public functionary, while retaining the form of government, and one that destroys the government itself" (IX, 122).

Calling for the King's head was traumatic, for Robespierre as well as for the hundreds of educated and civilized men who sat in the Convention. The extended debate the Convention was willing and even eager to hear during the trial is some indication of the deeply felt need to exhaust all possibilities, sample all options. For Robespierre, who carried the regicide case at a couple of crucial points, the conflict was seen in almost cosmic dimensions. He envisioned and articulated a great abstract struggle between tyranny and humanity, and although he spoke of the motions of his own heart, he transmuted introspection into general political maxims: "The hatred of tyrants and the love of humanity have a common source in the heart of a just man who loves his country." All natural feelings of tenderness and human kindness must be "immolated . . . for the health of a great people and oppressed humanity" (IX, 184). The King must die for the Revolution to live.

The King's trial offers a unique view of Robespierre. For the first time in a national forum he is not an isolated figure, but rather the self-conscious and acknowledged leader of a significant (and self-confident) group. He holds no office, no special position, in government or in the Convention. Indeed, it will be several months before he will be able to command enough votes even to be elected president of the Convention for a fortnight, a distinction enjoyed by a number of his rivals and several nonentities. He has only the weapons he has always had, his oratory, his reputation, the intimate enthusiasm of the Jacobins and now another newspaper, *Lettres à Ses Commettans*, whose first issue appeared in October. These are sufficient following the insurrection of August 10, as they had not been previously. Robespierre does not yet represent the majority. It is arguable whether he ever does represent the majority in the Revolution. But he certainly represents the most vital and aggressive wedge of the Revolution.

During the months of the trial, he emerges as an efficient and effective faction chief and a formidable parliamentary scrapper, roles denied to him until the Convention. Hitherto he had been essentially a prophet, an ideologue. Now his unexpected gifts as strategist and parliamentary politician, seen first at Arras when he stood as a deputy to the Third Estate, and more recently in the Paris elections to the Convention, are given scope. He continues to be an ideologue, to present reasons for what is to be done, to provide the moral dimension essential to revolutionary work; but his ideological work is increasingly practical. Robespierre puts the Montagnard case for regicide constantly before the *conventionnels* not as an abstract line that ought to be followed, but as a series of immediate political choices that have to be made and that imply, nay entail, further choices. The metaphysics of revolution he leaves, and apparently without regret, to the genius of Saint-Just. As in the confrontation with Louvet, and slightly later in another (and more intellectually satisfying) confrontation, with the subtle and stirring Pierre Vergniaud, thought the best speaker of the Girondins, Robespierre is concerned more with proposing tactics, putting precise choices before his auditors, than with envisioning the future benefits of a theory.

The considerable influence he exercises throughout the trial he exercises by persuasion. The Jacobins, not to mention their left wing called the Mountain, are a minority in the Convention. They alone are incapable of carrying any legislation or policy.[11] Men followed Robespierre's line in the trial because they were convinced it was correct or useful or at least marginally preferable to any other. The later accusation that he influenced because he was in a position to punish is simply not true during the trial, if it ever was true. The unlikely coalition of personalities and positions necessary to send Louis to the scaffold was forged as much by Robespierre as by anyone else. And his shrewd and immediate grasp of how politics works is clearly seen in the trial. The success he enjoyed, his first such outside the Jacobins, gave confidence. It turned out that regicide sentiment was widespread in the Convention, and in the least expected places, yet this fact was unpredictable. Robespierre sensed this. He had the gift of seeing political implications before they were apparent to most. He also had patience, tenacity, consistency, and practicality, those profane virtues in a politician that had given him the Jacobin Club. Political seduction, like its sexual version, is an art as well as a craft. Even those who are able and willing to yield expect and enjoy the excitement of the process. Robespierre had the lover's interest and intuition, while lacking his impatience. His attentions were assiduous, intense, and sensitive. When the four separate and difficult votes on the King's fate were taken, between January 16 and January 20, 1793, at which time the deputies had to stand up and be counted, the regicides realized they had won a great victory. It was a victory for Robespierre, for the Mountain, for Paris, as well as a profound and irreversible commitment to further revolution.

The King's trial and execution did not instantly convey power into the hands of Robespierre and the Mountain. Nor did it even radically change the balance of forces in the Convention. The presidents of the Assembly, until May 30, were predominantly moderates or, at best, those with left leanings. The regicide fire-eaters were not chosen.[12] But the battle lines were drawn ever more clearly. The Convention now split, immediately after the voting, into two antagonistic groups: the regicides and the so-called *appelants*, those who had voted to spare the King. This split was another of the inevitabilities of August 10. The divisions among the revolutionaries were becoming sharper.

The stunning successes of the King's trial may have convinced Robespierre not only that when correct principles were given expression, his ideas could be translated at once into revolutionary action, but also that he now had a following within the government. It is true that the regicide coalition was fragile, made up of radicals and moderates and those deputies who were willing to adhere momentarily to the left but who had no deep convictions and distrusted Robespierre anyhow. But he had overcome in open confrontation the best speakers of the Girondins and was the darling of Paris. He had successfully translated the shouts and corner harangues of the streets into a kind of parliamentary program by cloaking these imperious and uncouth ejaculations in an eloquence fit for the National Assembly. In a sense his patterns in the Constituent had been reversed. In place of addressing the Parisians over the heads of his colleagues, he was now addressing to his colleagues the demands of the Parisians. He had thus converted "the logical impasses of direct democracy" into representative, parliamentary currency.[13] The enormous question of sovereignty remained only partly answered with the elimination of the King in the name of the people, especially the people who had made the insurrection of August 10, but Robespierre's influence pointed toward a representative rather than a direct democracy. He had, so to speak, performed some legerdemain, transmuting the anger and impatience of the streets, backed by irresistible armed might, into the relatively smooth and familiar contours of parliamentary debates and a criminal trial, albeit an unprecedented, political trial.

Still, personal power did not come with the King's death, nor did Robespierre show any significant desire for such power. And all the enormous problems of the Revolution remained—the bitterness of faction, a still virile counterrevolution, a difficult war, and short rations. Robespierre's ascendance, made possible by August 10, remained incomplete on January 21, when the King's head fell. The Convention, like the Legislative before it, was hopelessly divided. The assumption that crisis draws men together, making workable alliances that would be impossible in peaceful times, does not describe the French Revolution. Each crisis, each new turning, only made the divisions deeper, more bitter, and beyond reconciliation. The unprecedented experience of regicide, no less than the earlier declaration of war, further divided the revolutionaries. The Convention, the only instrument of revolutionary government, survived the King's execution, but did not emerge strengthened from the ordeal. The Convention could not endure another such shock.

Robespierre now drew back from further aggression in the Convention. There could be no *rapprochement* with the Girondins and the antiregicides who had joined them, but similarly there must be no additional tests of the fragile and emotionally drained Convention, whether self-inflicted or emanating from the Paris streets. Robespierre now returned to the prudence he had so long clung to in the summer of 1792. There must not be another insurrection: "What we must do at this moment," he told the Jacobins, "is to oppose any kind of insurrection, because insurrection, which is the most holy of duties, would be dangerous against the Convention" (IX, 150). Such changes of direction or speed are not capricious. The Legislative had betrayed the people, in Robespierre's view. The people had risen. The Convention had yet to betray.

The new element in revolutionary politics was urban insurrection. It appeared to many that somehow all the problems confronting the Revolution could be solved by yet another successful upheaval in the Paris streets. But such an upheaval would now be directed, for the first time, against an organ of the Revolution, the Convention. The revolutionaries, at least those like Robespierre, now had a vested interest in preventing insurrection. The theorist of insurrection, whose career can be said to rest ultimately on insurrection although he never himself took to the streets, had now to keep the new and terrible weapon available for use while simultaneously preventing its use. This balancing act depended on the success or failure of the Mountain and Robespierre in making the kinds of laws that would realize the meaning of August 10. The republic remained to be created. The Revolution and the revolutionary had entered a new phase. Could social democracy be created in parliament rather than in the streets?

CHAPTER 8

Purging the Convention

PLATE X
(Phot. Bibl. nat. Paris)

THE RELIEF FELT at the end of the King's trial was in proportion to the strain the deputies had been under. For the Revolution there was no relief. The animosities and struggles that had marred the Convention from its first meetings remained. Although the Montagnard wing of the Jacobins had all been regicides, not all regicides were Montagnards. The moderate and uncommitted deputies who had voted with the Mountain to kill Louis lapsed again into an increasingly difficult neutrality. On every issue they had again to be wooed. Outside the Convention the situation was even more disturbing. The distrust felt by many deputies toward Paris continued and was reenforced by the city's nervous unease. Food remained in short supply, as did fuel. There were long and angry lines in front of bakery shops and groceries, and the usual level of consumer grumbling was intensified by dearth and the weather. The end of the monarchy did not fill any stomachs. Soon there was rioting in the markets. On February 25 the price of sugar instigated the first of these convulsions. The rioting continued, with growing intensity, until March 9–10. The discontent was uncoordinated, but still ugly and dangerous; and it seemed to be turning against the government, against the Convention. Only narrowly, and for reasons not altogether clear, did the rioting fail to materialize into insurrection.

At the same time the ongoing war, whose imperious demands on the economy could not be met without vast consumer sacrifice, was again intensifying, after the relative quiet of the winter months that halted the campaign with the French armies flushed with their great victory at Valmy in September 1792. European wars were fought between the end of the spring rains and the first frosts. With the approach of the campaign season, the beleaguered government called for larger troop levies, and in the west of France, in the old province of the Vendée, the recruitments led to riots and soon to a murderous civil war, long prepared by deep and widening social and economic gaps, regional dislocations and antagonisms, all sharpened by the Revolution. The rebellion broke out on March 16, 1793, and continued to plague the Revolution on into the Napoleonic period. The rebels fought in the name of the throne, and altar. Sympathizers of counterrevolution, so recently humbled and cowed by August 10, now emerged and were emboldened by the great western uprising.

The choices available to the Convention were few. Robespierre was convinced, and argued, that the Convention, whatever its faults, must be maintained. The Revolution could not sustain a foreign war and a civil war and simultaneously defend itself against Paris or ambitious factions. Any disturbance would "shatter the political machine" wherein "resides the first power that can accelerate the progress of public spirit, the pure citizens who are inspired only by the love of their country, which means everything that is virtuous in men and renders them worthy of regenerating the universe" (IX, 296). The machine in question was the Convention and the disturbance he imagined was insurrection. His fears were exaggerated, as it turned out, but not unreasonable. The insurrectionary threat of February–March 1793 sputtered, through no efforts of Robespierre, into some isolated food riots, which were insufficient to topple either municipal or national government. A relieved Robespierre scornfully detached himself from these agitations: "I am the partisan of all necessary and well-conceived insurrections against despotism and intrigue," not rioting "caused by the high price of sugar" (IX, 322).

This dismissal of food rioting as unworthy of revolutionaries did nothing to dispel the very real problems created when Paris was hungry. Nor did it deter those who emerged in the streets to agitate around the issue of dearth and the government's responsibilities. Here was Robespierre's first taste of serious competition for the favor of the Parisians since August 10. And he was instinctively hostile. Unlike earlier struggles, in the Constituent and at the Jacobins, he was not competing with men much like himself for the right to represent the people of Paris. His competitors were now men and women of the people. Robespierre's personal inclinations were toward restraint and discipline, qualities that he projected upon the people. On the Mountain there was the assumption that sacrifice and frugality were virtuous and that this distinguished patriots from counterrevolutionaries, whatever their class. Robespierre preached this axiom, as did others. "Let us make temporary economies," said Bertrand Barère, a man on the left and a future member of the Committee of Public Safety with Robespierre, but a moderate of great charm and ideological agility, "voluntarily impose upon ourselves a civic frugality in order to preserve our rights. Let us delay those pleasures of the table permitted to republicans, forgo the delicacies that belong only to sybarites. If the citizens spend only what is necessary for a few more months, a free France will bless its defenders and you will have founded, at the same time as republican mores, those of temperance and equality."[1] The middle-class Montagnards were vexed that the spirit of restraint and sacrifice had not everywhere prevailed in March.

The riots not only revealed a significant gap between Robespierre's view of how the people ought to behave and where they ought to look for leadership, but also undercut ideas he had formulatd in the summer of 1792 as he moved toward a theory of insurrection. "There is in the heart of the people a just sentiment of indignation" (IX, 274), he now reiterated, which is set in motion when the government has failed them. It is "natural for the people to seek means of relieving their misery," for they have "the right to provide for their needs" (IX, 272). But "when the people rise up, should they not have a goal worthy of them? Should they be concerned about a bag of groceries?" (IX, 275).[2] The people should rise up "only to save liberty" (V, 285).

He blames the March food rioting not on the people but on their seducers. He insists, without evidence, that "no merchant" in the radical neighborhood of Saint-Marcel "has been disturbed" by the rioters. The conquerors of the Tuileries are incapable of taking up arms for "a bag of groceries." The March riots are the work of "women who have come from distant neighborhoods" to mislead "the good and vigorous citizens" (V, 326–27). The rioters are not the true people of Paris, who remained "calm despite their misery" (V, 285). For the moment he has managed to preserve the integrity of his ideas about the people by resorting to a theory of conspiracy, by removing from the people those few he considers unworthy. It was an ominous distinction that he was incapable of sustaining. An ideology whose contradictions are cut away and discarded without being reconciled is in danger of collapsing from its own compromises and accommodations. Besides, those who spoke for the rioters had no intention of letting Robespierre monopolize the role of articulating the needs and demands of the Paris poor.

Those who now gave passionate voice to the victims of dearth were scornfully and incorrectly dubbed the *enragés* (the mad ones) by their enemies. It was, of course, only a matter of time before the *sans-culottes* would produce their own spokesmen, and in Robespierre's dealing with these new competitors we see him at his worst, we see him most limited by the social and economic realities of his life, his circumstances, and even his character. The *enragés* insisted that their constituents were hungry because of the policies of the Convention and that sermons on patience and discipline were worthless to starving patriots. The price of sugar might seem an unworthy concern to men who had sugar on their tables; to the poor all speculation and pettifoggery—and they considered dearth (as did the government) the creation of selfish manipulators— deserved punishment. These were potent arguments. The neighborhood agitators thought their cause legitimate and righteous, but their manner was obnoxious to the authorities of the city, the deputies, and Robespierre. Not only did he consider the *enragés* irresponsible and dangerous because they stirred up social discontent and turned grumbling into politics, a kind of popular politics that he held contemptible, but he also despised them personally as iconoclasts and troublemakers who dared challenge him as the embodiment and articulator of the popular will. If the *enragés* were successful (or if they were not stopped), the Revolution might well be returned to the streets, from whose tumultuous precincts it had been rescued after August 10.

With the *enragés*, as with so many of Robespierre's enemies, the personal and ideological are inextricably mixed. Because he mingled self with analysis, he invited personal rejection, criticism, and calumny. On this level his personality matters a great deal and may be said to have had an impact on history. The *enragés*, with their irreverent and embarrassing diatribes against a government whose members were well fed while the poor went on short rations, were disrespectful not only to Robespierre, who wanted and needed the polite rituals of social intercourse, but to all those who represented the people and were, in Robespierre's mind, willing to die for them. In addition to his distaste for the bad manners and low language, the lack of tact and the brazen glee some *enragés* took in giving offense to those who considered themselves socially superior, Robespierre considered them socially marginal. He expected such men and women to show some respect for a representative of the people who had proved himself in nearly four years of revolution. He was not accustomed to dealing with those who did not share his social expectations and assumptions. Here were self-proclaimed representatives of the people, not elected deputies as he was, who not only disputed his views of self and *subsistances* but did so bluntly, indecorously, crudely. The intensity with which he hounded the ex-priest Jacques Roux, one of the most articulate *enragés*, for example, reveals Robespierre's most unpleasant characteristic: his extraordinary priggishness. When priggishness is accompanied by power, it can be more than unpleasant.

What made *enragé* agitation and criticism most astringent for Robespierre, who had after all long been the target of calumny, was the accusation, both implicit and explicit, that he was as indifferent or heartless to the plight of the poor as any former nobleman. His integrity and his oft-proclaimed vision of self-sacrifice were under attack. His critics had found the chink in his armor. Robespierre was neither blind nor indifferent to economic matters, although his utterances are relatively free of these concerns. The truth is that he thought economics and economic questions essentially political. Paris would be provisioned when good laws were put in place and enforced; dearth would vanish when the republic was firmly established. His early optimism that the

King's death would resolve many problems, among them *subsistances*, quickly faded. But he continued to look for economic solutions through political action. Even on the left this view was orthodox. Shortly after the March riots there was much angry talk about purging the *appelants*, the antiregicides, from the Convention. The response to food shortages was political action. This talk Robespierre did not brush aside as he had the price of sugar. Here was social discontent directed, as it ought to be, into political channels. These were the terms in which he instinctively thought. Whether or not he began to consider purging the Convention of his enemies as a result of this agitation cannot be known. He continued to preach patience to Paris, as well as prudence and the need for personal sacrifice. Still, the suggested recourse to insurrection did not pass unnoticed: it was far too tempting a weapon to remain indefinitely sheathed. Revolutionary leaders had either to learn its use or become its victims. And since there was no longer a court against which insurrection could be directed, if the weapon was again used, it would be used by one group of revolutionaries against another.

It had long been thought an axiom that members of the various assemblies of the Revolution enjoyed some immunity while fulfilling their offices. In the course of the King's trial this principle had been tested. The Girondins had several times demanded expulsions and impeachments. Robespierre himself had been singled out. But the most serious attacks had been directed against the most vulnerable figures on the left, the obnoxious Marat and the politically suspect Philippe Egalité. Both had been defended by a reluctant Mountain led by Robespierre. He had insisted that impeachment or expulsion was an attack on the sovereignty of the people since it deprived constituents of representation. He disliked both Marat and the revolutionary prince of the blood but came to their defense on principle. The defense was successful, and for the moment the principle of parliamentary immunity remained intact. But during the winter crisis of 1793, in the midst of a deteriorating war situation, rebel successes in the Vendée, and food shortages in Paris, it was again attractive to contemplate the possibility of impeaching those deputies who were uncooperative. Ironically, it was Marat who was impeached and exonerated (April 13), but the Girondins, who had long been eager to purge their opponents and yet who had bungled the Marat impeachment, would obviously be the victims if the Mountain abandoned its resistance to impeachment.

Despite his continued opposition to impeachment and insurrection, Robespierre was less scrupulous and high-minded on this subject than he had been during Louis's trial. He now made no principled objection to any and all interference with the elected representatives of the nation. Rather, he opposed expulsions from the Convention on purely practical grounds. "Those you want to drive out," he told the Jacobins, "are known intriguers, and they would be replaced by intriguers still hidden by the mask of patriotism" (IX, 279). Among the *appelants*, he insisted, "only a few have been paid to vote in favor of the tyrant; the others are only a bunch of ignoramuses who have been misled by the eloquence" of the faction chiefs on the right. Only these chiefs deserve impeachment, and "it is useless and even dangerous" to confuse everyone on the right with "what the chiefs want" (IX, 370). Such utilitarianism put him with the more moderate Montagnards, but represented a retreat from his earlier view. A first step toward purge had been taken. The deputies were not sacrosanct; insurrection could serve as a mechanism for recall.

Immune to many illusions, Robespierre, like so many intellectuals, was at risk when it came to his own ideas. Once having thought through the place of insurrection in the Revolution, he remained uncritically loyal to his conclusions. Having discovered the general law amid the particular details, he was more prone to fit perhaps significantly different details into the general pattern than to question the aptness of the pattern. He had only to be convinced that the same or very similar circumstances had recurred in order to be persuaded that insurrection was the correct and necessary response. The continuity of crisis and personnel from the summer of 1792 to the spring of 1793 helped him to reach this conclusion. The King and the Court were gone, but the generals remained and so did many of the courtiers, as well as those segments of the population who had supported the Court or been tinged with some strain of royalism. The rich, for example, were protected (and represented) by those who "also protect Coburg and the rebels of the Vendée" (IX, 485). "There are only two parties in France: the people and its enemies." Hence there could be neither compromise nor accommodation: "It is necessary to exterminate all those vile and scoundrely beings who conspire eternally against the rights of man and against the happiness of all the people" (IX, 487–88). These enemies of the people are known at sight: "He who has *culottes dorées* is the enemy of all the *sans-culottes.*" These menacing antitheses, playing on class antagonisms, even hinting at social war, would become increasingly frequent in Robespierre's utterances. He himself continued to wear *culottes* but obviously not the hated *culottes dorées* (literally, golden knee-breeches) of the enemy. "He who is not for the people," he continues his analysis by antithesis, "is against the people," for "there are only two parties, that of corrupt men and that of virtuous men"; "the friends of liberty and equality, the defenders of the oppressed, the friends of poverty, and the supporters of undeserved opulence and tyrannical aristocracy. There you have the division that exists in France" (IX, 488).

The economic crisis and the food riots of March had sharpened Robespierre's awareness of social questions, and he had given the divisions of class and interest in France a formulation not radically different from that provided by the *enragés*. But he had included, by implication, only those parliamentary members opposed to the Mountain, who were presented as the friends of the *culottes dorées*. At the same time, he saw another Lafayette on the scene, this time in the person of General Dumouriez. With his pathological distrust of generals, he had never much liked Dumouriez, who was closely tied to the Girondins despite a brief interlude of wooing Robespierre and the Jacobins. All the fears he had announced in exposing and denouncing Lafayette he now transferred to Dumouriez and "the administrative corps of the government." For the moment he diagnosed the infection as local—he was speaking at the end of March 1793—confined to the *"feuillants,* or moderates." The remedy was "in the people and the National Convention" (IX, 348). But if treatment was not begun at once, the gangrene might spread. On April 1, Robespierre attacked Dumouriez at the Jacobins and on April 3 launched a series of attacks on his old enemies, Brissot in particular, who had protected and elevated the general. Some of the characters, some of the circumstances, and virtually all the nuances were changed, but Robespierre spoke as if he were back in the time of the war debates and his diatribes against Lafayette.

Then the war had not yet been declared; now the verbal battle was fought against a depressing backdrop of military defeat. Dumouriez's career and ambitions hinged, as did all the military careers of the Revolution, on continued success. But the Netherlands had had to be evacuated, and Dumouriez, unable to organize a substantial *coup d'état*, fled with part of his general staff, on April 5. He would eventually end his brilliant, restless, deeply flawed career advising the British on fortifications to resist Napoleon's planned invasion.

On April 15, partly in response to the news of Dumouriez's treason as well as the perpetually gloomy war news and the equally perpetual unrest of Paris, the sections called for a purge of the Convention. This, too, is reminiscent of 1792, when the sections (forty-seven of the forty-eight) signed and sent an ultimatum demanding the King's dethronement. Throughout the intensifying crisis Robespierre had played, as he would continue to play, a deliberately ambiguous game. His public stance was to insinuate the need for insurrection while at the same time insisting that he did not desire insurrection: "When I suggest firm and vigorous measures, I am not suggesting those convulsions that do to death the body politic." But the Convention, lulled into passivity and even supineness by "the enchantress voices of several intriguers," must bestir itself. If the representatives of the people could not save themselves, he ominously pointed out, the people "must save the Convention and then the Convention will save the people" (IX, 348).

With his passion for continuity and general historical laws, Robespierre may have insisted on the parallels with 1792 too vigorously, yet he was not altogether mistaken. The months following the King's trial were a time of flux, and he sought, like others, to make sense out of what was happening. He did not devote all his energies to discovering these parallels and advocating insurrection. He thought and spoke about much else. In March, for example, he demanded strict laws against the *émigrés* as "a political and revolutionary measure," a necessary hedge against any sentiments of commiseration that might plead "with us in favor of this or that individual" (IX, 290). He had not earlier shown much concern with the plight of the *émigrés*, nor would he ever again. He had little inclination to hound them throughout Europe, as some of his more rabid followers wished to do, but he thought them traitors beyond rehabilitation and mercy. The Girondins he several times chided for their misplaced charity. At the same time he reiterated an earlier call for Marie Antoinette's head (IX, 337–38), which had not been mentioned for months. These concerns bespeak an attack on sentiment, a hardening line toward the counterrevolution in whatever form it appeared. The broad, generous sentiments of the first year of revolution were disappearing. The world was increasingly harsh and hostile. Robespierre's utterances, the growing rigidity of his formulations, the more frequent use of war metaphors, signaled the change and reflected it. In April he spoke against unlimited freedom of the press, arguing that "revolutions are made to establish the rights of man" and that one must use "all necessary means to ensure success" (IX, 452).[3] Measures "contrary to an unlimited liberty, which should reign in a state of calm, are nevertheless necessary at this time" (IX, 453). Words were revolutionary weapons. He saw no reason why such weapons should not be confiscated. Nor were the *conventionnels* exempt from this hard line: "This gangrened portion," he said, using his favorite image of the moment, specifically indicating the Girondins, "will not prevent the people from combating the aristocrats" (IX, 492).

The changing tone of Robespierre's utterances from winter into spring is clear, but an unmistakable political line is not. At the same time as he is denouncing his colleagues, he proposes a new version of the Declaration of the Rights of Man and Citizen. He published his proposals in the final issue of his newspaper *Lettres à Ses Commettans*, which appeared around April 23, juxtaposed with a fierce denunciation of Brissot and the Girondins. This coupling of insurrection and constitution, purge and principles, recalls his 1792 position that insurrection, rightly understood, was a fulfillment of the constitution. The difference is that he is no longer defending a flawed document: he is offering his own, punctuated with deliberate and sincere appeals to the *sans-culottes*.

For Robespierre, as for many contemporaries, the republic was a regime whose principle was virtue. This was a tenet held by thinkers as divergent as Montesquieu and Rousseau. With the monarchy judged and destroyed, the Revolution had no longer the difficult task of striking an acceptable but uneasy compromise between the virtue inherent in a republic and the honor Montesquieu had taught was essential to monarchy. Henceforth the state could be consecrated to the creation of republican values, of virtue. Simultaneously this meant, at least for Robespierre, the eradication of all forms of vice, both moral and political. His proposed Declaration of Rights expresses these two aims. It is also a document that insists upon using the law and statements of principle as a manifesto for insurrection. Robespierre never completed the journey—an extraordinary one for any man to accomplish in the French Revolution—from seeing the enemy as the rich and the virtuous people as the poor, to seeing class war as the motor of history. The Declaration of Rights is filled with some extremely combustible thoughts on the natural enmities between rich and poor, but it does not advocate social war, nor will Robespierre ever propose a socialist solution for the Revolution's ills. "Internally," he notes privately, "the dangers come from the bourgeois. In order to convince the bourgeois, it is necessary to rally the people."[4] "We have got to get arms for the *sans-culottes*, stir them up, enlighten them. We must exalt republican enthusiasm by all possible means," and looking ahead to securing the fruits of insurrection, he insists "that the insurrection itself continue until the necessary measures to save the country have been taken."[5]

Rich and poor, bourgeois and worker, *culottes dorées* and *sans-culottes*, moderate and patriot, these are the poles in which he sees the struggle. The only solution, since compromise is out of the question, is for good to triumph over evil. The parliament must be purged. The "Girondin faction" represents and inspires "the bourgeois aristocracy."[6] But he lacks a program to realize this transformation by insurrection. He discovers the missing mechanism when he hits upon the formula of "a single will." Precisely when he scribbled the note to himself we do not know. "What we need," he wrote sometime in that difficult spring, "is a single will [*une volonté une*]. It must be either republican or royalist. If it is to be republican, we must have republican ministers, republican newspapers, republican deputies, a republican government. The foreign war is a mortal sickness, a fatal plague, so long as the body politic suffers from the Revolution and the division of wills."[7] The same imprecision of date mars another private fragment, the so-called catechism that derives from the same state of mind and seems as well to offer a program for realizing *une volonté une*.[8] What the Revolution needs is

1. *Proscription of perfidious and counterrevolutionary writers; propagation of patriotic writings.*
2. Punishment of traitors and conspirators, above all the guilty deputies and administrators.
3. Nomination of patriotic generals; removal and punishment of the others.
4. *Subsistence* and *social legislation* (*lois populaires*).

Reduced almost to slogans, this is Robespierre's revolutionary program. The order of items may not indicate priority or importance. The last item, "*Subsistence* and *social legislation*," is new. If it is true, as is likely, that this catechism and *une volonté une* date from sometime just before June 2, we can speculate that Robespierre's proposals for a new Declaration of the Rights of Man was also an appeal for the *sans-culottes'* support in the proposed insurrection. The difficulty, as always with Robespierre's social thought, is his ambiguity. Had the *sans-culottes* seen in his constitutional proposals and other public utterances a champion of their desires, they would not have been mistaken. But at the same time Robespierre had no desire to establish a *sans-culottes* government. Even more so than in the insurrection of August 10, the purge of June 2 had to be quickly regulated by the victors, made successful by being made orderly. Robespierre would mediate once again.

When the purge came, when the sections of Paris, encouraged and even incited by Robespierre, if not organized and set in motion by him, invaded the Tuileries, where the Convention was now sitting, and demanded expulsions, Robespierre stepped in. He opposed the intense minority agitation for the heads of "the infamous Brissot and all the clique of the Gironde."[9] They were placed under house arrest. It was merely a delay. The purge itself was the death warrant of the expelled deputies, whether they were confined in Paris or managed to escape to raise rebellion in the provinces. Robespierre could not spare the Girondin deputies, nor is it clear he wanted to. He did manage, however, because of his personal prestige, to spare the seventy-three additional deputies who had shortly afterward signed a protest against the purge and thus nearly shared the fate of those they sought to save. His was the only voice raised against Jean-Baptise Amar's proposal that the seventy-three be executed: "The Convention should not seek to multiply the numbers of guilty," he pleaded.[10]

Robespierre's willingness to use insurrection to purge the Convention came as slowly as had his original conversion to insurrection, and demanded some significant adjustments or deliberate blind spots in his theories. At the beginning of April he believed, half-heartedly, that persuasion would suffice. "There remains at this moment," he told the Jacobins, "one source of salvation for liberty; it is enlightenment, it is the true awareness of the cure,[11] and I tell you, from my heart, that the most fatal of all measures would be to violate the national representation" (IX, 355). It was only on May 29, two days before the actual movement in the streets began, that he advocated the attack on the Convention. By that time it is doubtful he could have stopped the gathering insurrection. His extreme reluctance in turning to the streets for salvation is expressed in the collapse of his health on the eve of the purge. "I am incapable of prescribing to the people the means of its salvation," he confessed to the Jacobins on May 29. "That is beyond me, exhausted as I am by four years of revolution and the oppressive spectacle of the victory of all that is most corrupt and vile." Once again the embodiment of the Revolution abdicated at the moment of action. No additional explanations were needed from him; the initiative had passed from his hands. He was superfluous: "It is not for me to indicate measures, consumed as I am by a slow fever and even more by the fever of patriotism. I have spoken and I have no other duty to perform" (IX, 537–38).[12]

On May 31 he supported the decree of accusation against the twenty-two Girondin deputies. To Vergniaud's taunt—"Finish already"—Robespierre snapped, "Yes, I'm going to finish, and against you . . . my conclusion is the decree of accusation against all the accomplices of Dumouriez and against all those who have been designated by the petitioners" (IX, 541). Then he retired from the scene.

The purge of June 2 went against many of Robespierre's instincts and intuitions and openly contradicted the arguments he had made during the King's trial. But it seemed to him the only possible tactic. He had sanctioned the use of force against the very body that had been itself created by an earlier insurrection, the only revolutionary body that remained in France that was capable of governing. For the first time in the Revolution the unique weapons of revolution had been used against itself. More important still, although ineluctable, was his use of the streets of Paris against the elected representatives of the nation. Until June 1793 he had been an anomaly: a popular leader who yet was unblemished by the excesses of his followers. Now he had overawed the sanctuary of the deputies. He had not precisely become a man of the streets, but he was henceforth closely identified with the streets. He would never be cleansed of this stain in the eyes of his parliamentary colleagues. They never forgave the invasion of their precincts and prerogatives. The fears of the Girondins, incessantly raised during the King's trial, that the Convention could not deliberate freely so long as it sat in Paris, and that the deputies were held hostage by the dangerous and uncontrollable city and its gruff population, had come true. What had appeared little more than factional posturing or exaggerated, even unfounded fears had become real.

Once the dirty work had been done by the Parisian crowd, Robespierre came forward to explain the victory and mediate it. The immediate results (and justification) would by "the most popular constitution that has ever existed." This great document could now be achieved because of the purge, and this "double miracle of renewal and purification" was the work of the people of Paris. The city was "worthy of achieving a Revolution that she has so gloriously begun" (IX, 601). These fine phrases struck far fewer resonances of sympathy, let alone elation, than had his equally enthusiastic celebrations of August 10.

The heritage of June 2 was riddled with contradictions. Robespierre correctly reasoned, but only with himself, only in his private notebook, that *une volonté une* was the means for transcending the contraditions of the Revolution in mid-1793. But the creation, not to mention the imposition, of a single will was not the legacy of this purge any more than it had been of the more substantial and popular insurrection of August 10. There was, certainly widespread in the Convention, deep suspicion of anything smacking of dictatorship. Having gotten rid of a king, the revolutionaries were not about to give themselves another absolute, if not arbitrary, authority. In addition, the faith in a republic held, although shaken by the purge. The creation of *une volonté une*, it became almost immediately apparent, was enormously difficult in a collegial government, which was the only government thought tolerable. Marat's earlier calls for a dictatorship had then fallen to the ground, and the purge did not revive them. Besides, Robespierre was the least likely man to exercise a dictatorship. He had a strong authoritarian streak to his thought, was always willing to use force to compel moral conformity, but simultaneously had faith in democracy. This paradox he shared with Rousseau. On another level his avoidance of personal authority is consistent throughout the Revolution. His biography is too fragmentary to permit an analysis in psychological terms. But politically he was a parliament man. Although in many ways temperamentally unfit for collegial government, he could not imagine any government that was not collegial. His support might come from outside the Convention, and he had clearly sided with the popular cause. But sovereignty was to be exercised, he insisted, only by the elected representatives of the nation assembled together. Originally he had embraced this article of faith out of expediency: it was impossible for the people as a whole to be assembled and consulted. In 1793 he would become convinced that the prevalence of counterrevolution, surviving in pockets everywhere, made popular government, some kind of direct democracy, an invitation to the forces of reaction to at least disrupt, and perhaps destroy, the Revolution. Even when he was elected to the Committee of Public Safety, one of twelve, he functioned as a parliament man, seeking majorities and consensus. A man who so consistently fled personal power cannot be charged with seeking the dictatorship.

There also remained the problem of faction. The purge had been at least partly justifiable to Robespierre as a bit of emergency surgery to cure gangrene, to cut away faction that, "by its nature, tends to immolate the general interest in the particular interest" (VIII, 316). But despite this assertion of Rousseauist orthodoxy, faction remained, and the purged Convention had no difficulty in excluding Robespierre from any direct participation in the government. It kept him off the new Committee of Public Safety for almost two months after the purge. In addition, a great many of his constitutional proposals, those he had promised the *sans-culottes* and spoken of as possible only in a purged Convention, were rejected by his colleagues. Robespierre might be admired for his exemplary behavior and habits, but he was also feared, especially so now that he had called the people out into the streets and the Convention to fight his battles. Even at the Jacobins the resort to purge had repercussions. He did not have to face any open hostility, for his dominance remained unaffected, but those to his left who had long preached a closer alliance with the populace of Paris, now felt emboldened to step foward and confront him. For the first time Robespierre found challengers within his own precincts who stood to his left.

François Chabot, for example, proposed that the rich be made to pay for the purge by having their property confiscated. The parliamentary purge was to be generalized outside the Convention: "if you don't push the wheel with us we will drive you from the republic, we will take your properties and divide them amongst the *sans-culottes.*"[13] This is not what Robespierre had in mind.

He now found himself the man in the middle, a position that was novel and would be increasingly forced upon him till the end of his life. The insurrectionists themselves were critical of their treatment, and the first signs of the "incompatibility of the revolutionary government, essentially Jacobin, and the democracy of the *sans-culottes*"[14] were discernible. The militant sections of Paris, having risen, were unwilling to return quietly to a passive role while *une volonté une* was imposed. Couthon thought the forty-eight sections, still flushed with their victory, presented "the hideous spectacle of federalism"[15] in the heart of the capital. Robespierre's desire that the Convention govern in the name of the people was in difficulty on all fronts. On the theoretical as well as the practical levels, the Convention and the Commune "represented forms of government (un-government might be a better term to describe the communalism of the popular militants) that could not co-exist for more than a few months."[16] Robespierre's exceptional powers of synthesis and mediation were about to be put to their most severe test.

The dilemma was clear: "I declare that nothing can save the republic [if] the National Convention is disabled and a legislative assembly put in its place" (X, 65). "It would be dangerous to change the Convention" (X, 77), to risk yet another insurrection. And the people in whose name the Convention was to govern, those it represented, were divided, as divided as their would-be governors. The rich could not be allowed to govern. In part the purge was directed against them; certainly the poor had been exhorted to rise up against those accused of representing the rich, and besides, the rich were "too egotistical." Nor could "the poor class, the class of the *sans-culottes,*" govern. They had no fit organs of government, a great nation could not be run from the streets of Paris, and they were "still too ignorant."[17] Only the purged Convention could govern. But how, in whose name, by what authority?

CHAPTER 9

Robespierre the Ideologue

PLATE XI
(Phot. Bibl. nat. Paris)

THE PERIOD FROM June 2 till July 27, 1793, from the purging of the Convention to the election of Robespierre to membership on the Committee of Public Safety, his first (and only) official position of authority, is the last time he can be contemplated performing the tasks he believed providence had set him. Once he joined the inner circles of government, disappeared into the Green Room of the Tuileries where the great committee met secretly, he not only spent less time in the public gaze, but he ceased to be a critic of the government. He had been made, he several times declared, to criticize and correct those who ruled, but not to rule himself. He was the representative of the people and had consistently declined all offices and appointments that might make him the representative of government. The purge changed everything.

"I am utterly tired of the Revolution; I am ill; the country was never in greater danger, and I doubt whether it will survive."[1] Thus did he lament on the eve of June 2, confounding self and circumstance. But the purge revitalized him as had August 10. His vigor of mind and body returned. Insurrection again made him whole. Urban uprising had rearranged the Revolution, created new possibilities. There was ideological work to be done. Running on nervous energy and willpower, he once more emerged to explain and cajole and seduce. The purge had to be given intellectual coherence, fit into the ongoing history of the Revolution. June 2 did not give Robespierre personal power but the purge destroyed the most stubborn opposition to the Mountain. The way to Jacobin dominance lay open, and Robespierre's years of cultivation of the Society were about to bear fruit. This is a good time to step back from the rush of chronology and events and examine Robespierre's thoughts before he joined the Committee and devoted an increasing amount of time and energy to defending not the best or most admirable government but a necessary and possible government, against a growing number of critics.

At the Jacobins and the Convention he simultaneously enunciated the line on the purge and provided detailed proposals for securing the victory.[2] On June 3 he exhorted the Club to explain the uprising to all the affiliates; on June 8 he launched a series of speeches in the Convention, partly intended to assuage fears and misgivings felt by those who had opposed the purge yet remained in the Convention. He wanted to assure them there would be no further amputations—and there was no talk at all of punishing the purged members—and he did so by speaking of the tasks that lay ahead.[3] France could now fulfill the dream of democracy, but it would be a democracy familiar to the eighteenth century "in which the sovereign people, guided by laws of their own making, do for themselves all that they can adequately do, and by delegates all that they cannot do by themselves" (X, 353). More significant than these commonplaces is his conviction that the Convention be unopposed in the exercise of power. It was not only inconceivable to him that France be governed from the streets, but equally inconceivable that the streets and the Convention govern together. He was a believer in representative, not participatory, democracy. He was convinced that "the people as a whole cannot govern themselves."[4]

A new constitution would fix the necessary arrangements of government. The constitution of 1791 had been an impossible and incomplete synthesis between aristocracy and democracy. Now, with the slate wiped clean, a proper constitution could be attempted, one that would incorporate the meaning of August 10 (as modified by June 2). As Robespierre envisioned it, the new constitution would have as its goal "the happiness of men, and consequently the conservation of their rights, of their security, of their liberty, of their property" (IX, 434). The addition of "happiness" to the customary political abstractions of the age is the originality of the Jacobins, which Robespierre so perfectly represents. Governments were to be instituted among men not only to legalize social relationships, regulate commerce, provide protection, and set the duties of citizenship and government alike, but also to assure human fulfillment and felicity, to spare men the humiliating destructiveness of poverty and dependence, whether legal or financial, on others. The preconditions of happiness are independence and self-sufficiency, which the Jacobins conceive of as the mundane and necessary dimension of freedom. This is not a utopian scheme, but rather a redefinition of social relationships. And the laws are to be used to force the creation of independence. Such a society, Robespierre argues, has no precedents. The American constitution he thought "quite imperfect" (IX, 434) and that of England only "offered . . . some feeble image of liberty" (IX, 499). He dreamed of nothing less than implementing the visions of human happiness propounded throughout his century. There was some admixture of the visionary in Robespierre's suggestions for achieving human happiness, but it is striking how realistic and practical he was as a legislator.

His specific proposals fall into two groups: those concerning a new Declaration of Rights of Man and Citizen, already presented before the purge, and those concerning the constitution proper.[5] Both show a new concern with social democracy; both are militant. "Kings and aristocrats," he declares, and "tyrants whatever they may call themselves, are slaves in revolt against the letigimate sovereign of the earth, which is the human race, and against the supreme legislator of the universe, which is Nature" (IX, 469). This utopian and revolutionary fustian, which Brissot sneeringly said was "unintelligibility posing as profundity," was in keeping with his views on sovereignty and authority. "The people is sovereign. The government is its property. Its functionaries are its employees."[6] Such a people, "when it pleases them, [can] change their government and revoke their mandatories" (IX, 456). "All infractions of the mandatories of the people," he logically insisted, "should be severely punished" since they were no "more inviolable than any other citizens."[7] Property, which in his proposed Declaration of the Rights of Man and Citizen he had defined as a social rather than a natural right,[8] is to be limited "by the obligation to respect the rights of others" and cannot be permitted to interfere with "the liberty, the existence, or the property of our fellow men."

Gracchus Babeuf, the most radical social thinker of the Revolution, a conspiratorial insurrectionist who would be executed in 1795, after a fascinating public trial for treason, a show trial conducted by the Thermidorians, had (in 1791) insisted that Robespierre was a fellow *agrarien*, a revolutionary devoted to the confiscation and redistribution of land.[9] The contrary is true. Robespierre's ideas on property were conventional enough that the majority of the Jacobins continued to consider him their spokesman, while the majority of the *conventionnels*, and other bourgeois loyal to the Revolution, did not feel themselves threatened in their pocketbooks.[10] Robespierre's strength and appeal lay not in his originality or radicalism as an economic thinker—in the French Revolution such deviations from convention were a hindrance to a popular leader—but in his providing familiar ideas with a moral intensity, giving them political articulation, and embodying some of the deepest and most passionate ideals of his age.

In economic matters Robespierre was content to reiterate the formulas of advanced bourgeois thought in his day. His use of a ferocious rhetoric, his denunciations of bourgeois greed and selfishness, might make his economic ideas appear more radical than they were, but he himself was unable or reluctant to draw extreme inferences. Above all, his economic ideas were thoroughly subordinated to political and moral ideas. He distrusted and disdained great wealth, he was angry at economic exploitation and was willing to use coercion against those who got rich off the Revolution, and he was equally willing to force the rich to deal justly with the poor, but none of these responses was given legislative form, and he certainly does not envision a society based on some distribution of wealth besides private property. He accepted material inequality as inevitable (and eternal). His contemporaries, themselves devoted to the same axiom, and willing to moralize about the social responsibilities of the rich—especially after the shock of the June 2 purge gave them little choice—thought Robespierre less radical than many. Still, they took little comfort in his fierce preamble and the proposed articles that followed:

I. Property is the right belonging to each citizen to enjoy and dispose of possessions and is guaranteed by law to him.

II. The right of property is limited, as are all other rights, by the obligation of respecting the rights of others.

III. This right cannot prejudice the security, nor the liberty, nor the existence nor the property of another.

IV. Any possession, any use that violates this principle is illegal and immoral. (IX, 461)[11]

Commercial and business interests too were made uneasy by Robespierre's pronouncements, although once again he did nothing to them despite the regular reiteration of forcing the rich to be charitable toward the poor: "the aid indispensable to him who lacks the necessities is a debt of him who has a superfluity. It is up to the law to determine the manner in which this debt should be paid."[12] Society has the responsibility of "assuring the means of existence to those incapable of working." This "is a debt of the rich to the people."[13] He adds that "society ought to salary public functionaries and make sure that citizens who live by their work can attend public assemblies to which the law summons them, without compromising their standard of living or that of their family."[14] All these constitutional proposals, with the exception of the rather innocuous giving of salaries to civil servants, were rejected. Robespierre's conspicuous lack of success as a constitution-maker continued. He had gone, without attacking private property, as far as he could, content to decry economic injustice as morally outrageous. Though he threatened coercion, he never used the repressive capacity of the state against landlords or businessmen specifically. The war economy forced upon France, of course, meant much government interference in the economy, but in overseeing production and commerce in the midst of war, the government (and Robespierre) had no intention of disrupting trade or discouraging enterprise.

The economic ideas he sketchily set forth on December 2, 1792, just as the formal indictment against the King was being readied and Paris was restless, impatient over the long delays in the trial, and grumbling about food prices and shortages, sprang from the conviction that the *laissez-faire* orthodoxy of the first years of the Revolution had failed.[15] To feed France, he argued, the decrees of December 31, 1791, and January 6, 1792, which assured free trade in grain, must be abrogated. They had necessitated "bayonets to subdue panic or to oppress hunger," while creating "profits for businessmen and property owners" at the expense of the populace. "The first right of man, the first object of society, is the right to exist" (IX, 112). He was willing to have free trade for luxury goods, but "all mercantile speculation made at the expense of a man's life is not commerce, it is brigandage and fratricide." The law must punish "the homicidal hand of the monopolist" as it does "that of the ordinary assassin." Men are entitled to the "enjoyment of the fruits of the earth that are necessary to their existence." They are also entitled to the fruits of their labor, but property itself ought not to bring its owner a profit beyond what labor has added to its intrinsic worth (IX, 113).

This is radical stuff, although well within the traditions of eighteenth-century economic thought, which had prepared for the revolutionaries a spectrum of speculation from the absolute sacrosanctity of private property to communism. Robespierre leaned obviously to the left, closer in his assumptions about the social responsibilities of private property to the *sans-culottes*, but never himself taking the next step and calling for confiscations. His actual proposals for feeding France are not very radical. They are the usual expedients resorted to by a government fighting for its life. He wanted each district "to declare the amount of grain" it produced and the amount that each property owner or farmer harvested. All would be compelled "to sell in the market" and forbidden "to move any purchases during the night" (IX, 114–15). "I am not denying them an honest profit, any legitimate property," he explains. "I am not destroying commerce, but only the brigandage of the monopolist. I condemn them only to the punishment of letting their fellow men live" (IX, 117). He then reiterates Rousseau's famous assertion that men must be forced to be free,[16] giving it a suitable twist: "the greatest service that the legislator can render to men is to force them to be *honnêtes gens.*" He concludes with a strident exhortation against "rich egoists" who may share the fate "of the nobles and the kings" if they continue to behave like them (IX, 117).

Robespierre shared with his age a deep respect for property and an equally deep regard for the values and virtues associated with it, especially small-property holding: thrift, uprightness, solvency, hard work, prudence, independence. He was a persistent and vigorous enemy of the agragrian law (*loi agraire*), with which Babeuf, and all those on the far left, were associated. The very mention of the agragrian law was "a phobia for the men of the Revolution."[17] "The aristocrats and the *feuillants,*" Robespierre lectured, "dare to impute the absurd project of the agrarian law to the friends of liberty" (IX, 52). His own views of the government's role in property relationships, which he expressed for the Mountain, was that of a policeman. It was not the function of the state to redistribute wealth, but "to protect the individual in the use" of it and "to protect other individuals from [the] misuse of it."[18]

From this followed several inferences. "The equality of wealth is a chimera" (IX, 459) and "essentially impossible in civil society" (IV, 117). His own efforts were, consequently, devoted to making material inequality endurable for the poor: "the rustic hut of Fabricius is as worthy as the palace of Crassus" (IX, 459). These views sprang from himself, from his own convictions and circumstances. On the dignity of poverty and the affliction of riches he spoke from his core. The resonances he set in motion were responses to self. "True independence," he insisted, "is relative not to one's fortune, but to needs, to the passions of men" (VII, 620–21). An artisan, a laborer, whose only property is his skill and sweat, is more independent than a rich man "because he is not burdened with all those ruinous passions, the offspring of opulence." The poor man's few hectares "are so much more sacred" than the immense holdings of the rich (VII, 622). Proportion, balance, tempered by austerity, make for happiness.

Robespierre was not much interested in changing fundamentally the economic complexion of France. He railed ferociously at the rich, but did little (besides frighten them) to deprive them of their privileges. He was obsessed with creating worthy citizens and was concerned that economic matters not interfere with this transcendental task, but he certainly did not think that landowning or business or commerce was as important as education, for example. He had the intellectual's disdain for business. There was not a single commercial case in his prerevolutionary law practice, he had no businessmen among his friends, and in both assemblies in which he sat he took virtually no part in commercial or financial matters. Indeed, he distrusted commerce and those involved in it, thinking the enterprise at best dubious, and more likely than not some form of chicanery. *Agiotage,* speculation in the rise and fall of public funds, he thought "the main source of our ills" (X, 336). Much of his Anglophobia sprang from his loathing for those who run a state as a business, who sell "to King George their conscience and the rights of the people" (X, 477). He spoke often and bitterly of the "bourgeois aristocracy," and Courtois singled out his detestation as worthy of denunciation.[19] There is no reason to assume he objected to the language used by his old Arras friend, Buissart, in speaking of businessmen: "We are dying of hunger in the midst of abundance. I believe it is necessary to kill the mercantile aristocracy just as we killed that of the priests and the nobles."[20] Robespierre himself never proposed killing the mercantile aristocracy, but his manner of talking about them was deeply offensive. Businessmen were another of the groups he offended with threatening and vituperative language without carrying through. This was a political blunder he often committed, and one for which he would pay.

Economic matters were not central to Robespierre's thought; the creation of a republic with republican citizens was. And this creation went far beyond economic or purely legal considerations. Nothing will be done for the people, Augustin Robespierre writes Buissart, if the Convention "limits itself to the drawing up of the constitution." What is needed is "a civil code, public education, which will in the future spare the Republic the misfortunes that weigh upon it in the Midi and in *ci-devant* Brittany."[21] Maximilien, too, sought the animating civic spirit of the republic, "a certain spirit of sacrifice . . . a certain spiritual energy."[22] He called for education and enlightenment, the great hopes of his century. At the same time he called for control of public administrators and officials. A quarter of the constitutional proposals he made are devoted to forcing officials to be virtuous, or at least outwardly honest.[23] Here again was his willingness (at least verbal) to use force, and he was much more deliberate in going after those holding the public trust. Doubtless he saw them as more dangerous to freedom than the businessmen. But above all he had faith in education. "Society ought to encourage, with all its power, the progress of public reason and put instruction within the reach of all citizens" (IX, 466). "This final task," Augustin confessed to Buissart, "is perhaps more difficult than we thought, and this final birth will perhaps be as painful as the first."[24]

When Robespierre presented the plan of national education on July 13, 1793, it was clear he considered this the key to republican regeneration. Prepared by his comrade and friend, the aristocrat converted to radical Jacobinism, Lepeletier de Saint-Fargeau, the plan had lain mute since its composition. Lepeletier had been murdered on January 20, 1793, just after he had voted for the King's death, as he dined at his favorite restaurant. The assassin, a royalist fanatic named Paris, thus created the first Jacobin martyr of the Revolution. Now, nearly six months later, Robespierre took up Lepeletier's education program and presented it with the full passion of his own conviction. Education was, in Lepeletier's blunt phrase, which Robespierre seconded, "the revolution of the poor."

There could be no republic without republicans. Those who had repeatedly fought to create the republic, the poor, the *sans-culottes*, the Parisians, who had recently renewed the Revolution by purging parliament, were the raw material out of which republicans were to be created, and education was the instrument that would make them the beneficiaries of their struggles. When he speaks of the people or republicans, he is using synonymous terms.[25] In a sense, true republicans are the people educated. "What thing above all should citizens learn?" he asks: "the rights of humanity . . . the duties of each man toward his fellows . . . the divine principles of morality and equality" (V, 209). This learning will be achieved if children are taken "at the age when they receive decisive impressions, in order to prepare men worthy of the Republic" (X, 70). The republic will educate them for seven years, between the ages of five and twelve, not in the idyllic isolation envisioned by Rousseau in *Emile*, but in schools resembling barracks. "It is no longer a question of forming gentlemen," he declares, speaking with the experience of one who went through the best schools of the *ancien régime*, "but rather citizens." "The nation alone has the right to raise children." So important a task cannot be left "to the pride of families nor to the prejudices of individuals," which only leads to "aristocracy and domestic feudalism" and eventually "destroys, equally, all the foundations of the social order" (X, 458).

Lepeletier's education scheme, rigorous and spartan, remained a paper one, but it declared the fervor of the Jacobin radicals for moral renewal, which Robespierre shared as unequivocally as he did the proposals themselves. "Considering how degraded human nature was by the vice of our former social system," wrote Lepeletier in his *Plan for National Education*, "I am convinced of the necessity for a complete regeneration and, if I can thus express myself, the creation of a new people."[26] Here more than in proposed constitutional articles is the authentic voice of the Mountain. Robespierre's championship of the plan is more than homage to a dead friend. On this most intimate issue Lepeletier spoke for the Mountain, and on the Mountain there was unison. Billaud-Varenne, an eventual colleague on the Committee of Public Safety, no friend to Robespierre and a man more closely connected to the *sans-culottes*, demanded a public education worthy of "a people regenerating itself."[27]

If sovereignty was the most persistent political category of the Revolution, the Jacobin passion for regeneration was the most radical. However one thought of regeneration, it was obvious that it could not be achieved with a few reforms, some modifications of the inheritance of the past. The Mountain may have underestimated its debt to the past, as Tocqueville argues, but its spokesmen were convinced nevertheless that they were involved in nothing less than creating a new people. The qualities inherent in the people, latent for so many centuries because of tyranny and oppression, were to be liberated. This great passive repository of virtue was to be made active. Here was the historical mission of the Mountain. And if its heights required the masses to look up for leadership, this was a perspective Robespierre and his friends thought appropriate and necessary.

Robespierre most often defined the people by their opposite, which is how he most often defined himself, by what he was not. "The people recognized themselves in him," writes a poet and politician and historian of the next century, Alphonse de Lamartine.[28] Robespierre himself believed his connection with the people is precisely what certified his authority. "I am not the courtesan, nor the moderator, nor the tribune, nor the defender of the people," he proudly announced. "I am the people myself!" (*Je suis peuple moi-même!* VIII, 311). And the people that he is are not the better sort, the refined; the people are "the *sans-culottes* and the riffraff"[29] (IX, 59). France was divided into two "great sections, the majority of citizens, the least powerful citizens, those least smiled upon by fortune and by the former government, those citizens we call the people," and their enemy, "who want to resurrect the old abuses or create them anew" (VIII, 24–25). There continue to be, even after August 10 and June 2, "those who oppress the people and those who love liberty" (IX, 438). Between them there can be no compromise. The rich are, by nature, "the lash of the people" (VI, 625).[30] Robespierre's people, however, are not so poor that they are indigent or mendicant,[31] and he almost never mentions the proletariat, which he thought a class below the poor, and by implication probably incapable of being republicans. Robespierre viewed the poor from a bourgeois perspective.[32]

Unlike Rousseau, Robespierre does not yearn for the imagined simplicity of a spartan society or a primitive society spared the ravages of civilization. But he does insist that the people are naturally simple in their needs and desires. "The people ask only for tranquillity, justice, the right to live," while their enemies demand "distinctions, treasure, voluptuousness." The interest of the people is in harmony with "nature and humanity"; their enemy is driven by "ambition, pride, cupidity, the most extravagant fantasies, passions harmful to society" (VI, 625).

These antinomies were common on the left. The terrorist Claude Javogues, who was no *robespierriste*—defined the people simply as those who had suffered from the *ancien régime* and who had issued from "the industrious part of society," including "the agricultural class." The people were thus the vast majority of Frenchmen who were excluded from privilege and opportunity and who, he is careful to add, were distinct from what he colorfully called *"la horde des praticiens,"* those who had some specific skill salable to the government or the bourgeoisie.[33] Collot d'Herbois, another confirmed terrorist who was also not fond of Robespierre, had a similar definition. The people were "the workers, the *sans-culottes* who made the Revolution; it is they who have sustained it and who have crowned it with success; it is they who will finish it."[34] Robespierre's views on the people were in harmony with the left, although he was much more insistent in declaring what he thought on the matter.

Describing the people as the antithesis of both old and new elites implied, and was meant to imply, their moral superiority. The grandeur of simplicity informed by virtue set them apart from their enemies. The people is "a stranger to all excess, is always of the party of morality, of justice and of reason" (X, 199). It possesses virtue (X, 355). The people is "pure, simple, avid for justice, the friend of liberty; it is this virtuous people that sheds its blood in order to found the Republic" (X, 476–77). From the people is drawn those who compose the advanced revolutionary warriors, who function as "a preservative against the vices and the despotism of government" (IX, 498). "Everything that the French Revolution has done that is sage and sublime is the work of the people" (X, 230). But they need not all act simultaneously. Just as he believed in representative government, so he believed sections of the whole people could represent and act for their brothers. The few who seized the Bastille or vanquished the Tuileries were a vanguard, but a fully representative vanguard. "The Republic belongs only to the people," he says, immediately qualifying: "only to the *sans-culottes*" (IX, 354). In all questions of patriotism, he tells the Jacobins, "the spirit of the people is good and alone capable of rendering justice to friends and enemies alike" (VIII, 180). The sections of Paris "have made the Revolution," sustained it against "all perfidious maneuvers, against all the aristocrats, against all the disturbers of the peace" (IX, 217).

The people are known by their deeds, which spring from an inner, innate virtue. Montesquieu, in *L'Esprit des lois*, had given virtue (*vertu*) the political connotations it would carry throughout the eighteenth century and into the Revolution. "What I call virtue," he writes in the

Avertissement to his treatise that would become a quarry for subsequent thinkers, "is love of one's country, that is, love of equality. It is not a moral or a Christian virtue, but a political one; and it is as much the mainspring of republican government as honor [*honneur*] is the mainspring of monarchies." In the course of his work this definition was integrated into his models. "No great amount of social integrity is needed for a monarchical or a despotic government to maintain itself," he argues. "But in a popular state one spring more is necessary, namely VIRTUE."[35] With the notable exception of Rousseau,[36] virtually all political thinkers of the French Enlightenment were pessimistic about the possibility of men living together in a democracy. There lingered about democracy the fear it had inspired since the Greeks: democracy was demagogy, class rule for and by the least educated, the least able, the most oppressed (and vengeful) members of society. Rousseau, with his extraordinary gift for paradox, for standing a familiar proposition on its head, insisted virtue was "the sublime science of simple souls." The people were not the least capable of government but the most worthy. This formula, the inseparability of poverty and virtue and democracy as the best form of government for their expression and realization, harmonized perfectly with Robespierre's thinking.

Throughout the whole of his thought one can find the threads of virtue woven in. The concept joins and enriches the dialectical tensions that characterize his ideas. Tyrants, aristocrats, rich bourgeois, the wicked and the scoundrels—and in the heat of struggle he was not scrupulous in making distinctions—were opposed to, locked in combat with, patriots, the friends of liberty, democrats, the poor, the good, the virtuous, the *sans-culottes*.[37] Virtue characterized all that was worthy about the Revolution just as vice characterized the counterrevolution. Virtue, in Robespierre's vocabulary and in the vocabulary of the left, had become a political term in a far broader sense than Montesquieu ever intended. And in Robespierre's case this was not an abstract vocabulary. Virtue was personal as well as public, and he often certified his exigeses by offering his own virtue as an example. He delighted in contrasting his qualities of character with those of his political rivals.

Before the Revolution, he argued, virtue was only a personal and private quality. There was no occasion for its public exercise. Those who possessed virtue could manifest it only privately; publicly they had to dissimulate. Hypocrisy was a mask worn by virtuous men during the *ancien régime*. The Revolution reversed this paradox: the virtuous man could now express his virtue in patriotism, for the Revolution had given him back his country. And patriotism was but one aspect of virtue, which in a healthy society informed every act, whether public or private. Paradoxically, the mask of hypocrisy which had been torn off by the Revolution had been replaced by another. Hypocrites now wore a mask of virtue. Previously it was essential to appear indifferent or cynical or sophisticated. Now one must appear virtuous. With hypocrisy masquerading as virtue, Robespierre proposed a test. If "once in his life" a man has revealed himself "base or without pity," he lacks virtue. If a man has been seen "clawing his way up at court or humiliating himself at the feet of a minister or a mistress," he lacks virtue. Such men may have changed their manner, but "their heart remains the same" (VII, 511).

Prior to August 10 and June 2, prior to the definitive entry of the people into revolutionary politics, Robespierre had reflected the smug conceit of his class, the professional bourgeoisie: virtue and talent were inseparable. The most he was willing to concede what that "of the two, virtue is still the most important." It would take him some time to abandon this bourgeois fetish and adopt Rousseau's view that virtue and simplicity were inseparable. Only in this way could he escape the narrow (and self-serving) limitations thus placed on virtue. What he could not escape, because self and substance were one in his politics, was the constant personification of virtue. A favorite means, especially when he was under personal attack, was to assume kinship with the virtuous men of the past. In the winter of 1792, around the time of the war debates, he wailed that "the defenders of liberty who still dare to raise their voices are only regarded as seditious." The virtuous would be forced "to drink the hemlock, like Socrates, or perish under the blade of tyranny, like Sydney, or else rip out their entrails, like Cato" (VIII, 91–92). "Read history," he begged his newspaper readers; "you will see that the benefactors of humanity were martyrs" (V, 114). He was a patriot, one of a long line of distinguished patriots whose deeds and deaths had illuminated history. Even in the Revolution virtue was in the minority. On December 28, 1792, in his oratorical contest with Vergniaud over the King's fate, Robespierre elaborated what he had long said only in phrase or aphorism. Underneath the development of the theme of virtue in the minority lay not only the recent verbal drubbings he had taken in the Convention and the Girondin press, but also the memory of his isolation during the spring and summer of the year. But in the speech he was moving away from the self-pity inherent in an imagined martyrdom (IX, 183–202).

He would return to the theme of virtue's minority and martyrdom, but only in the last months of his life, when he once again felt beset and isolated. But at the end of December he was trying to get away from the fatalistic notion that virtue was in the minority and to extend virtue to the majority, to the people, on whom all of his ideas depended. It would be absurd to maintain that the people were in the minority, and the people were virtuous. He now made the contrary argument: it was the rulers who were without virtue. Fortunately, the ruled were virtuous. There were "millions of citizens in our departments" who were worth "no less than" the deputies in Paris. Because of them "the victory of liberty is assured," since "a free man is worth more than 100 slaves, and the destiny of crime is to tremble before virtue" (IV, 290).

The notion of virtue being in the majority, arguably one of the definitions of the Revolution, also permitted Robespierre to dispose of the argument that a man could be privately but not publicly virtuous. "A man who lacks the public virtues," he insisted, "cannot have private virtues." Jacques Necker, the first minister of the crown when the Revolution began, was "a veritable tyrant in the bosom of his family," and "it is in vain that Roland praised his virtue to me and drew a picture of his private life." Even the "scandalous story of the private life of Barbaroux" mattered not at all. "I ask a man," Robespierre continued, proposing another test of virtue, "what have you done for the prosperity of your country?" If a man could answer the question in a satisfactory manner, "then I believe him virtuous" (X, 520). The enemies of the Revolution were satisfied with "a certain decent exterior and above all an equivocal probity, which consists in not breaking into the strongbox of another." This was not virtue, and never prevented men "from conspiring against liberty." "The generous devotion to the cause of the people . . . [is] the sole yardstick of the happiness of the human race" (X, 531).

On the Mountain virtue was invoked almost as a magical word.[38] There was general agreement that virtue was "a natural passion" driving its captives to "the most sublime and most holy love of humanity . . . the ravishing spectacle of public happiness" (X, 554). It was virtue that made the violence of the Revolution tolerable, no small matter to civilized, sensitive, intelligent men such as Robespierre. Without virtue "a great revolution is nothing more than a startling crime that annihilates another crime" (X, 554). This was not specifically an *apologia* for terror, but rather an article of faith. "The soul of the Republic is virtue, that is to say love of country, the magnaminous devotion that sees all private interests in the general interest" (V, 17). It belongs specifically to the "people, to men of all circumstances who have a pure and elevated soul, to philosophers who are the friends of humanity, to the *sans-culottes"* (IX, 377).

In the weeks after the purge of June 2, Robespierre returned, obsessively, to the theme of virtue and the people. There was now apparent a gradual inclination to see virtue as an essentially spiritual quality, independent of the world of politics and purges. As Robespierre's thought ripened in mid-1793, as he worked to harmonize the various elements of his ongoing synthesis of self and revolution, he came more and more to speak of the Revolution as being in men's hearts. His concern for education is one indication. The republic must, of course, be established on firm footing, endowed with lasting institutions and good laws, but its true genius lay "above all" in "the goodness of its mores" (X, 476). "The country is in the patriot; and the Republic is in those who defend it" (X, 297). Having rejected private virtue as a suspicious, or at least dubious, aloofness from society, which is the antithesis of virtue, and simultaneously having put Montesquieu's abstraction, modified by Rousseau's faith, at the center of the republic, Robespierre now established a close correspondence between the individual and society, between self and people: "Whoever is not master of himself is made to be the slave of another." This "is a truth for the people as for individuals." All those who "despise virtue, who corrupt public morality" are the enemy (X, 476). By internalizing the spirit of the republic and the Revolution, he had rendered them secure, safe from the machinations of the counterrevolution. The republic lived so long as there was a single republican who lived. He had ideologically preserved the Revolution by making it subjective.

He arrived at this intellectual haven after a precarious voyage. He had been unable to persuade either the purged or the unpurged parliament that *une volonté une* was necessary and entailed some serious concessions to social democracy. Nevertheless, he believed that the Convention, in its purged form, must have almost absolute power to govern.[39] Even his sincere passion for Lepeletier's education plan was a concession: had it been instantly adopted, without change, it would have been at least a generation before the republic would have been able to create the citizens Robespierre insisted were essential. In the long interim the purged Convention would have had to rule. The failure to reconcile the antithetical interests of parliament and Parisians, the failure to find some acceptable form of social democracy, the failure to regenerate through education, all meant that *une volonté une* would have to be imposed on the Revolution. Robespierre saw clearly what had to be done. He had serious doubts it could be done. These deep reservations he kept to himself, confining his fears to his private notebook:

> What obstacle is there to the enlightenment of the people? Its misery. When, then, will the people be enlightened? When it will have bread and the rich and the government will stop using hired pens and perfidious language to deceive it; when the interests of the rich and the government shall be confounded with those of the people. And when will these interests be confounded with those of the people? Never.[40]

This catechism of disillusionment he put aside. Election to the Committee of Public Safety, for the first time in the Revolution, brought him close to the power necessary for imposing his vision of a virtuous republic on France. There was work to be done.

CHAPTER 10

The Committee
of Public Safety

PLATE XII
(Photo Bibl. nat. Paris)

ON JULY 27 Robespierre was elected to the Committee of Public Safety, the executive committee of the Convention, a brilliantly successful improvisation that replaced the executive authority that had been guillotined with the King. Much of the wavering in the face of distractions that had afflicted the Convention since its beginning was thought to result from the lack of an executive. The Committee of Public Safety would have, by delegation, all the powers of the Assembly itself, with the significant exceptions that it could not declare war, make peace, or legislate. These required majority vote of the Convention. But otherwise, in carrying out the will of the Convention, the Committee was unrestricted. Robespierre's selection, so long delayed by reluctance, had now become irresistible. For the first time he shared a place at the head of the republic.

The Committee of Public Safety began life as the Committee of General Defense, in January 1793. By March it was commonly known by its now-notorious name and was charged with preparing all the laws and measures necessary for the interior and exterior defense of the republic. On April 6 the Committee of Public Safety, its new name and functions recognized, was officially created. Nine members were chosen by vote (eventually there would be twelve), and the legal basis for its immense powers were specified.[1] The Committee's authority was further enhanced by its meetings conducted in secret. No record of its proceedings was kept. Decisions were reached by majority vote of all the members present, but no tally was ever made public: only unanimous decrees were announced. There was also no specified quorum needed for legality. The Committee would become the virtual government of France for about a year, the year of the Revolution's greatest crisis, the year of the Terror, the year of Robespierre's preponderance. To prevent the usurpation of power, the Committee was subject to monthly renewal, dismissal, and control. Yet once it had achieved its definitive personnel, in September 1793, neither mandate nor membership were tampered with (although Hérault de Sechelles, the author of the 1793 constitution, would be guillotined in April 1794 and not replaced on the Committee).

The twelve members, elected by their colleagues from among the deputies, could hardly have been different. The twelve were not harmoniously disposed toward each other; their skills and aptitudes were varied, as was their conception of the Revolution and the work of the Committee. Robespierre's faction, which comprised himself, Saint-Just, and Couthon, was bound together not only by politics but by friendship, yet this was the only such group on the Committee. No individual ever dominated the Committee consistently, although on this or that issue the members might defer to the man thought to be expert in the matter at hand. The division of labor on the Committee was remarkable and perhaps the single most important reason for its survival and effectiveness. Seldom were all twelve members present in Paris at the same time, for much of the Committee's work was done by sending one or several of the members on mission, particularly to the war zones of the beleaguered republic. These missionaries carried with them the full authority of the Committee, often making, without being able to consult their colleagues, fundamental policy. The twelve were agreed only in the need to save the republic at whatever cost. In theory as well as practice the emergency government overseen by the Committee was to be collegial. It was a unique experiment in political authority and has never been repeated.

It took several months not only for the definitive membership of the Committee to be established, but for the Committee to function with any efficiency. The two issues are intimately related. On July 10 there was a major reshuffling of the membership of the first Committee. Danton was displaced. Robespierre had been, since June 2, a loyal supporter of the Committee, but he was not at this time made a member (IX, 561–62; 612–14).[2] At the beginning of August, Lazare Carnot and Prieur de la Côte d'Or—to the befuddlement of historians there was another Prieur on the Committee, distinguished also by his place of origin, Prieur de la Marne—both former captains in the prestigious engineering *corps de génie*, were added to the Committee. On September 6 two representatives of the left opposition, Collot d'Herbois and Billaud-Varenne, were also added. On September 20 Thuriot, the only remaining representative of the right on the Committee and one of the original nine members, resigned.

Robespierre's election to the Committee came a couple of weeks after Danton's displacement and was probably achieved on the proposal of Jeanbon Saint-André, himself a member and a Montagnard. Robespierre, then, did not replace Danton, but rather the obscure Thomas-Augustin de Gasparin, former soldier and talented military strategist, who resigned because of ill health. It is typical of Robespierre's career, as of his life, that his assumption of power should be veiled by ambiguity. The reasons why he was now acceptable to his colleagues are not clear, nor do we know what sort of pressure and arm-twisting may have gone on to get him elected. Nevertheless, it is from Robespierre's membership that we can date the beginning of the Committee's great work.

Essentially the Committee of Public Safety had two categories of members: specialists and theorists. The former were charged with specific administrative responsibilities because of specific skills. Jeanbon Saint-André, for example, had made himself familiar with maritime matters and was the naval specialist. Robespierre was one of the theorists, charged with formulating and explaining the policies of the Committee to the Convention and the nation.[3] Prieur de la Côte d'Or, another military specialist, reports that Robespierre felt some uneasiness in his new position and tended, in the beginning, to remain aloof from the business handled by the specialist bureaus. The specialists, in turn, paid some deference to his views on political matters because of his influence over public opinion.[4]

Robespierre's appointment to the Committee put him at the center of the Revolution. His immense prestige at the Jacobins and with the sections, as well as the respectful trepidation he inspired in the Convention, placed him at all the critical synapses of the Revolution. He was the living link between the Committee and the Convention, the Committee and the Jacobins, the Committee and the Commune, and Committee and the *sans-culottes*. For the moment he seemed about to reconcile all the terrible contradictions of the Revolution in his person.[5]

The first Committee of Public Safety had been dominated by the exceptional personality of Danton, but had been ineffectual, paralyzed by a Convention sunk in incessant bickering and factionalism that ended in purge. Those deputies who remained were stunned and cowed by the invasion of their hall and of their immunity.[6] With no other choices available, they formed a popular front, a fragile and unlikely alliance of individuals, factions, and remnants of older coalitions, that expressed all the social and political complexity of French society and of the Revolution in its fifth summer, and was held together by necessity as much as by will.[7] The new Committee of Public Safety would henceforth govern for this popular front.

The central task of the new government would be to hold the antagonistic forces of society together by any means until the emergency passed. No one better understood the proportions of this task than Robespierre, who spoke of the Committee as the Convention's "organ of action and combat," which was to "crush the rebels and intimidate conspirators."[8] At the same time no man was so temperamentally unfit to join, let alone eventually dominate, a collegial government, although no other could have done what he did.[9] Convinced for some weeks that the people could not govern themselves and hence all authority must be concentrated in the Convention, he simultaneously realized that all government would be by coalition. Equilibrium was the only possible policy. The antagonistic forces had to realize they shared a common enemy, a common destiny, and a common government. Robespierre remained consistent. The counterrevolution was the enemy, as it had been since 1789. The Revolution would not be secure until the counterrevolution was defeated, until each Frenchman could say to himself, "If today the aristocracy triumphs, I am doomed" (X, 523).

Robespierre's election to the Committee came late in his revolutionary career. Only in the midst of the Revolution's greatest crisis were his colleagues willing to grant him power. But although he was distrusted as too radical, although he was thought too uncompromising and too austere, still he was called to power. He had been difficult for most to tolerate when he was only a passionate and eloquent gadfly. But from the time of the King's trial he had become the necessary man. He gave the Committee what it had hitherto lacked: a revolutionary voice.

The Revolution remained at war, and if the war was lost, all would be lost. The sole justification for the Committee, the reason for its creation and the numerous emergency measures it was allowed to take, was the grim struggle for survival. Robespierre never lingered over the irony that the war he had originally opposed he would now have to fight to the death. The memory of General Dumouriez's treason in early April was fresh, and all the generals, especially those who had, like Dumouriez, aristocratic antecedents, were potential traitors. "*Victory or death* was the order of the day in the republican armies."[10] Over this slogan there was neither disagreement nor compromise. In essence the Committee of Public Safety was a war cabinet with extraordinary powers. Although Robespierre had no special knowledge of warfare, he had a sure grasp, both intuitive and reasoned, of the complexities of revolutionary war, particularly on the domestic front. Public safety, he had long insisted, was "the first of our laws." A people "advancing toward liberty ought to be inexorable toward conspirators," for "weakness is cruel, indulgence is barbaric, and a just severity is imperiously demanded by humanity itself." Liberty would come only with victory and be maintained by "laws protective of the individual rights of all citizens against the caprices and the despotism of the constituted authorities" (V, 170). The Committee was well named and Robespierre was well chosen. He was a hard man for a hard job.

While his bluntness and fervor fit him for the tasks set by circumstances in 1793, they did not fit him for collegial government. Only toward the end of their tenure did bits and fragments of the clashes and antagonisms and hatreds that nightly filled the Green Room leak out. From these seepages we surmise that only *la force des choses* held the

Committee together, that the members quickly broke into factions, and that Robespierre not only never held unquestioned sway but was a disturbing presence rather than a peacemaker.

To fight the war and simultaneously sustain the Revolution demanded experiment, improvisation, innovation. It seems unlikely that Robespierre was the sole architect of the so-called Revolutionary Government, but he was the man who most often came before the Convention and the nation to explain. He envisioned the new government as Montagnard, for a Montagnard "is nothing else but a pure patriot, reasonable and sublime" (X, 493). From the ranks of such pure and exclusive patriotism would come "a small number of strong commissioners, furnished with sound instructions and above all good principles" to lead all "to unity and republicanism, the only means of terminating the Revolution to the profit of the people."[11] This revolutionary vanguard would scour the country for men "worthy of serving the cause of liberty."[12] The corollary of this policy of identifying and recruiting a patriotic elite was the destruction of all factions, which had kept pace with the Revolution: "today all the royalists are republicans, all the Brissotins are Montagnards" (X, 166). He would tolerate no opposition. Attacks on the Revolutionary Government were counterrevolutionary: "One must not criticize the Revolutionary Government, but rather remind it of its principles, simplify it, diminish its innumerable crowd of agents, and everywhere purify them" (X, 569). His revolutionary program was summed up in the formula *une volonté une* earlier scribbled in his notebook.

Although difficult to ascertain precisely, Robespierre's place on the Committee is not now in much dispute. "The true head of the Committee is Robespierre," wrote the historian of revolutionary institutions.[13] His colleagues were forceful and intelligent and vigorous, and the majority of them were not acknowledged adherents of Robespierre's group nor even very fond of him. Still, he was the chief articulator of the theory of the new government because he expressed in his personal words their view of the Revolution. "The new government," Billaud-Varenne told the Convention on November 18, "will be terrible toward conspirators, coercive toward public servants, severe toward prevaricators, redoubtable to the wicked, the protector of the oppressed, inexorable toward oppressors, partial to patriots, tailored for the people. . . ."[14] Robespierre might have said the same thing: he had been saying it for years, which enhanced his prestige.

Despite his unquestioned revolutionary credentials, Robespierre was no Lenin whose personal prestige was so enormous and unchallenged that he seldom failed to get his way on issues he chose to insist upon. Robespierre exercised no such dominance over his colleagues. He had elements of the charismatic leader, but never enjoyed the personal authority of such leaders. He was *primes inter pares* at best, and maintaining this precarious primacy meant constant vigilance. In the collective leadership of the French Revolution, Robespierre's major advantage continued to be his voice. How it was heard in the Green Room is only a matter of conjecture; but in the Convention and at the Jacobins he continued to dominate through persuasion. He put his case and self incessantly before the nation. There is scarcely a major issue on which Robespierre did not declare his views, and he continued to be influential because he continued to draw nourishment and support from the people, from those outside the government. He continued to cultivate his popularity, and the applause he earned at the tribune reverberated in the Green Room. The Committee was a kind of primitive factory where labor was divided. Such is the nature of war cabinets. Robespierre did not harangue his colleagues there for hours, using a prepared script, but he proved the essential member, a kind of animating presence. His participation acted to direct the individual, specialized efforts.

Robespierre's presence on the Committee altered him and his sense of self as much as it affected the Revolution. His earlier metaphors of self, his whole imagery, was gradually replaced by the vocabulary of war and armed struggle. His thought turned from defense to attack. He saw himself metaphorically as he was in reality, active not passive. His urge toward stark distinctions was fully satisfied: those who were not actively defending France were the enemy. The world, the Revolution, were expressed in the language of dualism. His paradoxical cast of mind, which depicted reality as contradiction, tension, energy, which demanded synthesis through reason, now reached an extreme. The enormous struggles of the Revolution had, by 1793, burned away subtleties of discourse, leaving only the polarities of revolution and counterrevolution, war and peace. The Revolution, as he saw it, was a kind of spiritual crusade. So uncompromising were his views that they have been called "the ideology of Manicheanism."[15] The world was a struggle between the forces of light and darkness. His revolutionary allies found dualism compelling. The infant republic was locked in mortal struggle; its triumph would be that of good over evil. Only in such moral absolutes was it possible to explain and apologize for the brutality of the fight. Saint-Just gave this dualism succinct statement in his *Rapport* of April 15, 1794 (26 Germinal). The Revolutionary Government was "the change from bad to good, from corruption to probity, from bad to good maxims."[16] The stark realities of 1793–94, the Year II, made Robespierre's familiar and habitual preaching of this doctrine appear prophetic.

The theoretical (and moral) basis of the new government was provided by Robespierre and Saint-Just. Significantly, none of the three theoretical disquisitions—Saint-Just's on October 10; Robespierre's on December 25, 1793, and February 5, 1794—discussed popular sovereignty. No attempt was made to disguise the Revolutionary Government as democratic. It was to be both autocratic and temporary. All authority continued to reside in the people, but during the emergency they gave up, so to speak, to their elected represe.1tatives all direct and immediate control over decisions. These representatives, in turn, made a similar sacrifice to the Committee of Public Safety. This "theory of revolutionary government," Robespierre argued, aware that he was breaking with his own democratic past and the democratic expectations of his followers, "is as new as the revolution that brought it into being." There were no precedents, either "in the treatises of political writers" or "in the laws of tyrants" (X, 274). New times demanded new responses.

On October 10 Saint-Just delivered, for the Committee, a report, "On the Necessity of Declaring the Government Revolutionary until Peace." "The republic will only be founded when the will of the sovereign will have curbed the monarchical minority and will reign over it by the right of conquest," he told the Convention. Saint-Just then added a formula that Robespierre would subsequently use: "It is necessary to govern by iron those who cannot be governed by justice."[17] The Convention responded by voting Saint-Just's slogan as its policy: "the provisional government of France revolutionary until peace." With some exaggeration he also announced another theme of the Revolutionary Government: "All the enemies of the republic are in its government."[18] Robespierre had been making this argument since the beginning of the Revolution. France's struggle for regeneration might be lost on some foreign battlefield: it could only be won by destroying the counterrevolution at home. He had continued to think of the war as a kind of tragic adventurism. His own attention was fixed on domestic issues, the winning of the Revolution, and this would become revolutionary orthodoxy in later struggles.

Robespierre would elaborate and enrich these themes in much the same way he had the themes of regicide so brilliantly adumbrated by Saint-Just. Robespierre was the propagandist whose prestige and popularity, intensity and conviction, gave him a power beyond that of originality. In the complex relationship with the young Saint-Just, the two men depended on each other and complemented each other intellectually. Saint-Just had the more original theoretical intelligence, Robespierre was able to animate the spirits conjured by his comrade. Throughout the months of defending the Revolutionary Government, Robespierre returned again and again to a distinction he had made months earlier: the Revolution could not be judged by standards and values made for peacetime. "The goal of constitutional government is to preserve the republic; that of revolutionary government is to found it. The Revolution is the war of liberty against its enemies: the constitution is the regime of victorious and peaceful liberty" (X, 274). Constitutional and revolutionary government are the political analogues of peace and war. Constitutional government requires that individuals be protected from abuses of public authority. In a revolutionary government "public authority itself must defend itself against every faction that attacks it" (X, 274).

This novel and ferocious government "is supported by the most sacred of all laws, the welfare of the people; and by the clearest of all titles, necessity" (X, 275). Those who think the new government "arbitrary or tyrannical are stupid or perverse sophists . . . [who] desire the resurrection of tyranny and the death of la patrie" (X, 275). The tasks before this emergency government admits of no ambiguities for Robespierre: to save the Revolution by whatever necessary means. Still, in the midst of this total war he calls for a substantial program of public education. Citizens are to be created in the midst of the crisis, for only with their emergence in sufficient numbers can coercion be relaxed and then ended. He makes no attempt to mitigate the harshness of the Revolutionary Government. He apologizes for it as a form of patriotism, insisting "Patriotism is ardent by nature" (X, 276). Among the functions of the new government will be "to protect patriotism, even when it errs," and he now sees patriotism to reside only on the Mountain and with the sans-culottes. All the more reason to bolster the few while recruiting others to fill their thinning ranks.

The general policy he proposes, with an uncharacteristic resort to sexual imagery that was bland by eighteenth-century standards, is equilibrium:

> We have to row between two sand banks, weakness and audacity, moderationism and excess; moderationism that is to moderation what impotence is to chastity, and excess that resembles energy in the same way that hydropsy resembles health. (X, 275)

This is to be a government extreme in its methods but not its policies. The report concludes with a call for the heads of specific victims (Custine fils, Biron, Des Brulys, Barthelémy, Lamarlière, Houchard) as well as "strangers, bankers, and other individuals suspected of treason and complicity with the kings leagued against the French Republic." The *Rapport*, made in the name of the Committee of Public Safety and thus having official status, also proposed the improvement of the Revolutionary Tribunal, that special instrument created, along with the Committee, to administer the new legal system of revolutionary justice, augmentation of assistance to wounded soldiers or their surviving dependents, the creation of a commission to aid disabled defenders of *la patrie* (X, 281–82). In Robespierre's mind the Terror is already inextricably associated with the Revolutionary Government, a necessary arm of the new authority: "The Revolutionary Government owes to citizens protection; it owes the enemies of the people nothing but death" (X, 274).

The occasion of this *Rapport* of December 25 was to answer the attacks in the Convention against the increased powers granted to the Committee by the law of December 4 (14 Frimaire).[19] Much of Robespierre's ideological productivity was stimulated by circumstance. His followers expected him to perform when necessary, to help them understand what they had done and what remained to be done. The *Rapport* of December 25 was among Robespierre's most successful *pièces d'occasion*. The report of February 5, 1794 (17 Pluviôse), was a much more ambitious matter, a profound explication of "the principles of political morality that ought to guide the National Convention in the internal affairs of the republic." This *Rapport*, too, was presented in the name of the Committee of Public Safety, but the range of invention and speculation indicates that he probably was given a free hand by his colleagues to explore the meaning of the new course. Here he deals broadly and theoretically with the Terror. "At this remarkable moment of human history," he announces, the Revolution will fix "without appeal the destinies of the world" (X, 356).

In the weeks since his last *Rapport* little has changed. The war continues at home and abroad, as do the factions: "One of these two . . . wants to make liberty a bacchante, the other wants to make her a prostitute" (X, 359). When caught between such enemies, the Revolutionary Government cannot relax its vigilance, Terror cannot be moderated. But there is much more here than the familiar justification by necessity. Terror now seems to Robespierre not merely a defensive weapon but an instrument for realizing the imagined and desired republic. The dreams the revolutionaries inherited from their philosophical predecessors are to be realized with the guillotine. Robespierre sets forth the grandeur of this imagined republic in a series of contrasting abstract nouns:

In our country we want to substitute ethics for egoism, integrity for honor, principles for habits, duties for protocol, the empire of reason for the tyranny of changing taste, scorn of vice for the scorn of misfortune, pride for insolence, elevation of soul for vanity, the love of glory for the love of money, good men for amusing companions, merit for intrigue, genius for cleverness, truth for wit, the charm of happiness for the boredom of sensualism, the greatness of man for the pettiness of the "great," a magnanimous, strong, happy people for an amiable, frivolous miserable people, that is to say all the virtues and all the miracles of the republic for all the vices and all the absurdities of the monarchy. (X, 352)

More perhaps than anything he did, certainly more than anything else he said, Robespierre has never been forgiven for furnishing the Terror with a philosophical and moral pedigree. Yet he was not, despite subsequent slanders, a bloodthirsty man. By contemporaries, at least before his fall when it became so fashionable to decry his excesses and blame all on Robespierre, he was not generally classed among the "drinkers of blood," the "tigers," the "wild beasts," and the "cannibals" who terrorized with gusto and at times with macabre imagination and invention. Only in counterrevolutionary legend was France during the Year II peopled exclusively by monsters and their victims. Contemporaries made a number of precise distinctions, and Robespierre was not counted among the sanguinary who made careers and reputations by killing. He worried about the deeds thrust upon him by history, and he worried in public while others kept their reservations to themselves. He sought for himself and for the Revolution some kind of intellectual and moral respectability. In his quest he crossed an invisible line of what is tolerated. He gave the Terror intellectual form, he harmonized it with the concerns of his age and his class, he took account not only of the *philosophe* and ancient heritage but also the new sensibilities that had been softening assumptions throughout the century. Along with the invasion and purge of the Convention this *apologia* for the Terror was beyond the forgiveness of his colleagues. Their withholding of charity has endured.

The only acceptable explanation for revolutionary violence is necessity. Anything else is seen, sooner or later, as expediency or cruelty or weakness bedecked in the jewels of philosophy, whether political or moral. Such ornaments do not hide hideousness. The lamentable but inescapable spasms of popular violence and revenge, *la volonté punative*, largely spontaneous in outbreak and limited in duration, accompanied all the mass uprisings of the Revolution. Men, or most men, were able to live with these bloody riots, even to endow them with some grandeur, as with the Fall of the Bastille. But the Terror, the official policy of the

Revolutionary Government, with its considerable apparatus of administration and bureaucracy, with its cold-blooded efficiency and long duration, not to mention its deliberate use as a weapon of parliamentary political struggle, presented other problems. Robespierre voiced the concerns of the majority when he celebrated July 14 or August 10; and even his defense of the September Massacres as a force of nature beyond men's manipulation was thought plausible, a ghastly episode but generically related to the earlier urban uprisings that had made and saved the Revolution. But when he provided the instituted violence of the new government with the patina of philosophical propriety and utopian longings, he ceased to speak for most men. Although men were willing to use the Terror or merely tolerate the Terror, they did not want to hear that it was philosophy teaching by example. Self-defense, maybe even in the form of *raison d'état*, would have been more acceptable.

On September 5, 1793, terror was made the order of the day in response to yet another invasion of the precincts of the Convention. This uprising, the so-called Hébertist uprising, took its name from the rabid journalist René Hébert, whose notorious newspaper, *Le Père Duchesne*, had long called for an act to intimidate the parliament. He hoped also to enhance his position at the Commune, for Hébert, along with his odd gift for brilliant yellow journalism, obscene and vituperative language that captured the flavor and power of the talk of the *sans-culottes*, was possessed by enormous political ambitions. The attack itself, it is worth a pause, was carried out despite an eclipse of the sun that threw a great darkness over the militants who gathered at the Hôtel de Ville preparing to march on the Convention. For the men of Paris omens held no significant power or terror.

It is impossible to say how much support there was in the Convention for terror, but the invading crowd was irresistible. The riot was fueled by dearth, by social discontents, by the disastrous and deteriorating war effort, by the failure of the purged Convention to deliver on what were thought promises of social democracy made on June 2. These real grievances, almost daily repeated with much shrillness by Hébert and others, appeared immune to the treatments so far prescribed by the Convention. All could be set right, Hébert and the radicals of the Commune now insisted, by a vigorous government and the guillotine. The Convention capitulated and tried to salvage something out of the confrontation by directing the Terror themselves lest it fall into the hands of the sectional militants and be turned against the *conventionnels*.

Once again insurrection had intervened. That of September 4–5 wedded social democracy, especially its economic component, to the

Revolutionary Government and the Terror. This would prove a profound but turbulent union. Terror was now to be used to accomplish the social ends of the Revolution. Robespierre might announce that the scheme for national education was "the revolution of the poor," but the poor were impatient and hungry and angry and had their own ideas of what constituted their revolution.

At the beginning of the Revolution the dominant economic view had been that of economic liberalism, *laissez-faire*. There was no serious competition to this view at the time, and its proponents were blessed by the good harvests of 1789 and 1790. The question of dearth and bread did not trouble the young Revolution. Throughout 1791 bread prices gradually diminished until by the end of the year they were below two sous per pound, an immense decline. The markets, following the shortages of 1789 that were among the immediate causes of the Revolution, remained full as a result of the good harvests, and what pillaging there was could be attributed to disgruntled aristocrats. The stockpiles of the cities and towns were substantial and in some cases even overflowing. It was easy to believe all these blessings were the result of the economic policies of the Constituent. The illusion was destroyed in 1792 with the menace of war and the rumors of a mediocre harvest. It is dearth, the inheritance and bane of the Revolution, that forced the abandonment of *laissez-faire* economics and the creation of some kind of controlled economy. There were those, like Roland, who continued to cling to the theology of a free market, long after experience had exploded the reality of such views.[20] But for most it was clear that something had to be done: if there was no bread, there would be riots.

The assumption, throughout the Revolution as throughout the *ancien régime*, was that French agriculture was adequate to the population. There was no objective basis for this assumption, but a leap of faith substituted, and made the question of dearth one of distribution and not shortage. Distribution could be regulated.[21] "Dearth is not the result of the lack of grain, because the French soil produces more than is necessary for the nourishment of its inhabitants" (IX, 149). "Dearth can only be attributed to the vices of the laws themselves or their administration." Both causes "have their source in false principles and bad mores" (IX, 110). In Robespierre's orthodox views is inherent the belief that dearth was a political problem; in September of 1793 this meant coercion could feed France.

Subsistances and *lois populaires*, scribbled months earlier in his notebook as necessary to the revolutionary program he envisioned, were now on the agenda. The Terror would, naturally, embrace the food question. The Revolution had reverted to the policies of the monarchy: it was determined to regulate the grain trade. Robespierre, as always, gave the new policy reasons and purpose. "Let us make beneficial laws that tend to equate the price of necessities with the earnings of the industry of the poor," he wrote. "Let us block the flow of the great sources of hoarding, stop the brigandage of the bloodsuckers, and restore order to our finances by reestablishing the credit of our *assignats* and in severely punishing all the prevaricators and all the scoundrels" (V, 344). Shortages and high prices—and here he was in harmony with popular perceptions—he attributed to "the perfidious designs of the enemies of liberty, the enemies of the people" (IX, 275). Hoarders and speculators were counterrevolutionaries. They deserved similar treatment. "The opulent farmers only want to be the bloodsuckers of the people; we will deliver them up to the people themselves" (X, 93). He meant this threat literally: "If we should find too many obstacles to bring the traitors to justice, we shall say to the people, 'Bring them to justice yourselves' " (X, 94).

These fulminations and threats of lynch-law he never acted upon. Here, too, his words were far more ferocious than his deeds. And while he thundered anathemas and proposed vigilante justice, he simultaneously preached sermons on patience and sacrifice, the audience determining the rhetoric. On August 26, 1793, shortly before the Hébertist uprising, he lectured a deputation from Vincennes on the evils of "aristocracy, avarice, and tyranny." This deadly coalition had been abetted by those functionaries who had "too often betrayed their duties," but he specifically forbade the people to riot (X, 82). For all his talk of street violence, he had no intention of letting anyone but the Revolutionary Government enforce the law. The elected deputies of the people would exercise, by representation, their just wrath.

The specific intrusion of economic questions into the program of the Revolutionary Government was beyond Robespierre's control. He proved a reluctant champion of *subsistances*. Bread alone did not make citizens, he argued in a manner reminiscent of his remarks about the food riots of March 10: "despots provide it to their subjects." Bread is less important than "liberty cemented by humane laws" (V, 287). He did not actively support the two laws of the maximum, which fixed price ceilings on foodstuffs and supplies of first necessity—bread, fuel, tallow, for example—and provided the basic legislation for a controlled economy. He remained aloof when the first maximum was decreed on May 4, 1793, equally aloof when the second, more far-reaching law was enacted on September 29, 1793. "The maximum had been," writes the historian Georges Lefebvre, "from the social point of view, the great hope of the *sans-culottes*, a legal expression of the right to life."[22] There is much truth in this judgment. When the Thermidorians removed all controls on the economy and returned to *laissez-faire* economics, the poor were reduced to "atrocious misery."[23] But Robespierre was never able to put economic matters at the center of his ideology or his concerns. Yet if he himself did not propose or actively champion the laws of the maximum, his popular prestige was such that he got considerable credit for what successes there were. "Under Robespierre," said a joiner from section République, Richer, "blood ran and we had bread. Blood does not run today and we don't have any bread. We ought to make some blood flow to get some."[24]

The maximum laws worked best in those areas of France where ferocious men did not hesitate to use force. Where Fouché and Taillefer and Laplanche and Javogues operated, Richer's chilling formula was in effect.[25] In Javogues's department, the Loire, which has been carefully studied, there was intensive repression brought on by chronic shortages. The repression was wielded equally by "the violent, insubordinate terrorist Javogues and the governmental Montagnard, Bassal."[26] In the Loire also, the hated bands of armed men determined to enforce what they considered revolutionary orthodoxy (which often meant confiscations at bayonet point), the so-called *armées révolutionnaires*, operated with some freedom. As the spokesman for the Revolutionary Government, Robespierre found himself administering and defending an economic policy that not only was alienating the countryside but was largely out of his control and created sinister and potentially dangerous satraps.

Even in Paris, where his grip was firmer, there were serious problems. The laws against hoarding, so passionately desired by the *sans-culottes* and verbally supported by Robespierre, were difficult to enforce. Juries were reluctant to send hoarders to the guillotine. The *conventionnels* well remembered that the royal government had infested the market with armed soldiers, and felt uneasy about doing the same. Besides, the new policy had been forced upon them by rioters. Parliamentary opposition took the form of sullen and selective inertia. On the Mountain itself there were resentments that Robespierre found it increasingly difficult to ease. The bourgeois Mountain was not entirely comfortable being associated with the policies of an unruly Paris that might be more beholden to the Commune or sectional militants,[27] some of whom called for economic equality to be realized by massive confiscations of individual wealth, a program that did not draw clear distinctions between the comfortable and the rich as the proposed victims.

The policy of equilibrium Robespierre had fixed upon shortly after June 2 was under increasing strain; the gap between ideology and events was ever widening. Save among the militants of Paris, the controlled economy was unpopular, as controlled economies always are. It did not, like the later and more thoroughgoing (and efficient) War Communism of the Russian Revolution, destroy the French economy. But the controlled economy did create bitterness and dislocations that would take years to disappear, especially in the countryside. More than any other aspect of the Terror, the controlled economy carried the interventions of the Revolutionary Government into the most obscure corners of France. Those who had hitherto escaped the grasp of the new government now found themselves beset by the hated and often undisciplined *armées révolutionnaires*—sometimes legally constituted and empowered, sometimes not—as well as with threats of terrible punishments, acts of confiscation and expropriation, rituals of bizarre cruelty. The common commercial intercourse of daily life was rendered harsh and brutal and filled with deprivation by the war; now Terror was added to hardship. The Revolutionary Government, which Robespierre most completely represented and defended, was blamed.

It is ironic that Robespierre earned more opprobrium than advantage from the economic aspects of the Terror, for he was primarily concerned with other, more strictly political aspects. It was generally more dangerous to speak ill of the Revolution or well of the *ancien régime* than to disregard the food regulations. The most frequently invoked laws "were those concerning sedition in all its forms and embracing opinions as well as acts."[28] Treason, intelligence with the enemy, and rebellion, along with sedition, account for 93 percent of the indictments of the Terror.[29] This was not exclusively, or even significantly, Robespierre's doing. There was little enthusiasm in the Revolutionary Government to use the Terror to work a social revolution, and on this enormous question Robespierre was with the majority of the Mountain, even the majority of his colleagues.

His thinking on economic matters remained frozen, even suffered from contraction, from his speculations of December 1792 and May 1793. Once entered into the Committee of Public Safety, his economic ideas withered and he returned to an earlier manner of self-righteous moralizing coupled with philosophic celebrations of the benefits of poverty. The poor, he insisted, "have never sought an equality of goods" but only "an equality of rights and happiness."[30] Poverty is preferable to wealth because morally superior: "I consider opulence not only as the reward for crime but as the punishment for crime, and I want to be poor in order not to be unhappy" (IX, 488). Although he recognized a necessary connection between material equality and liberty, he was unable to express it except in almost purely moral terms. "The blood of 300,000 Frenchmen has already flowed," he cried with exaggeration, and "the blood of another 300,000 perhaps will have to flow so that the simple laborer will be able to sit in the senate next to the rich grain merchant; so that the artisan can vote in the assemblies of the people alongside the illustrious businessman or the presumptuous lawyer, so that the poor, the intelligent, and the virtuous can assume the dignity of men in the presence of the rich, the imbecile, and the corrupt!" (IX, 498).

On occasion he liked to remind that the Terror had predominantly struck the rich and was thus a weapon of social democracy. "You see," he lectured the Jacobins on November 21 (1 Frimaire), "that the rich have been destroyed to feed and clothe the poor."[31] But if this was his intention, he had only pursued it intermittently and inconsistently and had taken little initiative on the Committee of Public Safety to see that policy ran in this direction.[32] His old obsessions—treasonous generals, hostile factions, irresponsible journalists—were much more important targets than the rich and the hoarders and speculators. His personal involvement in the Terror, as distinct from his ideological justifications, makes this clear.

As early as August 11, 1793, before Terror had become the order of the day, Robespierre denounced the commanders and deplored the delays in General Custine's trial (X, 60–65).[33] The next day he explained to the Convention, in the broadest terms, the lines along which the Terror should be organized, stressing the removal of nobles from the army, the reorganization of the Revolutionary Tribunal to speed deliberations, and punishment for those responsible for the recent massacres in Marseille, Toulon, and the Vendée, as well as the arrest of all suspects and the purification of provincial administration (X, 66–68). This is not a program for social democracy. After the Hébertist uprising put Terror on the agenda, Robespierre did not significantly alter these concerns, but in both the Jacobins and the Convention he tried to restrain those who called for more and still more terror. He opposed his comrade Claude Royer at the Club (X, 87) and withdrew from revolutionary confrontation on September 5 by yielding the president's chair when the Hébertists burst into the Convention. He departed to join the Committee of Public Safety, in the Green Room, and was absent when the decrees of arrest of suspects to purify the revolutionary committees were passed.[34] When he could no longer influence or change the direction of

events, he absented himself, on September 5 as at all the previous uprisings of the Revolution. He was, so far, untainted personally by the
Terror.

His first specific involvement in the Terror, after encouraging efficiency in Custine's trial, concerned the Girondins. On October 3, Amar,
speaking for the other great committee of the Year II, the Committee
of General Security, which was charged with police functions, presented
a report calling for forty-eight of the expelled Girondins to be tried.
Hébert demanded an additional seventy-three victims in his *Père Duchesne* and at the Commune. The slack left by Marat's assassination had
been quickly taken up by Hébert, among others. Amar also wanted a
roll-call vote on his decree, which would once again have forced the
Convention to stand up and be counted, to relive the agony of the June
2 purge. "I don't see the necessity," said Robespierre, "of supposing that
the Convention is divided into two parties, of which the one is composed of friends of the people and the other of conspirators who have
betrayed the people" (X, 134). The motion for a roll-call vote was defeated, and the additional victims were spared. Perhaps in revenge for
this parliamentary setback Billaud-Varenne, who had moved the motion for a roll-call vote, later that same day induced the Convention to
try Marie Antoinette immediately.[35]

This action does not exonerate Robespierre from a share of the guilt
for the Terror. There was certainly an adequate amount to besmirch
all. Certainly his nurtured bitterness toward political foes is one of his
least attractive characteristics, but in his first direct intervention in the
Terror he proposed restraint. He did nothing to save the original group
of purged Girondins. He, in fact, proposed speeding up their trial, although for months he had been in no hurry to see them punished. It
was not, it appears, some impatience for the blood of his enemies that
motivated him. Rather it was that much more cold-blooded motive of
political usefulness or necessity. "Citizens," he introduced his proposals
for truncating the Girondins' trial, "written proofs are weakest of all; it
is the history of the Revolution that condemns them; it is public opinion
that has struck down the conspirators we are about to decree accused"
(X, 136). He proposed that the trial stop as soon as the jury announced
"they are ready to pronounce a verdict" (X, 159).

The deaths of the Girondins might be laid to Robespierre's account,
but not exclusively. It is one of the melancholy facts of revolution that
there is no provision for a loyal opposition; there is only victory or
death. The Girondins were dead when they were purged. Those who
survive the purges of a revolution enjoy the delicious malice of bes-

mirching the reputations of their vanished foes. In Robespierre's case it is his words that created his demonic reputation rather than his deeds, which were considerably less ghastly than those of many colleagues. But he has spoken so often, so well, and so ferociously about the Terror that in doing so he had prepared his own indictment. He was an easy and obvious (and necessary) target. Once again the power of his person reaped its bitter harvest.

On February 5, 1794, long after the Terror had become the main weapon of the Revolutionary Government, Robespierre gave it ideological and theoretical credentials. This was not prudent. The hostile and the skeptical and the cynical have chosen to see his words as no more than an elaborate rhetorical presentation of the dictum that the ends justify the means. Rather, these utterances, which are among his most original, should be thought a hopeless undertaking, a *tour de force* of dialectics and oratorical skill that no one wanted to hear. The revolutionaries did not like to be reminded of the deeds they were doing, and especially these deeds that ran so counter to so much they had grown up with, so much they had appealed to in making the Revolution. Least of all did they welcome an unsought moral and philosophical justification for the Terror.

Montesquieu had accustomed Robespierre's century to seeing certain governments and institutions and laws as expressions or emanations of abstract qualities. He had sought to create a social and political science; he had created a moral one. Republics were inspired by virtue, despotisms by terror. These two were mutually exclusive. Montesquieu's generous spirit got the best of his objectivity: he considered despotism and terror unnatural and hateful. By inference the use of terror was the destruction of virtue. Robespierre, in one of this most original juxtapositions, put *"virtue and terror"* together. The theme runs through his utterances in the period of the Terror, sometimes issuing in slogans— "the Terror is nothing but prompt, severe, inflexible justice" (X, 357)— sometimes in elaborate arguments about the nature of patriotism. Love of country "necessarily includes the love of equality" (X, 353), he insists in a manner that would have been acceptable to Montesquieu. Then he elaborates and conflates. In founding the republic and in consolidating it, all political conduct must tend toward "the maintenance of equality and the development of virtue." Every act that "tends to excite love of country, to purify mores, elevate souls, direct the passions of the human heart toward the public interest, ought to be adopted or established by you" (X, 354). Terror is one such act. As inflexible justice "it is consequently an emanation of virtue, it is less a particular principle than a consequence of the general principle of democracy applied to the most pressing needs of *la patrie*" (X, 357). This is more, far more, than treating Terror as an expedient, an outgrowth of the violence that inescapably accompanies revolutions; nor is it Terror as a domestic self-defense. This is Terror given a theoretical and moral legitimacy that men do not want to admit or be reminded of.

The need to fix by explanation was an obsession with Robespierre, and his justifications of the Terror spring in large part from a Manichean cast of mind whose dualistic inclinations were only sharpened with the Revolution. More and more he saw the Revolution as "the domain of the true and the false, of good and evil."[36] He did not create these polarities any more than he created the Terror. But he gave both frequent and eloquent expression. Long after the historical universe in which he lived and thought, which formed him and which he helped form, had vanished, his words remain to remind men of the deeds of violence they have done, that needed doing. Most prefer to forget.

CHAPTER 11

A Mortal Blow
to Fanaticism

PLATE XIII
(Phot. Bibl. nat. Paris)

IN THE LATE FALL of 1793 the irresistible rush of events, the almost perpetual crisis of the Revolution, kept men from looking too closely at their circumstances, at the contradictions and strains, both inherent and created. Riveting distractions may be one of the definitions of revolutionary activity. Men function by falling back on the familiar and essential. Jean-Victor Colchen, head of a division in the Ministry of Foreign Affairs, a functionary of the *ancien régime* who stayed on to serve both the Revolution and Napoleon faithfully—he was made a count by the latter—had an interview with Robespierre in November and set down his impressions.[1]

Robespierre in power was, externally, the same polite and proper provincial lawyer who had come up to Versailles in the wonderful springtime of 1789. Colchen found him "extremely polite" and dressed "in a suit that came from an earlier time." His hair was carefully combed and powdered. "He called me *Monsieur* and not citizen, and refrained from using the familiar 'you' [*tu*]." Robespierre listened carefully to Colchen's report, without interruption, for forty-five minutes. The division chief remarks, with obvious satisfaction, that he had been heard "with interest and pleasure." A second interview was then arranged, and it, too, passed with politeness, attention, a flattering interest directed to the reporter, and a formal yet easy sociability made a bit charming by the manners of the *ancien régime*. The information thus gathered from Colchen, as well as others, would serve as the basis for Robespierre's formidable *Rapport* of November 17 (27 Brumaire) on "the political situation of the republic" (X, 167–88). The episode also reveals the conscientiousness with which he worked.

Colchen might have concluded, though he does not, that Robespierre was little affected by the burdens he carried, that he had remained the same charming and thoughtful man, if somewhat fastidious in dress and manners, he had always been. He certainly did not look like a revolutionary nor behave like one. Nor did he look like a man passionately, desperately, in search of some comprehensive formula that would draw together all the scattered phenomena of the Revolution, along with the warring factions, into a single whole, the desired *une volonté une* that had eluded him for so many months.

By early December, after nearly five years of struggle, he was in a position to oversee the creation of a republic. Part of the act of creation was returning the government to a constitution, replacing the emergency government he had helped create with the government men had dreamed of, certainly since August 10, perhaps from the beginning of the Revolution. The Revolutionary Government declared by Saint-Just and Robespierre he now conceived as the instrument for the transfer of sovereignty to the people. But the times were not right, the omens were inauspicious. The Revolution had passed, unnoticed by those guiding it, into a juggernaut phase. Its course was determined less and less by the will and reason of men, more and more by *la force des choses*, complex circumstances set in motion and bound to run their course. When this shift occurred is a matter of dispute. From the point of view of Robespierre's revolutionary career, October 12, 1793 is a plausible moment.

Shortly after the Convention had determined to try the Girondin deputies long under house arrest in Paris—those who had fled would be condemned *in abstentia*—and Marie Antoinette, but before the trials began, Fabre d'Eglantine, a poetaster (and one of the creators of the new revolutionary calendar with its heavy natural symbolism), a dandy, a figure of some importance on the left, a friend of Danton's, and, in Robespierre's bitter characterization, "that artisan of intrigue," began unfolding a "Foreign Plot." Much of the plot derived from Fabre's imagination and exaggeration, much of it from his growing fear that he himself would be found out, his thefts and pettifoggery and connivance at the wholesale misuse of funds belonging to the Compagnie des Indes, the old trading company being dissolved by the Revolution, discovered. If caught, he would go to the guillotine.[2] Rather than lose his own head, Fabre was willing to see others killed, and he provided, through his vile fabrications, a good deal of the fatal evidence. His disclosures inaugurated the war between the factions and, more significantly, revealed the Mountain—the sacred Mountain, in the exalted language of the day—as riddled with scandal. These revelations were profoundly shocking, especially to Robespierre. The discovery of corruption on the Mountain deprived the Revolution of virtue. The people, of course, remained virtuous, but their virtue was passive and dependent upon the Montagnard vanguard for realization. Enlightenment and education and the creation of a democratic republic were the necessary means for releasing this vast potential. Now Fabre had undermined the vanguard.

"Not only is virtue the soul of democracy," Robespierre insisted, first echoing and then diverging from Montesquieu, "but it can exist only in such a government." Only in a democracy was one both "a citizen and a member of the sovereign" and thus able to exercise and realize virtue, which "is nothing other than the love of *la patrie* and its laws" (X, 353).[3] Virtue was active and worldly, for it was the "ardent love of liberty" (X, 250). But if those whose historical mission it was to release this ardent love while simultaneously creating the institutions for its expression, the republic, were corrupt, then both reasoning and vision fell to pieces. It was a shattering experience for Robespierre. Only purification of the Mountain would save the situation.

On November 9 (19 Brumaire) he insisted that only those affiliated clubs that had undergone a recent and rigorous purification of membership, an examination of patriotism conducted in public and following the procedures established by the Paris club, be permitted to remain in the Jacobin Society. On November 28 (8 Frimaire) he proposed a public purification of the Club, and then made several proposals establishing the criteria of exclusion: all nobles and all rich men were to be purged. "Can we consider a German baron a patriot?" he asked, singling out Anacharsis Cloots, a Prussian nobleman who had thrown himself into the Revolution and was the prophet of a fervent revolutionary internationalism that had gradually diverged from the official Jacobin line. Cloots was exactly the kind of man Robespierre disliked, and besides he made an easy target. He was politically isolated and not important to Club or Convention. "Can we consider a man," Robespierre continued his denunciation, "who has more than 100,000 livres in rent to be a *sans-culotte?* Can we believe that a man who is seen only with bankers, the counterrevolutionary enemies of France, is a republican?" (X, 248). No Jacobin responded in the affirmative.

Henceforth an enormous amount of Robespierre's time and energy would be taken up with these purifications (*scrutins épuratoire*) at the Club. He was personally involved at every level, spurning the proposed affiliation of neighborhood patriotic clubs that had not undergone an acceptable purification, refusing to cooperate with an unpurified Cordeliers Club, denouncing, expelling, defending, constantly watchful, overseeing the necessary rebuilding of his Society, nursing it again through crisis.

Purge may be inherent in revolutions. It was in the French Revolution. The ardor, the danger, the moral fervor and exaltation, all contributed to silence or overwhelm any spirit of compromise or accommodation. There was no room for even a loyal opposition. So it had been with the Jacobins from the beginning of the Revolution. The preamble of the first rules drawn up by the Society made clear the basis of membership and the intolerance of divergence. "Fidelity to the constitution, the duty to defend it, respect for and submission to all the powers that it will establish" were "the first laws imposed on those who would be admitted to these societies." Members were required to have (and show) a "love of equality and this profound feeling for the rights of man" that called one "to the defense of the weak and the oppressed."[4]

Those who joined not only accepted these conditions but tacitly announced their desire for exclusiveness. In the early years of the Society the expelled, who usually left on their own initiative, set up rival clubs of their own that were as exclusive as the Jacobins, if not more so, or joined clubs that were exclusive.[5] The Jacobins had not undergone, until 1793, the rigors of expulsion and exclusion. Earlier membership purges had been accomplished through schism and secession.

The theoretical justification for the purification had been brilliantly formulated on November 13, 1792, in another context, when Saint-Just opened the debates on the King's trial with his maiden speech. His novel thesis was that Louis was an alien amidst the French. He belonged neither to the nation nor to the body politic, and was certainly not of the people. He thus had no claims on the protection given citizens nor any of the civil liberties and rights, including the right to a trial, that pertained only to citizens. This highly original break with the tradition of social-contract theory, by which most of the political analysis of the century was conducted, established a basis for exclusion that would work as well for lapsed Jacobins as for the King. Those who were not ardent patriots had put themselves outside society and outside the Society. They must be purged lest they pollute. On November 26 Merlin de Thionville proposed to his colleagues the catechism for purification:

> What were you in 1789?
> What have you done till 1793?
> What was your fortune in 1789?
> What is it now?
> If your fortune has increased, how do you explain it?
> What have you done for the Revolution?
> Have you ever signed a counterrevolutionary petition?
> If you are an administrator, journalist or representative of the people, have you devoted your efforts only to the service of liberty?[6]

Nor was a man's private life to be left out of account. This, too, would be revealed and reckoned. "I want us to know each other," an unnamed Jacobin told his colleagues, "as I know the five fingers of my hand. I want each member to be able to say, looking at his neighbors, there is an honest man, a good patriot, or there is an intriguer we must expel."[7] The Manichean cast of mind so well represented by Robespierre was not his alone. There were now thought to be only two kinds of Jacobins, and by implication of Frenchmen: "those who were irrevocably suspect and those whose publicly challenged records qualified them as exemplars of republicanism."[8] It is noteworthy that the discovery of the two was to be made in public.

Robespierre himself underwent this public scrutiny and emerged with his reputation unsullied. In all, more than four hundred Jacobins were subjected to the rigors of scrutiny in Paris, whose rituals were carefully reported to all the provincial affiliated societies, for they were expected to imitate and emulate. It was not specifically stated, but Robespierre assumed, and so presumably did others, that his own was an exemplary career and others could and should be judged against his achievements and self. There was thus created a politics of revolutionary biography and autobiography.[9] The Jacobins would prove their worthiness by approximating their leader's character and acts. Robespierre's insistence on his exemplary character as a revolutionary model had given him prestige and influence. Now his established reputation would give him supreme authority in the purges: he himself would be the final judge of revolutionary worthiness. His insistence on being scrutinized first, and in a sense not merely before the Jacobins but before the entire nation, indicates the ritualistic nature of the purges. Yet for all the emphasis "on cleansing, sweeping, purging, purifying, and policing," only a dozen Jacobins failed to pass scrutiny. Robespierre, in fact, was unexpectedly tolerant toward his friends and comrades, a fatal benevolence in revolution. Those he did not defend, the few unvirtuous, were expelled from the Society, and their insignificant numbers has led the historian of the process to speculate that expulsion may not be the only or even the most important goal of these purifications and purges.[10] "Instead, the rites promoted by Robespierre in the fall of 1793 served, throughout the Terror, to involve the Jacobins in an ongoing demonstration of the standards of republican behavior by subjecting them to a public scrutiny by their colleagues."[11]

This use of ritual to call attention to oneself as politically and morally worthy, while simultaneously suggesting one's enemies are corrupt and counterrevolutionary, is the formalization of habits familiar to the Revolution. Robespierre had long paraded his virtue for political advantage, had long made invidious comparisons between himself and his less austere opponents. Now not only was this self-righteousness generalized and regularly enacted at the Jacobins, but it assumed an educational purpose. He had insisted, when presenting Lepeletier's educational proposals to the Convention, that here was the Revolution's most important work. Now he could extend this belief. In the purges he was educating by example. His lectures on virtue and republicanism continued, but increasingly his pedagogical bent depended upon presenting himself as exemplary. His every word and act, conducted in public, carried an increasingly heavy symbolic burden. He was a living emblem of

the Revolution: an assertion and posture that was widely shared by his comrades, by some of his colleagues, and by a large number of the people. Not only did he speak more often of self than he had earlier, but his public life completely absorbed the private man.

The politics of revolutionary biography, the purifications, assumed there were two Mountains: one "personified in Robespierre" and the other guided only by "the lowest passions."[12] At around the same time that Robespierre insisted on a dichotomy on the Mountain, he also stressed a split in the people. It was an article of faith for him, and for the Mountain, that the people was not a faction, could not "in any way belong to a faction" (IX, 217). This axiom came from Rousseau but was indispensable to Robespierre's ideology. Those who were enemies of the Revolution, of the people, were factions, self-interested parts of the whole. But in late 1793 the seamless fabric began to show rents. One of the justifications for the Terror now became the need to exercise it against the gangrened portion of the people: "One leads the people by reason, the enemies of the people by terror" (X, 356). The appalling spectacle of the revolutionary vanguard of the Mountain riddled with backsliders was a warning that the people whom they represented also lagged behind their leaders. The mass of the *sans-culottes* "remained very much behind the political views of those who wanted to be their leaders."[13] The same dualism that troubled the Mountain existed in the streets of Paris. The sections wavered between "terrorist repression or the appeal to the reconciliation of classes."[14] It was impossible to build a coherent policy on such quicksand. At the outset of his career Robespierre had appealed to the people, over the heads of the deputies. Then he had assumed the Jacobins were representative of the people. Now he discovered, to his horror, that both people and Mountain were split along the same lines. The people had been successfully and successively wooed by demagogic journalists, sectional militants, members of the Committee of Public Safety, street-corner orators, hawkers of social schemes, would-be dictators (both military and civilian), and alienated cranks. None had held them for very long, but Robespierre had been and remained the most faithful and persistent of all these lovers. Now even his attentions were unreciprocated.

Robespierre saw the Revolution's enemies as belonging to one of three groups: moderates, extremists, and a new and shocking category, the *pourris* (the putrid or morally corrupt). This recent political group was not strictly a faction, like the others. Graft and peculation proved attractive to all shades of opinion. Roughly, the extremists stood to Robespierre's left, had important spokesmen in the Convention and on the Committee of Public Safety (especially Collot d'Herbois and Billaud-Varenne), and had considerable strength in the Paris Commune. The moderates stood to his right, were similarly represented by important revolutionaries (most conspicuously Danton and his considerable number of friends), and had the significant strength on the Committee of General Security. The extremists wanted to intensify the Terror and perhaps even organize a "third revolution" to their own advantage, completing the work they considered left undone by August 10 and June 2. The moderates wanted an end to the Terror, or at least a modification, and a quick return to constitutional government. Each persuasion, it is important to remember, was led or defended by veterans of the Revolution, men with solid credentials, men Robespierre had fought with and trusted, or at least tolerated. To him it mattered not that "one group or the other be victorious, since both systems," he insisted, "will equally destroy the republic" (X, 313). Here speaks the government man, who sees no difference between right and left, between *ultras* and *citras*, as they were called: he saw only disequilibrium, critics and competitors. The putrids were equally dangerous, but not for the same reasons.

The right and the left and the putrids tore at the social fabric, attacking and undermining the Revolutionary Government and the popular front on which it ultimately depended. Aside from their capacity for destruction, the three groups had in common contempt not only for the emergency government, but for religion. Their desire to dechristianize France was one of the few points of agreement. Robespierre thought all his enemies could be attacked on this issue, faction could be transcended and unity achieved, first in the spiritual realm (which was especially significant to him) and then in the mundane. In addition, the synthesis he envisioned, besides being his most ambitious scheme for reconciliation, for the reestablishment of equilibrium, was also very close to his heart.

For all his radicalism directed against the institutions and ideas and men of the *ancien régime*, Robespierre was extremely reluctant to tamper with basic institutions. The monarchy and aristocracy deserved destruction. Otherwise he believed in regeneration, and especially now when the new revolutionary growths were so fragile: "The republic has been proclaimed rather than established." An attack on Christianity would "put new arms into the hands of malevolence and fanaticism" (V, 118-19). It was better to be tolerant: the politic was also desirable. The old church, he insisted, would wither away with the apostosy of its devotees. He wanted to stop the dechristianizers. The Committee of Public

Safety, or at least its majority, was in general agreement. It was embarrassing for the Revolutionary Government to have representatives on mission in the provinces, such as Fouché, stripping churches of their ornaments (which he ostentatiously sent to the Convention as a general might have sent captured flags), banning religious ceremonies, committing sacrilege, conducting a campaign to compel clergymen to marry, adopt a child, support an elderly person, or resign, when these were not the policies of the government. In the town of Nevers Fouché had celebrated a Feast of Brutus in the local church and had placed above the cemetery the motto "Death Is an Eternal Sleep."[15] And he was not alone. Another government agent, André Dumont, at Abbeville, conducted similar rites in the local church and by the end of the month was in the substantial town of Amiens, dominated by its great cathedral and a long history of piety. There were other outbreaks as well.[16]

Robespierre was charged, probably at his own request, with drawing up the Committee's policy of moderation in religious matters. "The religious prejudices, which the people adore, should not be attacked head-on," he wrote. "Time must prepare the people, slowly wean them from prejudice" (VIII, 26). This early view, which he several times reiterated (V, 270; X, 235–36, for example), remained throughout the Revolution. He was able to persuade the Committee that it was the correct view and drafted their circular letter to be sent to all agents on mission. "Accept this truth, one does not control men's consciences," the letter lectured. Some men were weak in understanding, unable to accomplish "the rapid passage from superstition to truth." These citizens were not to be punished: "They are the ill who must be prepared for healing by reassuring them; one makes them fanatics by forcing a cure on them."[17]

In fact, his personal views went well beyond the expediency expressed for the Committee. Robespierre imagined a revolutionary deism that would outbid the dechristianizers, seduce the believers away from their Christian superstitions, give the masses an object for faith, create a civic devotion, and transcend the contradictions of the Revolution. He was not the only revolutionary to imagine using the resonances and rituals of Christianity for a revolutionary purpose, but his turning to such potentially risky means is the result of his failure to close the ranks of the revolutionaries by more traditional means.

On November 10 (20 Brumaire)—at approximately the same time the purifications began at the Jacobins—there was celebrated in Notre Dame cathedral in the center of Paris a festival of reason. The festival had been preceded by a remarkable session of the Convention held three days earlier, at which the bishop of Paris, Gobel, had divested himself of his office and insignia under considerable pressure from the Commune radicals and dechristianizers. The festival that was planned was to have been celebrated outdoors, in the old Palais Royal—the palace of the Duc d'Orléans, renamed Equality Palace—but at the insistence of Pierre-Gaspard Chaumette, who had changed his given name to Anaxagoras, a Christian thief hanged for his republican sentiments and eventually sanctified (for Chaumette loved to blaspheme), and it was transfered to the venerable cathedral. Chaumette and his comrades were determined to be provocative. Among the articles of his dechristianizing faith was that women were the churchgoers and went to breathe "the cadaverous odor of the temples of Jesus." They would continue to do so even after the churches had become homes of the new cult.[18] Sacrilege he considered one of the few useful weapons against such devotion.

During the three days separating Gobel's resignation from the ceremony, Notre Dame was decorated with an artificial mountain, atop which stood a temple of philosophy ornamented with four sages of the Revolution. Nearby burned a torch of truth: the scene was surrounded by young girls in white robes, crowned by flowers. The figure of Reason was portrayed by an actress. Music was provided by Gossec to words by Chénier.[19] The celebrants, following the rituals at the cathedral, went in procession to the Tuileries, where the Convention was sitting awaiting them, entered the hall (led by Chaumette), and reenacted their ritual for the deputies, some of whom accompanied the procession back to Notre Dame. Robespierre took no part in the debates or the planning or the ceremony itself. He had been deeply offended by the festival, with its strongly provocative tone, pagan flavor, and calculated mockery of Christianity. He may even have felt some satisfaction at the rain that marred the day.[20]

The atheists and the dechristianizers (Robespierre did not scruple to distinguish them) he loathed equally.[21] "To preach atheism is only a way of absolving superstition and accusing philosophy. The war declared on divinity is but a diversion that favors royalty" (X, 361). The Mountain, as the instrument of a special providence, must fulfill its mission. It had proclaimed its Declaration of the Rights of Man "in the presence of the Supreme Being," and "this vague pseudonym of God" was more than a prudent verbal compromise for Robespierre; it was a Montagnard declaration of faith.[22] The dechristianizers were militant atheists. Atheists were aristocratic (or so they had been under the *ancien régime*). Aristocrats were counterrevolutionary. Thus did he syllogize. But neither his personal power nor his support was supreme.[23] As with all his political maneuvers, he left nothing to chance. On November 21 he denounced atheism as aristocratic. The next day the Commune, ignoring or challenging him, ordered all Paris churches closed. Robespierre jotted in his notebook: "Destroy the decree of the municipality that forbids the mass and vespers. They do not have the right. It is going to cause trouble."[24]

He was unwilling to back down. The Committee of Public Safety had no taste for a confrontation with the dechristianizers at the Commune: Robespierre did. He who prevents the saying of mass, he threw down the gauntlet, "is more fanatical than he who says mass" (X, 196). He slandered the dechristianizers as recent revolutionaries who created "trouble and discord" only to win "a false popularity." "By what right" did they "disturb freedom of worship in the name of liberty, and . . . attack fanaticism by a new fanaticism?" And, in a fine image, he added: "Why are they allowed thus to toy with the dignity of the people, and to attach idiotic noisemakers to the very scepter of philosophy?" (X, 196). "Under the pretext of destroying superstition, they want to make atheism itself into a kind of religion." It was not the task of the Revolution to look into the beliefs of others. "The Convention is not a maker of books, an author of metaphysical systems. It is a political and popular body, charged with seeing that not only the rights but also the character of the French people is respected" (X, 196). Besides, the policy endangered the Revolution. Such provocations in Paris, fueled in part by the anger felt at the counterrevolution in the Vendée, being fought in the name of Throne and Altar, would not help win that grueling civil war. Quite the contrary. The Vendée was "the last refuge" of religious fanaticism, not its cause. "It is the politics, the ambition, the treasons of those who formerly governed, that have created the Vendée" (X, 195), not the saying of mass. Counterrevolution was the spawn of irreligion, not religion. "True religion," he argued, "consists in punishing, for the general welfare, those who undermine society" (VII, 72). His was neither an irenic nor a Christian theology.

Robespierre was less inclined than many to see religious fanaticism as the most serious problem confronting the Revolution, perhaps because his own life had been so little touched by religious upheavals. He seems not to have suffered the wrenching and scarring experience of having lost his faith, for his was essentially a secular character whose spiritual needs could be, and were, fulfilled from other sources. The malicious view of him as a priest, made by some contemporaries and taken up by Michelet, is metaphorically striking but not accurate. He was much more a pedagogue than a priest, and his views were decidedly profane. He was anticlerical, but less vehemently so than many contemporaries; and although he may have talked of the need for religion in society with less cynicism than had Voltaire, there is no significant evidence that he was much moved by religion, had any religious vocation, or aspired to rule through religion. His synthesis of the deism of his century (and his youth and young manhood), although deeply important to him, sprang from other sources than a traditional religious sensibility.

Circumstances in Year II fixed attention on religious questions. In Robespierre's case these questions had already intruded into politics. He had first revealed the depth of his feeling at a meeting of the Jacobins, on March 26, 1792. In the midst of the war debates, deliberately goaded by Guadet, who provided but the final exasperation inflicted by the flamboyant, provocative, and sophisticated irreligion of several of his opponents, Robespierre took the offensive, pouring out his unrehearsed profession of faith:

> . . . to invoke the name of providence and to express an idea of the eternal being who essentially influences the destiny of nations, who seems to me to watch over the French Revolution most especially, is not an ill-considered idea but a sentiment of my heart, a sentiment that is necessary to me.

He would not be restrained from pursuing so embarrassing a topic before the silent, even shocked Jacobins:

> How could it not be necessary to me who, abandoned to all the passions and to all the vile intrigues in the Constituent Assembly, surrounded by so many enemies, yet sustained myself? Alone with my soul, how could I sustain labors that were beyond human capacity if my soul had not been exalted? (VIII, 234–35)[25]

Then, realizing he had been carried away by his *cri de cœur*, he retreated to the safer ground of analysis, insisting that he called "providence what others would perhaps rather call chance; but the word providence," he could not resist making all too clear, "is closer to my feelings" (VIII, 235). The damage had been done. A generation earlier, when Rousseau had answered Voltaire on the same subject, many already thought such declarations unfashionable and dubious.[26] Robespierre's outburst became at once, and has remained, a subject of mockery to his enemies, embarrassment to his friends. He himself was aware these views caused some consternation among his comrades. "Some will perhaps say," he explained in a later profession of faith, "that I have a narrow mind, that I am a man of prejudices, that I am a fanatic." But the "idea of a superior being [*grand être*] who watches over oppressed innocence and who punishes triumphant crime, is completely popular. The people, the unfortunate, applaud me. If I have critics, they will be from the rich and the guilty" (X, 196).

His views on religion that he believed so representative of the masses he had acquired before the Revolution. His eclectic deism was unoriginal, literary, refined, abstract, private, intellectual, and had no social dimension. None of these characteristics is popular. He came to Versailles believing in God the Creator, in providence, in the immortality of the soul, and that religion, so long as it was not fanatical, was not harmful to individuals and probably necessary for society. He considered the priesthood socially parasitic and dependent upon superstition, thought that the church's wealth rightly belonged to the people, and considered the social gospel the most worthy part of Christianity. The God of this youthful deism owed a good deal to the ongoing critique of religion carried on by the *philosophes*, whose concerns he had imbibed and embraced. But above all it owed a good deal to Rousseau's Savoyard Vicar, an important character in his treatise on education, *Emile*.[27]

Robespierre's deism underwent so enormous a transformation during the Revolution that it scarcely resembled that preached by Rousseau. From a derivative deism he arrived at an original conception of God. He was no theologian, but what his conception lacked in philosophical shrewdness or consistency was made up for by the ardor and ferocity, only slightly mollified by compassion, of his God of revolutions, his God of the Mountain. "My God," he proudly proclaimed, "is he who created all men for equality and for happiness; he who protects the oppressed and who exterminates tyrants. My cult is that of justice and humanity!" (V, 117). His God is a "director of nations, and a patron of the Revolution . . . a consolation in trouble, and the inspiration of a work-a-day life."[28] The attributes of this curious deity are liberty, virtue, and justice (X, 482), the very attributes of the Revolution. He is a God who easily would have survived a purification scrutiny at the Jacobins, who would have sat on the Mountain. He is, Robespierre insists, a popular God, a God of the people, because a natural God. The Christian God is the artifice of priests who "have created God in their image. They have made him jealous, capricious, rapacious, cruel, implacable." The priests are to "morality what charlatans are to medicine" (X, 196).

A return to principles perverted over the centuries, a return to what is natural, is what Robespierre advocates. Atheism, he connects the theme to social and economic considerations, is not only aristocratic (X, 196), it is a luxury reserved for the wealthy. "What part of society is detached from all religious ideas? The rich." What part is most attached?: "the weakest and the least well-off citizens." The irony of employing a catechistic format in denouncing religion was surely unintentional, a habit he never bothered to escape. The church, once divested of priests and priestcraft, should then return to "the moral teaching of the son of Mary," which he thought compatible with the ideals of the Revolution. The son of Mary, he continues, preached "anathemas against tyranny and against pitiless opulence, and [gave] consolation to misery and to despair itself" (V, 120).

It is customary to see Robespierre's deism as a variation on that preached by Rousseau's Savoyard Vicar. This is possibly true only of his early deistic speculations; by the time of the festival of the Supreme Being, Rousseau's irenic theology had been overwhelmed by a more severe vision, which more resembled the embattled determination (and ferocity) of some of the primitive Christian communities. He was closer to the Donatist schismatics of Roman North Africa than the Savoyard Vicar. "If God did not exist," Robespierre reiterated, "it would be necessary to invent him" (X, 196). His own invention, carrying a "torch of philosophy," had banished all the "ridiculous phantoms that the ambitions of priests and the politics of kings have commanded us to obey in the name of heaven." In place of these clerical absurdities he offered "the sublime and touching doctrine of the virtue and equality that the son of Mary taught" (V, 117). He did not, in interpreting the meaning and nature of the social gospel, go quite so far as Hébert, who declared Jesus was a *sans-culotte*, but he came close. The tenets, the only necessary tenets, of his religion were a belief in a revolutionary God and the immortality of the soul: the former would lead the patriots to victory; the latter was "a constant call to justice" (X, 452).

Robespierre did not preach his rebellious deism in the wilderness. On religious matters, too, he gave voice to deep and important and widespread feelings, both on and off the Mountain, and he presented his contemporaries not only with a highly original synthesis of hitherto separate themes, but with himself as votary and, simultaneously, embodiment of the new cult. "Man," wrote the Montagnard Levasseur, who did not much like Robespierre although he was in many ways a representative Jacobin, "cannot be republican if he is not first and foremost moral and religious."[29] His religious ideas were not an aberration but a consistent concern. Moral regeneration, moral revolution, the necessary remolding of men, these driving passions seemed to Robespierre to have no chance of realization unless somehow enmeshed in a providential scheme.

Having made God in his own and the Mountain's image, Robespierre adored him. The exaltation, the occasional rapture, the energy, the intensity that he felt and that made possible his continuous and superhuman struggle, came not from himself but from some transcendental force. Like the prophets of the Old Testament, he saw himself as but the chosen (and even unworthy) vessel. He was the instrument of a revolutionary, divine providence, a juxtaposition of his own making. And he was a willing instrument. There was no question of his sincerity. As in all he did and said, Robespierre was transparent. This total lack of pretense was one of the sources of his hold over contemporaries. All his earlier metaphors of self were summed up in his revolutionary God. It only remained for him to explain this vision to his comrades.

In an extraordinary speech on 18 Floréal (May 7), Robespierre proclaimed the cult of the Supreme Being to the Convention.[30] Along with the two speeches of 20 Prairial (June 8), this oration is the fullest presentation of his religious ideas.[31] "This beautiful morality" was "the only rule by which public reason separates the defenders from the enemies of humanity," he announced. A revolutionary people needed more than "the uncertain favors of fortune," more than "the law of the strongest or the most cunning" to sustain it (X, 456). The cult of the Supreme Being would "deliver a mortal blow to fanaticism." All fictions would evaporate "before the Truth, all stupidities fall before Reason." Without "constraint, without persecution, all the sects should be obliterated in the universal religion of Nature" (X, 457). The festival of the Supreme Being followed soon afterward.

It was "the most brilliant and popular of all the festivals of the Revolution."[32] Robespierre himself was elated, enthusiastic, rapturous. The great day had been carefully planned by Jacques-Louis David, and the guillotine was thoughtfully dismantled for the ceremony.[33] "Joy radiated" from Robespierre, writes his friend Vilate.[34] From the vantage point of Vilate's room, Robespierre "was astonished at the enormous crowd that covered the Tuileries garden." He was able to eat little, absorbed as he was in staring out the window at the spectacle below, "plunged in the drunkenness of enthusiasm." His entire conversation consisted of a single emotional outburst that Vilate recorded: "There is the most interesting part of mankind. O Nature, how sublime and delicious is your power! How the tyrants will pale at the very idea of this festival!"

Robespierre's address to the enormous crowd, probably as little heard beyond the first several ranks of spectators as Peter the Hermit's call to crusade, was similarly inspired.[35] Like all his great speeches, it had been carefully written out. "French Republicans," he shouted out his exordium to the multitude, "it is for you to purify the earth that has been soiled, and to recall to the Earth Justice which has been banished. Liberty and virtue spring together from the breast of the divinity; neither can live among men without the other" (X, 482). Not only did the educated, the connoisseurs of oratory, appreciate the speech, so too did the people. His eloquence continued to know no social barriers. A certain Birbal, of section Guillaume-Tell, reports that he saw "simple citizens shed tears, so much were they struck by the eternal truths that God had put into the hearts of all men of goodwill" and which Robespierre articulated.[36]

The day of 20 Prairial, unlike the rain-marred ceremonies of the celebration of the cult of reason, was of unparalleled beauty, such that might tempt a man given to musing about a special providence to see the hand of the Deity. As president of the Convention, Robespierre had the first place in the procession, carried not one but two bunches of flowers, and alone of the celebrants wore a suit of dark blue: the other deputies wore cornflower-blue coats. But for all the splendor of pageantry and weather, the day did not pass without blemish. Accusations, sometimes delivered in a stage whisper, reached Robespierre's ears: "There's the dictator! He wants all the people's attention fixed on him! It's not enough to be king! He wants to be God!"[37] Robespierre later accused Bourdon de l'Oise of being responsible for "the grossest sarcasms and the most indecent statements" during the ceremony.[38] Yet despite such flaws he thought 20 Prairial one of the greatest days of the Revolution. In his enthusiasm he elevated the festival to the incomparable level of July 14, 1789, and August 10, 1792: along with the Fall of the Bastille and the overthrow of the monarchy, the celebration of the Supreme Being was one of the founding acts of the Revolution. It completed Robespierre's Trinity. There had been no fighting on 20 Prairial, and it was the only one of the great revolutionary days in which he had participated.

The festival "left on France a profound impression of calm, of happiness, of wisdom, and of moral goodness." For the few hours when the people were assembled in "this sublime gathering," no one "would have believed that crime still existed on this earth." But Robespierre's elation soon yielded to pessimism. As the celebrants dispersed and returned to their mundane activities, as the people dissolved into its component parts, Robespierre's habitual distrust of individuals and their motives returned. He had always considered social man, man in the abstract, preferable to the individual, had always contrasted the people with egoists. Quite uncharacteristically for his century, he believed humanity was realized in the collectivity, not in individuality. He believed a qualitative change took place when individuals became a people.

Furthermore, the festival had "advanced the final hour of tyranny by a half century," by showing the Revolution to the world "in all the magnificence of its heavenly beauty" (X, 561). This judgment appeared correct. The conservative and intelligent Swiss journalist Mallet du Pan wrote that the festival "produced an extraordinary effect outside France. Men truly believed that Robespierre was going to close the abyss of the Revolution."[39] "It is not religion you have created," gushed the *robespierriste* Claude-François de Payan, who was not the only convert, "but simple, eternal principles." Who, he asked, would "not prefer these principles, simple and eternal as Nature herself, to a mysterious, inexplicable cult? a just and benevolent God to the God of the priests . . . ?"[40] The answer, provided by history, was a great many.

The cult of the Supreme Being did not transcend or unify. It did not even restore some working semblance of the popular front on which the Revolutionary Government had originally rested and which was its only legitimate support. Without such a social base the emergency government had only the Terror to sustain itself. But only momentarily were Robespierre's words and vision, interpreted by David's genius, able to reinvigorate the Revolution. He had lost none of his exceptional hold over contemporaries, his words still worked alchemically on his auditors, but the gap between an increasingly grim reality of murderous strife and envisioned regeneration was widening. Religious symbols and resonances were still potent, even if their purpose was secular. The deism of Robespierre's century, the deism of his youth especially, was not only a last attempt to compromise with Christianity, but at the same time an attempt to preserve the morality of religion with none of its more "superstitious" aspects. Deism legitimated, so to speak, the strong current of anticlericalism that ran so uninterruptedly through the thought of the time. Deism would preserve the ethical basis of Christianity by giving it rational form and simultaneously eliminating the priests and their church. Robespierre's deism expressed the moral universe of the Revolution in the Year II. The Supreme Being was more than a metaphor. It was the Revolution in the sense that adoration of the Supreme Being was adoration of the Revolution. It was not, however, adoration that was needed or lacking.

Once embarked on, Terror now became the essential and indispensable weapon of the Revolutionary Government. Reconciliation could not be accomplished by ritual. Only for a brief moment did the festival of the Supreme Being interrupt the political trials of spring 1794. The dismantled guillotine was almost immediately erected. Some even thought the festival a cynical attempt to wash away the blood of so many important or admired revolutionary rivals, Danton and Hébert chief among them, who had been executed.[41] It is doubtful that this was Robespierre's purpose. Not only was such hypocrisy out of character, but the political trials followed a hideous logic of their own. The Revolutionary Government had become the most centralized and unchallenged and powerful that France had ever seen: no one was immune from its Terror, and it could not tolerate acquittal. There remained no buffers between this terrible power and its victims.

No one wanted to end the Terror except on his own terms. All who called for an end to the killing meant that they would agree to a halt only if their safety and vengeance were assured. Dufourny, at the Jacobins, put it well. If the Terror did not continue, the Convention would be "inundated by petitions from those related to the victims demanding the arrest and death of their persecutors."[42] If the Mountain for a moment relaxed its grip, it would be exterminated by a coalition of its enemies and those it had spared. This is precisely the coalition that eventually brought down the *robespierristes*. Robespierre was a cautious man. His policy of equilibrium was not merely dictated by considerations of political expediency; it sprang as well from his character, from self. One false move would finish him and with him any hopes he had for a return to normal government. If there was to be an amnesty, its prelude would have to be not the festival of the Supreme Being, but the elimination of all those "who were too heavily compromised" by the Terror and were hence committed to its continuation lest they themselves have to pay for their excesses.[43]

Not only did the Supreme Being not bring the Terror any nearer an end, it brought Robespierre closer to his own death. His religious views and policies were seen by many as committing the Revolution to a state religion, and the deliberate (and malicious) neglect the Convention—as well as the two earlier assemblies—had shown for Catholicism was ample evidence that having gotten rid of one religion, men did not want another in its place. Robespierre misread the signs, but increasingly his gaze failed to reach beyond the Mountain. The Committee of General Security, long hostile to the Committee of Public Safety, was especially concerned. Its Protestant members feared a revival of Catholicism, while the skeptics and Voltaireans on the Committee, such as Marc-Guillaume-Albert Vadier, detested Robespierre's "fanaticism."[44] His enemies on the right and on the left remained and, although cowed by the Terror, were growing restive.

The festival of the Supreme Being was the apotheosis of Robespierre's career. Two days afterward was passed the dreadful law of 22 Prairial (June 10), which announced the final, most murderous spasm of the Terror.

It is arguable that the two terrorist episodes in the Revolution before 1794—August 1792 and spring 1793—were tied to the national peril, the war. These convulsions could be seen, and often were by both participants and subsequent observers, as the domestic reflex of national trauma. Repression at home in the face of defeat abroad is a familiar enough phenomenon. This explanation simplifies reality without parodying it. The same argument cannot, however, serve for 1794. During the so-called Great Terror, which began on June 10, the military situation was not deteriorating. The Great Terror coincides with an improving war. The other significant difference between the Great Terror and those earlier outbursts is that it was not spontaneous, not a popular expression of the instinct for self-defense and the need to punish those feared. The Great Terror is not another grim episode of *la volanté punative* that animates the masses: it is the official policy of government.

The triumph of the Revolutionary Government, won through its efficiency and the successful elimination of many enemies and critics, gave an institutional structure to the revolutionary habit of putting things in the most stark and uncompromising way. Since 1789 the men of the Revolution had seen their work as a life-or-death struggle between good and evil, the Revolution and the counterrevolution. Robespierre's cast of mind did not create but rather reflected and expressed the dualism. But in the midst of the inexorable workings of the machinery of Terror, on May 23 and 24 (4–5 Prairial), two singularly inept assassination attempts were made, against Robespierre and Collot d'Herbois. The assassins themselves were unlikely characters. Aimée-Cécile Renault, the twenty-year-old daughter of a stationer, was caught carrying a couple of small knives near the Duplays'. Henri Admiral, a former servant, unable to get close enough to Robespierre to carry out his obsession, turned upon Collot. Both were guillotined, plots were imagined though not proved, and young Renault went to her death clothed in the red shirt of a parricide, which had also been worn by Charlotte Corday, the assassin of Marat. The ill-prepared and unrelated attempts set off "a kind of generalized social panic" not closely related to "the reality of struggles, but [rather to] a Manichean ideology."[45]

The fear of assassination, long a stock image borrowed from Stoicism, became more than literary with the murders of Lepeletier and Marat. On the Mountain these martyrdoms were remembered and often invoked. When the attempts of Prairial were made, Robespierre, in the name of the Committee of Public Safety, wrote to Saint-Just, who was then away on mission: "Liberty is exposed to new dangers. The factions are bestirring themselves with an even more alarming character than before . . . an insurrection in the prisons, which could have broken out yesterday, the intrigues that we saw when Hébert was alive, are now combined with assassination attempts . . . against the members of the Committee of Public Safety; the other factions, or rather the factions that have always existed, redouble their audacity and perfidy. We fear an aristocratic uprising, fatal to liberty."[46] Here are all the fears and hysteria and imagined plots of the earlier panics of the Revolution. This official letter, from responsible men of government to one of their colleagues, might have been written by some ignorant and incendiary street orator attempting to inflame the mob.

The response to the assassination attempts, the law of 22 Prairial, "looks like the result of a violent terrorist thrust which, originating with the *sans-culottes*, had mastered the government."[47] But there was nothing of the sort. The Great Terror was cold-blooded, legalized, ritualized, bureaucratic, administered with gruesome efficiency. The new law abolished the old immunity that had hitherto protected deputies from the guillotine.[48] Couthon, expressing his own views and probably those of the Committee, declared: "It is not a question of providing some examples but of exterminating the implacable satellites of tyranny or of perishing with the Republic."[49] Robespierre was more coldly procedural in his panic: "A man is brought before the Revolutionary Tribunal. If there are material proofs against him, he is condemned; if there are no material proofs, in this case witnesses are called" (X, 486). Robespierre and the Committee had taken fright.[50]

There were 1,376 victims of the Great Terror (from June 10 to July 27). Panic wed to governmental centralization made it possible and marked a significant shift in the nature of revolutionary violence.[51] On March 13 (23 Ventôse) "for the first time in over five years, central authority asserted itself, and instead of yielding to insurgents put them in jail." The Revolution would henceforth "be the work of government, not an upheaval from below."[52] The dictatorship of the Revolutionary Government was no longer contested, at least openly. There were a few minor adjustments made in the machinery of Terror, but otherwise this terrible weapon functioned smoothly. The temporary government enjoyed stability and showed no signs of stepping aside, the Convention voted without discussion, the Jacobins quietly acquiesced, there was virtually no movement in the streets or at the Commune: "The Revolution is frozen," said Saint-Just.[53]

CHAPTER 12

Thermidor

PLATE XIV
(Phot. Bibl. nat. Paris)

ALONE OF THE REVOLUTIONARY DAYS, the *grandes journées* during which the course of the Revolution was changed, 9 Thermidor is inextricably associated with Robespierre. It is his day, the day of his fall. Thermidor is also the most paradoxical of the great revolutionary days. It is a day of unrealized potential, of aborted insurrection, of unpredictable consequences. It is an episode without design, stumbled through by men who more resemble sleepwalkers than conspirators and their victims. It has entered revolutionary legend for both the right and the left, while the ingenuity of historians has been devoted to explaining why the expected did not happen. The action of 9 Thermidor is static, its drama internal and psychological. Above all 9 Thermidor is an end, an abrupt and unexpected end, and our catharsis is incomplete.

The Revolution rejected Robespierre on 9 Thermidor not for his failures, but for his successes. A small and unlikely parliamentary conspiracy, substituting desperation for planning, toppled and executed Robespierre, his friends and followers. He had never been a parliamentary leader popular among his colleagues. His hold over the Convention was tenuous; support was grudging. His authority in the assembly rested on the real or supposed popularity he enjoyed on the Committee of Public Safety, at the Commune and the Jacobins. Since joining the great Committee he had been able to spend less time with the deputies. Because his political sense was tactile, dependent on almost daily stimulation so that he could maintain the feel of a situation, his absences undermined his sensitivity to parliamentary politics. In addition the longest of his many illnesses had kept him at home for weeks before Thermidor. Nevertheless it is remarkable how easily the conspirators overthrew him.

But the ease with which Robespierre was destroyed was apparent only afterward. Thermidor's outcome was in doubt until the very end. Robespierre was the victim as much of his own character as of the efforts of his enemies. During the hours at the Hôtel de Ville, before his definitive capture, when he might have done something on his own behalf, he could not or would not. He seems to have misread or surrendered to the sudden shift of circumstance. His fall is more ironic than tragic, although the personal side of the drama has a strong tragic component.

That a conspiracy so hastily patched together should have succeeded reveals the serious weaknesses in Robespierre's position. Robespierre was thirty-six years old, but the Revolution had worn him out. "The Revolution," writes Trotsky of his own experience, "has its own system of chronology, where months are decades and where years are centuries."[1]

Robespierre was similarly aware of the difference in temporal scale. "The French people have advanced by two thousand years over the rest of mankind," he writes (X, 444). Boissy d'Anglas, somewhat more modest, thought the Revolution had done the work of "six centuries in six years."[2] By whichever chronology one calculated, Robespierre had been in power for at least a century: the Terror had lasted almost as long. By the summer of 1794, although military victory now seemed possible, and hence much that the Revolutionary Government had done justified, there were some ominous developments, and much reluctance to restore the suspended constitution. With France no longer in danger of invasion and occupation, with the Revolution apparently secure from military destruction, it was widely held, the emergency government could be terminated. But Robespierre was gloomy, Saint-Just downcast, and the Jacobins were without energy. It was not, as has sometimes been argued, that Robespierre and his friends wanted to remain in power and that meant perpetuating the Terror despite the relaxation in the war crisis. Rather, the problem of returning the government to some peacetime basis seemed insoluble. The Revolution had become the work of committees. Convention, Club, and Commune had lost the initiative. The extraordinary and resilient energy that had been generated by his tripartite division of revolutionary activity was gone. To whom could authority be restored?

The Revolutionary Government ruled unchallenged; no countervailing power remained to buffer. This became apparent when the hysterical law of 22 Prairial was passed in response to the attempted assassinations of Robespierre and Collot d'Herbois. In June and July the Committee of General Security, the other great committee of the Terror, arrested 1,814 citizens.[3] Among those arrested were a number of popular militants. The Terror was turning its hideous attention to those who had been the staunchest supporters of the Revolutionary Government and Robespierre's political and ideological engineering. These new victims had always been unruly allies, but necessary ones. Now, with the centralization of authority, the alliance was burdensome: "the government had discovered that it could not only run the Terror without popular support, but also use it against the popular militants."[4]

The Terror, whatever its inspiration in the psychology of the crowd and the need for protection coupled with a desire for revenge, was tied to the war. The sporadic outbursts of popular violence could not have been organized into the Terror had it not been for the ongoing crisis of war, a war whose outcome was doubtful until the spring of 1794, when French revolutionary armies were everywhere on the offensive.

Now that the war was being won, many saw no reason to continue the emergency government, and especially no need to cater any longer to the demands of the *sans-culottes*. Robespierre's few implementations of the social democracy he envisioned had been tolerated, but barely. It was time, his enemies thought, to be done with this dangerous social tampering; it was time to reassert the rights of those who had hitherto sacrificed their own interests because they were frightened and thought they had no choice. Once the secret was out that the country was no longer in danger, those who had been forced to submit could seek their revenge.

Robespierre himself liked to insist that the Terror was being used to create social democracy. There is some evidence to support the contention, but not enough to prove it. In proportion to their numbers in the population, the upper classes suffered "more than the lower classes, in fact the ratio is about eight to one."[5] But these upper-class victims went to the guillotine for counterrevolutionary activity and sedition, not for violating the social or economic laws of Year II. They were certainly not systematically eliminated as part of a policy of egalitarianism. This was true both in Paris and the provinces. There might be, here and there, a man such as the violent and colorful Javogues in the Loire, who believed "Terror was undoubtedly the next and final step forward into the Democratic Republic," and that "the enemy of the people, by definition poor, were the Rich," who were called, in his vocabulary, "these wretched reptiles."[6] But Javogues was not typical; he was no *robespierriste* who might reinvigorate the fading Jacobin faith in social renewal— he referred to Robespierre and Couthon disparagingly as *"Messieurs"*— and his fulminations do not pass for a social policy. Rather, Javogues was close to those Parisian neighborhood militants who had been destroyed by the Terror. Just as no buffer stood between the Terror and its victims, so no buffer stood between Robespierre and his enemies. The work of the Revolutionary Government undermined his popularity, he became more and more exposed to his enemies in the Convention.

Although he did not create lasting social democracy in France, Robespierre was sincere in his desire to do so. The most explicit attempt he made to realize this dream of an egalitarian republic was given form on February 5 in the so-called Ventôse laws. This extraordinary scheme, proposed by Saint-Just, is obscure and controversial.[7] Saint-Just planned to distribute, without cost, the seized lands of suspects, to indigent patriots. This radical proposal was never put into practice, but the historian of the Ventôse laws, arguing in part from surviving fragments of

Saint-Just's treatise *Institutions républicaines* (Republican institutions), insists "the *robespierristes* were sincere; the majority of the Convention and the Committee of Public Safety were not."[8] In theory the laws of Ventôse were the most audacious yet sanctioned by any revolutionary assembly. They could not, nor were they intended to, lead to the disappearance of the rural proletariat and to put an end to the agrarian crisis, a task beyond any eighteenth-century government. The laws had the more modest, yet still daring goal of realizing the Jacobin ideal of a democracy composed of small property owners and artisans. Saint-Just gave this dream epigrammatic expression: "Man must live independently."[9]

Opposition was strong, and no effective means for realizing such independence were ever found. The experience of all the social and economic legislation of 1793 had made it clear to Robespierre that the Convention had not budged from its resentments of June 2. The intervening months had done nothing to break down the widespread fear of any additional concessions to the rioters who had purged the Convention, summoned by Robespierre. The Marais, who looked with horror on the vast confiscations of land carried out under the Terror, which took the lands of traitors and *émigrés* under the law of suspects, were even more horrified at the proposal that these lands be distributed to the indigent. The idea was repulsive.

Robespierre had no coherent policy of social democracy. His thoughts on the matter are marked by dramatic and acute observations and analysis, the raw materials for a policy he never formulated. Perhaps the distractions of governing kept him from completing so central a task. He was always angered that his foes looked upon him as a social leveler, for this had never been his intention. But his passionate and impressionistic depictions of the desired republic were easily construed as an attack on property by the *conventionnels*, by the bourgeoisie, by all those who feared any further drift to the left. The coalition against Robespierre was gathering adherents, while he was losing his grip. His health, his nerves, his stamina were again slipping into prostration, and the Jacobin Club reflected the declining vigor of its leader. The Paris club, once the home of advanced revolutionaries who had nightly debated tactics as well as theory under the watchful and paternal gaze of Robespierre, had gradually abandoned any revolutionary initiative. The role of the Society became increasingly that of a kind of political police attached to the Revolutionary Government.[10] The meetings at the rue Saint-Honoré monastery lost their character and came to resemble civic reunions "where personal causes were the subject of debate and global issues the object of discussion." These debates in the library, where once had been fought some of the great oratorical battles of the Revolution, gradually acquired "a self-consciously exemplary character" and were carried out "as if models for repetition." It was "a pose struck for imitation throughout the realm."[11] All the business that came to the Jacobins was referred to the committees, especially the Committee of Public Safety. A special secretary was assigned to handle this enormous rerouting of correspondence.[12] Letters from the provinces, from affiliated societies, "once the Jacobin's vanity," now passed perfunctorily through the Society proceedings, "pausing only long enough to be rerouted to their proper destination."[13]

Robespierre himself suffered the same revolutionary lethargy as his creation. He was often absent from the Club, the Convention, and the Committee. There were now weeks of silence, mute stretches spent at the Duplays', perhaps gazing into the pleasant courtyard while exploring his mind, self, and heart.[14] These retreats, a kind of internal emigration, signaled not only physical and psychic exhaustion, but times of depression, doubt, disgust, manifestations of the felt unattainability of all he had dreamed and preached.[15] His prostrations were becoming longer, his resiliency less. His frequent and extended absences revealed another of the unexpected, and unwelcome, aspects of his revolutionary work. During these long silences all the synapses of the Revolution, which he had so carefully tended, were left unwatched. Yet the Revolutionary Government continued to function, indeed with grim efficiency. The organism had no further need of his voice. It still demanded the ability to speak, but others could provide the droning noises of uninspired human utterance. No more was now necessary. The heroic, creative days of the Revolution were over. Heroes were no longer needed.

He himself—and his last speech, on 8 Thermidor, is the evidence—knew or felt his approaching end. Premonitions of death had long been on his lips, varying in intensity with circumstance. Certainly since the attempt on his life, and probably much earlier, these fears were real rather than conventional or literary. The speech, with its fatalism and self-pity enveloping all arguments and tinging all phrases, is unmistakably a testament. His enemies did not know they were going into battle with a beaten and self condemned man. Robespierre did not appear vulnerable. His enemies attacked not because he was defenseless but because they believed they were doomed unless they destroyed him.

It is altogether fitting that Robespierre's last deliberate revolutionary act should have been a speech, and a speech unlike any other he had yet delivered. At this moment he retained his remarkable powers of analysis and oratory. The speech of 8 Thermidor, although bearing resemblance to earlier utterances, is unique among his creations. Rambling, filled with self-pity, scintillating with memorable turns of phrase, repetitive, redundant, angry, maudlin, priggish, it stumbles along with a kind of grandeur and brilliance. It reveals the isolation and despair of a man beyond human aid, "wandering self-blinded at Colonnus."[16] The *leit-motif* of his speech is his death. But if he appears at moments resigned to death at the hands of his enemies, deeply concerned to ensure his apotheosis or at least write his own epitaph, yet he has not surrendered. The speech bristles with the old energy of anathema, the thunder of denunciation. He is resigned only to deliverance from the burdens of the Revolution, from responsibilities disproportionate to his strength, perhaps to his genius.

The stupendous problem that he now confronted, whose solution had evaded him since the beginning of the Revolution, was the creation of equality. With the tenacity that marked his entire revolutionary career, he continued to chew on this bit of bone, trying to reconcile the contradictions inherent in creating equality while retaining private property. His last thoughts revealed no startling rethinking of the problem, no attempt to examine the dilemma from a new angle, not even any reexamination of the potentially fruitful speculations about the social basis of private property he had made more than a year earlier, then abandoned to enter the Revolutionary Government. He was content with reflecting pessimistically on the difficulties of creating equality and with rehashing some of the old arguments for his auditors. "My reason, but not my heart, is on the point of doubting that virtuous republic whose plan I had traced out for myself,"[17] he announced. On the question of equality, at least, he had no energy or originality left. He reiterated the failed and familiar policies of terror and purification, along with his homilies of patience and sacrifice.

He did give some thought to economic questions, for the first time in months. He fixed his attention momentarily on the financial system of the Revolutionary Government, and hence of France, and insisted there could be no liberty and no equality without the creation of a reasonable system. The current one was "worthless, prodigal, vexatious, rapacious, and absolutely independent of your supreme power." The administration of this financial chaos was the final refuge of the counterrevolution, since the economy benefited "the rich creditors by ruining and reducing to despair the poor" while "despoiling the people of the confiscated land [*biens nationaux*] and leading, inevitably, to the ruin of the public wealth" (X, 570). The brutal and violent measures, of necessity taken by the Revolutionary Government, had alienated the people while not adequately punishing the commercial criminals (X, 571). It was not the lack of good laws, he summed up on a moral note, but corruption in high places: "The laws are revolutionary; those who execute them are not."[18]

The building of the new society, as in all revolutions, proved more difficult than overthrowing the old. Robespierre had glimpses of the close relationship between economic and social questions, but he seemed unable to pursue the implications of his intuitions. In his last speech he returned to threats and exhortations, which was where he began the Revolution. He vaguely denounced "all the insidious maneuvers of our enemies" (X, 571) while at the same time calling upon the hungry to be patient. "The people," he continued, attributing his own belief that discipline makes a man free, "can endure hunger, but not crime. The people know how to sacrifice everything except their virtues" (X, 560).

The speech is a fit testament, redolent with the themes sounded throughout Robespierre's life, enriched by the harmonic overtones of a familiar rhetoric evocative of earlier efforts, and, more than any of his other speeches, deliberately cast as a kind of revolutionary autobiography, a summing up, Robespierre's *res gestae*. Had these autobiographical remarks been conveyed in memoirs written years after the Revolution, in the leisure of retirement or exile, Robespierre's judgment would have been tempered, if not substantially altered, by the subsequent events of the Revolution. His central metaphor of self, to which he returned in this final speech—the representative of the people—would doubtless have been refined.[19] The rougher edges would have been knocked off and his aesthetic sensibility, so committed to consistency and lucidity and proportion, would have imposed more pleasing patterns. The speech of 8 Thermidor is self-revelation in a raw state.

Not only is refinement lacking, but the purpose of these revelations is different than that usually pursued by the autobiographer. Robespierre is revealing himself to the nation, to the Revolution, as part of his ongoing ritual of self-purification. His whole revolutionary life is offered up for scrutiny.

Robespierre concentrated, understandably, on his doings since he joined the government, almost exactly a year earlier. Unlike so many autobiographers who return to savor the remembered joys or sorrows of their childhood and youth, Robespierre remains a man without a personal past. He was wholly absorbed by the Revolution and recalled the part most on his mind, most in need of explanation. In a sense his biography until he joined the government needs no defense. Much, perhaps most, of what he advocated or predicted had been done or realized. Besides, when he was out of power there was not much interest in his activities, and in Year II few wanted to hear about how right he had been in this or that past crisis and how mistaken had been his enemies, many of whom were now dead.

Surveying his year in government, Robespierre judged his work, on balance, successful. More, of course, remained to be done, but the "Revolutionary Government has saved *la patrie*," which was the reason for its creation. It now remained "to save the Revolutionary Government itself from all dangers." He was aware of the growing support for what had been, some six weeks earlier, Danton's premature desire to dismantle or at least modify the emergency government since the war was improving. Robespierre remained convinced of its necessity and made no mention of any improvements in France's military situation. So long as crime continued, he insisted, so too must the terrorization of crime: "It is the terror of crime that makes innocence secure" (X, 570). For him the Terror was not exclusively, and maybe not even largely, tied to the foreign war. Certainly in recent months he had seen it as a means of purification more than victory. These distinctions mattered a great deal to Robespierre, and he diverged from a number of those who had supported the Terror with the reservation that it would last only as long as the war. Robespierre insisted it would last as long as the counterrevolution lasted, which has taken its final refuge "in all parts of the political economy." All the efforts of genius are now needed to lead the republic to a natural and harmonious [*doux*] regime (X, 571). This would be accomplished, he revealingly said, not "by the phrases of a rhetorician, nor even by the exploits of warriors . . . but by the wisdom of our laws, by the majesty of our deliberations, and by the grandeur of our character" (X, 568). Only republicans can make a republic.

This view implies that revolution is a permanent mode of government. Robespierre had not formulated any theory of permanent, ongoing revolution, but he did not, like so many contemporaries, see or imagine a return to regular parliamentary government immediately. This divergence from what most believed or wanted to believe was threatening to many of his colleagues and pregnant for future revolutions and revolutionaries. Once again Robespierre had hit upon one of the enduring essentials of revolution. To make these arguments, or rather to suggest permanence, for he had not worked out the implications of his insight, before an audience inclined to moderation was politically inept. Although he retained to the end his exceptional powers of persuasion, he seemed to have lost, on 8 Thermidor, his grasp of political manipulation. He told his auditors what they did not want to hear and he offered them no compromise. His revolutionary autobiography was a self-righteous challenge to those with less rectitude.

Robespierre's stubborn insistence that the Revolution was not yet won, that it must be fought to its conclusion (which included an assault on the administrative corps of the emergency government), found few adherents. Even on the Mountain there was war weariness. Robespierre's stance isolated him as he had not been isolated since the war debates, and as it did then, the theme of virtue in the minority found its way into his utterances. His call for more sacrifice, more terror, more governmental intrusions, sparked no enthusiasm save among a shrinking group of confirmed *robespierristes*.

Unlike so many earlier orations, that of 8 Thermidor was addressed primarily to his colleagues in the Convention, not the inhabitants of poor Paris. The people appeared now and again, but they did not occupy the central place in his final thoughts, nor did he make any appeals beyond the walls of the Assembly. He was publicly brooding over how well or ill he had fulfilled the duties of a representative of the people, more concerned that he be vindicated by his colleagues than those he represented. There was also some attention to posterity. Throughout the Revolution any loss of personal popularity had set off in Robespierre the need to justify his actions by some standard more enduring than momentary reputation. In the war debates and again in Thermidor he turned to the future.

His life, as he unfolded it on 8 Thermidor, was a destiny more than a biography. His work was set by forces external. The Revolution made him the representative of the people, and he remained now what he had always been: "I prefer my quality as representative of the people to that of member of the Committee of Public Safety, and I put my quality as French citizen above all" (X, 565). He was hurt and angry that he must defend this self "against the most vile of all tyrannies," which is calumny. It was the republic itself that his enemies were attacking in his person. All those who exaggerated his importance were like "the impious man who denies the existence of the divinity he holds in awe" (X, 553). "Who am I?" he asked: "A slave of *la patrie*, a living martyr of the republic, the victim and the scourge of crime. . . . The faults of others will be pardoned: my zeal for *la patrie* is made into a crime."[20]

The oscillations between the heroic and the pathetic were frequent on 8 Thermidor. He was a victim, a martyr, slandered and suffering, powerless to repulse the bullies. "I have the experience of the past and I see the future," he explained. "What friend of *la patrie* could desire to survive into a time when it is no longer permitted to serve and defend oppressed innocence?" The defense of "oppressed innocence" was one of the first characteristics he insisted upon for a representative of the people. He saw himself a martyr to his own integrity. It would be left for posterity to decide "which of the enemies of my country was the most wicked and the most atrocious" (X, 566–67). He himself would be vindicated, for he would fulfill his destiny: "A representative of the people cannot let himself renounce the obligation to defend the interests of the people. No power can take it from him. Only depriving him of life can silence him" (IX, 198).[21]

The most presumptuous aspect of autobiography is the desire to influence how the future will think. Robespierre had not the leisure to contrive his own apotheosis, fix the general outlines of his reputation; but he took some care on 8 Thermidor to cleanse himself of all the filth that had been flung. The historian of revolutionary oratory insists that Robespierre kept an "imperturbable confidence in the omnipotence of the tool he had forged and polished ceaselessly, one which led him to believe he had a talisman for vanquishing his enemies, without the need to act. This is why, at the session of 8 Thermidor, he carried no other weapon but a sheaf of papers."[22] It is true he went into battle thus armed, for he had always done battle with the same weapons, self, reason, and rhetoric. What is curious is not that he appeared thus but that he left so much to chance, that he spoke without first having taken all necessary steps to see that things went his way. In this, too, he had returned to the relative political innocence of the first months of the Revolution, when he believed his sincerely felt words would persuade unaided. It is because he was often concerned more about the future than the present on 8 Thermidor that he innocently appeared before his colleagues.

"I have seen in history all the defenders of liberty attacked by calumny," he said, adding a peevish consolation: "but their oppressors are also dead!" (X, 567).[23] It was the calumnies surrounding the festival of the Supreme Being that still rankled, for the festival was "the most sublime," making "probity and virtue the order of the day" (X, 519). "It is from this time that date the assassinations and the new calumnies"— an interesting juxtaposition—"even more criminal than the assassinations" (X, 560). The paradox of apotheosis and destruction intrigued Robespierre. Of no other creation, of no other moment in the Revolution, was he more proud. None was more uniquely his. The festival left "on France a profound impression of calm, of happiness, of wisdom and well-being. Seeing this gathering of the first people of the world, who could have believed crime still existed on the earth?" (X, 561). Even more revealing are the lines he scratched out:

> Whoever could have watched this spectacle with dry eyes or an unmoved soul is a monster. The silence of the feeling imprinted more eloquently than discourse the soft and profound emotions with which all hearts were filled, and this cry escaped all hearts, *that whoever had seen this great spectacle could have died without regret.*[24]

In spite of its self-serving pathos—and Robespierre had enough restraint to strike out some of his more excessive flights—and all his tedious harping on his approaching martyrdom, in spite of his unabashed celebration of his own achievements and the customary presumptions of autobiography, he had, on 8 Thermidor, a remarkably accurate view of himself in the Revolution. His illusions and delusions were not blinding. He, and in a sense the Revolution, had reached an impasse. The representative of the people had done his work. The price of stability now seemed to be the elimination of Robespierre. This was his destiny, and he was prepared but not reconciled. "I am the most miserable of men," he wailed (X, 556).

After more than two hours of justification and analysis and passionate outbursts, Robespierre concluded with a peroration containing this analysis of his tragedy: "I am made to fight crime, not to govern over it" (X, 576). More than five years of revolution had passed since he had first sketched himself as a revolutionary. The Robespierre of 1789 and of 1794 are closely related:

> I have a stout heart, a resolute soul. I have never known how to bend under the yoke of baseness and corruption. . . . If I can be reproached, it is for never having said yes when my conscience told me to say no . . . of never having given my heart to the mighty ones of my province, from whom I have always believed myself independent, whatever efforts they have made to persuade me that it would cost me nothing to present myself, in an attitude of supplication, in the antechamber of an influential man. . . . There, my dear compatriots, you have the man who speaks to you.[25]

The ironies in Robespierre's last speech were unintentional. He was overwrought, emotionally and physically drained, and more than usually morbid. But he did not know this would be the last political act of his own will. He knew, he had fragmentary but disturbing evidence, that there was formidable opposition in the Convention and on the committees. He surely suspected a number of those who would shortly conspire against him, although when challenged, from the floor of the Convention, to name them, he refused. This was a political blunder beyond repair. The other blunder was his uncharacteristic disregard or contempt for mundane politics.

"The history of 9 Thermidor," said the bitter and brilliant reactionary Joseph de Maistre, "is not long; some scoundrels destroyed some other scoundrels."[26] It is the details behind Maistre's witticism that are necessary.

After delivering his remarkable speech to the Convention, Robespierre witnessed a long and acerbic debate concerning its publication and distribution. He might have seen in this procedural wrangle significant diminution of his influence. Decrees to publish his speeches (and those of other important members of the government) were routinely voted. But he did not see much significance. He was peeved, even angry that he was being asked to submit his speech to those he had attacked, but he did not stay to fight. He left the Convention with the ultimatum still reverberating in his auditors' minds that they must join with him in yet another purge, whose intended victims he had refused to name.[27] Whatever else it may have been, the speech of 8 Thermidor was a kind of referendum on himself and his politics, a gauntlet he threw down to the *conventionnels*. They were offended.

That night Robespierre delivered the same speech to the Jacobins. At the Club he was bathed in applause, and his supporters cast Collot d'Herbois and Billaud-Varenne out: the Jacobins were willing and anxious to read Robespierre's mind as the Convention was not. In the past, purge had preceded destruction. While Robespierre, lulled by the affection of the Jacobins, went home to sleep, satisfied that he had overcome the blunders of the day or unaware he had committed any, his enemies conspired. Central to their designs, indeed the only part of their plot they seem to have considered carefully, was the determination to prevent Robespierre from again speaking to the Convention. Collot and Billaud were convinced, and rightly so, that they were doomed if they failed.

There was a third option, pursued the night of 8–9 Thermidor by Saint-Just. He hoped to effect a reconciliation between the feuding committees of Public Safety and General Security and through this compromise or accommodation stop or at least moderate the factional war. The two committees had long been antagonistic over personalities, policies, and jurisdictions. Saint-Just had worked out some compromise a few days earlier. On 6 Thermidor (July 24) Couthon had told the Jacobins that the two committees were now working together. Either this agreement had broken down, or was not yet final, or Robespierre's speech of 8 Thermidor had destroyed it.[28] At any rate Saint-Just spent the night in the Green Room of the Tuileries writing the speech he would deliver in another attempt to patch up the feud. It appears that both Saint-Just's attempts at mediation and Robespierre's speech of 8 Thermidor were not coordinated efforts. Even the inner circle of the *robespierristes* was disintegrating.

On 9 Thermidor the Convention's session began, as usual, at 11 A.M. At noon Saint-Just was ready to speak. Collot d'Herbois was in the president's chair, having been elected on 1 Thermidor (July 19). Saint-Just was allowed only to deliver a few sentences of his prepared speech before the chair recognized Tallien, one of the conspirators, on a point of order. None of the *robespierristes* would again have the floor. Tallien did not, in fact, make a point of order. He started denouncing Robespierre. Collot then recognized several conspirators who continued in this vein, denouncing Robespierre and his friends, who stood mute and dumbfounded around the speaker's tribune. Robespierre, soon roused from his stupor, tried to shout over the noise and invectives, but was unable to make himself heard. His anger and near-hysteria caused his voice to freeze up. "You are choking on Danton's blood!" shouted Garnier de l'Aube. "Down with the tyrant!" came the prearranged unison cry of the conspirators. And all parts of the Convention joined in. Robespierre was silenced. His arrest was decreed and carried. His brother, Augustin, demanded to share the same fate. His wish was granted. Couthon was then vilified and arrested. So, too, was Saint-Just. Le Bas, deeply devoted to Saint-Just, followed Augustin Robespierre's act of sacrifice. He, too, was arrested. The whole confused scene was enacted in a little more than an hour. The spontaneous enlistment of the *conventionnels* in the braying denunciations and vilifications of Robespierre gave the conspirators their victory. But 9 Thermidor was only beginning.

The prisoners, five in all, were escorted to different prisons, after being forced to listen to a moralizing harangue by the momentarily triumphant Collot d'Herbois. The jailers of Paris were under the control of the Commune, which was widely thought to be *robespierriste* in sympathy and personnel. The keeper of the Luxembourg prison—the old Bourbon Palace that today houses the French senate—refused to incarcerate Robespierre. His four comrades were also released in the course of the late afternoon by jailers unwilling to hold them. Eventually the condemned men ended up at the seat of the Commune, the Hôtel de Ville. The Convention, which remained in session throughout the night, declared the five outlaws at 9:00 P.M. This act meant that the fugitives had only to be taken and identified before being executed. No trial was necessary.

The night, in Paris, at the Convention, at the Hôtel de Ville, was confused and confusing. Robespierre and his friends, taken by surprise, had no plans and were unable to make any. The Convention, for several hours, was equally inactive. The council of the Commune deliberated, but as the night wore on it became clear the city would not, could not, rise to save the *robespierristes*. Even the exploits of François Hanriot, Robespierre's hand-picked commander of the Paris guard and one of the heroes of June 2, failed to raise the city. Of the forty-eight sections, only twenty-four sent partial delegations to the Hôtel de Ville. There was no unitary will in Paris. The centralizing Revolutionary Government had not only destroyed sectional spontaneity and insurrectionary zeal, it had also stripped the sections of their artillery, whose loss made successful street fighting out of the question.[29]

The outlawed quintet was as incapable of its salvation as was Paris. They sat, in the meeting room of the Commune's council on the second floor, paralyzed. Saint-Just was sunk in an impotent stupor—he who, accompanied by Le Bas, had revitalized the army in Alsace, set up the Strasbourg guillotine to restore the authority of the Committee of Public Safety in the rebel city, destroyed the self-proclaimed satraps of the region, and spurned the Austrian's request for a parley with the words "The French Republic takes from and sends to its enemies nothing but lead."[30] Le Bas was similarly supine. Couthon, who despite crippling (and progressive) meningitis, which confined him to a wheelchair and imposed a life of pain, had, in his natal department of Puy de Dôme, where he was sent by the Committee of Public Safety, recruited troops and supplies from a region deeply disaffected from Paris and its problems, who had wielded his unchallenged authority as revolutionary proconsul with vigor touched with kindness, Couthon too was incapacitated. Even Augustin Robespierre, who had discovered personal courage at the siege of Toulon (where he had also discovered Napoleon), could only pace the room, possessed and rendered impotent by rage turned inward. These men of action could not act. They were enthralled. Only Robespierre's passivity was in character.

At 2:00 A.M. the newly raised forces of the Convention converged on the Hôtel de Ville. When the guardsmen broke suddenly into the room where the outlaws and the insurrectionary committee sat, Augustin Robespierre climbed out a window and fell, nearly killing himself, to the street below. The totally helpless Couthon, trying to move, tumbled down a stone staircase and injured his head. Saint-Just, inert, yielded without a struggle. Le Bas gave one of his pistols to Robespierre, turned the other on himself, and died almost at once. Robespierre shot himself in the lower left jaw.[31] He was alive but gravely wounded.

Couthon and Saint-Just were held until morning at the Hôtel de Ville. Robespierre was borne on a plank to the Convention, which refused to receive him: "the body of a tyrant can bring nothing but pestilence,"[32] they declared. He was deposited on a table in the waiting room of the Committee of Public Safety, where he lay unconscious for a long time, his head resting on a sample box of army bread the Committee was examining. When he suddenly roused from his unconsciousness, he awakened to insults and taunts, as well as some acts of kindness. A few of the spectators gave him pieces of paper—there was no linen available—to staunch his wound. It is reported that he thanked one citizen, addressing him, with his customary (and unrevolutionary) politeness, as *"monsieur."* Eventually a doctor arrived, extracted some broken teeth, and bandaged his shattered jaw.

Around midday Saint-Just, his hands bound behind his back, Couthon, his crippled body carried on a stretcher, and Robespierre, carried in an armchair, were taken from this place where formerly they had performed their extraordinary labors.[33] At the Revolutionary Tribunal the legal ritual of identification was enacted. Then the death procession assembled.

The guillotine, which had been moved on June 12 (24 Prairial) to the outskirts of Paris, had, for such illustrious victims, been reassembled in the Place de la Révolution in the center of Paris, where Louis XVI, the first of many distinguished victims, had been executed. The day of execution, 10 Thermidor, was a *décadi,* a tenth day in the revolutionary calendar, and thus set aside for patriotism. The gathering crowd, free to attend, was numerous and lively. When Robespierre was strapped to the plank, only semiconscious, the bandage holding his jaw together was torn off. He died screaming with pain.

The bodies were put in a common grave, in the cemetery of Errancis, and covered with quicklime. The spot was unmarked by a gravestone.

CHAPTER 13

The Incorruptible

LÉGISLATEUR INCORRUPTIBLE

M . M . J . ROBERSPIERRE

Député de Paris à la Convention Nationale en 1792.

Élu Président le 22 Aoust 1793.

à Paris chez Villeneuve *Graveur*, Rue Zacharie St Severin Maison du Passage, Nº 72.

PLATE XV
(Phot. Bibl. nat. Paris)

IN DEATH, TOO, ambiguity clings to Robespierre. Enough of the Thermidorian legend remains that he is remembered as a man of blood. The 16,000 death sentences of the Terror, the thousands of additional deaths attributed directly and indirectly to the Terror, the hundreds of thousands of arrests and imprisonments and interrogations and confiscations, the harassments, the cruelty, the fear that were the work of the Revolutionary Government, all demanded explanation while being perpetrated and expiation afterward. Robespierre had defended the Terror: after 9 Thermidor his reputation was enthusiastically sacrificed. He was made, as Napoleon and others said, the scapegoat. "Robespierre's trial," added the regicide Jean-Jacques-Régis Cambacérès, who eventually became archchancellor of the Empire, "was judged without being heard."[1]

But if Robespierre's name is linked, reflexively, with the Terror, his name simultaneously is associated with rectitude, devotion to duty, loyalty, sincerity, and moral purity. Robespierre is familiar, in textbook and legend, to expert and amateur, as The Incorruptible. It is an epithet affixed to him during the Revolution, and it has endured. Odd and unique among political leaders, "The Incorruptible" is reminiscent of nicknames given to princes. Goodness, piety, boldness, lion-heartedness, these were the qualities fit for kings. But they, whatever else was thought flattering or enhancing, were never dubbed incorruptible. By common understanding of the word, a prince could not be corrupt, hence its opposite was not a noble virtue. Robespierre's singularity was recognized at the time of the Revolution and is still recognized by any good French dictionary, which has a separate entry for "L'Incorruptible," defined as Robespierre's surname.

The Incorruptible is not a term of endearment or familiarity. It distances the man from us by elevating him into a moral entity. It is difficult to have great emotional affection for someone who is incorruptible. Then (as still), men felt uncomfortable with the power of virtue. But long before the epithet was attached to Robespierre it had acquired political application of a very limited sort. In the seventeenth century in France the incorruptible judge was a stock figure of literature both popular and polite. He was the necessary counterpart of that other stock figure, the corrupt judge.[2] This, of course, implies widespread judicial corruption. In the Revolution the word, particularly when given to Robespierre, would be considerably enriched in implication and resonance, but that a man was singled out thus indicates not only that incorruptibility was honored, but that its opposite was prevalent among the revolutionary leadership. Robespierre himself never used the epithet. He preferred his own creation, "the representative of the people," who, by definition, was incorruptible. Memory, however, has chosen The Incorruptible.

Exactly when Robespierre was anointed is a matter of conjecture. The epithet is not fixed to an event or a single episode. It first appears in a letter he received on July 11, 1790. A certain Lefetz, an otherwise obscure monk from Amiens, wrote Robespierre, begging him to use the "force of reason and reasoning to annihilate everything that nourishes the people in their superstition." All Europe, Lefetz assured his correspondent, was looking on. "As *incorruptible* as courageous," he continued, "you have always openly manifested your sentiments. Only the general good, not the interest of the few, has ever caused you to act or speak."[3]

Already incorruptibility had a far broader applicability than that given it in the seventeenth century. The public welfare, religious enlightenment, and moral sincerity were now included in the properties of incorruptibility. Still, it would be a year before circumstances and Robespierre's deliberate flaunting of his rectitude would allow the designation to stick. By early summer of 1791 the circumstances and his reputation came into the necessary harmony. Mirabeau's sudden death in April, the nearly simultaneous condemnation of the church settlement by the Pope, Robespierre's ordinance excluding deputies in the Constituent from sitting in the Legislative, the flight of the King to Varennes, and the massacre in the Champ de Mars, all had made a desperate situation in France. Robespierre's personal ascendancy was acknowledged: he was an important figure on the left, someone to be reckoned with although literally years away from personal power. And his ascendancy was coupled to his virtue. He was, for the first time, described in the newspapers as incorruptible, and the description already had transcended the narrow sense of the word as immunity to bribery. Sometimes the usage was ironic, but Robespierre was being seen as morally unique. "M. Robespierre, the incorruptible man, the God of Marat, Garat, Gorsas, and Martel, the great Robespierre, in a word" is how the *Journal Général,* a conservative, even counterrevolutionary newspaper, edited by the Abbé Fontenai, a former Jesuit, refers to him in early June.[4] Shortly afterward another newspaper, *Le Défenseur du Peuple* (in July), spoke of "M. Robespierre, the irreproachable, the incorruptible friend of Marat, whom he pretends not to know, can denounce and denounce in Paris with so little success; but what a man of such an enormous reputation says is unsettling in the provinces."[5] The linkage with Marat, who was then thought the more notorious and dangerous man, as well as his provincial influence are significant. Stridently moral politics, with the self revealed and offered as exemplary, were united in the public mind.

It was around this time that the word was taken up by some of his aggressive supporters. The extreme disgust of those on the left with the Constituent and the Revolution generally created the need for a figure above the intrigues. Camille Desmoulins, then Robespierre's infatuated friend and disciple, published a tribute to his hero that had been sent him by a women's society. "In the midst of corruption," reads the extract in *Révolutions de France et du Brabant*, "you have not ceased to be the unyielding support for truth. Ever firm, ever incorruptible, ever in harmony with your conscience, you have fought to prevent any impure alloy from being incorporated in a constitution that should be dictated by philosophy for the happiness of the human race."[6] Incorruptibility was becoming a revolutionary trait with meaning beyond bribery.

Marat himself, stressing the moral over the pecuniary aspects of corruption, offered a variation on Desmoulins's enthusiasm in his own paper, *L'Ami du Peuple*. "After the outrages that the incorruptible Robespierre has had so many times to swallow for defending the rights of the people against an Assembly almost entirely prostituted to Louis XVI," he declared, "and the little influence that he has had on most of the decrees passed over his objections, can he hope to find a single judicious patriot who does not have for the work of our senators the just scorn they deserve!"[7]

Here are all the ingredients for Robespierre's epithet. They were first combined, it appears, not in print but in the visual arts, in the Salon of 1791, held that summer. Two portraits of Robespierre were shown: one by Joseph Boze, a former court painter whose most famous work would be his portrait of Marat;[8] the other by Adélaïde Labille-Guiard, another artist who easily adjusted to painting rebels rather than courtiers. Her pastel, which has since disappeared, carried the title *The Incorruptible*.[9] Labille-Guiard had the habit of doing her oil portraits from her pastels, and the surviving canvas of *The Incorruptible* depicts a pleasant, smiling (albeit somewhat ironically), composed young man with fine hands and carefully curled hair, dressed in the somber and simple black of a deputy to the Third Estate.[10] His growing popularity and reputation for moral elevation and distinction made him not only a fit subject for a respectable Salon painter but meant that the artist might expect to see her work soon issued in the inexpensive engraving, "on display in the windows of all the print dealers." This is precisely what happened. Labille-Guiard's charming "Incorruptible" was readily available, bearing as caption this quatrain:

> Du superbe oppresseur redoutable
> Incorruptible ami du peuple qu'on accable,
> Il fait briller au sein des viles factions
> Les vertus d'Aristide et l'âme des Catous.[11]

By the end of the Constituent Assembly, Robespierre had become The Incorruptible.

On September 30, 1791, as the deputies filed out of the final session of the Constituent, the crowd gathered on and about the Feuillants' Terrace of the Tuileries, anxiously awaiting their champions, Robespierre and Pétion. When they emerged, arm in arm, the crowd cried Long live Liberty! Long live Robespierre! Long live The Incorruptible![12] The epithet, so joyously shouted in public, stuck. On November 28, when Robespierre entered the Jacobin Club after his return from Arras, he was greeted with loud applause. Collot d'Herbois, who was presiding, proposed "that this member of the Constituent Assembly, rightly called 'The Incorruptible,' should preside over the society." The proposal was carried unanimously.[13]

Robespierre had by his conduct and his speech impressed his contemporaries with his moral qualities, which he lived and described. Even his fastidiousness of dress and manners did not detract from what was perceived as his sincere and austere virtue. He was able to persuade others to see him as he saw himself, to value in him what he himself thought most valuable, and to tie these qualities of self to the Revolution and to a particular political line. Not only was he morally more worthy than most of his colleagues, but his principles were also more worthy. Indeed one could not have moral principles without oneself being moral. There were others as poor as (or poorer than) Robespierre who did not get rich off the Revolution, but none of these so intimately bound together self and ideas. Only Marat—and later Saint-Just, who was in 1791 too young to sit in the Legislative Assembly—so persistently insisted on the unity of self and principle, and the self Marat offered, although never suspected of being corruptible, was repellent to many. He was violent and bitter and histrionic. Robespierre, more controlled and socially respectable, exploited his moral edge to good advantage in the bitter parliamentary struggles by sneeringly contrasting his life with the frivolities pursued by others (IX, 79). That he was able to do so was determined by circumstance as much as the nature of the man.

It is useful to see Robespierre's revolutionary career as a series of confrontations with rivals.[14] The stages of his emergence are marked by his clashes with the most significant men of the Revolution. Mirabeau was the first of these, and set a pattern of moral comparison Robespierre would subsequently follow. The two men did not like each other. Their most famous encounter, at the Jacobins (December 6, 1790), when Mirabeau challenged his supporters to stand physically with him against the upstart Robespierre, ended in public humiliation when a majority left their seats to rank themselves with Robespierre. The episode did not undermine Mirabeau's authority, although it did compromise him somewhat with the Jacobins, who already seem to have preferred the austere Robespierre to more flamboyant leaders. This was the major confrontation between the two men, for as long as Mirabeau lived and dominated, Robespierre was correct and polite. But when he died, at the height of his popularity (April 2, 1791), the long-stifled rumors of his personal corruption, his deal with the Court to have his debts paid in exchange for support, circulated without hindrance. Robespierre was one of the beneficiaries of Mirabeau's scandalous finances. He did not come to power with Mirabeau's death. That mantle was inherited by Barnave, Lameth, and Duport (whom Mirabeau had once called a *triumgueusat*, a trio of beggars). But it was remembered that Mirabeau had praised Robespierre's sincerity, and the austere provincial offered a useful and telling contrast with the morality of the *ancien régime*.

Robespierre's self-regarding virtue, his sincere simplicity of life, his persistent championship of democratic causes, especially of equality, all contributed to creating The Incorruptible. He had a kind of transparency of self. Although his revelations of self were public and even theatrical, he was without pretense. There was no suspicion of deviousness or duplicity. In revolution, much more quickly than in peacetime, affectation as well as self-seeking are exposed. Partly the intensity of political activity, partly the risks involved, partly the expectation that revolutionaries be different, that they be better than those they have overthrown, expose the charlatan. It is personal morality and integrity that are especially valued. In the French Revolution those who perpetuated the duplicity, the hypocrisy of Court politics, or were suspected of secret allegiances to the *ancien régime*, were tainted. The new manner and significance of politics demanded by the Revolution also benefited Robespierre. The Court was thought secretive, beset by gossip, animated by the competition for place, and corrupted by the need of favors to support ruinous personal expenditure. The Revolution was anithetical to all these characteristics, and Robespierre, with his need to reveal himself, constantly reminded that he was not tied to this despised past. He was a new man, a revolutionary.

His moral pedantry was not his most pleasant characteristic, but it was fundamental to his success and his character. Incorruptibility was a means of achieving recognition from an amorphous assembly and a notoriously preoccupied and fickle Paris. At the Jacobins his right and ability to lead were first apparent. At the time of Mirabeau's death his ascendancy there was nearly complete, and the members chose "to follow, by preference, an irreproachable, poor, austere man" rather than anyone compromised by "a bad reputation of intrigue and violence, and sinister rumors (however untrue)."[15] In Robespierre men saw manifest one of their deepest convictions: the Revolution was morality in action. He was a just and righteous man, set apart from so many contemporaries. He was a man formed by the regenerative energy of the Revolution.

Despite his own efforts at enshrining himself as "the representative of the people" and those of his enemies at making him a monster, he is remembered as The Incorruptible.[16] Because of the complexities of his character the epithet itself took on a richness of meaning. Robespierre died a poor man,[17] but his incorruptibility went far beyond his honesty. He was chaste, immune to virtually all the seductions of the flesh. He was contemptuous of the pleasures and attractions that lured many a revolutionary from his austerity and then from his duty. He could be inflexible, deaf to the pleas of former friends, as when he shut his ears to the pleas of Lucile Desmoulins, the wife of his former comrade, at whose wedding he had stood witness. She shortly followed her husband to the guillotine. All these characteristics, both pleasing and repulsive, were expressed by The Incorruptible.

The Revolution produced a number of formidable moral athletes, most of whom sat with the Mountain. Robespierre was not alone in his austerity and his devotion to the Revolution, but he did more talking about it than most. Along with Marat, Robespierre created a new kind of leadership. Marat understood that his appeal lay in his self as much as in his denunciations:

> Learn [he lectured Robespierre] that my reputation with the people rests, not on my ideas, but upon my boldness, upon the impetuous outbursts of my soul, upon my cries of rage, of despair, and of fury against the rascals who impede the action of the Revolution. I am the anger, the just anger, of the people, and that is why they listen to me and believe in me.[18]

Robespierre would not have minimized ideas in his revolutionary career, for he was far less a demagogue than Marat, but he would have agreed— and in this Marat had nothing to teach him—that authority resided in the self. Marat's was a much more tormented soul than Robespierre's and consequently had a far narrower appeal. Robespierre's was the voice of reason, of equality, of liberty as well as "of rage, of despair, and of fury against the rascals who impede the action of the Revolution." Unlike Marat, he did not talk at all about details of his daily life, yet his leadership was as personal. He was revered among the rank and file not for the simplicity of his life[19] but because his ideas and self were inseparable.

His self, which gave him popularity and authority, also gave him his enemies. Robespierre was a living rebuke to many. The grossly exaggerated stories of men trembling in his presence lest he discern their thoughts are both preposterous and revealing. Men who live with flamboyant virtue make others uneasy. Robespierre, once he had authority, made men tremble, both for their deeds and for their moral shortcomings, since he was incapable of separating the two. But he was no Stalin, who delighted in intimidating his comrades. Although Robespierre was feared by many, he was less treacherous and deadly than both the cool administrators and passionate terrorists of the Revolution. It is often what a man says rather than what he does, that influences. Robespierre talked a good deal about punishment and Terror and moral laxity in others and consequently earned a sinister reputation. He morally browbeat his contemporaries, and they never forgot how unpleasant an experience that was. For the period of Robespierre's ascendancy, during the final year of his life, men felt powerless before his superior virtue because it was enforced by the Terror. Moral intimidation is humiliating; physical intimidation is not.

Revolutionary leadership, more than leadership in normal times when habit and passive allegiance obtain, is a matter of morality and will. Men endure and do the work that must be done only if they can believe that their actions have moral sanction as well as being necessary. Great revolutionary leaders provide the explanations and justifications that help the people transcend their suffering, steel their endurance, vindicate their dreams, justify their deeds. Revolutions, along with wars, seem greater (to participants and historians alike) than the sum of their parts. Robespierre had the gift to articulate the grandeur of purpose and the moral form of the new world born of the Revolution. René Levasseur, an intelligent doctor, a civilized man, a devoted Montagnard, pondering the Revolution from the exile enforced against all regicides by the restored monarchy of Louis XVIII, thought the Terror a series of "legal acts of vengeance, whose necessity seemed clearly demonstrated." None who sat on the Mountain "recoiled before the consequences of [Robespierre's] principles, however deplorable they might appear." Robespierre was a hard, ruthless man, but this is not to his discredit as a revolutionary leader. He was not, for Levasseur and a number of other thoughtful Montagnards, a cruel or capricious man, or one who enjoyed the work of killing: "The difference between a Robespierre, a Saint-Just, and a Carrier, a Collot, a Le Bon, was that which separates a just but inflexible magistrate from a hangman stained by the blood he has been paid to shed."[20]

Levasseur, of course, wanted desperately to see his part in Year II as different from that of the more extreme terrorists, most of whom turned on Robespierre in Thermidor. Robespierre provided this desired perspective. He saw beyond the practicalities, beyond the mundane and often brutal aspects of the Revolution, into a world not yet born. He was able to show this world to his contemporaries and to persuade them that the birth trauma of liberty and equality was unavoidable, would be survived, would not permanently disfigure the future, and, although painful and bloody, was not evil. He nowhere celebrates bloodletting as purifying. The Revolution is the price men must pay for freedom. The great speeches—with a few notable exceptions—are not tactical analyses of what has been and is, but descriptions and apotheoses of a world yet unrealized. These visions of the future, this ability to express the restless longings of contemporaries, was another of the gifts of The Incorruptible.

Robespierre's prophetic, sometimes messianic invocations of things to come were acts of his faith in man's salvation through history. Longer and more consistently than any of his comrades or rivals, he insisted that fallen man could, must, "be made to want his painful redemption."[21] He himself manifested and declared this faith, and willed it, exhausting himself.[22] Much of the work of the Revolution was accomplished by febrile missionaries, believing their willed actions would change the course of human history. Billaud-Varenne, interrogated in his Saint-Domingue exile by Dr. Chervin, spoke for the Committee of Public Safety and its motives:

> The decisions for which we are so much reproached were most often taken by us in two days, a single day, sometimes in a few hours. The crisis itself made this necessary. Decisions were made in the midst of the exhaustion of our long night sessions at the Committee. . . . We wanted to triumph

at whatever price, to be the victors in order to give reality to our principles.[23]

Robespierre's revolutionary credo is scattered throughout his utterances, from his first political pamphlet in Arras to his final speech. He was the prophet of the uniqueness of the French Revolution, and its uniqueness was apparent only when the Revolution was seen in historical context. If man's redemption was to come in and through history, as he insisted, then the Revolution must be put into history. Robespierre's Revolution was without precedent. It could not be found "in the books of Tacitus and Machiavelli" (X, 351) nor in any modern revolution. The English Revolution had been presided over by "ambition and fanaticism" (V, 56), his euphemisms for Cromwell and the Puritans. The American Revolution was "founded on the aristocracy of riches" (V, 17). There was nothing in antiquity to compare. "Our destiny, much more sublime," he argued, "is to found on earth the empire of wisdom, of justice and of virtue" (X, 521). The Revolution "is new . . . equally unknown to free peoples as to those subjugated by despotism" (VI, 617). No court, no monarchy, with its pomp and circumstance, inhabited the same universe. In a despotism "everything is small, petty, the range of vice, like that of virtue, is circumscribed." But with the Revolution "it is no longer individuals, it is humanity itself" that is the object of government (IX, 44).

Despite its singularity, the Revolution is part of the nature of things, prodigious but not freakish. It is the *ancien régime* that was unnatural. Before the Revolution "anarchy reigned in France from the time of Clovis to that of the last Capets," a vast social disorder "that forces nature and the law off the throne to replace them with men!" (IX, 496). "In the system of the French Revolution, what is immoral is contrary to politics, what is corrupting is counterrevolutionary. Weakness, vice, prejudice, these are the way of royalty" (X, 354). So different was the Revolution from the *ancien régime* that none of the values and judgments of the old society obtained. Not only must the laws and customs and morality be made anew, but the entire world would represent a new order, a revolutionary order. When men and a nation struggle for liberty and equality, they cross a barrier and enter a new and different universe. A revolution "is nothing more than the efforts of a nation to conserve or to conquer liberty" (VII, 746), whose principles "are engraved by nature in the hearts of all men" (IV, 111). "All reasonable and magnanimous men" belong to the revolutionary party, "all perfidious and corrupt men belong to the faction of our tyrants" (X, 320).

When the people rise in revolution, they are obeying "the voice of reason" (X, 231).

Following Rousseau, he insisted, "Nations have only a moment to become free" (VI, 243). History itself would reveal the right moment. Men could be mistaken—although once they had begun there could be no turning back—but history was never wrong. The judgments of history were moral and definitive:

> If this generation was destined only to thrash around in the filth into which it had sunk through vice and despotism . . . a future generation, purer than ours, more faithful to the sacred laws of nature, will undertake to cleanse this land soiled by crime; it will bring not the false peace of despotism nor the horrible agitations of intrigue, but the sacred fire of liberty, and for tyrants the exterminating blade. (VIII, 109)

Robespierre gave fortune, that force in history that had so well served political thinkers in antiquity and the Renaissance as a check to overreaching human ambition, small sway. For Robespierre revolutions were made by the willful acts of men, so long as their acts were informed by moral fervor. "If fortune favors the cause of virtue, of courage and of liberty," he said, "the victory is ours." But even if fortune was against the Revolution, "the Republic and liberty are imperishable and . . . we [the revolutionaries] will not all be destroyed" (X, 146). If revolutionaries endured, so would the Revolution, for just as the republic lay in the hearts of republicans, so the revolution lay in the hearts of revolutionaries. The spirit of revolution is imperishable.

Robespierre's revolutionary universe is fraught with risks. Not least of these is the tenacious endurance of old habits of mind and heart: "It is the misfortune of a people who pass rapidly from servitude to liberty that it carries with it, unperceived, into the new order of things the prejudices of the old, for there has not been time to shed this burden" (VII, 173). This is the original sin, so to speak, of revolution. The counterrevolution is internalized in the unshed habits of the *ancien régime*. Or, as Robespierre puts it: "We have raised the temple of liberty with hands still scarred by the chains of despotism."[24] Until the Revolution was fully victorious, the government of France (and those living under it) would be "a monstrous mixture of the old and the new regime" (VIII, 418). "Frenchmen," Robespierre pleaded, "you have only one way to escape the vengeance of the kings: victory. Vanquish them or perish; these are your only choices" (V, 61). In revolution there are no compromises.

The Incorruptible was a being who did not compromise with the enemy. For Robespierre the Revolution was an enormous civil war that had to be fought to its end. Only the unconditional surrender of the counterrevolution was thinkable: "To stop before the end is to perish" (X, 572). The correct line was not one of accommodation and could not be abandoned. Others had changed, others had deserted, but not Robespierre, not The Incorruptible.

The intensity, conviction, and ferocity of this faith Robespierre conveyed to his followers, simultaneously arguing one of the earliest versions of a familiar nineteenth-century myth: France was the natural home of revolution; other nations could but follow the French lead. Robespierre, for all his exceptional political and ideological sophistication, was parochial. A provincial lawyer who had not traveled outside his country, he shared the xenophobia of his petit-bourgeois followers. The invasions of France, the interference of England, all contributed to French isolation. Cosmopolitanism had no place in the Revolution; nor has it in any revolution. The only way to deal with the enemy, abroad as well as at home, was to destroy him. For Robespierre it was not so much French arms as French ideas that would conquer Europe. When the Revolution had created a free society at home, there would be "peaceful conquests in the rest of the world." When a people "want to be free they will be" (IX, 310). "The tyrants will fall themselves when they are ripe. The contagion of our principles, the spectacle of our glory and our happiness," would create world revolution (IV, 251). The corollary was that France's failure or defeat would deprive Europe "of this powerful and necessary ally," and the world would be "reduced to servitude." France was the home of "philosophy and humanity" (X, 179). "Let liberty perish in France, and all of nature will cover herself with a veil of mourning, and human reason will retreat into the abyss of ignorance and barbarism." Europe would be returned to "the Huns and the Tartars" (X, 180). "The French people have to bear the weight of the world . . . they must be among the people what Hercules was among the heroes" (IV, 331). Just as he offered himself as example of republican virtue, so he offered France. The Revolution would triumph not by France becoming "the Don Quixote of the human race" but by establishing "in our midst liberty, peace, abundnce, and laws" (V, 60). He believed that men, once shown the good, would choose it: "The laws of eternal justice that were contemptuously called the dreams of humanitarians, we have turned into imposing realities. Morality lay in the books of philosophers; we have put it into the government of nations" (X, 229).

This essentially idealist view, insisting on reason and reasonableness, on the power of ideas rather than arms, Marat, with his usual shrewd malice, criticized. "The Revolution," he argued, "has aborted because many wanted to fight it only with the weapons of philosophy. . . . As if the most driving passions were under the control of reason!"[25] Marat himself relied upon rage and anger to make the Revolution. Vergniaud, also critical of Robespierre but from the right, wanted compassion. "There are those who have sought to achieve the Revolution by Terror," said the Girondin orator. "I would have preferred to achieve it by love."[26] Robespierre's was the rationalism of the Enlightenment made militant, undiluted by sentiment, sentimentality, or skepticism. These aspects of the Enlightenment tradition Robespierre had successful cut away to fight the Revolution, leaving the remaining flesh healthy.

Robespierre's emphasis on ideas and their power made his view of the Revolution spiritual and subjective. He talked often of these aspects of the Revolution and many, during and after the upheaval, complained that his elation, his elevation of rhetoric, was a lapse from clarity and lucidity, maybe even a flight from rationalism.[27] He sometimes borrowed the language of religious faith, just as he sometimes borrowed the language of stoicism; but his was a secular mind. When speaking of intangible matters, when speaking of one's own liberation and exhilaration as well as that of a nation and its people, the language of the spirit is unavoidable. "Who among us does not feel all his faculties enlarged?" Robespierre asks. "Who does not believe himself elevated above humanity itself in knowing that it is not only for a people that we fight but for the universe, for the men alive today and for those who will live in the future?" (X, 180). Victory would come "above all from the energy of our souls, the elevation of our characters, the purity of our principles, the prudence of our undertakings" (V, 266). Here is a grandiose vision and purpose. There is nothing mean-spirited about Robespierre's understanding of revolution or history or self. His ideas have a grandeur that comes of spaciousness as well as precision.

The counterrevolution, on the contrary, mired man in his vices and prejudices. Egoism became the most significant word in Robespierre's vocabulary of denunciation. The antidote to this poison was truth. The Revolution was "as immortal as truth, as invincible as reason" (X, 180). The enormous struggle of reason with egoism was the essence of Robespierre's Revolution. The transcendence of egoism would bring liberation, for the individual, for himself, for the people. The logical difficulty arose when Robespierre became convinced that some men had been deprived of a "profound horror of tyranny" and had no "sacred love of country" (X, 544). Reason, it appeared, was not universal. Some men, deprived by nature, as some are born blind, can only go through the external motions of revolution and liberation. Their natural inclination is toward counterrevolution. These uneducable counterrevolutionaries, these unregenerate egoists, these natural enemies of liberty and equality, must be destroyed or there would be no end to the Revolution. Here, too, Robespierre was The Incorruptible.

Among those who followed Robespierre there was general agreement: he was a moral force whose exemplary life and words assured and certified his authority. His voice appeared bigger than the man: "it is because it is not that of a man; a great people speaks through him, that of the Jacobins."[28] The faithful awaited his clarification. "Robespierre, who is never deceived about political events," says the Montagnard ex-butcher Louis Legendre, "will descent from the Mountain, will excite all hearts by the force of his eloquence."[29] Many of those who marched with him were not confirmed *robespierristes*. "I marched with confidence in his footsteps," wrote Jean Dyzèz, a regicide deputy from Landes who resumed a quiet (and lucrative) career after Robespierre's fall. "The reason is simple: I believed I saw in him a man who truly loved liberty, who was impassioned for liberty. The route he took did not seem to me very far from the correct route."[30]

There is considerable evidence of this sort, from men who were loyal because their own revolutionary passion was approximated in Robespierre. These witnesses all mention the combination of moral energy and reason. Dubois-Crancé, a fair man despite having been proscribed by Couthon, thought Robespierre had too much presumption and pigheadedness, and too little of Danton's physical presence and sheer lung power, but was able to lead because he "was the sworn foe of every kind of oppression, the fearless champion of the rights of the people." Even though he carried all his strengths to an extreme, "He was a proud and jealous man, but fair and upright. His principles were austere to a fault, and he never deviated from them a hair's breadth." Consistency was his guarantee of sincerity: "Such as he had been from the beginning of his career, such he was to the end of it; and there are mighty few men to whom such praise can be given."[31] Billaud-Varenne, a complicated and confused character who stood to Robespierre's left, stressed rectitude. Robespierre achieved his "ascendance over public opinion" by embodying "the most austere virtues, the most absolute devotion, the purest principles."[32] He rose to such heights that men were persuaded "that the public prosperity resides in his very person," and thought his fall "the greatest calamity that they had to fear."[33] Even from his enemies it is what made Robespierre The Incorruptible that is significant.

The Incorruptible also impressed those who saw him only as observers. W. A. Miles, the English political writer who met all the leading

French revolutionaries in 1790–91, who later suggested digging a Suez canal, wrote political tracts as well as two comic operas, corresponded with Pitt, and died at Paris while collecting materials for a history of the Revolution, left one of the better of these observer reports:

> The man held of least account by Mirabeau, by Lafayette, and even by the Lameths, and all the Orléans faction [he is writing in early 1791] will soon be of the first consideration. He is cool, measured, and resolved. He is in his heart republican, honestly so, not to pay court to the multitude, but from an opinion that it is the very best, if not the only form of government which men ought to admit. He is a stern man, rigid in his principles, plain, unaffected in his manners, no foppery in his dress, certainly above corruption, despising wealth, and with nothing of the volatility of a Frenchman in his character. . . . I watch him very closely every night. I read his countenance with eyes steadily fixed on him. He is really a character to be contemplated; he is growing every hour into consequence.[34]

Here is none of the afflatus of a follower, or even of a Frenchman. Nor is there any in the observations of Cassat, an intelligent and conservative Swiss journalist. Cassat considered Robespierre a dictator, but insisted that his dictatorship "far from being founded on his ambition rested only on the justice that one was compelled to render to his republican virtues. He was looked upon as the palladin to whom was attached the destiny of the public welfare. When he spoke it was patriotism itself that dictated the laws through his oracular pronouncements."[35]

The moral force emanating from Robespierre, the force that made him The Incorruptible, is what matters. It either attracts or repels, and can do so differently at different times. Revolutions, writes Jean Jaurès, "are the barbarous form of progress." He longed for a day when "human progress will be truly human." But until that time the grandeur, the creativity, the hopefulness of revolutions would be scarred by origins in a "semi-bestial epoch of humanity."[36] Such primitiveness and brutality would coarsen men while simultaneously heightening the need for moral sanction for the repulsive deeds thrust upon men in revolution. This moral force, which inspired and impelled, instigated and forgave, explained and encouraged, Robespierre provided in himself and his words. He was, he remains, the man of Year II. He then bore and has ever since borne the affliction of all the excesses of the Revolution in its greatest crisis. Perhaps it is too great a price to have paid. But as the theocratic reactionary Joseph de Maistre said, "The ferocious genius of Robespierre saved the integrity of France."[37]

Epilogue

PLATE XVI
(Phot. Bibl. nat. Paris)

D EATH BROUGHT ROBESPIERRE another career. His fame, whatever the efforts of his successors, was assured: now it had to be explained. His career had to be fit into the new revolutionary tradition that began with the French Revolution. Robespierre, who had so self-consciously revealed himself posthumously, became the subject of analysis and interpretation. His own revelations, his own words, which he had intended as the basis for evaluation, were largely disregarded. For many years his reputation oscillated between hatred and hagiography, between the views of the Thermidorians and the Socialists, between the anecdotes of Abbé Proyart and those of Charlotte Robespierre. On the most superficial level one either liked or disliked Robespierre, and usually such feeling was accompanied with views of the Revolution that matched. Those with more sophistication tried to judge the man and his career in terms of the Revolution, and all such efforts followed the changing politics of nineteenth- and twentieth-century France, the changing fortunes of revolutions and revolutionaries.

But the central issue is not whether one likes or dislikes Robespierre. Political tastes are as inexplicable as other varieties. Our task is the one Robespierre himself set: to explain why this particular man enjoyed this particular career. With the exception of Napoleon Bonaparte, Robespierre is the most written-about figure of the Revolution. This fact explains the ratio: only Napoleon's career is more exceptional.

Robespierre's unique gifts and personality, his industriousness and dedication to the Revolution, his words and ideas, have been the subject of this book. I have asked the reader to view the French Revolution through the consciousness of Robespierre. I have presented Robespierre's Revolution, which is not identical with that seen by others who lived it, nor with the Revolution now seen by historians. Robespierre's Revolution is simultaneously idiosyncratic and compelling. He sometimes miscalculated the mood of the nation, as in his opposition to the war, or misread the significance of political activity, as in his reluctant (and late) conversion to insurrection. He was overly sensitive to ridicule and slander, was hesitant to strike, whether through orchestrated riot or in the Convention, and consequently sometimes allowed matters to reach a crisis. The most notorious example is his failure, on 8 Thermidor, to do anything to check the conspiracy against him. He furthermore had the fatal habit of threatening without carrying out the threats. He tended to make his colleagues uneasy with his categorical virtue, and because he so closely identified self and ideology, he mistook his own will for that of the masses, as he did in the cult of the Supreme

Being. Yet for all these errors of judgment, these limitations of personality and perception, he triumphed.

Robespierre was called to power only in 1793, when his fellow deputies elected him to the Committee of Public Safety. He dominated the Revolution only during the last year of his life, and we forget, because of the significance of his career, that his apprenticeship was exceptionally long, his ascendancy exceptionally slow. He was chosen only after many others had had a chance to lead, only when his choice was unavoidable, when he could no longer be ignored. The choice came in the fifth summer of the Revolution, in the midst of a crisis that surpassed all earlier crises. It had become a choice between Liberty or Death, and Robespierre was the essential man. In choosing him to lead, the deputies (and the Revolution) rejected, either tacitly or deliberately, those who had earlier led and those who aspired to lead.

Although Robespierre has been here much talked of as a literary intellectual in revolutionary politics, and as such an archetype, his triumph was not that of an author whose work is suddenly, or finally, recognized as worthy. Robespierre's skills had been long recognized. Since the early weeks of the Constituent Assembly he had been acknowledged a man to reckon with, a voice to be feared and respected. He was kept from power not because he was thought incapable but because he represented ideas that were unacceptable to the majority in the assemblies of the Revolution. Had he been another man, or had this been a later revolution, he and his followers might have seized power, as the Bolsheviks did in October 1917. Such an action was unthinkable to Robespierre and his contemporaries, with their distrust of all faction. The only men who did attempt a *coup d'état* in the Revolution were the generals, Lafayette, Dumouriez, and finally Napoleon. Robespierre had to wait to be summoned. Before he was summoned, many had failed, from the King and the Court, to parliamentary coalitions and factions, to the emergence of powerful individuals. Once he was summoned to power, several additional men and groups would challenge him. All would be struck down until the unlikely Thermidorian coalition, which quickly disintegrated, toppled Robespierre himself. After his fall there would not be another leader of the Revolution from the ranks of parliament.

Revolutionary struggle knows no quarter: those who fail die. The competition for leadership of the French Revolution was, literally, murderous. Robespierre survived longer than most. It is important to see his career in the context of the savage competition of the Revolution.

Parliamentary politics, between 1789 and 1794, not only left little or no room for an opposition and for maneuver, it also left precious little room for error. The slightest hesitation or miscalculation could cost a man his life, and with him a long line of followers, for the Revolution struck down not only the leaders but their comrades and anyone who might eventually seek revenge. Robespierre, ironically enough, did not destroy his enemies as comprehensively as the Thermidorians destroyed him and his adherents. One of the realities that made 9 Thermidor possible was the widespread existence in the Convention of men who hated Robespierre, men who had sympathized with the Girondins, or with Danton, who saw a chance for revenge. The harsh truth is that when Robespierre was finally chosen to lead, it necessarily meant that others were not chosen, and some of these were doomed by his ascendancy.

Robespierre himself, I have stressed, was ever ready to explain and analyze, and he attributed his choice to his principles and to providence, which latter he understood in a unique and non-Christian way. Yet in retrospect there is much to recommend this interpretation. His was an irresistible destiny and simultaneously a demonstration that virtue was more powerful than vice, that men, once given the choice, would recognize this truth and cleave to virtue, which was the basis of all Robespierre's principles. Surely he saw his rise to power as confirmation of this interpretation. It is not a bad explanation, but it tends to disregard or undervalue the mundane circumstances of his career. Robespierre's inclination toward abstraction, toward seeing moral principles behind men's political behavior, had led him to attribute too much to the power of ideas and self. These were forces of exceptional potency in the French Revolution, but Robespierre had long expressed his principles, long revealed his self, long preached virtue, before he was chosen. More significant, I think, is the course of the Revolution itself. Robespierre was vindicated in July 1793 when he was chosen. His view and self were approved, and at the same time the views and selves of many others were rejected. This is the dialectic of his preponderance.

From the beginning to the end of the Revolution there were men who sought to impose themselves, to influence the course of events, direct the virile energies released by the upheaval. Many of these aspirants were remarkable men, worthy to lead, deserving of followers, capable of representing substantial aspects of France and of the Revolution, admirable men with attractive personalities and obvious gifts. Only compared with these men does Robespierre's career make sense.

Brains and courage and patriotism, talent and passion and devotion, these were not lacking in the French Revolution. But as with a great wine, it is a question of the blend, the proportions, as much as the quality of the vines and the benevolence of the weather. Mirabeau is often contrated with Robespierre, and the contrast is useful. Not only was Mirabeau the first of the great tribunes of the Revolution, the first to lead from parliament through his voice and self, but his career is the prototype of Robespierre's, although the two men could not have been different. Even leaving aside Mirabeau's dubious finances, he was a flawed and compromised character, although a man of the first rank in intelligence, oratorical skills, and political genius. But in habits of mind and morality he was a man of the *ancien régime*, and he never completely shook off his past. The synthesis he hoped to forge between the old France and the new, in which he was the necessary mediator, was probably doomed. Revolutions do not make compromises until they become unavoidable.

The odor of old France did not cling to Mirabeau in superficial ways, such as dress and manners, as it did with Robespierre. These outward manifestations of a vanished world Mirabeau shed easily enough. Rather it was his scandalous prerevolutionary life that appeared symptomatic of his values and those of the *ancien régime*. He had been a victim of the arbitrary justice of the monarchy, having been imprisoned under a *lettre de cachet*, one of those hated royal warrants by which absolutism operated and intimidated its critics. Yet Mirabeau retained a profound belief in the necessity of monarchy, for he had considerable skepticism about the ability of the people to govern (or the advisability of their doing so). He had also a certain spiritual shallowness on moral matters that issued in cynicism. He attached himself to the monarchy and quickly discovered what so many before him had discovered: Louis XVI was a treacherous ally. All Mirabeau's schemes came to naught, his penetrating advice was disregarded, and given his chosen master it is doubtful that even had he lived longer he could have saved the monarchy from ruin. His incomplete career, somehow unworthy of his great gifts, his equally great personality, was, along with Lafayette's, and to a lesser extent that of the Duc d'Orléans, a demonstration that the values and style and men of the *ancien régime* could not accommodate themselves to the Revolution. They understood politics as it had been practiced in the last decades of the monarchy, but this understanding was ultimately irrelevant to the Revolution.

With Mirabeau's death the scramble for power resumed. All who would henceforth lead the Revolution would be new men, men untainted by the old society, or rather men who had not enjoyed prominence or prestige during the *ancien régime*. The Revolution was fecund in generating its own leaders. The most talented of Mirabeau's immediate successors was Barnave, "the spoiled child of the Revolution," as he described himself at his trial for treason. He came first to national attention in his native province of Dauphiné, where he established himself as a revolutionary leader, taking a prominent part in the agitations of 1787–89, now conventionally spoken of as the prerevolution. Yet for all his personal charm and oratorical brilliance and political shrewdness, for all the prestige he brought to the Revolution for having defied the King and Court when they were still unquestionably powerful, Barnave, too, could not conceive of a France without a monarchy, could not imagine the people in power. He, too, was entrapped by a fatal dependence on Louis XVI. He was further compromised by his infatuation with Marie Antoinette. He had been sent by the Constituent to accompany the returning coach carrying the King and Queen back to Paris from Varennes. Riding with the royal couple, he came to adore the queen; and she was a more treacherous ally than her husband. Barnave was a passionate man, still attached to some of the vanished supremacies of France. He hoped to preserve, in the constitutional settlement, a socially stable nation whose many fundamental reforms— a monarchy under a constitution, an expropriated church similarly subordinated, and an outlawed nobility—would be sufficient to prevent any further upheaval. The instruments of control against further revolution would be the constitution and the King. In addition, Barnave had personal and emotional ties with commercial and banking and colonial interests, which he frequently defended in the parliament—against Robespierre as well as others—and which helped undermine his personal popularity. Barnave wanted the Revolution frozen, prematurely as it turned out. Mirabeau was undone by his character; Barnave was undone by history.

The careers of Lafayette and the Duc d'Orléans are a special case. There were a number of nobles who joined the Revolution. The two most famous aristocratic Jacobins were Lepeletier de Saint-Fargeau, the first Jacobin martyr and the author of the educational scheme, and Hérault de Sechelles, the sophisticated connoisseur of life and the author of the 1793 constitution. Both had the most distinguished aristocratic credentials, but neither aspired to personal power and neither was as great, in the old feudal sense of the word, as Lafayette or Orléans, who may have inherited the two most substantial fortunes in France. Lafayette was a political rather than a fighting general; the Duke was the King's first cousin and the inheritor of a long family tradition of meddling in politics. Lafayette had the prestige of his participation in the

American Revolution and wanted to be the arbiter of his country's destiny. Not so much a kingmaker, as he might have been in an earlier age, but a constitution-giver whose army and wealth and personal prestige would regenerate France, Lafayette dominated the Revolution in 1791. The Duke used his immense fortune, reckoned as the greatest in France, to indulge his taste for devious political intrigue. He seems to have aspired to the throne, although his motives are sometimes difficult to follow through the labyrinthine turnings and oblique motives of his activities—he voted for his cousin's death in 1793—from which he was incapable of extricating himself. He never sat upon the throne, but in a sense his career was fulfilled by his son, who in 1830 ascended the throne as Louis Philippe.

Both Lafayette and the Duke failed to grasp the politics of revolution. Enormous wealth and personal prestige, expressed through a vast patronage, these were the essential attributes of an important personage during the *ancien régime*. They proved a hindrance in the Revolution. Both men had narrow social bases on which to build a political career, and although both were detested by the Court, both failed to establish a reliable constituency elsewhere. Lafayette ultimately depended on the army, which he thought of as his own; yet only his general staff joined him in an attempted *coup d'état*. The Duke ultimately depended on the manipulation of those he had bought or who were beholden to him, and on ingratiating himself with the Jacobins, with whom he had few affinities, hoping they might put him on the throne in place of Louis XVI. His new revolutionary friends did not ever trust him unquestionably, momentarily defended him from expulsion from the Convention, then abandoned him and sent him to the guillotine. For both men politics was the art of force and fraud. Both were discarded as the Revolution passed them by, victims, with Mirabeau, of the ruin of the *ancien régime*.

The faction that gathered around Brissot and would pass into history as the Girondins, are different from these other would-be leaders. Not only did they actually exercise revolutionary power for several months, but they were confirmed republicans and revolutionaries. They rose to prominance and power through the Revolution, and in their bold initiatives exercised a profound impact on the course of events. Roland (and even more so his brilliant wife, Manon), Brissot, Guadet, Buzot, and Vergniaud, to mention only a few of the more prominent Girondins, were personally ambitious and talented. Roland was the dullard of the faction, but he brought a certain personal stature and prestige and rectitude—he was a functionary of the *ancien régime* who emulated the Quakers in dress and manners—and his wife supplied the brains, the passion, and the inspiration Roland himself lacked. Guadet and Buzot and Vergniaud were all exceptional men, Vergniaud being considered the greatest orator of the Revolution by many. Brissot himself came from the poorest background, had an unimpeachable character for honesty, was hard-working, and had some cleverness. His singular gift was for enthusiasm and ebullience. His ideas were often scatter-brained, but he had a keen sense of what interested his contemporaries, and he inspired others. Here were men capable of leading the Revolution, and in addition to oratorical genius and political shrewdness the faction had, in the fiery Barbaroux, a genuine militant hero, one of the few men of action among the parliamentary revolutionaries. Barbaroux had led the Marseillais in the attack on the Tuileries on August 10, and despite his scandalous personal life (women, not money, were his weakness), his exploits reflected well on his friends.

It was ambition and impatience, coupled with an odd combination of political sensitivity and audacity, that undid the Girondins. They were willing to resort to the most dangerous and extreme political means to gain their ends and consequently appeared to many as exclusive, cynical, and devious. One contemporary dubbed them the Jesuits of the Revolution, a particularly bitter characterization in a country were the Jesuits had been recently expelled (1763) and were thought meddlesome, untrustworthy, and unpatriotic. In addition the Girondins, although of the same social *milieu* as the Jacobins, had little generalized support in the populace, especially in Paris, where the Jacobins had so successfully courted the Commune and the *sans-culottes*.

But some of these criticisms arise from later developments. When the group first sought power, in the Legislative Assembly, they enjoyed considerable popularity. The Girondins preached an enormously popular war, and they were borne to power on the popularity of their politics. The war, Brissot and his friends argued, would expose Louis XVI's duplicity. When this failed they resorted to urban insurrection (June 20) as a means of intimidating the Court. During the King's trial they tried to abort the process rather than capitulate to the demands of Paris and the radicals. They looked upon Paris as the home of assassins and social scum, and claimed support in the provinces. But they had done little to cultivate this provincial support, and found themselves often uncomfortably allied with royalists and reactionaries who saw in the Girondin cause views capable of exploitation. These were all dreadful errors of judgment, contradictions they could not resolve and so sought to transcend with more and more risky policies.

In addition to these collective bunglings, this irresponsibility of policy, the group did not have a single individual who might have led it, let alone have led the Revolution. Vergniaud was the most attractive of the group, and in many ways the most generously endowed with the gifts essential to a leader of the French Revolution. He had brilliance and humanity, he was personally liked, he had a commanding physical presence, and there was nothing mean-spirited about him. But he lacked the core of single-mindedness that was so essential. When roused to fight, he was incomparable; but he was seldom roused.

Even more damaging than these personal shortcomings was the example of the Girondins in power. They entered the Convention with a majority, perhaps twice as many deputies as the Jacobins. True, provincial and not Parisian voters had elected them, but because of their numbers and their prestige they came at once to dominate the committees and offices of the Convention. Their ineptitudes in the King's trial, the first test of leadership, were damaging, as was their alienation of Paris. In a sense their high-handed manipulations of the Convention created a more cohesive Jacobin Society and made of Robespierre the official ideologue of the group. They did nothing to ease the food shortages and rioting of March 1793, and General Dumouriez, hand-picked by the group, delivered the fatal blow to its fortunes when he turned his coat. The purge of the Girondins marked the abandonment of moderate republicanism. For the cautious and the timid the Girondins offered revolution without any accompanying social revolution. But this compromise proved impossible. Although it took nearly two months after the purge for the stunned Convention to turn to Robespierre, the collapse of the Girondins signaled the need for new leadership. This would mean accepting some (as little as possible is what the majority desired) of the dreaded social changes long threatened and delayed.

In July 1793 Robespierre was preferable to some street militant. It is true that none of the street radicals had sufficient social support outside the Paris neighborhoods to command the Revolution, and the fears they inspired were widespread. Those who sat in the Convention well remembered the weeks when the Commune had governed, between August 10 and September 21, from the attack on the Tuileries to the sitting of the newly elected Assembly, which included the September Massacres. Most recently they had witnessed the purging of the Convention. At least in choosing Robespierre, leadership would remain in the Assembly. He was preferable to the fire-eaters Chaumette or Vincent or Hébert. He was clearly superior to Marat, who had anyhow been assassinated by Charlotte Corday on July 12. Actually only Hébert had ambitions to govern. He was a member of the General Council, the governing body of the Commune of Paris, as well as the editor of the *Père Duchesne*, the most notorious newspaper of the period. In the pages of his newspaper, vastly popular among the *sans-culottes*, he regularly blew his own horn, advertising his fitness to rule. But he offered little in the way of politics and ideology. He had an especially murderous and bloody vision of the kinds and degree of coercion that should be used to accomplish the work of the Revolution, but otherwise he had little substance. His failure to achieve power (he was guillotined in the spring of 1794) was not only a judgment of his abilities, but an instance of the general fact that journalism was not, in the French Revolution, a road to power.

When Robespierre was summoned in July 1793, there were others in the Convention who might have been chosen, but with the exception of Danton, to whom I shall turn in a moment, not one of these *conventionnels*, a number of whom would join the coalition that toppled Robespierre, had a following that could support him. That several of the conspirators wanted to lead became apparent during Thermidorian governments when egotism was a significant factor in the indecorous shifting of alliances of the years from Robespierre's fall to Napoleon's *coup d'état*. Those, of course, who fell with Robespierre, although they did not go to the guillotine—Collot d'Herbois, Billaud-Varenne, Bertrand Barère—might have aspired to personal power, but were rendered incapable by 9 Thermidor.

Of all those who challenged Robespierre, Danton was the most serious rival. The convention of contrasting the two men, seeing in them not only a personal struggle between opposed personalities but a struggle over the nature of revolution itself, has validity. During the Revolution Danton was seen by many as an alternative to Robespierre, and he was twice given power: first by being made the Minister of Justice in the interim government that succeeded the destruction of the monarchy on August 10, and again as one of the original members of the first Committee of Public Safety. He had extensive friendships, a considerable personal following, unimpeachable revolutionary credentials. He was a riveting speaker and had the advantage over Robespierre of being a man of action whose words and deeds made him the incarnation of the militant Revolution. He had, in addition, an organization, the Cordeliers Club, where he was a dominant force, although he had never cultivated that weapon with the assiduity Robespierre had lavished on the Jacobins. He was a man of many parts, some of them larger than life. He had a fine physique, a pockmarked yet compelling face, and his upper lip was pulled into a sardonic smile by a childhood scar from a bull's horn. These attributes were enhanced by the most respected pair of lungs in the Revolution. He was forceful, gruff, dominating, and good-humored. He was overpowering in intimate as in public dealings and debate. Even his faults—his coarseness, his love of low company and vulgar humor, his boisterousness, his occasional cynicism—were thought endearing or harmless. He not only had ideas and energy, he had a personality to match.

There were rumors of his dubious finances. After so many years it is not easy to say for certain, but he seems to have taken money from the Court. In 1789 he was at least 43,000 livres in debt, a substantial liability for anyone: a crippling burden for a not very successful lawyer. In 1791 he paid off his many creditors and bought an estate for 80,000 livres. There was no visible improvement in his law practice or his prospects. But if he took bribes, he was not thought a traitor (then or now), and the rumors not only were unsubstantiated in his lifetime, but did not compromise his popularity. Then as now, Danton occupied a warmer place in his countrymen's heart and imagination than did Robespierre.

It is Danton's very self that compromised him and finally led him to a serious political miscalculation that exposed him to his many enemies. He was too much of an egotist to put up with the laborious, oblique movements of legislative and administrative bodies, too brilliant to deal patiently with those who staffed them. Like so many clever and quick-witted men, he was impatient with the pace of others whom he considered (often correctly) inferior to himself. Robespierre, interestingly enough, although a very intelligent man, had no such intellectual arrogance. Danton was visibly bored by the sameness and tedium of daily politics. He depended on inspiration rather than habit and discipline. His oratory shows this characteristic perfectly. Not one of Danton's speeches has survived in manuscript, for he spoke extemporaneously. His oratory was scintillating, and those who heard Danton on a great occasion, as when he called the country to defend itself against the invading Prussians and Austrians, in September 1792, never forgot the impression he made. But because he had no patience with preparations, he often let slip opportunities that would not come again, as when he was absent during the final weeks of the King's trial and hence did not join in that great national debate. He assumed that, with his abilities and self-confidence, he could restore his popularity almost at will.

Danton had exceptional political intelligence. When he concluded, in the winter of 1794, that the Terror could not be moderated, the local militants (in Paris and the provinces) controlled, and consequently government returned to the Convention under the constitution of 1793, until the war was either concluded or a negotiated truce was made, his analysis was correct. Probably on no other basis could the Terror be stopped. But his timing was premature by several months; and in revolution time is everything. His personal probings among the allies made him vulnerable at home. Contempt for his own vulnerability was another of Danton's miscalculations, and proved fatal. It is always a mistake to underestimate one's enemies. It is not Robespierre, strictly speaking, who destroyed Danton, although the writers Hugo and Büchner and Dickens, as well as many historians, have made it seem so. Robespierre, in fact, was reluctant to sacrifice Danton; but his colleagues on the Committee of Public Safety prevailed. Danton destroyed himself.

Robespierre's preponderance is a complex matter. The failure of his possible rivals to seize or hold the initiative or to command the necessary social support, or to possess the peculiar combination of gifts necessary to a revolutionary leader, these are all significant considerations in judging his career. All those who might have led, who did temporarily lead, or who lusted to lead, were flawed or incomplete in person or perception or principles. None enjoyed Robespierre's sustained popularity, and none was able to institutionalize popularity as Robespierre did at the Jacobins. And if none had his popularity, none had the social range of that popularity. Similarly, none had the unique combination of ideological genius and a keen grasp of mundane political action. None could have mediated the Revolution as Robespierre did, controlling and articulating the flow of energy from Committee to Convention to Commune to countryside. Robespierre's command of the Revolution was the most comprehensive, whether exercised at the tribune of the Convention or that of the Jacobins or in the Green Room of the Committee. History, both personal and general, had conspired in making the circumstances for such a revolutionary career, the first of its kind and a prototype for later careers. Robespierre himself was a man exceptionally fit for these circumstances. The question of whether Robespierre exploited circumstances, tailored himself to the Revolution, or was in happy harmony with the Revolution, is moot. As with all great careers, the lines separating design from chance are impossible to discern.

Danton has his statue in the center of Paris; and dozens of lesser men have their streets. But Robespierre dominates the memory of the Revolution and the history of the Revolution. This is a fit, worthy, enduring memorial.

APPENDIX

Portraits of Robespierre

There are two basic representations of Robespierre: one in three-quarters full face, the other in profile. Each of these perspectives is in turn varied by depicting his turning either to the right or the left. Virtually all the portraits, even those used to caricature the man, are derived from these basic views. All the formal portraits, as well as the sketches made from life and a great many of the caricatures, reveal the same features. In terms of shape of head, size and shape of eyes and nose and mouth and ears, jawline and chin, there is general agreement. Robespierre had large, almond-shaped eyes set off by long eyebrows that curved slightly. He had a high forehead and in some images appears to have had a receding hairline. His nose had prominent nostrils, and appeared flat in full face and sloped upward to a slight point in profile. His mouth was large, his upper lip prominently bowed, and he had large ears. His chin was articulated but was not especially prominent. His expression derived almost entirely from his eyes and his mouth, and by slight emphasis of one or the other an artist could change his appearance. There is one curiosity about the face: in full face it is fleshy, in profile angular and lean.

In whatever medium the artist worked—oil, pastel, pencil, ink—and in whatever circumstances—a formal sitting, a sketch from life, a lithograph based on a painting—Robespierre's features are familiar but his expression varies. Perhaps his was a difficult face to depict; perhaps the artists were influenced by what he was or the circumstances in which they made their images. Whatever the case, we have several variations on a basic theme, for Robespierre's face was capable of expressing or revealing quite different characteristics.

The two oils done of him during the time of the Constituent (VII, chapter 5, and I, frontispiece) make these variations clear. The former is attributed to Joseph Boze, the latter to Adélaïde Labille-Guiard. The Boze portrait is of an intense, frank young man with exceptionally prominent eyes and a neutral expression. Perhaps because of the background Robespierre appears solid, almost sculptured. The Labille-Guiard portrait emphasizes the mouth rather than the eyes and shows us a congenial, sweetly smiling young man whose elegant hands add to the overall impression of conviviality and ease. On first glance one might not think these portraits of the same man, but all the features are the same if the spirit informing them is not. The Labille-Guiard portrait is the only one of Robespierre smiling, and the gentleness of expression and the open congeniality are characteristics we do not normally associate with Robespierre.

The portrait Charlotte Robespierre apparently thought best captured her brother's likeness is a lithograph by Delpech (VIII, chapter 6), which closely resembles an anonymous oil now in the collection of the Carnavalet Museum (II, Prologue). This oil is probably the most frequently reproduced portrait of Robespierre. There is no way of knowing whether the lithograph was based on the oil or done independently, nor can the approximate date of the painting or the lithograph be established.

In both, Robespierre looks out with his face turned to the right rather than the left, as in the two portraits discussed above. Both Delpech and the anonymous artist emphasize the flamboyance of Robespierre's clothing: the oil has him wearing a striped coat as well as a striped vest. The oil portrait concentrates on the eyes and mouth. The eyes are bright, steady in gaze and with no hint of irony. The mouth is set in what might be described as the faintest hint of a smile, a smile about to begin. It is this detail that gives a touch of irony to the expression. The ironic lips cause him to appear a bit distant, and since this characteristic, more or less emphasized, appears in several portraits, it was doubtless a quality he possessed. But if he is painted as slightly reserved, it is not the reserve of aloofness or arrogance. The Delpech lithograph offers less detail, partly because of the medium, especially in the eyes. The face is somewhat fleshier and the lines at the corners of the mouth less obvious. The face has less irony, its dominant impression being that of frankness.

The other full-face portrait is a sketch from life done during the Convention (IX, chapter 8). Again the eyes and mouth make the expression; the mouth is here set in a slightly forward direction, and the lines or indentations where the lips end are prominent. This configuration is enough to create an aloof, distant, even arrogant Robespierre. The eyeglasses, characteristically pushed up on his forehead, are a detail that gives the portrait immediacy, as if the subject had been photographed at the end of one of his speeches. The vest and coat appear to be the same as those worn for the anonymous oil discussed above. The artist, Gérard, has drawn Robespierre with his least-attractive qualities emphasized: his coolness, his distance, his detachment. In a nineteenth-century version of the Gérard sketch (XII, chapter 10) the face has been made more somber, the expression less haughty. This has been accomplished by making the lips less fleshy and the eyes a bit larger. These minor alterations make for a more appealing Robespierre.

In profile Robespierre's face is both more angular and sculptural. In the nineteenth century it was his profile that appealed to those anxious to rehabilitate his reputation. The bronze medallion by Ruhière (XVI, Epilogue) is an example of how these characteristics, with some slight emphasis, could be made to yield an austere, determined, heroic, and virile Robespierre. The contemporary profiles from which Ruhière, and others, made their Robespierre, are a bit less severe and heroic. The most elegant of these (XV, chapter 13) presents a man whose nose is his most prominent feature and whose forehead slopes back noticeably, revealing not only a quite prominent forehead, but also what may have been a receding hairline. (Could Robespierre's preference for wigs owe something to vanity about the loss of his hair?) This is a serious face, with none of the affability of the Labille-Guiard portrait nor the aloofness of the Gérard drawing nor the ironic hint of the anonymous portrait in the Carnavalet. The inscription, "Legislateur Incorruptible," fits. Here is a determined and dedicated men. This profile, like all the profiles, also reveals that Robespierre had large ears as well as a large mouth.

An earlier profile (V, chapter 3), is of a younger man, although it is worth noting that only a few years separate the portraits. The Revolution aged its votaries. This earlier profile has the hint of a smile, and the face has not yet been as intensely lived in as it soon would be. The head is tilted forward rather than inclined backward, so the slope of the forehead is not as obvious, and the nose appears a bit more pointed. It might be reasonably argued that in these two profiles we have the Robespierre of the Constituent and the Robespierre of the Convention, the young deputy and the mature ideologue. The contrast is essentially one of purification. The youthfulness has been shed; the face is more austere and determined. The Revolution has taken its toll.

The last sketch we have of Robespierre is that made during the extraordinary Convention session of 9 Thermidor (XIV, chapter 12). It is important not only because it is a historic document of a great moment, but because it offers a comparison with the formal profiles. Gérard's sketch has vitality and intensity, as well it might, given the circumstances. The mouth is set in a straight line, and we see here the lines of the muscles at the corner of the mouth that had played so important a part in other portraits, where the slightest relaxation or contraction of these muscles significantly altered Robespierre's expression. The eyes are emphasized by Gérard in a curious way. He does not stress their shape or size. Rather, he calls attention to them by having Robespierre wear his glasses. His wig, usually so immaculate, is a bit frazzled, and the high forehead is particularly prominent. The face is sharp, vital, intense, and seems the face of a man well beyond Robespierre's thirty-six years. But if Géard's sketch depicts a Robespierre we have not seen in the other, earlier and more formal portraits, still the features are those of all the portraits. There is not a good deal of agreement on Robespierre's dominant expression, but there is agreement on what he looked like, or rather what his individual features looked like.

All the many portraits of Robespierre, whether contemporary with the Revolution or subsequent copies, are variations on these basic types. The illustrations chosen for this book I consider either representative images of Robespierre or historically significant in their own right.

FRONTISPIECE (Plate I): Oil portrait, now in a private collection, thought to have been painted from her original pastel (now vanished) by Mme. Adélaïde Labille-Guiard. Robespierre is dressed in the black suit of a representative of the Third Estate, his hat under his arm, his hand on an ornamental sword. His fine hands, carefully done hair, and knotted cravat, all lovingly painted, convey the man's fastidiousness. The engaging smile appears in no other portrait. This is the portrait shown in the Salon of 1791 (see page ii above) that first dubbed Robespierre "The Incorruptible." According to Buffenoir (p. 9), at its showing "The sound patriots applauded the inscription with all their hearts." Buffenoir also quotes a letter from Robespierre to the artist (p. 10), dated February 13, 1791 (from the Egerton Papers in the British Museum), which accepts her proposal that he sit for a portrait. The letter is typical of his flamboyant and elusive rhetorical style when writing to women.

PROLOGUE (Plate II): Oil portrait now in the Carnavalet Museum. This is the most famous portrait of Robespierre, artist unknown. The same gray-on-gray striped coat and vest, as well as the formal high cravat, appear in several other portraits. These may have been copied from this canvas, or Robespierre, who had so small a wardrobe, may have often worn this coat and posed in it. His smile here is less charming and open than that of the Labille-Guiard oil.

CHAPTER 1 (Plate III): One of the many caricatures done circa Thermidor. The caption reads: "Robespierre guillotining the executioner, having sent all the French to the guillotine." The letters, corresponding to the forest of guillotines behind him, are keyed in the caption to identify slain groups: A. The executioner. B. The Committee of Public Safety. C. The Committee of General Security. D. The Revolutionary Tribunal. E. The Jacobins. F. The Cordeliers. G. The Brissotins. H. The Girondins. I. The Phlipotins (followers of Mme. Roland). K. The Chabotins (followers of Chabot). L. The Hébertists. M. The nobility and the priests. N. Men of ability. O. Old men, women and children. P. Soldiers and generals. Q. Constitued authorities. R. The National Convention. S. Popular societies. The pyramid at whose base he is sitting (dressed in the costume of a deputy) bears the inscription "Here lies all France." Robespierre is tramping underfoot the constitutions of 1791 and 1793. (Bibliothèque Nattionale)

CHAPTER 2 (Plate IV): I reproduce this oil portrait, supposedly the earliest done of Robespierre, with some trepidation. Its identity and provenance are very well attested, but it does not resemble the other portraits. The face here is more oval than round, the forehead is higher, the nose longer and sharper. The eyes, although almond-shaped, are smaller than otherwise depicted, and this does not appear to be the portrait of a twenty-four-year-old. According to Paris, appendix, p. cxiv, who reproduces this portrait as his frontispiece, the oil was painted at Arras, around 1783, and carries the signature of the artist, Louis-Léopold Boilly. Paris insists he reproduces the portrait from the collection of a descendant of Robespierre's: "we can thus affirm its authenticity." Despite the weight of this evidence, I am not convinced this is Robespierre; or if it is, he underwent a remarkable and inexplicable change in the Revolution.

CHAPTER 3 (Plate V): One of the many mass-produced portraits of the deputies, issued in series by various booksellers, inexpensive, and intended for a broad distribution. This one is from a volume entitled *La collection de Jabin* (Jabin was the publisher). The original drawing was done by Gros, the engraving by Beljambe. The medallion at the bottom of the ornamental plinth, "la Loi et le Roi," represents the cachet of the Constituent Assembly. Robespierre's date of birth is wrong: he was born in 1758, not 1760. Gros's original sketch is in the Bibliothèque Nationale. The wig he is wearing here appears in many portraits. (Bibliothèque Nationale)

CHAPTER 4 (Plate VI): A contemporary sketch of Robespierre at the Convention's tribune. The formality of his dress, including a wig, is apparent. The small, circumscribed gesture captured by the anonymous artist agrees with the verbal descriptions of Robespierre's manner at the tribune. His text (here drawn as only a few sheets of manuscript) is too short to be complete, but otherwise it is an authentic detail, since he almost always spoke from a text. The glasses he habitually wore when reading his speeches are here absent or eliminated. (Bibliothèque Nationale)

CHAPTER 5 (Plate VII): Oil portrait attributed by Buffenoir (p. 30) to Joseph Boze, a former court painter whose most famous portrait was of Marat. This was done, arguably, during the Constituent, thus around the time of the war debates. The portrait has a kind of intensity that is lacking in most of the portraits. Partly this is created by having the figure emerge so starkly out of a black background. (Bibliothèque Nationale)

CHAPTER 6 (Plate VIII): This may be the portrait referred to by Charlotte Robespierre, in her *Mémoires*, as the best likeness of her brother. At her death, on August 1, 1834, an inventory of her few possessions was made. Among them was (Buffenoir, p. 69) "A portrait of Robespierre." Buffenoir argues that the portrait meant in this inventory was a lithograph by Grevedon, which he reproduces (plate 49). But the portrait Charlotte mentions in her *Mémoires* is by Delpech, which I reproduce here. The differences between this and the one reproduced by Buffenoir are that a facsimile of Robespierre's signature is not included in the Grevedon lithograph (I have here deleted it) and that Robespierre's name is in the Roman alphabet, not in script. Otherwise the portraits are identical, although the Delpech version is rougher in execution, lacking some of the detail apparent in the Grevedon version. (Bibliothèque Nationale)

CHAPTER 7 (Plate IX): Drawing from life by Gérard, done at a session of the Convention. This may possibly have served Gérard as a study for an oil portrait that survived until 1815, when Simon Duplay destroyed it. This is only conjecture, but if correct, then it is this likeness that Robespierre himself had with him at the Duplays' when he was killed. The note attached to the drawing (another indication that it was a study for a painting) says: "Green eyes, pale complexion; coat of green stripes, vest, blue stripes on white, cravat red stripes on white." The colors are somewhat different, but this was probably the same coat and vest that appear in several portraits. Robespierre's eyeglasses are, characteristically, pushed up on his forehead. (Bibliothèque Nationale)

CHAPTER 8 (Plate X): Another of the caricatures done after Thermidor. The portrait itself is based on an earlier one by Bonneville, which served as a model for a number of likenesses. To this model the engraver, Fassart, has added the cup into which Robespierre is squeezing blood from a heart. "Le Triumvir Robespierre" does not make much sense unless it refers to his faction on the Committee of Public Safety, composed of himself, Couthon, and Saint-Just. Otherwise he was not referred to as a member of a triumvirate. (Bibliothèque Nationale)

CHAPTER 9 (Plate XI): A composition rich in symbolism, and one that served as a setting for the portraits of several deputies around the time of the acceptance of the constitution of 1793 by the Convention. In the center is the constitution, with tricolor flags draped at the sides, enveloping the fasces on the left, Robespierre on the right. The *coq hardi*, symbol of France, is perched atop the scales of justice. The design is by Bérnard, published by Binet, and probably quite near the June 24, 1793, date announced under the Acte Constitutionnel. (Bibliothèque Nationale)

CHAPTER 10 (Plate XII): This is a nineteenth-century version inspired by Gérard's sketch, engraved by Gouault. The face has been made less arrogant and aloof. The Gérard sketch was a favorite throughout the nineteenth century. (Bibliothèque Nationale)

CHAPTER 11 (Plate XIII): Again a nineteenth-century lithograph but useful for the details of a deputy's costume as well as its commemoration of the Festival of the Supreme Being. Because this was a state occasion, all the deputies wore their costumes. A long-tailed coat of blue, wrapped around the waist by a tricolor sash knotted on the left, falling to the ornamental sword whose decorated guard is surmounted by a bonnet of liberty, a large white cravat with ample knot, top boots (not here visible), and a plumed hat (also not depicted) were the costume of a representative. (Bibliothèque Nationale)

CHAPTER 12 (Plate XIV): A historic document in its own right, this sketch, the last we have of Robespierre, was made during the session of 9 Thermidor by Parceval Grandmaison. The liveliness of the face and the grim set of the jaw well reflect the drama of the occasion. (Bibliothèque Nationale)

CHAPTER 13 (Plate XV): This engraving by Fiésinger, after a drawing by Guérin, was at least twice published during the Revolution. An earlier version listed Robespierre's accomplishments as "deputy for Artois to the National Assembly in 1789. Public prosecutor of the Criminal Tribunal for the department of Paris." Buffenoir (p. 52) says, "This portrait is considered by connoisseurs as the most elegantly executed of those of Maximilien." And (p. 53) he adds, "I believe this one is truly the most characteristic portrait of the great man, the most reflective of his role in government, of his republican mission, and his philosophical discipleship of Jean-Jacques Rousseau." (Bibliothèque Nationale)

EPILOGUE (Plate XVI): A bronze medallion done around 1835 by François-Théodore Ruhière, from a portrait belonging to Charlotte Robespierre (which is not specified by Buffenoir, pp. 38–39). The inscription surrounding the image reads: "We desire that France become the model of nations, the scourge of oppressors, the consolation of the oppressed." The verses are from p. 450 of Laponneraye's edition of Charlotte's Mémoires. Here is the face of a hero, austere, distant, idealized, determined, self-confident. It signals the beginning of the rehabilitation of Robespierre in the nineteenth century, especially by the Socialists of the 1830s, of whom Laponneraye was a leading figure. (Bibliothèque Nationale)

Notes

1. A. Z. Manfred, "Robespierre dans l'historiographie russe et soviétique," *Actes du colloque Robespierre*, pp. 237, 250.

Notes

Prologue

1. A. Z. Manfred, "Robespierre dans l'historiographie russe et sovétique," *Actes du colloque Robespierre*, pp. 237, 250.
2. Because the list of biographies would be excessively long, I arbitrarily select those I think most worthy. The several approaches to Robespierre's life indicate some dissatisfaction with earlier attempts, or the quest for a perspective adequate to reveal the complexities, or both. The first scholarly life, written by Ernest Hamel, was undertaken as an act of piety. This is a work conceived and executed on an enormous scale, in three volumes and more than a couple of thousand pages. It is a history of Robespierre in the Revolution rather than a biography, and when Robespierre is not on stage, the history of the Revolution is unfolded for us. Hamel was reluctant to discard any scrap of information concerning his hero, and his work remains a mine of information. Another nineteenth-century classic, this one keenly hostile, is J.-A. Paris's study of Robespierre's early years in Arras, which ends as Robespierre departs for the Estates-General. It is the most scrupulously detailed account of these years of obscurity. Albert Mathiez, alas, died before he could fulfill the contract he signed to write Robespierre's life. But his essays, both scholarly and popular, indicate the kind of book he would have written. Mathiez was determined to rehabilitate Robespierre and was inspired by the Boshevik revolution. His sharp intelligence and scholarly diligence, as well as his excessive love for controversy, inform his work. Louis Jacob's collection of contemporary opinions and impressions of Robespierre is not, strictly speaking, a biography, but the cumulative impact gives us a picture of the man as he was seen before and after Thermidor. More traditional are the biographies of J. M. Thompson and Gérard Walter. The former is the most extensive and reliable life in English, conventional in approach and presentation, intelligent and sensitive, but with a tendency

to overrationalize, to see in Robespierre's every move and gesture a reason. Walter runs to the other extreme. In his first as well as his "definitive" versions of Robespierre's life, the enormous amount of information collected, sometimes almost encyclopedic in quantity and quality, is not fully integrated into the biography. The overflow is relegated to appendices. Walter seems more concerned with collecting the materials for a biography than with writing one. Still, these are the best traditional lives, in French and English.The best short life is Marc Bouloiseau's, whose few pages are redolent with Robespierre's essence: a smooth *demi-glace* carefully reduced. The best biography from a Marxist perspective, and a fine book in any comparison, is Jean Massin's study. The best psychological study is Max Gallo's, and Norman Hampson has written an original book that shrewdly considers, and muses on, the relationship of the surviving evidence to Robespierre's life.

Chapter 1

1. Mme. de Staël, XII, 142, has Robespierre in agony "on the very table he used while writing his name on those fateful warrants." The table is preserved in the Musée des Archives Nationales in Paris.
2. We do not know what or how much was destroyed by Courtois's Committee of Twelve. We do know that a great deal was "edited" or abridged or published out of context. Some of these editorial liberties can be checked by consulting Berville and Barrière, *Papiers de Robespierre*, a necessary supplement to Courtois.
3. Courtois, p. 14.
4. On the social views of the Thermidorians and their reliability as historians of the Revolution, see Cobb, *Police and People*, especially pp. 48, 173, 175.
5. Berville and Barrière, I, 154.
6. Courtois, p. 27.
7. Berville and Barrière, I, 157.
8. La Reveillière-Lépeaux, I, 115.
9. Only a bit later in his account, without troubling about the contradiction, Fréron has Robespierre laughing till tears flowed, hopelessly amused at the clever absurdities of Camille Desmoulins (Berville and Barrière, I, 158).
10. Berville and Barrière, I, 155.
11. Proyart published his biography at Augsburg in 1795. There is some dispute as to whether Le Blond de Neuvéglise, the putative author, is the same man as Abbé Proyart, vice-principal of Louis-le-Grand when Robes-

pierre attended. It is now generally accepted that the two men are one and the same.

12. Proyart, pp. 67, 61, 55, 63. Also cited in Hampson, *Life and Opinions,* p. 3.

13. Mme. de Staël, *Considérations sur les principaux événements de la Révolution française,* II, 130, quoted from Thompson, I, 52.

14. Berville and Barrière, I, 159.

15. Villiers, pp. 1–6, is perhaps the most notorious of the inventors because his supposed recollections are both plausible and circumstantial, are presented as those of an eyewitness to Robespierre's most obscure revolutionary days in Paris, and contain information not otherwise available. His anecdotes have been widely repeated. René Garmy, especially pp. 22, 31, convinces that Villier's evidence is highly questionable if not worthless, the clever arrangement of hearsay. Biographers have proved reluctant to give up this source. Gallo acknowledges Garmy's argument and retains the anecdotes. Hampson, *Life and Opinions,* dismisses the testimony (p. 51).

16. Montjoye, p. 230.

17. Proyart, p. 279.

18. Choudieu, p. 290; also in Jacob, p. 203.

19. Quoted from Mathiez, "La politique de Robespierre . . . ," p. 271.

20. Debates were opened on November 13, 1792. The trial itself began with the reading of the accusation against the King, on December 10. Louis appeared on December 11 to respond to the charges, and again on December 26 to present his defense. The votes were taken, by roll call, from January 15 to January 20. The king was executed on the morning of January 21, 1793.

21. Walter, *Robespierre,* pp. 130–31.

22. The first edition of 1832 contained only the speeches from 1789 to 1792. A more complete edition, *Oeuvres choisies de Maximilien Robespierre, avec une notice historique, des notes et des commentaires,* in three volumes, was published in 1840. Until the Société des Etudes Robespierristes began its great edition, completed in 1967, only selections were available of Robespierre's speeches and journalism. Laponneraye's remained the most complete of the several selections. The others are *Discours et rapports de Robespierre,* edited by Charles Vellay (Paris, 1908,), and *Les plus beaux discours de Robespierre,* edited by Charles Vellay (Paris, 1908), and *Les plus beaux discours de Robespierre,* edited by F. Castres (Paris, 1929), which includes only five speeches from the Constituent. Jean Poperen, *Robespierre, Textes choisis,* 3 vols. (Paris, 1957–58), is the most useful of the short collections.

23. For a full account of the story of the genesis of the *Memoires,* see Fleisch-

man, which also contains a critical edition of the work. There is an abbreviated account in Walter, *Robespierre*, pp. 596–601. On Albert Laponneraye and the Socialists of the 1830s, see Jacques Godechot's short introduction to a big subject, "L'Historiographie française de Robespierre," pp. 173–74.

24. Fleischman, pp. 189, 198, 202.
25. Charlotte reports he resigned as a humanitarian gesture against capital punishment. Paris, p. 45, finds no record of this resignation: "At the time when this old judicial organization was suppressed (1790), his name still appeared on the list of men having a *fief gradués* in the Episcopal court."
26. Fleischman, p. 210.
27. He regularly saw Le Bas, Saint-Just, and Couthon, his closest political comrades, all of whom (with his brother) would go to the guillotine with him. In addition he regularly saw the artist and Montagnard Jacques-Louis David, and Buonarotti. See Stéphan-Pol, p. 84. These close friends were sometimes joined by a more specifically Duplay inner circle, whom Robespierre also counted among his intimates. See Hampson, *Life and Opinions*, pp. 90–91, and Lenôtre, pp. 123–27. Here, as in so much else, the Thermidorians sacrificed easily verifiable facts for political and propaganda effect.
28. Only ten of the speeches he made have survived in printed versions. Four of these were published at his own expense, the other six (three each) by the Jacobins Club and by the Assembly itself. Only in these few instances can we know at least what he wanted on the record, for he saw these speeches through the press.
29. On one occasion (Hampson, *Life and Opinions*, p. 50) he complained about a published speech attributed to him which he had not made.
30. Robespierre's manuscripts were apparently hidden by Eléanor Duplay at the time of her fiancé's arrest and death. They thus escaped the ravages of Courtois's commission. The papers remained in the Duplay family until 1815. Simon Duplay was at that time a minor functionary in Paris, working for the Restoration Government. He took fright that the compromising manuscripts might be found and ruin his career. He burned them—papers, manuscripts, letters, holographs of speeches—along with a portrait by Gérard. Only three manuscript speeches, along with a few letters, escaped this destruction. Of the holograph speeches, only that of 8 Thermidor, Robespierre's last, is in his own hand (Hamel, I, 303, note). Robespierre's modern editors, in reconstructing his utterances, have had to rely upon reports of the speeches, except in those cases where the author had them published. In many cases several versions, owing to the accuracy or speed of the stenographer, have survived. It is impossible to choose between them save on impressionistic grounds, and in matters of taste no man should

claim unquestioned authority. See the introduction, by Marc Bouloiseau, in IV, xi–xxx.

Chapter 2

1. Charlotte was born in 1760. Henriette, who died in her teens, was born in 1761; Augustin in 1763.
2. Fleischman, p. 194.
3. Only a few of the revolutionaries lashed out retrospectively against the "barbarism" of the schools. Among these were Brissot, Condorcet, and Billaud-Varenne. For a short documentary history, see Palmer, *School of the French Revolution*. The standard work on Louis-le-grand is Dupont-Ferier.
4. The episode is well documented, but the details, as with almost every episode in Robespierre's life, not to mention the interpretation, have been inflated, elaborated by many. The symbolism of the occasion is irresistible. The King and Queen apparently took no more than a passing notice of the young prize student kneeling in the rain and reciting his memorized Latin speech than they would have of any other ritual performed by a commoner at the end of a long day of the brilliant and tiring ceremonies of coronation. There is no way of knowing whether the King "looked kindly at the boy" as Thompson, I, 8, maintains.
5. Biographers have seldom been considered by contemporaries of their subjects. Maurice Goudeket, who went to school with Jean Cocteau, subsequently told Francis Steegmuller, the poet's biographer: "If we had known that he was going to become Jean Cocteau, we might have paid more attention to him then and would now remember more of what he was in those days" (p. 15).
6. *Correspondance*, p. 22 (April 11, 1778).
7. Quoted in Paris, pp. 28–29, and translated in Palmer, *School of the French Revolution*, p. 72.
8. For the hash some of Robespierre's contemporaries made of their lives and dreams in attempting to conquer Paris see Darnton, "The High Enlightenment."
9. Quoted from Paris, p. 42. Lacretelle *ainé* (he had a brother, also distinguished as an intellectual) was a respected man of letters and a legal scholar as well as a reactionary. The episode is elaborated in Walter, p. 43.
10. See Shulim, "The Shulim, "The Youthful Robespierre," who amasses all the evidence but is so bound to a later conception of what a revolutionary is—his model seems to be some of the Bosheviks—that he reaches feeble

conclusions. Robespierre "must have been dissatisfied. . . . His briefs, furthermore, read like those of an angry man" (p. 417). "Thus, as history was to show, Maximilien de Robespierre, along with so many other French intellectuals, had the potentialities for revolution, but he was not a revolutionary before the Revolution" (p. 420).

11. All these details are from Charlotte's recollections. Many of these habits, trivial patterns, are later confirmed by those who saw him in Paris. They are plausible, reveal only superficial aspects of his personality, cast little light on his revolutionary career, and are among the very few aspects of his life liberated from controversy.

12. Walter, pp. 35–37, presents the argument that the two *plaidoyers* relied almost completely upon Buissart's collection of scientific documentation. Robespierre limited himself "to replacing some turns of phrase with others that are equivalent, or in accenting for personal preference the praise given to certain illustrious personages." Hampson, *Life and Opinions*, p. 9 agrees. The practice was not unusual, nor did Robespierre seek to take credit for Buissart's work. Quite the contrary. Both friends sent presentation copies of their texts to Ben Franklin (see *Correspondance*, p. 29, for Robespierre's covering letter) and to the *Mercure de France*. Buissart may have recognized Robespierre's gifts as an orator, hence the division of labor. The two remained close friends until Robespierre's death and exchanged letters that became increasingly infrequent with the burden of revolutionary work but remained warm, candid, and friendly. When Robespierre himself could not write, his brother, Augustin, was delegated. There is a good summary of the case by Vellay, "Robespierre et le procès de paratonnerre." A judgment in M. de Vissery's favor was rendered by the Conseil d'Artois on July 31, 1783.

13. Quoted from Thompson, I, 34. Vellay, "Robespierre et le procès de paratonnerre," dates the letter to have it refer to the famous case. The redating has been generally accepted.

14. The entire case is in *Oeuvres*, II (*pour Pagès*), as well as in Barbier and Vellay. An account and summary is in Thompson, I, 38–40.

15. He pleaded thirteen in his novice year, ten in 1788. In his best years in Arras he had pleaded more than twenty cases. For a detailed list of the cases before both the *conseil d'Artois* and the *Echevinage*, see Paris, appendix, pp. xii–xxiii and xxiv–xxvii. Paris also points out (appendix, p. xxiii, note 1) that Robespierre was seventh among local lawyers in 1782. By 1788 he had fallen to eleventh. Some argue (among them Thompson and Massin) that the decline signals a growing discontent with the provincial practice of law, the implication being that as the Revolution approached, Robespierre became more alienated from his society. Hampson, *Life and Opinions*, p. 24, points out that there is no specific evidence of discontent, either early or late, in his Arras practice. The view that his practice fell

off because of his habit of taking only "just causes," which did not pay well and discouraged those with money from seeking him out, comes from Charlotte, Fleischman, p. 198.

16. There is a good account of the Rosati in Reinhard, pp. 87–106, and an unfriendly but detailed one in Paris, pp. 158–89.

17. For the facts in the case Barbier and Vellay, pp. 573–79.

18. Barbier and Vellay, p. 613.

19. Barbier and Vellay, p. 609.

20. Barbier and Vellay, p. 561.

21. Barbier and Vellay, p. 661.

22. Barbier and Vellay, p. 645.

23. Barbier and Vellay, p. 660.

24. Hampson, *Will and Circumstance*, p. 141.

25. Robespierre was mistaken, but the error is revealing. Brissot and Mercier, for example, were Rousseauists (see Hampson, *Will and Circumstance*). But his need to oppose vice and virtue with logical consistency transformed them into Encyclopedists. His enemies could not share the same inspirations or philosophy he did.

26. Fleischman, p. 194.

27. The *Dédicace*, in Robespierre's hand, cannot be precisely dated. Walter, *Robespierre*, p. 72, puts it in the first weeks of the Estates-General, but he offers no proof. There is no internal evidence that would suggest when he might have read the *Confessions*. The moment of conversion must remain obscure. It is certainly not a physical encounter with Rousseau that Robespierre has here commemorated. Cobban, "Fundamental Ideas," p. 151, dismisses the meeting as "almost certainly suppositious." Aulard, *Orateurs*, p. 218, reports "an interview which perhaps decided for him his vocation and destiny." Hampson, *Life and Opinions*, p. 15, citing an early and enthusiastic biographer, M. Graterolle (*Robespierre* [1894]), gives a verbatim account of the conversation that supposedly passed between the two. Despite this unique evidence, he concludes "there is no evidence that Rousseau saw him."

28. Hampson, *Will and Circumstance*, p. 145.

29. Hampson, *Will and Circumstance*, p. 142.

30. Lefebvre, "Discours sur Robespierre," p. 493.

31. Mercier, I, 19.

32. *Confessions*, I, ix (Pléiade edition), I, 405.

33. *Emile*, I, iv.

34. Hampson, *Will and Circumstance*, p. 218.

35. Cornette, p. 39.

36. The facsimile is reproduced by Paris between pp. 280 and 281.

37. See Paris, pp. 280–82, for a discussion and quotations from Robespierre's "Doléances du corps des Cordonniers mineurs de la ville d'Arras."

38. The full title is *A la nation artésienne, sur la necessité de réformer les Etats d'Artois.* Both versions are dated Arras, 1789, but carry no month. The first is fifty pages in octavo; the second eighty-three pages in duodecimo. The Bibliothèque Nationale in Paris has only the first version. I have not been able to see the second, and quote it here from Paris. The other pamphlet in question is *Les ennemis de la patrie, démasqués par le récit de ce qui s'est passé dans les assemblées du tiers-état de la ville d'Arras,* fifty-eight pages in octavo, published anonymously and attributed to Robespierre by most of his biographers.

39. Quoted from Hamel, I, 69.

40. Quoted from Paris, p. 237.

41. Quoted from Hamel, I, 77.

42. Quoted from Paris, p. 246.

43. Quoted from Paris, p. 242.

44. Quoted from Paris, p. 339.

45. Lenglet's report, in a letter, written on 16 Thermidor (a week after Robespierre's death) to Lequinio, one of Robespierre's enemies, says, "Robespierre intrigued to have himself named to the Constituent Assembly." It is reprinted in Paris, appendix IV. Devienne's testimony is quoted from the same work, p. 414, which states that "he vigorously intrigued to have himself chosen a representative." Proyart's testimony (p. 145) accuses him of incendiary speeches that seduced the simple country folk.

46. Cobb, "Robespierre," p. 54, shrewdly points out that the "only time he did leave things to chance was 9 Thermidor."

47. Abbé Proyart, p. 81, note (I quote from Paris, p. 415, note 2), says he obtained from the woman who packed Robespierre's trunk the following list of possessions:

> A suit of black wool (its texture worn smooth); a suit of black sculptured velour (bought used in Paris [which he had left eight years earlier] and redyed).
> A quite good satin jacket; another (passable) of *raz de Saint-Maur.*
> A *culotte* of black velour and cotton, a *culotte* of black wool, a *culotte* of serge and silk (the three very worn).
> Six shirts, six collars, six handkerchiefs (of which most were in good condition)
> Three pairs of silk stockings (of which one was almost new).
> Clothes brushes, shoe brushes, a sack of powder with its applicator [for his hair].
> A small black coat, a small hat to be carried under the arm.
> An advocate's robe.
> Several pieces of different material.
> A box of silk thread, wool and sewing needles.

A packet of papers for a Paris *procureur*.
A quantity of copies of his printed *Mémoires*.

At his death he would have a similarly pathetic collection of worldly goods. It is worth noting the absence of books from his trunk.

48. Quoted from Bouloiseau, p. 20: "Il ira loin, il croit tout ce qu'il dit."

49. Throughout I use *ideology* in what might be called its pre-Marxist or original meaning. What Robespierre and his fellow ideologues thought they were doing, what they aspired to do, was to offer an objective, rational, maybe even scientific understanding of the logic of the human mind that would replace false, superstitious reasoning and identify the basis for a rational and, in Robespierre's case, moral social order. See Baker, especially pp. 202–3.

50. Hampson, *Will and Circumstance*, p. 202.

51. *L'Ami du Peuple*, no. 648 (May 3, 1792). Massin, p. 102, shares Marat's view, as does a contemporary, Choudieu: "Of all the Montagnards Robespierre is the one who has been most subject to accusations of all sorts" (quoted from Jacob, p. 202). The libels began even before Robespierre was elected a deputy, and appeared in Arras during the elections to the Estates-General. The slanderer called Robespierre "the windbag" (*le long braillard*) and "the venomous advocate" (*le plaideur enfiélé*). These insults are quoted from Gallo, p. 64.

52. Hampson, *Life and Opinions*, p. 18, and *Pour Dupond*, in Barbier and Vellay, pp. 639 and 641 especially. Cobb, "Robespierre and the Year II," p. 63, is upset with this habit and complains, with as much malice as some of Robespierre's enemies: "He was like a sort of moral juke box: you made your choice, and out came Virtue, Sin, Corruption, Purity, Plots, Plots, Plots, Imminent Self-Immolation (on this or that altar), *je, je, je, mon, mon, mon, ma, ma, ma, moi, moi, moi*, as though the needle had got stuck."

53. From section VI of *Beyond Good and Evil*.

54. Furet, p. 66.

55. Revault d'Allonnes, p. 593.

56. Quoted from Jacob, pp. 200–201.

57. IX, p. 28. Hamel (II, 474) attributes these words directly to Robespierre. They may be those of Léonard Bourdon, from whom the information comes.

58. There is no way of knowing what Robespierre's illnesses were, although the symptoms seem to fit some kind of neurasthenic. Perhaps he was a serious migraine victim, which affliction would correspond with a number of his symptoms. See Sacks, especially parts I and II.

59. *Correspondance*, p. 110 (to Buissart).

Chapter 3

1. See Baker.

2. Thompson, I, 50. "*C'est parfaitment exact*" are the King's words. The letter is in *Correspondance*, p. 57.

3. *Contrat social*, II, 7. See an interesting discussion on what distinguished the Jacobins from the liberals in Revault-d'Allonnes, pp. 586, 598–99 especially.

4. Thompson, I, 52. The June 6 intervention, concerning the clergy, is reported in VI, 29–31.

5. Among the mispellings were Robert-Pierre, Robes-pierre, Rabesse-Pierre. On the question of the accuracy of the reporting of parliamentary proceedings see VI, xi–xxxii.

6. Quoted from Walter, *Robespierre*, p. 140.

7. Cobban, "Fundamental Ideas," p. 144.

8. Marat, who knew something about poverty—and not as a rather benign deprivation, which is the way Robespierre experienced it at Louis-le-Grand, not to mention his later, literary, imaginings of what constituted poverty—thought that eighteen livres a day (more than an average worker's salary) was a substantial sum, and for the enormous amount of work it bought from the deputies the Revolution had a bargain. Thompson, II, 271, has the quotation. For a number of Robespierre's contemporaries and comrades—Desmoulins, for one—who did hack journalism as their only source of income, a deputy's stipend was something to be envied not only because it was regular, but also because it was considerable.

9. Michelet, III, iii, 318, sees a paradox. The October 22 decree said that no man could vote unless he paid, in direct taxes in a single year, an amount equal to three days' work. This decree, Michelet argues, deprived the landowning aristocracy of "a million country electors." The "friends of the ideal, Grégoire, Duport, Robespierre," in objecting that this violated natural law, were only playing into the hands of the counterrevolution. "The utopians, in the name of equality, would give a million electors to the enemies of equality."

10. "Absolute or suspensive," said Abbé Sieyès, making an epigram, "the veto is nothing but a *lettre de cachet* against the general will."

11. See Hamel, I, 219ff, for Robespierre's treatment by the press during the Constituent. For his treatment during the Legislative and the early Convention, see Bouloiseau, "Robespierre d'après les journaux girondins," pp. 2–17.

12. Cobb, "Robespierre and the Year II," p. 62, suggests "there was a *réseau Robespierre* that has not been sufficiently studied and that is at least revealing of the extent of his informants."

13. Courtois, p. 122 (pièce XXIII).
14. The suggestion is Gallo's, p. 79. This geopolitical aspect of Paris still prevails.
15. See Gusdorf, pp. 269–70, on the significance of dress and costume.
16. See an interesting suggestion of Gallo, pp. 39–40 and 136.
17. On the testimony of Madame Le Bas, quoted from Jacob, p. 119. See Goutor, p. 323, for the tradition that criticizes Robespierre as a bourgeois whose views and habits undetermined the popular revolution in Paris.
18. Soboul, "Robespierre ou les contradictions de Jacobinisme," p. 5.
19. Louvet, I, 26–28, and in Jacob, p. 162.
20. These characterizations are from (respectively) Gallo, p. 170, and Hampson, *Will and Circumstance*, p. 115.
21. Soboul, *Sans-culottes*, p. 694.
22. Lefebvre, "Discours," p. 493.
23. Soboul, "Robespierre ou les contradictions de Jacobinisme," pp. 4–5; Lefebvre, "Discours," p. 493.
24. Hampson, *Life and Opinions*, pp. 72–73.
25. Quoted from *Les Révolutions de Paris*, by Massin, p. 49.
26. Massin, p. 58.
27. Mathiez, "La popularité de Robespierre en 1791," p. 488.
28. Massin, p. 69, calls it Robespierre's *apologia pro vita sua*.
29. Wolfe, p. 228.

Chapter 4

1. Quoted from Massin, p. 32. The episode referred to is the session of October 21, 1789. See VI, 121–30, for the various contemporary accounts of the speech. No text has survived. The Comte de Castellane thought "never had he spoken so well, or sustained such detestable principles." The deputy quoted by Massin is Duquesnoy. This intervention seems to have been an improvisation and demonstrates, as do several others, that Robespierre could, when necessary, speak without a text.
2. Michelet, I, 102.
3. Mercier, *Tableau de Paris*, I, 196, makes this distinction. See also Thompson, I, 40. "A reading of Robespierre's *plaidoiries*," writes Trahard, p. 43, "reveals that the young lawyer of Arras did not shy away from the sentimentality then in vogue, nor pathos, nor theatrical rhetorical effects. For him the art of convincing was, first and foremost, the art of moving."
4. These details are provided by J.-J. Dussault, quoted from Jacob, pp. 191–92.

5. Quoted by Hamel, I, 60, and Trahard, p. 189.

6. Etienne Dumont has left this account (quoted from Thompson, I, 51): "At this speech, which was so well suited to the passions of the moment, there arose, not a torrent of applause, . . . but a confused murmur, which was more flattering. Everyone asked, Who was that orator? He was not known, and it was only after some minutes of investigation that a name was repeated from mouth to mouth which, three years later, was destined to make France tremble." Compare this with VI, 29–31. Mathiez, "Robespierre orateur," pp. 59–60, reprints a fragment, *a brouillon*, in Robespierre's hand, from which he spoke on April 24, 1793. The *brouillon* is more than laconic; it is only a few words hastily thrown down on paper. The speech has Robespierre's usual complexity and density of argument and development as well as a vigorous yet carefully controlled style.

7. Courtois, p. 25.

8. Thompson, II, 215. "Both methods," he concludes, "were equally characteristic of the man."

9. Walter, *Neuf thermidor*, p. 48.

10. Quoted by Walter, *Robespierre*, p. 132, from *Journal général de la Cour et de la Ville*.

11. Cobb, "Robespierre," p. 45.

12. Fréron to Courtois, in Berville and Barriére, I, 155. The legend of Robespierre's inability to command attention, overcome the tumult and ridicule, which is repeated by some modern biographers (Gallo, for example), seems to have originated here with Fréron. It was taken up and given authority by both Michelet and Aulard.

13. Dumont, p. 250, quoted from Jacob, p. 88, and also quoted by Hamel, I, 115.

14. Quoted from Walter, *Jacobins*, p. 36.

15. Walter, *Jacobins*, pp. 223–24.

16. Quoted by Thompson, I, 221, from Reichardt's contemporary diary. The description dates from April 1792, when Robespierre was isolated at the Club. Dubois-Crancé (quoted from Jacob, p. 83) makes a similar observation: "The Jacobins have contributed more to Robespierre's glory than the National Assembly. At the former he had friends, he was listened to, encouraged, and often there developed excellent ideas. Rarely had he this advantage in the National Assembly." See also Anatole France, *Les dieux ont soif*, p. 134, for an imaginative (but historically accurate) description of Robespierre at the Jacobins.

17. Kennedy, p. 298.

18. Kennedy, p. 30.

19. Kennedy, pp. 296–98.

20. Kennedy, p. 247. "Gentlemen!" he wrote the Lille affiliate, "If I knew more

citizens like you, I would count upon the regeneration of my country."

21. Kennedy, p. 248.

22. Hampson, *Life and Opinions*, p. 72.

23. Kennedy, p. 107.

24. Kennedy, p. 123.

25. Kennedy, p. 300.

26. Kennedy, p. 268.

27. Quoted from Brinton, p. 189. The oath is from a slightly later period of the Revolution, but it is still typical of earlier oaths.

28. Furet, p. 236. None of the early "deviationist groups" that seceded from the Jacobins—the Society of 1789, the Social Circle, the Club of *Fédérés*, the Club of Victors of the Bastille, the Fraternal Society of the Two Sexes— posed any substantial threat to Jacobin unity.

29. The pamphlet is *Addresse de la Société des Avis de la Constitution, séant aux Feuillants, aux sociétés qui lui sont affiliées*, quoted from Kennedy, p. 285.

30. Quoted from Walter, *Jacobins*, p. 250. Typically, Robespierre was away from the action. It is true he had opposed the petitioning as ill-advised and he lacked the capacity for shoulder-to-shoulder solidarity in the streets. Gallo, p. 131, argues this is not "the traditional solitude of the leader" but "that of a man on the margin . . . who is willing to die, but alone, as an individual hero who sacrifices himself, as an exemplary witness, to the abstract idea of a 'good people.' " The suggestion, in keeping with Gallo's thesis, is overstated. Virtually none of the revolutionary leaders was willing to die at the barricades, for none of them had any notion that he belonged there.

31. Kennedy, p. 294.

32. Kennedy, p. 295, says Toulouse, Beauvais, and Dieppe were all swayed by Robespierre.

33. Walter, *Jacobins*, p. 215.

34. Quoted from Jacob, p. 97.

35. Walter, *Robespierre*, p. 132.

36. Walter, *Robespierre*, p. 158, quoting the newspaper *Lendemain*.

37. Ratinaud, p. 55, for the comment: VII, 368-77, for the session.

38. The charge would reappear, two years later, when an auditor shouted from the gallery of the Jacobins: "I see, in addition, that for a long time the Jacobin Society has allowed itself to be dominated by a despotism of opinion." Quoted from Gallo, p. 301.

39. Walter, *Robespierre*, p. 211.

40. Walter, *Robespierre*, pp. 290-91.

41. There are some similarities to Lenin's style of speaking, which "was completely free of histrionics and striving for effect." According to one witness,

Max Eastman, it was as if "he was taking us inside his mind and showing us how the truth looks." See Tucker, pp. 38–39.

42. Quoted from Lacretelle by Walter, *Robespierre*, p. 251.

43. *Journal d'une bourgeoisie pendant la Révolution*, quoted from Jacob, pp. 113–14. This analysis is of the first four numbers of his newspaper, *La Défenseur de la Constitution*, but applies equally well to his oratory, for his style was not capable of substantial modification: he wrote as he spoke.

44. Aulard, *Orateurs*, p. 238.

45. *Les Révolutions de France et de Brabant* 65 (February 21, 1791). Cobban, "Fundamental Ideas," p. 152, puts this same point in another way, stressing the future: "It would be best, perhaps, to say that Robespierre and Rousseau represented, each in his own way, a new attitude to the problems of political life, which was arising toward the end of the 18th century, and for the sources of which we must look beyond both."

46. VII, 523, note 13.

47. Quoted from Thompson, I, 51.

48. Matrat, p. 104. The session here is that of May 16, 1791 (VII, 377–82). The speech was so successful that it was ordered printed, as was his subsequent speech on the same subject (VII, 404–12).

49. Quoted from Thompson, II, 115.

50. The pamphlet is *L'intrigue dévoilée ou Robespierre vengé des outrages et des calomnies de ambitieux*, quoted from Jacob, p. 110.

51. Quoted from Trahard, p. 188.

52. Gallo discusses the issue at several points, pp. 16, 322–23, for example, relating these obsessive concerns to Robespierre's sad and lonely childhood. There is obviously some connection, but identifying it with precision is difficult. Gallo does as well as can be done, and his is the most intelligent and sensitive treatment of Robespierre's psychology.

53. Since I am not a native French speaker with an instinctive feeling for the overtones of words and rhythms, my remarks are both cautious and general. Lanson, p. 862, give a lucid statements of the traditional view, or at least the view held by those who shared (and share) his deeply conservative politics: "In the second place the speeches of the revolutionary period do not contain many original ideas or theories. He who knows Montesquieu, Voltaire, Diderot, Rousseau, the Encyclopedia, has not much to learn from the orators; they repeat what the philosophers have said." Lanson considers Mirabeau the greatest speaker and repeats about Robespierre (p. 896) what was the common view, at least since Michelet: "Robespierre's eloquence is a verbose catechism of civil religion in which an edifying theology is mixed up with bitter diatribes against the wicked and the impious. This bilious, spiteful, pontificating Picard reminds me of his compatriot, Calvin, to whom he is, in all things, inferior—intellectually, morally, and in literature." Aulard, *Orateurs*, goes even farther along this same muddy road,

excommunicating Robespierre (whom he thinks a mystic) from French culture. Robespierre was incomprehensible or frightening (or both) to many of the men of the early Third Republic who embraced the Revolution and the revolutionary tradition, but preferred that it be made less violent.

54. Here are two examples, one from his Arras days, the other from 1794:

Plusieurs refusèrent la gloire de s'associer à son entreprise [petitioning to have lightning rods destroyed]. Cinq ou six seulement, plus complaisans ou timides, signèrent la requête. Décoré de ces noms dignes d'être transmis à la postérité la plus reculée, le noble écrit fut présenté aux officiers municipaux de Saint-Omer. (II, 141)

And:

Nos sublimes voisins entretiennent gravement l'univers de la santé du roi, de ses divertissemens, de ses voyages; ils veulent absolument apprendre à la postérité à quelle heure il a dîné, à quel moment il est revenu de la chasse; quelle est la terre heureuse qui, à chaque instant du jour, eut l'honneur d'être foulée par ses pieds augustes; quels sont les noms des esclaves privilégiés qui ont paru, en sa présence, au lever, au coucher de soleil. (X, 445)

Voltaire's list of what a courtier must know about his master includes the time the king goes to stool. The puritanical Robespierre deletes the scatology.

55. See Parker, pp. 17–19, 156–57, 164–67, 172–73.

56. Here are two examples:

Je ne croirai jamais au républicanisme des princes quelqu'ils soient, parce que je ne crois point au miracles. (V, 345)

Or:

Il n'y a pas deux manières d'être libres; il faut l'être entièrement ou redevenir esclave. (VII, 164)

57. Again a couple of examples:

La moindre ressource laissée au despotisme rétablira bientôt sa puissance. (VII, 164)

And:

L'Europe prodigue son sang pour river les chaînes de l'humanité; et nous pour les briser. (X, 445)

58. As when he made a neologism to describe the politics of his enemy, Brissot: "On disait 'brissoter' pour 'intriguer' " (V, 111).

59. It is hard to resist quotation, so I won't. Here are two examples.

La raison et l'intérêt public avoient commencé et l'ambition l'ont arrêté; les vices des tyrans et les vices des esclaves l'ont changée en un état douloureux de trouble et de crise. (IV, 1)

Or, as he thundered at the rich;

Si vous ne respectez ni l'humanité, ni la justice, ni l'honneur, conservez du moins quelque soin de vos trésors, qui n'ont d'autre ennemi que la misère publique, que vous aggravez avec tant d'impudence. (IX, 498)

60. There is no need to quote here one of these tedious rhetorical passages. There is a characteristic one in *La Défenseur de la Constitution*, IV, 232. Lafayette always brought out the worst in Robespierre.

61. Manuel's words are taken from Walter, *Robespierre*, p. 265. Robespierre's speech is in VIII, 57–90.

Chapter 5

1. Narbonne was appointed on December 7, 1791, to replace the resigned Duportail. On Narbonne, see Lefebvre, "Etudes sur le ministère de Narbonne."

2. During the five months following his return to Paris, on November 28, 1791, till the declaration of war against Austria, Robespierre intervened in the debates at the Jacobins some sixty-five times, or at most of the four meetings a week. Thompson, I, 202, has some discussion. The interventions vary in length and importance, but if only for their bulk they are important. They fill 271 pages of his *Oeuvres complètes*, and some of these speeches have been preserved only as summaries. In addition, in the same period, he began his newspaper. The first five numbers (another 164 pages) should be added to these totals. It is a significant amount of speaking and writing, even for Robespierre. Jean Jaurès, himself the greatest orator of his generation, declared the speeches of January 2 and 11 to be Robespierre's most extraordinary: "What a marvellous sense of reality, above all what a sense of the difficulties, of the obstacles, we see in this man we usually think of as an ideologue, an abstract theoretician." Quoted from Michon, p. 59.

3. Berville and Barrière, I, 158. No date is given: "During the Legislative Assembly," writes Fréron, "at a dinner at the Duplays' with several patriots, the talk turned to armies and generals."

4. Robespierre was gradually abandoned by even those few journalists who supported his views, chiefly Marat, whose *Ami du Peuple* did not appear between December 15, 1791, and April 12, 1792. See Michon, p. 31. Of the most widely circulated papers on the left, the *Chronique de Paris*, *Patriot Français* (Brissot's paper), *Annales Patriotiques*, *Courrier des 83 Départements*, *Thermomètre de Jours*, and *Les Révolutions de Paris* were all in the hands of political foes or had been converted to the war.

5. *Journal d'un étudiant pendant la Révolution*, pp. 287–89. For a survey and analysis of the newspaper attacks, see Michon, pp. 105–14.

6. Quoted from Sydenham, p. 91.

7. Quoted from Michon, p. 29.

8. Quoted from Michon, pp. 128–29.

9. See his letter attacking Robespierre in Buchez and Roux, XV, 69. Robespierre's response is in *Défenseur de la Constitution*, VI ("Réponse de M. Robespierre, citoyen français à Monsieur Lafayette, Général d'Armée), and VII ("Deuxième lettre . . .").

10. Robespierre believed his life was endangered, which may account for some of his hysterics. On April 9 he told his colleagues the story of a Jacobin (unnamed) who "had been insulted by a man attached as *aide de camp* to Lafayette" and told that "in three days' time we'll be done with you" (VIII, 260). It sounds autobiographical. The threat was reported in the press. Was Robespierre cleverly using the newspapers? (VIII, 260, note 4). He mentions assassination at Lafayette's hands or those of hired killers a couple of other times: VIII, 277 and 380.

11. In very few cases did Robespierre—or the more radical Jacobins—forgive or acknowledge an aristrocrat as revolutionary. Only Lepeletier had Robespierre's unreserved endorsement: "Instead of prostituting his remarkable talents, already celebrated before the Revolution, as so many others did, to ambition and intrigue, he consecrated them indefatigably to the defense of eternal principles of morality and philosophy" (IX, 257).

12. The extended attack is in IV, 77–89, especially p. 83. Brissot's response is in *Patriot Français*, nos. 1031 and 1032.

13. *Correspondance*, p. 135.

14. There is a useful list of ministers in Thompson, *French Revolution*, p. 526.

15. *L'Ami du Peuple*, no. 648 (May 3, 1792).

16. Quoted from Mathiez, "Le patriotisme de Robespierre," p. 103. The authority to declare war was specifically given to the legislative branch of government in chapter III, article 2, of the 1791 constitution.

17. On January 25, 1792 (VIII, 143), Robespierre had, in general terms, foreseen the emergence of a man very much like Dumouriez, or rather had foreseen the role Dumouriez would fulfill: among "a people disarmed, divided, exhausted, fatigued, hungry, don't you fear that a general, that a victorious army, drunk with enthusiasm for this general, could easily tip the balance in favor of the ministerial faction, moderate and antipopular, of which he would be both the chief and the instrument?" Dumouriez, too, was an aristocrat, although not as important nor as influential nor as rich as Lafayette.

18. Bourgeois, II, 80. Quoted from Michon, p. 127.

19. Quoted from Jaurès, VIII, 298.

Chapter 6

1. There were twelve issues of *La Défenseur de la Constitution*, appearing between (approximately) May 19 and August 20, 1792. The sequel, which he entitled *Lettres à Ses Commettans*, since he was once more a member of the National Assembly, followed the same format as the first newspaper, and began appearing on October 19, 1792. It had a run of twenty-two issues, in two series, and ceased publication in April 1793, on the eve of yet another insurrection.

2. For a good discussion of these first journalistic efforts, see Gustave Laurent's introduction to *Oeuvres complètes*, I, i–vi. For a general discussion of the press in the Revolution, see Godechot et al., pp. 405–85.

3. Sydenham, *Girondins*, p. 108, suggests May 27, 1792, as "a likely date for the beginning of the ascendancy of Robespierre's supporters in the Club." Walter, *Robespierre*, p. 291, prefers the end of April.

4. Lafayette arrived in Paris on June 28, the same day Brissot returned to the Jacobins after a long absence. The reconciliation apparently depended on Brissot's assuring Lafayette's impeachment in the Legislative. This he was unable to do. The Legislative eventually exculpated Lafayette (August 8) for his attempted march on the Jacobins (June 29), in which only thirty officers joined. The exculpation was among the immediate causes of August 10.

5. By comparison a subscription to Brissot's popular *Patriote Français*, a daily, was thirty-six livres; Prudhomme's *Révolutions de Paris*, a weekly (which often ran to fifty-six pages) cost the same. On the other hand, mere price did not necessarily indicate audience or popularity. Hébert's enormously popular and successful *Père Duchesne* sold for eight sous an issue, quadruple the price of Brissot's paper, and it was deliberately aimed at a poorer segment of society. The rarity of complete runs of *La Défenseur de la Constitution* may indicate that few survived because few were printed. Some contemporary newspapers, like Brissot's, had runs in the thousands.

6. Nicolas eventually died with the second batch of *robespierristes*, on 12 Thermidor (July 30, 1794). The *robespierristes* were a considerable group, widely dispersed in the population, and to date have been little studied.

7. *Les Révolutions de Paris*, no. 147 (April 28–May 5, 1792), pp. 205–12.

8. Deslandres, I, 83, describes the Constitution of 1791 as "*fortement antidémocratique.*"

9. "*Les mouvements tumultueux de la rue.*" Lefebvre, "Discours sur Robespierre," p. 504.

10. *Correspondance*, p. 44.

11. *Correspondance*, p. 42 (italics added). The entire passage is: "La Révolution actuelle, mon cher ami, nous a fait voir en peu de jours les plus grands événémens qui l'histoire des hommes puisse presenter. Il y a quelques jours,

le despotisme et l'aristocratie déconcertés par la fermeté peut-être inatten-
due de 600 représents du Tiers-Etat, réunissoient tous leur efforts pour
échapper par les derniers attentats à la ruine dont ils se croient menacés."

12. Tocqueville, II, vii: "Thus Paris had become the master of France and already the army that would master Paris was gathering." The gathering
army was composed of *sans-culottes*. Rudé, p. 12, gives these figures: ". . .
the clergy numbered about 10,000, the nobility 5,000 and the financial,
commercial, manufacturing, and professional *bourgeoisie* about 40,000; the
rest—the great majority—were small shopkeepers, petty traders, journeymen, labourers, vagrants, the city poor, who formed what later became
known as the *sans-culottes*."

13. Morris, I, 546 (entry for June 20, 1792).

14. *Correspondance*, p. 150.

15. I stretch the meaning of *avouée* in translation to retain metaphorical consistency.

16. Thompson, I, 251. The Central Committee met in the room of Anthoine,
the mayor of Metz, who was Robespierre's personal friend and at this time
was lodging at the Duplays'. When the direction of the insurrection passed
to the Bureau Central des Sections, Robespierre may have lost access to
secret information, although it is hard to imagine there was much that so
notorious and respected a radical leader did not know or could easily find
out.

17. Walter, *Jacobins*, p. 255. Those most anxious to accuse Robespierre of cowardice were themselves absent, with the exception of Barbaroux and Louvet. We do not know how or where Robespierre passed the night. His
enemies averred he hid himself in a dovecote at the Duplays'. The victors
of the Tuileries did not hold this nonparticipation against Robespierre.
Quite the contrary. Thompson, I, 257, describes a medal, designed by
Dupré to commemorate the Revolution of August 10, inscribed *Régéné-
ration française—10 août 1792*. "It shows a fountain in female form with
water flowing from the breasts: a patriot stoops to drink from a cup held
by a standing figure; it is that of Robespierre." His brother, Augustin, was
ecstatic to discover in himself physical courage and wrote Robespierre an
enthusiastic letter on the subject (*Correspondance*, p. 229). Neither Danton
nor Desmoulins, who did fight, later accused Robespierre of shirking.

18. See Furet, p. 73, for a description of this revolutionary *métier* as new with
the French Revolution.

19. According to Sagnac, p. 158.

20. In addition to having "the sublime sentiment of liberty" animate every
face, Robespierre implies that he was a witness to the Fall of the Bastille,
hence able to offer this visual comparison. He saw both events only through
the eyes of others. See his description of the Bastille in a letter to Buissart
(*Correspondance*, pp. 47–48).

21. The insurgents lost 324 men, mainly from the neighborhoods of Saint-Antoine and Saint-Marcel; 60 victims were Marsellais who had marched from the south.

22. There were perhaps 800 killed at the Tuileries, of whom about 600 were Swiss guards. Many of these were murdered in cold blood after they had surrendered, or were hunted down in the neighborhood for hours after the Château had fallen. It is quite possible Robespierre heard the cries of the hunted and the hunters from the Duplay house, if that is where he spent the night and the day of August 9–10. Assuming he stayed at home, he could easily have seen the grotesque sight of heads on pikes or mutilated bodies left to be stripped of their clothes, had he emerged from the courtyard at the Duplays'. Even if he was not at home on the day of the attack and massacre, the gruesome mopping-up operations went on into the night of the tenth and the following day. Corpses littered the neighborhood.

23. Westermann seems to have inflated his own role in the telling. In fairness to Robespierre's account of his friend's deeds, it is in the "Détails inté-réssans . . . ," not in the more sober and somber and carefully written account of what happened.

24. Roederer's is the most circumstantial account of the events by an eyewitness, although the author's focus on himself and the happenings in the Tuileries rather than on the insurgents is myopic.

25. Gustave Laurent (IV, xviii) thinks August 20 is the likely date of publication.

Chapter 7

1. At the Commune (September 1) "M. Robespierre went to the rostrum and developed, in an eloquent speech, all the manoeuvres used to deprive the General Council of the public confidence, and everything the Council had done to render itself worthy of such confidence" (VIII, 448, note 6).

2. Walter, *Robespierre*, p. 316, quoting the "Registre des délibérations de la section des Piques."

3. There is a good account of the elections in Hampson, *Life and Opinions*, pp. 127–30. Robespierre was elected by 64 percent of the votes, which he split with his former comrade, Pétion. Indeed, Pétion was one of those who could not be elected in Paris. Of the twenty-four Paris deputies, several had distinguished reputations for radicalism, several were Parisians recently risen to prominence in the insurrection, and two were radical journalists. All were beneficiaries as well as supporters of August 10. Patrick, pp. 325–26, identifies twenty of these deputies as Jacobins and adherents of the Montagnard group. In the King's trial only two Paris deputies voted against death.

4. Quoted from Gallo, p. 196.

5. Fear of Paris was born with the Revolution. "It is amusing," remarked one of the wits of the Constituent while it was still sitting in Versailles and about to move to Paris, "to contemplate how many illnesses have been caused by the approaching move to Paris." Quoted from Hamel, I, 150. Hundreds of deputies had applied for passports to leave the country, pleading illness.

6. In the growing catalogue of counterrevolution, Robespierre included the desire of his enemies "to flee Paris with the royal family and the treasury" when news of the fall of Longwy and Verdun (IX, 345) reached the capital. Earlier, on the eve of August 10, there had been another Girondin proposal for flight. Robespierre (VIII, 426) had then called the proposers "the Maurys of the Legislative," recalling the brilliant royalist orator from the days of the Constituent. He thought all such proposals a species of high treason.

7. Brissot and Roland both made this argument. Hampson, *Life and Opinions*, pp. 124–25, presents the evidence that Brissot's apartment was searched while he himself was in hiding and there was an order for his arrest. Louvet, Robespierre's enemy, maintained this arrest warrant was the result of Robespierre's denunciation. Sending Brissot to jail at the time of the massacres would certainly have been tantamount to a death sentence. But even if Louvet is an accurate witness, it does not prove that Robespierre instigated the massacres and hired assassins to do in his enemies. According to the historian of this grim episode, Pierre Caron, it is impossible to fix blame with such precision. Put another way, there is enough guilt to go around. The press was inflammatory, and Marat was no more so than several colleagues. No one, and no group or agency of government, tried to stop the murdering. Roland (a minister at the time) did not use his office to stop the killing, and his friends, who would soon be most vociferous in calling for punishments, were as silent and invisible during those five days as were those they accused.

8. The full title is *Accusation intentée dans la Convention Nationale, contre Maximilien Robespierre*. There is a version in the *Moniteur* for October 30, 1792, and a couple of pamphlet versions. The first was published by order of the Convention; the second (in 1795) by Louvet himself, for he is one of those who survived the Girondin purge inflicted by Paris. Shortly after the accusation was presented, Roland, then Minister of the Interior, used public funds to disseminate the speech throughout the country. Some 15,000 copies were printed. The Jacobins took up a collection to have Robespierre's December 28 speech (not his reply to Louvet) similarly distributed. See Bouloiseau, "Robespierre d'après les journaux Girondins," p. 5.

9. See Hampson, *Life and Opinions*, p. 118, for an elaboration of this argument.

10. Here is another deviation from Rousseau, who did not think sovereignty could be delegated.

11. On the strength of the Jacobins and the Mountain, see Patrick, especially the extremely useful tables.

12. See a list of the presidents in Thompson, *French Revolution*, p. 529.

13. Furet, p. 81.

Chapter 8

1. Quoted from Mathiez, *Vie chère*, p. 504.

2. Thompson renders Robespierre's "*de chétives marchandises*" as "a bag of groceries." Mathiez, *Vie chére*, p. 47, quotes a certain Conchin of Saint-Antoine (a friend of Brissot's): "Legislators, the citizens of the faubourg Saint-Antoine leave it to the women, to old men, to children to shriek for sugar. The men of July 14 don't demonstrate for *bonbons!*" It's interesting to note that Conchin makes it the men of 1789, whereas for the neighborhood militants, after August 10, one must have participated in that most recent insurrection for one's radical credentials to be acceptable.

3. Godechot et al., pp. 508–15, has a list of the newspapers that disappeared after June 2.

4. Courtois, p. 181, singles out this sentence in his introduction as particularly revealing of how dangerous Robespierre was to the Revolution. None of this notebook scribbling, apparently used when making his speeches, can be precisely dated, but from internal evidence they all appear to come from the time of June 2.

5. Courtois, p. 181. The note concludes: "The people must ally themselves to the Convention and the Convention must serve the people." He had no desire to overthrow the Convention, but wished to preserve it, and to do so he needed the continuing support of the *sans-culottes*.

6. Courtois, p. 207.

7. This famous fragment was published by Courtois, p. 181. There are excellent analyses in Jaurès, VIII, 146–47, and Thompson, II, 33–34. The fragment doubtless concerns the insurrection of June 2. On this there is no dispute. But exactly when it was written is a matter of some dispute. Sainte-Claire Deville, p. 44, dates it to May 16–19. This would prove that Robespierre had approved of the purge well in advance. Hampson, *Life and Opinions*, p. 150, calls this "clearly wrong since the Montagnards at that time were under the impression that things were going well at Lyons [there would be a *coup d'état* there on May 30, which would detach the city from the Revolution] and did not hear about the event there until June 1. Almost certainly the memorandum was written between June 1 and the arrest of the Girondin leaders on the following day." If "*une volonté une*" is taken in the narrowest sense, as it is by Hampson, his argument is persuasive. I think, however, it represents a general theoretical conclusion

that sums up and synthesizes the anguished analysis of the months before the purge. For me it is less significant exactly when he formulated *une volonté une* since it was in preparation, so to speak, at least from mid-March 1793.

8. Courtois, p. 181, calls the fragment "Espèce de catéchisme de Robespierre." The italics are in the original. He goes on to explore some implications. "What can be concluded from this? 1. That the writers must be proscribed as the most dangerous enemies of *la patrie*. 2. That patriotic writings must be distributed in abundance. What are the other obstacles to the establishment of liberty? The foreign war and the civil war. How can the foreign war be terminated? By putting republican generals at the head of our armies and punishing the traitors, *above all the guilty deputies and administrators*; by sending patriotic troops, led by patriotic officers, to destroy the aristocrats of Lyons, Marseilles, Toulon, the Vendée, the Jura, and all the other places where the standard of rebellion and royalism has been raised and to make terrible examples of the scoundrels who have outraged liberty and shed the blood of patriots." Hampson, *Life and Opinions*, p. 228, argues, having examined the original "catechism" in the Archives Nationales (F^7 4436), for a later date of composition. "Robespierre crossed out his various marginal points with vertical strokes, presumably as he incorporated them in a speech. The word 'never' is obliterated in a different way and perhaps reflected no more than a passing fit of pessimism. The 'catechism' as a whole probably served as the basis for the speech he made in the Assembly on 12 August which takes up all these points with the significant exception of *subsistances et lois populaires*." The speech in question is in X, 66–67.

9. Quoted from Soboul, *Sans-culottes*, p. 210.

10. Massin, p. 206. Robespierre's intervention came on October 3, 1793 (X, 134–35). The seventy-three were arrested, but Robespierre successfully resisted clamorings for their heads. Soboul, *Sans-culottes*, p. 236, suggests that Robespierre sought not only to check the terrorists in the Convention but also to have some potentially useful hostages from the Plain. None of the seventy-three showed themselves grateful to their savior.

11. I translate *moyens de salut* as "cure" to maintain the consistency of medical imagery that is so prevalent in Robespierre's thought at this time.

12. Thompson, II, 21–22, wonders about this and offers an explanation that appears to preserve consistency: "This curious withdrawal, at the moment when those he had incited were in danger of losing their heads, and it is uncertain which way the day will go, is so characteristic of him that it is difficult not to think it calculated. But it cannot be explained simply by moral cowardice. . . . He remembers July 17, August 10, and March 10. If things go wrong, if reaction once more triumphs, he must be in a position, as the leader of official democracy, to disown the insurrection, and to save the insurrectional machine." Walter, *Robespierre*, p. 440, and Mas-

sin, p. 66, are in fundamental agreement. In addition, it is worth noting that on June 2, as in earlier uprisings, the Jacobin Club took no direct part in events (Walter, *Jacobins*, p. 300). Those who participated, whether they thought of themselves as Jacobins or Montagnards, did so as individuals. Not only had Robespierre taken himself out of the combat zone, but he had at least by example, also removed the Society. Compare what he says on the eve of June 2 to what he wrote to Couthon on July 20, 1792, on the eve of another insurrection (*Correspondance*, p. 149).

13. Quoted from Walter, *Jacobins*, p. 301.
14. Soboul, *Sans-culottes*, p. 890.
15. Quoted from Soboul, *Sans-culottes*, p. 905.
16. Cobb, *Police and People*, p. 184.
17. Jaurès, VIII, 259.

Chapter 9

1. According to Garat, the Minister of Justice, Robespierre said these words to him in late March or early April 1793. I quote from Thompson, I, 21, note 2. The original is in Buchez and Roux, XVIII, 339.

2. His brief remarks to the Jacobins are in IX, 543–44, his June 8 speech in IX, 544–47. This latter is a critique of the proposals made by the Committee of Public Safety and presented to the Convention by Bertrand Barère on June 6. The overwhelming number of speeches made by Robespierre in June, as well as his substantial number of interventions in debate, is remarkable. Almost all this effort is confined to the Convention, where he speaks thirty-six times, while speaking only nine times at the Jacobins in the same period, and only three of the Jacobin interventions are of any length. This same pattern continues up to his appointment to the Committee of Public Safety. He makes literally twice as many appearances at the tribune of the Convention as at the Jacobins.

3. Mathiez, *Vie chère*, p. 210. He adds that acceptance of the constitution by the Convention (June 24, 1793) was necessary to take out of the hands of the Girondins and their sympathizers and supporters any pretext for civil war.

4. Quoted from Soboul, *Sans-culottes*, p. 38.

5. The discussion of the Declaration occupied the Convention through much of April. Robespierre offered three versions: the first to the Jacobins on April 21 (IX, 454–56); the second to the Convention on April 24 (IX, 459–63); and the third and definitive version, comprising thirty-eight articles and ordered printed by the Convention, also on April 24 (IX, 463–69). His extended speech on the constitution, on May 10, is in IX, 495–510. The order in which he presented the several articles in the April 21 and

April 24 versions is quite different. It is hard to see that this is very significant.

6. IX, 456. In his final version, clause XIV, he softens the bluntness: "The government is [its work] and its property."

7. IX, 456. In his final version, clause XXXIII, he adds "and promptly" punished.

8. IX, 455, and clause VI.

9. Quoted from Mathiez, "Babeuf et Robespierre," p. 237. The occasion was Robespierre's expression of his views on inheritance (VII, 187–88) in 1791, which Babeuf recounted and analyzed in a letter to a friend.

10. Saint-Just was more original than Robespierre in theoretical matters. He called for the sale of *émigré* lands, taxes paid in kind, the drawing up of regulations for commerce in grain, free circulation of grain within France, and laws on river navigation (*Moniteur*, XV, 604). See the complete speech in his *Oeuvres choisies* (Paris, 1968), pp. 84–92. The intellectual relationship between the two men is as complicated (and dependent) as their emotional relationship. In a very general sense it can be argued that Saint-Just provided the theses on which Robespierre would then discourse. His brilliant speech of November 29, 1792, is filled with fertile suggestions about the relationship of economic matters to the Revolution, although he, too, failed to produce a comprehensive economic view of the Revolution. This is part of the reason the complaints of orthodox Marxist historians that the Mountain did not adequately understand or consider economics are both true and beside the point. Economics were subsumed under other categories, in Robespierre's case what might be called political concerns, in the most general sense.

11. For the property clauses finally adopted, see *Les constitutions de la France depuis 1789*, pp. 33, 35, 80, 81. The articles dealing with property are II, XVII (1789 Declaration) and II, XVI, XIX (1793 Declaration).

12. Clauses VII, VIII, and XI.

13. IX, 456, and clause X. The Convention ultimately settled for a bland general formula: "The goal of society is general happiness. Government is instituted to guarantee to man the enjoyment of his natural and imprescriptible rights."

14. Clause XXIII.

15. Aside from December 2, 1792, Robespierre did not again deal exclusively with economic questions, although the subject, naturally, finds its way into his utterances. Political matters overwhelmed all others. On February 25, 1793, responding to the food riots, he spoke to the Jacobins on the pillaging of shops. On March 9, again responding to rioting in Paris, he addressed the Convention, calling for an end to imprisonment for debt. On April 12 he supported a decree in the Convention freeing all those so imprisoned. On June 17 he called for all citizens to pay a graduated tax, even the poor-

est. On June 25 he attacked Jacques Roux, which he again did at the Jacobins on August 5. On September 18 he opposed Collot d'Herbois's motion against merchants who overcharged. He spoke on neither the first maximum (May 4) nor the General Maximum (September 29). He did not speak on the creation of a central food commission (October 22) nor on the Ventôse decrees (February 26–March 3, 1794). Nor for that matter did he speak on the introduction of wage regulations in Paris (July 23, 1794). "From his entry to the Committee of Public Safety," Massin, p. 231, points out, "we do not find a single text of Robespierre where he considers at length and carefully social and economic questions; and this is true up to the time of his death (leaving aside his attack on the financial policies of Cambon on 8 Thermidor)." Despite some scattered interesting remarks, he "never again returned to the originality he permitted himself from June 1792 to July 1793." This is precisely the period before he joined the Committee of Public Safety.

16. *Contract social*, I, vii: "ce qui ne signifie autre chose sinon qu'un le forcera d'être libre. . . ."

17. Brunot, IX, 706. "The idea of the agrarian law," Carnot told the Convention, "spread by the enemies of the public welfare, sowed the Terror."

18. Thompson, II, 52.

19. Courtois, p. 207.

20. Berville and Barrière, I, 252–56.

21. *Correspondance*, p. 172.

22. Lefebvre, "Discours sur Robespierre," p. 499.

23. These measures (articles XIV–XVIII) were not thought necessary by the *conventionnels*, who showed no anxiety to regulate themselves or their friends.

24. *Correspondance*, p. 172.

25. Quoted from Lucas, p. 90, note 7.

26. Quoted from Revault d'Allonnes, p. 586.

27. From his *Rapport du 1ᵉʳ floréal*, in the *Moniteur* 29, p. 267.

28. Quoted from Godechot, *Un jury*, p. 131. The observation has been oft-repeated. Lefebvre, "Discours sur Robespierre," p. 493, makes it even more precise: "It has been said that he was only a petit-bourgeois. This is true and is part of the reason for his popularity. The French petit-bourgeois, which formed the majority of the Jacobins and the sans-culottes, found in him its probity, its diligence, its dignity of manners, its decent exterior, its scorn for excessive wealth and ostentatious luxury."

29. These terms are especially difficult to translate. I have rendered, with some hesitation, *les honnêtes gens* as "the better sort"; *les gens comme it faut* as "refined people"; and *canaille* as "riffraff."

30. He uses almost these identical words when arguing against a money qualification for active citizenship (VII, 166).

31. Brinton, pp. 161–62, quotes the Jacobin Club deploring the mendicants outside its windows, "odious as it is to all lovers of equality and fraternity." The club of Le Havre asked to have all beggars expelled, while another got the municipality to expel three persons "without domicile or calling."

32. Robespierre insisted (June 17, 1793) that unless all paid taxes, proportionally adjusted to poverty, the poor would become "a class of proletarians, a class of Helots, and equality and liberty [would] perish forever" (IX, 576), This is an interesting juxtaposition.

33. Lucas, p. 89.

34. Collot d'Herbois, quoted from Mathiez, *Vie chère.* p. 590.

35. Montesquieu, III, 3 ("Du principe de la democratie").

36. Even Rousseau, who prefered democracy in theory, had reservations. See *Contrat social*, I, III, iv. There is a brilliant historical survey of changing views of democracy in Macpherson.

37. Massin, p. 227.

38. Trahard, p. 66.

39. Cobban, "Political Ideas of Robespierre," p. 162. Cobban adds that this notion of sovereignty "is the outstanding feature in the political theory of Robespierre in the last two years of his life."

40. Quoted from Lefebvre, *Questions agraires*, p. 44.

Chapter 10

1. See Godechot, *Institutions*, pp. 303–8, along with the extensive bibliography.

2. Hampson, *Life and Opinions*, p. 157, speculates that he "may not have wanted to seem to be challenging Danton, or he may have changed his mind after an earlier refusal."

3. See Palmer, pp. 2–22, for shrewd portraits of the twelve, their skills and functions.

4. Hampson, *Life and Opinions*, p. 225, and his quotations from M. A. Baudot.

5. Furet, p. 86.

6. The constitution of 1791 had declared that national representatives could not "be arrested, charged, or convicted for anything they may have said, written, or done in the exercise of their functions as representatives." See chap. 1, sec. v, art. 78, and 43–44. Although the constitution no longer

existed, the deputies continued—with a few notable lapses for political advantage and vengeance—to believe they were immune.

7. The notion of a "popular front" I borrow from Massin, p. 190.

8. "*Voilà*," says Jaurès, VIII, 149–50, "on the day after June 2 is Robespierre's
plan, his political program."

9. Jaurès, VIII, 178.

10. Soboul, *Histoire*, II, 57.

11. Mathiez, "Robespierre terroriste," p. 72.

12. Courtois, p. 112.

13. Godechot, *Institutions*, p. 309.

14. Quoted from Godechot, *Institutions*, p. 293.

15. The phrase *l'idéologie manichéenne* is Furet's, p. 168.

16. Quoted from Revault d'Allonnes, p. 586.

17. Saint-Just, p. 168. See Hardman, pp. 159–60.

18. Saint-Just, p. 171.

19. Jaurès, VIII, 300, calls these "the organic laws of revolution." See a selection of the laws in Hardman, pp. 161–68. Robespierre, incidentally, did
not speak on the laws of Frimaire when they were presented to the Convention.

20. See his report (January 9, 1793) in the *Moniteur* as well as Mathiez, *Vie
chère*, p. 113.

21. Mathiez, *Vie chère*, p. 607, is unequivocal: "It is not the lack of food that
causes the dearth. France, an essentially agricultural country, produces
enough for its own consumption. The English blockade will begin only in
February 1793 and will never hermetically seal off France. In the midst of
the Terror France imported grain from America, Barbary, the Hanseatic
towns, from Genoa and Livonia." See also Cobb, *Police and People*, pp.
257–63.

22. Lefebvre, *Révolution française*, p. 408. "The government of Robespierre,"
Mathiez, *Vie chère*, p. 484, quotes Lefebvre (a quotation I have been unable
to locate), "saved working-class France from famine."

23. Soboul, *Histoire*, II, 38, 98, 103.

24. Quoted from Soboul, *Sans-culottes*, p. 455.

25. Mathiez, *Vie chère*, p. 389.

26. Lucas, p. 136.

27. Lefebvre, "Discours sur Robespierre," pp. 486–87.

28. Greer, pp. 14–15. As early as March 29, 1793, seditious language, seditious
cries, and seditious writings were made capital crimes.

29. Greer, p. 81.

30. The historian of the *sans-culottes* specifically contradicts this. "The demand

for equal incomes corresponded to one of the essential currents of popular thinking: egalitarianism. Particularly sensitive to the rampant inequality accentuated by riches during times of shortage, the *sans-culottes* first of all claimed equal distribution of staples. This stage was quickly superseded by another: equality means nothing it is not applied to all the conditions of existence. The rich man should not live better than the poor; he should give what he does not need for himself to the poor and share his good with him" (Soboul, *Sans-culottes*, pp. 459–60).

31. Quoted from Soboul, *Histoire*, II, 45.
32. Walter, *Robespierre*, p. 536, found only a single order concerning *subsistances* drawn up by Robespierre, and that was on August 7, 1793.
33. Custine's trial has received a recent and thorough treatment in English from Kelly, pp. 93–145.
34. See the *Moniteur* 18, p. 524, for the session.
35. Hampson, *Life and Opinions*, p. 200, says, "It is difficult to know whether the Committee as a whole tried to save Marie Antoinette and the Girondins from a trial by the revolutionary tribunal that would admit of only one verdict. There was so much intrigue surrounding each trial, with bribery cutting across political conviction and all parties pretending to the ferocity that revolutionary *bienséance* demanded, that it is impossible to know when any of them were sincere. . . . It was perhaps in revenge for this that, on the same day, Billaud induced the Assembly to vote for the immediate trial of Marie Antoinette."
36. Furet, p. 43.

Chapter 11

1. Quoted from Walter, *Robespierre* (def. ed.), II, 304–5, who quotes from the fragments of Colchen's memoirs published by H. Montbas in the *Revue des Deux Mondes* (September 15, 1952).
2. The plot is enormously complicated. There is a good account in Hampson.
3. Montesquieu, III, 4, argues that just as virtue is necessary in a "popular government, it is also useful in an aristocracy," although "it is true that it is not so absolutely required." Robespierre also modifies Montesquieu's theory that honor is the mainspring of aristocracy. For the revolutionary, hypocrisy is the mainspring of aristocracy.
4. Quoted from Walter, *Jacobins*, p. 39.
5. Furet, p. 236, puts it more abstractly: ". . . it is the small urban groups who form the skeleton [of the patriot party] who, by a mechanism of exclusion and purification inseparable from 'pure democracy,' soon monopolize the representation of the social body."

6. Quoted from Walter, *Jacobins*, p. 330.

7. Quoted from Walter, *Jacobins*, p. 326.

8. Carter, p. 223.

9. I paraphrase Tucker, where he speaks of "the politics of biography" as an apt description of the bitter struggles over Lenin's legacy that began while Lenin was still alive. The analogy is not strictly apposite, but it is useful. In the Russian context the point of the presentation of one's revolutionary biography was to prove to the party that one was with Lenin at crucial moments, followed Lenin's line always, and had been approved of by Lenin. Deviations were variously judged (and punished).

10. Walter, *Jacobins*, p. 335, cautions against the automatic assumption that those who were excluded went to the guillotine, or rather appeared before the Revolutionary Tribunal. "One should be very careful about generalizing from individual cases." Michelet insists that in Jacobin terminology *épurer* meant to guillotine (*guillotiner*) (Walter, *Jacobins*, p. 374, note 55). In the same tradition is George Masson's definition of a Jacobin in *A Supplement to Johnson's English Dictionary: Of Which the Palpable Errors Are Attempted to be Rectified, and Its Material Omissions Supplied* (London, 1801): "Jacobin: [So called from meeting at a monastery that had belonged to Jacobine Friars.] One of a faction in France that holds diabolical principles, and thinks it meritorious to murder any one, whose political opinions do not perfectly co-incide with their own. To be permitted to do this with impunity is their idea of liberty."

11. Carter, p. 223.

12. Fleischman, introduction, pp. 164–65.

13. Soboul, *Sans-culottes*, p. 221. Cobb, *Police and People*, is a brilliant critique of the view that there was an identifiable "movement" with political goals. "Our concern has been to outline what happened to the popular movement during these years, and even to question whether such a thing could be said to have existed at all" (p. 118; and pp. 118–71 passim).

14. Soboul, *Sans-culottes*, pp. 689–90.

15. The feast was held in the church of Saint-Cyr, where Fouché preached against "religious sophistry." Three days later he denounced ecclesiastical celibacy and ordered priests to adopt a child or old person. The October 10 decree is in Jaurès, VIII, 283–84, and asserts the French recognize no religion but morality, no dogma but its own sovereignty.

16. Even Couthon, Robespierre's friend and ally, while on mission in his natal province of Puy de Dôme, had indulged in some dechristianization, although he was otherwise unsympathetic to Fouché or Dumont or their friends. For a description and discussion, see Palmer, pp. 143–45.

17. *Correspondance*, p. 214. The circular is in Robespierre's hand and signed by him, along with Carnot, Couthon, Robert Lindet, C.-A. Prieur, Barère, Billaud-Varenne, Saint-André, and Collot d'Herbois. He had, a bit earlier,

drafted a letter to André Dumont, also calling for restraint (pp. 203–4). This letter, too, is in Robespierre's hand and signed by him, along with Collot d'Herbois, Carnot, and Billaud-Varenne. The opposition to dechristianization was significant on the Committee of Public Safety. "It seems to us that in your most recent activities you have struck too violently against . . . Catholic rituals. A part of France, and especially the Midi, is still fanatical. It would be wise not to provide the hypocrite counterrevolutionaries, who want to ignite civil war, with any pretext that seems to support their calumnies." It is essential to punish "seditious priests" but "not openly to proscribe the title of priests itself." In a region where patriotism is "tepid and lethargic" one should not apply "the violent remedies necessary in regions that are rebellious and counterrevolutionary." The letter concludes exhorting Dumont to strike the traitors and spare "the weak and ignorant mass."

18. Quoted from Jaurès, VIII, 288.

19. See a description in Aulard, *Culte de la raison*, pp. 52–60.

20. It rained for most of the day, not letting up until the deputies arrived back at the cathedral. Aulard, *Culte de la raison*, p. 53, note 1.

21. In his last speech he specifically attacked the atheists and defended the doctrine of the immortality of the soul. "No, Chaumette, no, death is not an eternal sleep . . . *death is the beginning of immortality*" (X, 567). The emphasis is Robespierre's.

22. Jaurès, VIII, 136. Robespierre stresses the point: "It is not for naught that the Convention proclaimed the Declaration of the Rights of Man in the presence of the Supreme Being" (X, 196).

23. Jaurès, VIII, 150: "He clearly foresaw the impatience and ambition of the Commune, he felt the intense Hébertist desire. How could he retard or moderate the disorganizers, those who, by their incessant suspicions, their continual disorder, would destroy the menaced Revolution without, at the same time, exposing to injury the very revolutionary essence, diminishing the energy and the *élan* of the people? A terrible problem. . . ."

24. Quoted from Mathiez, "Le carnet de Robespierre," p. 64.

25. See VIII, 229–41, for the session. Discussions and analyses are in Massin, p. 99, Thompson, I, 216–17, and Mathiez, *Cultes révolutionaires*, pp. 110–11.

26. "All the subtleties of metaphysics," Rousseau wrote Voltaire in answer to his Lisbon earthquake poem, "will not make me doubt for a moment the immortality of the soul or a beneficient Providence. I feel it, I believe it, I want it, I hope for it, and I should defend it to my last breath." Quoted from Gay, p. 125.

27. Published as an integral part of *Emile*, the "Profession de foi du Vicaire Savoyard" is a capital text in Rousseau's ideas on education. In his later writings he treats it as a work deserving of consideration, and in his *Rêveries*

says it was the result of "the most ardent and sincere researches on religious questions." There are two distinct parts to the "Profession de foi": the first deals with the essential principles of "natural religion," the second with a criticism of revealed religion and practical consequences. Virtually every Robespierre biographer acknowledges his subject's debt to Rousseau in religious matters. But two qualifications are necessary. So enormous was Rousseau's impact on his century that no deist and probably no one concerned with religion could be said to have remained immune. And, even aside from the ambiguities in Rousseau's religious thinking, Robespierre's religious ideas underwent considerable change in the course of the Revolution, his final expressions only partly derived from Rousseau. It would be more accurate to see Robespierre's mature religious ideas to be inspired by the chapter on the state religion in the *Contrat social* than the Savoyard Vicar.

28. Thompson, I, 217–18.

29. Levasseur, quoted from Jacob, p. 156.

30. "If one is looking through Robespierre's writings for the one that most intimately, that most profoundly reflects his thought," writes Walter, *Robespierre*, p. 399, "it is, without doubt, the report of 18 Floréal." The text of the decree is in X, 462–65. Not all, perhaps not even the majority, of his colleagues, not to mention his contemporaries generally, were similarly impressed. "The religious hypocrisy of this discourse," Bertrand Barère later wrote in his *Mémoires* II, 201), "revealed to the men of state and to observers the plan of making some kind of new revolution and of creating a crisis favorable to a transformation of power and of the Revolutionary Government."

31. The two speeches of 20 Prairial were much admired. Boissy d'Anglas wrote, some weeks later, "Robespierre, speaking of the Supreme Being to the most enlightened people in the world, reminded me of Orpheus teaching men the principles of civilization and morality." LeHarpe, "the academic judge *par excellence*, wrote to Robespierre to congratulate him." See Aulard, *Culte de la raison*, p. 317. Neither man was a friend to Robespierre.

32. Dowd, pp. 123–34. Even Michelet, usually so hostile to Robespierre on religious matters, says (II, 868): "no festival ever excited so sweet an expectation, none was ever celebrated with so much joy."

33. David had originally proposed a plan for a system of festivals on March 31, 1794, which would provide the basis for a new religion of patriotism The complete text of the artist's plan is in Buchez and Roux, XXXIII, and the *Moniteur* 20, pp. 653–56. Walter, *Robespierre*, pp. 686–87, note 19 reproduces two contemporary descriptions of the festival. There had been twenty executions on the 19th; there would be twenty-three on the 21st.

34. Joachim Vilate (or Vilatte) was a young teacher at the Collège de Limoges who became converted to Robespierre and served as an informer for the

Committee of Public Safety. After 9 Thermidor he was arrested and, despite the most craven abandonment of old ideals and friends, went to the guillotine, with the hated public prosecutor, Foquier-Tinville, in 1795. He spent 20 Prairial with Robespierre and recorded his impression in *Causes secrètes de la Révolution du 9 au 10 thermidor.* The entire text is in Buchez and Roux, XXXIII. I quote here from Aulard, *Culte de la raison*, p. 311.

35. Ben Franklin, when he heard the English minister Whitefield preach in 1739 in Philadelphia, tried to calculate how many might have been able to hear such an outdoor harangue. Here is his report (p. 119): "He had a loud and clear voice, and articulated his words and sentences so perfectly that he might be heard and understood at a great distance, especially as his auditories, however numerous, observed the most exact silence. He preached one evening from the top of the courthouse steps, which are in the middle of the Market Street and on the west side of Second Street, which crosses it at right angles. Both streets were filled with his hearers to a considerable distance. Being among the hindmost in Market Street, I had the curiosity to learn how far he could be heard by retiring backwards down the street towards the river, and I found his voice distinct till I came near Front Street, when some noise in the street obscured it. Imagining then a semicircle, of which my distance should be the radius, and that it were filled with auditors, to each of whom I allowed two square feet, I computed that he might well be heard by more than thirty thousand. This reconciled me to the newspaper accounts of his having preached to twenty-five thousand people in the fields, and to the ancient histories of generals haranguing whole armies, of which I had sometimes doubted."

36. Quoted from Soboul, *Sans-culottes*, p. 924, note 26.

37. Quoted from Jaurés, VIII, 400.

38. Courtois, p. 191. François-Louis Bourdon, called Bourdon de l'Oise to distinguish him from the more famous Léonard Bourdon, was an ambitious man who, despite these public sarcasms, survived Robespierre, who had noted in his private notebook that the quarrelsome Bourdon de l'Oise "joined perfidy to ferocity." Here is yet another bit of evidence that Robespierre was fatally tolerant of many. Bourdon got his revenge in Thermidor, becoming one of the most ferocious and malicious members of the new government, while at the same time a cynical (and successful) speculator in public funds. He later declared himself a royalist, and this political miscalculation earned him deportation to Guiana after the *coup* of 18 Fructidor.

39. Quoted from Mathiez, "Le culte de l'Etre suprême," p. 126.

40. Quoted from Mathiez, "Le culte de l'Etre suprême," p. 123.

41. The Russian revolutionary Alexander Herzen repeats this view with a slight variation, I, 153: "In the autumn of 1826 Nicholas, after hanging Pestel, Muravëv, and their friends, celebrated his coronation in Moscow. For other

sovereigns these ceremonies are occasions for amnesties and pardons Nicholas, after celebrating his apotheosis, proceeded again to 'strike down the foes of the fatherland,' like Robespierre after his *Fête-Dieu*."

42. Quoted from Mathiez, "Robespierre et le déchristianisation," pp. 343–49.

43. Hampson, *Life and Opinions*, p. 269.

44. Hampson, *Life and Opinions*, p. 273.

45. Furet, p. 168. A contrary view, argued by Lefebvre, "Sur la loi du 22 prairial," p. 129, is that the murderous law "was the last spectacular manifestation of one of the traits that dominated the revolutionary mentality since 1789." He is talking about what he calls "*la volonté punative*," the reflexive resort to violence in the face of real or imagined danger. This reflex Lefebvre traces from the Great Fear of 1789 (on which he has written the classic study) to Prairial. Although he sees Prairial as a panic of the bourgeoisie and the government, he does not sufficiently convince that this is the same panic that had earlier in the Revolution been the work of popular uprising springing from the popular mentality.

46. *Correspondance*, p. 288. See Lefebvre, "Sur la loi du 22 prairial," p. 126.

47. Soboul, *Sans-culottes*, p. 930.

48. On April 1, 1794, the Convention had decreed it could send to trial "any of its members who are strongly suspected of complicity with the enemies of liberty, equality, and republicanism."

49. Quoted from Lefebvre, "Sur la loi du 22 prairial," p. 129.

50. There is much argument designed to mitigate Robespierre's part in the law of 22 Prairial. Mathiez speaks of a "kind of feverish exaltation" he suffered, which, with the attempted assassination, caused his health to break. In other words, he sees a psychosomatic cause ("Robespierre terroriste," p. 79). But later in the same essay (p. 85) he argues that the new law was "to punish five or six corrupt and sanguinary proconsuls who had used the Terror as a weapon for their crimes." There is no reason to suppose delirium removes responsibility, nor that delirium occurred. It certainly does not flatter Robespierre to say he is not a murderer, let alone a monster, because he was out of his mind. The political part of the argument, too, has its difficulties. The existing machinery of Terror and the old law of suspects were adequate for the destruction of these proconsuls, according to Lefebvre, "Sur la loi du 22 prairial," p. 129.

51. Conservative and radical historians have both traditionally explained the Terror as popular, coming from below. Tocqueville (pp. 315–16) says the contrast between "the benign theories and the violence of the acts" is to be explained because "this revolution had been prepared by the most civilized classes of the nation and executed by the least cultivated and the rudest." It makes a nice aphorism. Many who would not like to associate themselves with Tocqueville's political views yet see the Terror in these same social terms.

52. Palmer, p. 293.
53. Saint-Just's original words are: "*La Révolution est glacée*," Soboul, *Sans-cu-lottes*, p. 918, surely had an echo in mind: "The sectional and political life had coagulated, the popular revolution was frozen."

Chapter 12

1. Trotsky, p. 142.
2. Quoted from Deymes, p. 57.
3. Godechot, *Institutions*, p. 313, who is anxious to point out that the *bureau de police* of the Committee of Public Safety, given so sinister a reputation during Thermidor, was responsible for only 250 arrests during the same period. Following Ording, he argues that Robespierre cannot be personally blamed for all these killings, or even a large number of them. Here are his conclusions on the work of the Committee of General Security during the twelve months of Montagnard dictatorship (p. 311): ". . . they had charge of all the great political *affaires*: the trial of the Girondins, of the federalists, of the case of the *Compagnie des Indes*, of the foreign plot. It was this Committee that directed the Terror and bears responsibility for having accelerated its functions after the vote on the law of 22 Prairial."
4. Cobb, *Police and People*, p. 117.
5. Greer, p. 108. The ratio of rich to poor, with adjustments made for percentages of the population, is "about two and one third to one." In June and July (p. 118) 57 percent of the victims belonged to the upper classes. The percentage of noble victims rises to 20 percent (from about 11 percent). At the same time the percentage of working-class victims shrinks from 34 to 21 percent. These figures are, in class terms although not in absolute percentages, reversed after Thermidor. When the Terror picks up again, in August 1794, it is, from the social background of its victims, directed against the lower classes.
6. Lucas, p. 89.
7. Cobban, "Political Ideas of Robespierre," p. 168, says, "At best they can hardly be regarded as more than a gesture, and even so there is nothing to associate them particularly with Robespierre. We have no reason to believe he had any more thought of economic revolution at the end than at the beginning of his political career."
8. The report, "Sur le mode d'éxécution du décret contre les ennemis de la Révolution," is in the *Moniteur* 19, p. 565, and also in *Oeuvres choisies*, pp. 205–7. The quotation is Lefebvre's, from *Questions agraires*, p. 5; and for the Saint-Just fragments, see Soboul, "Les *Institutions républicaines* d'après les manuscrits."
9. Quoted from Lefebvre, *Questions agraires*, p. 45.

10. Walter, *Jacobins*, p. 322.

11. Carter, p. 120.

12. Carter, pp. 235–36.

13. Carter, p. 287.

14. In the midst of the factional war, having envisioned the new republic (February 5/17 Pluviôse), and again during the Great Terror, shortly after proclaiming the Supreme Being, Robespierre fell silent. After participating in the Convention debates on February 10 (22 Pluviôse) he did not again speak in public until March 13 (at the Jacobins), and not again at the Convention until March 15 (25 Pluviôse). He then resumed his normal, remarkable level of activity for the remainder of March and till about mid-April. He spoke to the Convention on April 18 (29 Germinal) but did not again speak there, or anywhere, until May 7 (18 Floréal). He was again silent for more than a week (May 7/18 Floréal to May 15/26 Floréal) before he appeared at the Jacobins. There was another silence lasting until May 25 (6 Prairial), another from May 27 to June 8 (8 Prairial to 20 Prairial), during which he was probably preparing the great speech on the Supreme Being. From June 12 (24 Prairial) to June 21 (3 Messidor) he was silent, and although he was at the Jacobins from June 21 to July 24 (3 Messidor to 6 Thermidor) he did not speak in the Convention from June 12 till July 26 (24 Prairial to 8 Thermidor). Throughout this period he was more silent than not. The voice of the Revolution was seldom heard in these crucial months, and only on two occasions (February 5/17 Pluviôse and June 8/20 Prairial) was his voice heard with its familiar prophetic tone, explaining the Revolution, revealing himself. The rest of the time his utterances, mostly in the form of short interjections at the Jacobins, were concerned with denunciations, the ongoing purification of the Mountain.

15. See Hampson, *Will and Circumstance*, pp. 237, 239, and Cobb, "Robespierre and the Year II," p. 63.

16. The phrase is Isaiah Berlin's, from his characterization of Tolstoy in old age, p. 82.

17. Hampson, *Will and Circumstance*, p. 243, thinks this is the "key" to the speech.

18. Quoted from Mathiez, *Vie chère*, p. 414.

19. "It is difficult to imagine," writes Palmer, p. 132, "the effect produced in 1793 [or 1794] by the phrase "Representative of the People." Neither word today sends a thrill through anyone's spine. Both words were then alive with emotions of a new belief. A Representative of the People, for Frenchmen of the First Republic, was the most august being that could exist on earth."

20. X, 555. The passage has an interest beyond its meaning. The passage quoted is crossed out by him and subsequently inserted two paragraphs later in a slightly different version: "Who am I, me whom they accuse? A slave of

liberty, a living martyr of the republic, the victim as much as the enemy of crime. All the scoundrels outrage me; the most indifferent actions, the most legitimate, when performed by others, are crimes for me. A man is calumniated as soon as he knows me. Others are forgiven their faults; they make my zeal a crime" (X, 556). My own feeling is that in rewriting this revealing passage, Robespierre sacrificed some of the energy of his first version to achieve more pathos. I like the discarded version better, although it whines.

21. I translate in order to maintain the linkage between *répresentant du peuple* and speech. Here is the original: "Un répresentant du peuple ne peut se laisser dépouiller du droit de défendre les intérêts du peuple; nulle puissance ne peut le lui enlever, qu'en lui arrachant la vie."

22. Aulard, *Orateurs*, p. 291.

23. The same sentiment, expressed a bit differently, is at X, 574.

24. X, 561, note 20. The italics are in the original.

25. *Au peuple de l'Artois par un habitant de la province*, attributed to Robespierre by Hamel, I, 76, from whence I quote.

26. Quoted from Paris, p. 415.

27. His refusal to name the conspirators referred to is generally considered his chief blunder, the assumption being that he could have thus rallied the majority of the Convention to his cause while at the same time eliminating his enemies. For a discussion of this traditional view, see Thompson, II, 250–51. The most recent study of 9 Thermidor, Walter, *Thermidor*, has a useful collection of documents, including some contemporary impressions, pp. 373–440, as well as a survey of the reactions, or lack thereof, of the sections. For a brilliant analysis of the curious significance of the day in revolutionary historiography, see Furet, pp. 84–85.

28. The split between the two committees was long-standing, and according to Lefebvre, *Questions agraires*, p. 53, the coalition that would eventually destroy Robespierre could be discerned already in late March 1794.

29. See Walter, *Thermidor*, p. 154, and Soboul, *Sans-culottes*, p. 1012.

30. Quoted from Palmer, p. 184.

31. Even at the end of his life there is vexation over what happened, as well as what it means. The question is whether or not Robespierre attempted suicide or was shot by a certain Sergeant Méda, who burst into the room with the armed troops sent by the Convention. For a survey of the evidence, see Deville Sainte-Claire, pp. 295–97. Jaurès has him wounded by Méda; Mathiez insists on an attempted suicide; Ratignaud has him wounded. Palmer attempts a compromise: he has Méda fire at almost exactly the moment Robespierre did, so that in insisting he had wounded the tyrant, he genuinely believed it to be true. The modern consensus, including most recently Hampson, *Life and Opinions*, is for suicide. For some there is a political or moral issue involved: suicide would be the stoic

response and a fit end for a republican. As with much else in Robespierre's life and career, the ambiguity of the evidence calls for interpretation, which means views and values drawn from sources outside the history of the French Revolution.

32. Quoted from Palmer, p. 379

33. The details of what happened are from *Faits recueillis aux derniers instants de Robespierre et de sa faction, du 9 au 10 thermidor.*

Chapter 13

1. Quoted from Walter, *Robespierre*, p. 590.

2. Antoine Furetière's *Dictionnaire universal* (1690) says: "Incorruptible, used figuratively in moral matters. A good judge ought to be *incorruptible*, a subject ought to have *incorruptible* devotion." *Le Robert* says the word was first used in this figurative way in the seventeenth century and meant "He who is incapable of allowing himself to be corrupted, seduced, to act against his duty." The examples are *fonctionnaire* and *juge incorruptible*. Larousse, *Grand dictionnaire universel de XIXe siècle* retains these earlier meanings, and is virtually identical to the *Robert* definition. The word has the same meaning in English, and the *Oxford English Dictionary* cites Milton's *Paradise Lost*, published in 1667, as its seventeenth-century authority. "Incapable of being morally corrupted; that cannot be perverted or bribed," is the definition there given. The application to Robespierre is first made in English by Carlyle, in 1837.

3. Quoted from Gallo, p. 88. Lefetz's letter was found among Robespierre's papers.

4. This is the earliest such usage found by Walter, *Robespierre* (def. ed.), II, 358. On the *Journal Général*, see Godechot, et al., pp. 466–67 where the newspaper is described as somewhat moderate in tone but violent in content and virulently anti-Jacobin.

5. Walter, *Robespierre* (def. ed.), II, 357–58.

6. Walter, *Robespierre* (def. ed.), II, 365.

7. Walter, *Robespierre* (def. ed.), II, 355.

8. This well-known portrait hangs in the Carnavalet Museum in Paris. There is a reproduction in the catalogue for the exhibition held at the Grand Palais in Paris, November 16, 1974–February 3, 1975, which subsequently appeared in Detroit and New York. See the catalogue, *French Painting, 1774–1830: The Age of Revolution.*

9. According to Hamel, I, 559, note 1, "to which, said a critic of the period, 'the good patriots applauded with all their heart.'" Hamel is here quoting *Les Révolutions de Paris*, no. 119. He does not otherwise describe the painting.

10. The vanished pastel was copied by Pierre-Roch Vigneron and engraved by Pajeut. There is an oil, now in a private collection, and it is speculated the artist copied it from the pastel, for she often worked in this way. See a discussion by Pierre Rosenberg, one of the organizers of the exhibition mentioned in note 8, in the catalogue, pp. 518-9. It is from this source that I reproduce this portrait. It is regrettable that Robespierre's friend and comrade David never did his portrait.

11. Hamel, I, 559. Here is a rough translation:

    Superb to the redoubtable oppressor
    Incorruptible friend of the people under attack
    He causes to shine in the midst of vile factions
    The virtues of Aristide and the soul of the Catos.

12. Thompson, I, 174, following *Les Révolutions de Paris*, no. 116, which has a long description of the scene. Hamel, I, 559, following the same source, adds the cry *Voilà les véritables amis du peuple, les législateurs incorruptibles! (There are the true friends of the people, the incorruptible legislators.)* Rudé, p. 25, is less circumstantial and adds, vaguely, "He had already won the title of 'Incorruptible': it was a tribute both to the 'purity' of his principles and to his modest way of living and to his refusal to accept financial rewards (he was living on an annual income of about 600 livres at the time)." This is about two to three times the wages of a domestic servant.

13. Thompson, I, 165-66, quoting Aulard, *Société des Jacobins*, III, 364.

14. Walter stresses this convention by titling chapters and subdivisions of chapters "Robespierre contre Duport," "Robespierre contre Barnave," "Rupture avec Mirabeau," which follows the tradition established by Hamel. Thompson, on the other hand, arranges his biography by subject rather than personal confrontation. In general, and there are notable exceptions, the French follow Hamel, the English Thompson.

15. Michelet, I, 567.

16. Walter, *Robespierre* (def. ed.), II, 351, 352, quotes two bits of testimony from 1794, from foreign observers. The first is from W. A. Miles, Pitt's correspondant, the second from Mallet du Pan, the Swiss journalist. "I believe Robespierre incorruptible," writes Mills on January 5, "but he appears vindictive and little inclined to avoid bloodshed." "He hasn't an *ecu*," writes Mallet du Pan in March. "His incorruptibility contrasts with the graft of his associates." It is worth noting that Brissot, among Robespierre's competitors, was similarly above suspicion, but his honesty was never a significant political detail for him or his friends or his faction.

17. On the sale of Robespierre's personal property after his death—and it would then have fetched a higher price as a collector's macabre item—see documents of the auction of three coats left behind by Robespierre and his brother. They brought 855 livres.

18. Quoted from Gottschalk, p. 178.

19. Furet, p. 82.

20. Quoted from Jacob, p. 157. This Montagnard, who was no friend of Robespierre, argues (p. 155) that the Terror was a policy of circumstance and not men's will. "And above all, concerning all the excesses that created demoralization, one simply should no longer maintain they were part of Robespierre's strategy, because he constantly opposed these excesses and their authors were his cruelest enemies."

21. Hampson, *Will and Circumstance*, p. 31.

22. "The political life of a Robespierre, a Saint-Just," says Trahard, p. 12, "is consequently little more than an uninterrupted act of will." The Constituent meeting of June 21, 1791 (to consider what to do about the fled King), lasted twenty-one hours, at which time the session was suspended to permit the deputies "to take some nourishment and to sleep for a couple of hours on the benches" (Trahard, p. 102). The Convention session of January 16–17, 1793, at which the voting on the King's punishment was taken, lasted even longer.

23. Quoted from Walter, *Thermidor*, p. 75.

24. Quoted from Cobban, "Political Ideas of Robespierre," p. 172.

25. Trahard, p. 46.

26. Trahard, p. 20.

27. Aulard, *Orateurs*, p. 237, provides the classic statement of this view, seeing a strong religious side to Robespierre's appeal: "However, by a mystical eloquence, each day more grave and measured, he exercised a religious influence over souls and marched to sovereign power." This quality, this quasi-religious aspect, was remarked by contemporaries, and always with disapproval. *La Chronique de Paris* asked why there were "so many women attached to Robespierre, at his home, at the tribune of the Jacobins, at the Cordeliers, at the Convention? Is it because the French Revolution is a religion and Robespierre a cult? Is he a priest with his devotees? Whatever the case it is obvious that all his power come from the distaff." Quoted from Jacob, p. 126. Michelet takes up this impression and gives it brilliant expression in his perverse portrait of Robespierre as the high priest of the Revolution. See Goutor, pp. 58–76, for a discussion.

28. Michelet, I, 566, Cassat *ainé*, among others, remarked that this proved part of his downfall (quoted from Walter, *Thermidor*, p. 427): "He ceased to be the man of the Revolution and became only the man of his faction."

29. Quoted from Walter, *Robespierre*, p. 376.

30. Quoted from Lefebvre, "Sur la loi du 22 prairial," p. 115.

31. Quoted from Thompson, I, 113–14.

32. Quoted from Walter, *Robespierre*, p. 464.

33. Quoted from Walter, *Thermidor*, pp. 470–71.

34. Quoted from Thompson, I, 142–43. See the entry for this fascinating man in the *Dictionary of National Biography*, XXXVII, 379. Miles's "nothing of the volatility of a Frenchman in his character" is a curious addition to the mosaic portrait of Robespierre. It may be a variation on the adage that France begins at the Loire River and northerners, Robespierre included, are somehow not characteristically French. Aulard, *Orateurs*, p. 296, is the only scholarly historian I know who takes the view that Robespierre is un-French, and his expression of this attitude is informed by well-known hostility to Robespierre: "I have already said, what strikes me about Robespierre, what is disconcerting, is that he is of another race than the other French statesmen. One will find, I think, in the series of our remarkable political men—and I cite at random Henry IV, Richelieu, Danton, Napoleon himself (who knew how to make himself French)—one will find, I say, fundamental resemblances; a clarity of thought, little imagination, the taste and gift for action. Robespierre, who governed France by persuasion, was, on the contrary, a mystic, and passive. I find this same anti-French temperament in the oratorical style of the pontif of the Supreme Being."

35. Quoted from Walter, *Thermidor*, p. 425.

36. Jaurès, VIII, 243–44.

37. Quoted from Mathiez, "Robespierre, l'histoire et la légendre," p. 31.

List of Works Cited

Actes du colloque Robespierre (Paris, 1967).

Aulard, Alphonse, *Le culte de la raison et le culte de l'Etre suprême (1793–1794)*, 3d ed. (Paris, 1909).

―――, *Les grands orateurs de la Révolution* (Paris, 1914).

―――, *La Société des Jacobins: Recueil de documents*, 6 vols. (Paris, 1889–97).

Baker, Keith Michael, "On the Problem of the Ideological Origins of the French Revolution," in Dominick La Capra and Steven L. Kaplan, eds., *Modern European Intellectual History: Reappraisals and New Perspectives* (Ithaca, 1982).

Barbier, Victor, and Vellay, Charles, eds., *Oeuvres complètes de Maximilien Robespierre*, vol. 1 (Paris, 1910).

Barère, Bertrand, *Mémoires*, 4 vols. (Paris, 1842–44).

Baudot, M. A., *Notes sur la Convention nationale* (Paris, 1893).

Berlin, Isaiah, *The Hedgehog and the Fox* (New York, 1953).

Berville and Barrière, eds., *Papiers inédits trouvée chez Robespierre, Saint-Just, Payan, etc.*, 3 vols. (Paris, 1828).

Bouloiseau, Marc, *Robespierre* (Paris, 1957).

Brinton, Crane, *The Jacobins: An Essay in the New History* (Cambridge, 1930; republished 1961).

Brunot, Ferdinand, *Histoire de la langue française, des origines à nos jours: La Révolution et l'Empire*, vol. 9 (part 2) (Paris, 1967).

Buchez and Roux, eds., *Histoire parlementaire de la Révolution française, ou journal des Assemblées nationales, depuis 1789 jusqu'en 1815. . .* 40 vols. (Paris, 1834–38).

Buffenoir, Hippolyte, *Les portraits de Robespierre* (Paris, 1910).

Caron, Pierre, *Les massacres de septembre* (Paris, 1935).

Carter, Michael Phillip, *A Study in Terror: The Jacobin Club of Paris in the Year II* (unpublished manuscript).

Champion, E., *Rousseau et la Révolution française* (Paris, 1909).

Choudieu, Pierre-René, *Mémoires et notes*, publiés . . . par V. Barrucand (Paris, 1897).

Cobb, Richard C., *The Police and the People: French Popular Protest, 1789–1820* (Oxford, 1970).

————, "Robespierre," in *Tour de France* (London, 1976).

————, "Robespierre and the Year II," in *Tour de France* (London, 1976).

Cobban, Alfred, "The Fundamental Ideas of Robespierre," in *Aspects of the French Revolution* (New York, 1968).

————, "The Political Ideas of Maximilien Robespierre during the period of the Convention," in *Aspects of the French Revolution* (New York, 1968).

Cornette, André, "Arras et sa banliue, étude d'une evolution urbaine," *Revue du Nord* 42 (July–August, 1960).

Courtois, E. B., *Rapport fait au nom de la commission chargée de l'examen des papiers trouvés chez Robespierre et ses complices* (Paris, 1795).

Darnton, Robert, "The High Enlightenment and the Low Life of Literature in Prerevolutionary France," *Past and Present* 51, (May 1971).

Deslandres, Maurice Charles, *Histoire constitutionelle de la France de 1789 à 1870*, 2 vols (Paris, 1932–37).

Deymes, J., *Les doctrines politiques de Robespierre* (Bordeaux, 1907).

Dowd, David Lloyd, *Pageant-Master of the Republic: Jacques-Louis David and the French Revolution* (Lincoln, 1948).

Dumont, Etienne, *Souvenirs sur Mirabeau et sur les deux premières Assemblées législatives* (Brussels, 1832).

Dupont-Ferrier, Gustave, *Du collège de Clermont au lycée Louis-le-Grand, 1563–1920*, 3 vols. (Paris, 1921–25).

Fleischman, Hector, *Charlotte Robespierre et ses Mémoires* (Paris, n.d.).

France, Anatole, *Les dieux ont soif* (Livre de Poche, Paris, 1968).

Franklin, Benjamin, *The Autobiography and Other Writings* (Signet: New York, 1961).

Furet, François, *Penser la Révolution française* (Paris, 1978).

Gallo, Max, *Robespierre, histoire d'une solitude* (Livre de Poche, Paris, 1968).

Garmy, René, "Aux origines de la légende anti-robespierriste: Pierre Villiers et Robespierre," in *Actes du colloque Robespierre* (Paris, 1967).

Gay, Peter, "The Unity of the French Enlightenment," in *The Party of Humanity* (New York, 1964).

Godechot, Jacques, "L'Historiographie française de Robespierre," in *Actes du colloque Robespierre* (Paris, 1967).

————, *Les institutions de la France sous la Révolution et l'Empire*, 2d ed. (Paris, 1968).

————, *Un jury pour la Révolution* (Paris, 1974).

————, et al., *Histoire générale de la presse française: Des origines à 1814* (Paris, 1969).

Gottschalk, Louis R., *Jean Paul Marat: A Study in Radicalism* (Chicago, 1927; republished 1967).

Goutor, Jacques Roger, "*Robespierre and the French Historians*" (unpublished Ph.D. dissertation, Urbana, 1960).

Greer, Donald, *The Incidence of the Terror during the French Revolution* (Cambridge, 1935; republished 1966).

Guérin, Daniel, *La lutte de classes sous la première République: Bourgeois et "bras-nus,"* 2 vols. (Paris, 1946).

Gusdorf, Georges, *Découverte de soi* (Paris, 1948).

Hamel, Ernest, *Histoire de Robespierre*, 3 vols., (Paris, 1865–67).

Hampson, Norman, *The Life and Opinions of Maximilien Robespierre* (London, 1974).

————, *Will and Circumstance: Montesquieu, Rousseau and the French Revolution* (Norman, 1983).

Hardman, John, ed., *French Revolution Documents, 1792–95* (Oxford, 1973).

Herzen, Alexander, *My Past and Thoughts: The Memoirs of Alexander Herzen*, translated by Constance Garnett, revised by Humphrey Higgens, 4 vols. (New York, 1968).

Jacob, Louis, *Robespierre vu par ses contemporains* (Paris, 1938).

Jaurès, Jean, *Histoire socialiste de la Révolution française*, édition revue par A. Mathiez, 8 vols. (Paris, 1922–24).

Kelly, George Armstrong, *Victims, Authority, and Terror: The Parallel Deaths of d'Orléans, Custine, Bailly, and Malesherbes* (Chapel Hill, 1982).

Kennedy, Michael L., *The Jacobin Clubs in the French Revolution: The First Years* (Princeton, 1982).

Lanson, Gustav, *Histoire de la littérature française*, remaniée et complétée pour la periode 1850–1950 par Paul Tuffrau (Paris, 1951).

La Reveillière-Lépeaux, Louis-Marie, *Mémoirs*, 3 vols. (Paris, 1895).

Lefebvre, Georges, "Discours sur Robespierre," *Annales historiques de la Révolution française* 10 (1933).

————, "Etudes sur le ministère de Narbonne," *Annales historiques de la Révolution française* 19 (1947).

————, *Questions agraires au temps de la terreur*, documents publiés et annotés par Georges Lefebvre (Strasbourg, 1932).

————, *La Révolution française*, 6th ed. (Paris, 1968).

————, "Sur la loi du 22 prairial," in *Etudes sur la Révolution française* (Paris, 1963).

Lenôtre, G., *Robespierre et la Mère de Dieu* (Paris, 1926).

Levasseur, René, *Mémoires*, 4 vols. (Paris, 1829–31).

Lockroy, Edouard, ed., *Journal d'une bourgeoise pendant la Révolution* (Paris, 1881).

Louvet, Jean-Baptiste, *Histoire pittoresque de la Convention nationale* (Paris, n.d.).

Lucas, Colin, *The Structure of the Terror: The Example of Javogues and the Loire* (Oxford, 1973).

McDonald, Joan, *Rousseau and the French Revolution, 1762–1791* (London, 1965).

McNeil, Gordon H., "The Cult of Rousseau and the French Revolution," *Journal of the History of Ideas* 6, no. 2 (April, 1945).

Macpherson, C. B., *The Real World of Democracy* (Toronto, 1965).

Massin, Jean, *Robespierre* (Paris, 1956).

Mathiez, Albert, "Babeuf et Robespierre," in *Etudes sur Robespierre* (Paris, 1973).

————, "Le carnet de Robespierre," in *Robespierre terroriste* (Paris, 1921).

————, "Le culte de l'Etre suprême," in *Autour de Robespierre*.

————, *Les origines de cultes révolutionnaires (1789–1792)* (Paris, 1904).

————, "La politique de Robespierre et le 9 thermidor expliqué par Buonarroti," in *Etudes sur Robespierre*.

————, "La popularité de Robespierre en 1791," *Annales révolutionnaires*, 1 (1908).

————, "Robespierre, l'histoire et la légende," *Annales historiques de la Révolution Française* 49 (1977).

————, Robespierre et le déchristianisation," *Annales révolutionnaires* 2 (1909).

————, "Robespierre terroriste," in *Etudes sur Robespierre* (Paris, 1973).

————, *La vie chère et le mouvement social sous la Terreur* (Paris, 1927; republished 1973).

Matrat, Jean, *Robespierre, or the Tyranny of the Majority*, trans. Alan Kendall, with Felix Brenner (New York, 1971).

Maugras, Gaston, ed., *Journal d'un étudiant pendant la Révolution*, 2d ed. (Paris, 1890).

Mercier, Sébastien, *De J. J. Rousseau, considéré comme l'un des premiers auteurs de la Révolution*, 2 vols. (Paris, 1791).

————, *Tableau de Paris* (Amsterdam, 1792).

Michelet, Jules, *Histoire de la Révolution française*, édition établie et annotée par Gérard Walter, 2 vols. (Pléiade, Paris, 1952)

Michon, Georges, *Robespierre et la guerre révolutionnaire, 1791–1792* (Paris, 1937).

Montesquieu (Charles Louis de Secondat), *Oeuvres complètes*, 2 vols. (Pléiade, Paris, 1951).

Montjoye, Galart de, *Histoire de la conjuration de Maximilien Robespierre* (Paris, 1796).

Morris, Gouverneur, *The Diary and Letters of Gouverneur Morris*, ed. Anne Cary Morris, 2 vols. (New York, 1888).

Ording, M. A., *Le bureau de police du Comité du salut public* (Oslo, 1930).

Palmer, R. R., *The School of the French Revolution: A Documentary History of the College of Louis-le-Grand and Its Director, Jean-François Champagne, 1762–1814* (Princeton, 1975).

————, *Twelve Who Ruled* (Princeton, 1941).

Paris, J.-A., *La jeunesse de Robespierre et la convocation des Etats-généraux en Artois* (Arras, 1870).

Parker, Harold T., *The Cult of Antiquity and the French Revolutionaries: A Study in the Development of the Revolutionary Spirit* (Chicago, 1937).

Patrick, Alison, *The Men of the First French Republic: Political Alignments in the National Convention of 1792* (Baltimore, 1972).

Proyart, Abbé [Le Blond de Neuvéglise], *La vie et les crimes de Maximilien Robespierre* (Augsburg, 1795).

Ratinaud, Jean, *Robespierre* (Paris, 1960).

Reinhard, Marcel, *Le Grand Carnot: de l'ingénieur au conventionnel, 1753–1792* (Paris, 1950).

Revault d'Allonnes, M., "Rousseau et le Jacobinisme: Pedagogie et Politique," *Annales historiques de la Révolution française* 50 (1978).

Robespierre, Maximilien, *Correspondance de Maximilien et Augustin Robespierre*, recueillie et publiée par Georges Michon (Paris, 1926).

————, *Oeuvres complètes*, 10 vols. (Paris, 1903–68).

Roederer, P.-L., *Chronique de cinquante jours: Du 20 juin au 10 août 1792* (Paris, 1832).

Rousseau, Jean-Jacques, *Oeuvres complètes*, 5 vols. (Pléiade: Paris, 1958–69).

Rudé, George, *The Crowd in the French Revolution* (London, 1958).

————, *Robespierre, Portrait of a Revolutionary Democrat* (New York, 1976).

Sacks, Oliver, *Migraine, The Evolution of a Common Disorder* (Berkeley, 1973).

Sagnac, Philippe, *La Révolution du 10 août: La chute de la royauté* (Paris, 1909).

Saint-Just, *Oeuvres choisies* (Paris, 1968).

Sainte-Claire Deville, P., *La Commune de l'an II* (Paris, 1946).

Shulim, Joseph I., "The Youthful Robespierre and His Ambivalence towards the Ancien Régime," *Eighteenth Century Studies* 5, no. 3 (Spring 1972).

Soboul, Albert, *Histoire de la Révolution française*, 2 vols. (Paris, 1962; republished 1968).

————, "Les *Institutions républicaines* d'après les manuscrits," *Annales historiques de la Révolution française* 111 (1948).

————, "Robespierre ou les contradictions du Jacobinisme," *Annales historiques de la Révolution française* 50 (1978).

————, *Les sans-culottes parisiens en l'an II* (Paris, 1958).

Staël, Madame de, *Oeuvres complètes de Mme. la Baronne de Stael*, 17 vols. (Paris, 1830–21).

Steegmuller, Francis, *Cocteau, A Biography* (Boston, 1976).

Stéphan-Pol, *Autour de Robespierre: Le conventionnel Le Bas* (Paris, n.d.).

Sydenham, M. J., *The French Revolution* (New York, 1965).

————, *The Girondins* (London, 1961).

Thompson, J. M., *The French Revolution* (London, 1946; republished 1966).

————, *Robespierre*, 2 vols. (Oxford, 1935).

Tocqueville, Alexis de, *L'Ancien régime et la Révolution*, 8th ed. (Paris, 1877).

Trahard, Pierre, *La sensibilité révolutionnaire (1789–1794)* (Paris, 1936; republished 1867).

Trotsky, Leon, *1905*, trans. Anya Bostock (New York, 1972).

Tucker, Robert C., *Stalin as Revolutionary, 1879–1929: A Study in History and Personality* (New York, 1973).

Vellay, Charles, "Robespierre et le procès de paratonnerre," *Annales révolutionnaires* 2 (1909).

Vellay, Charles, and Barbier, Victor, eds., *Oeuvres complètes de Maximilien Robespierre*, vol. 1 (Paris, 1910).

Villiers, Pierre, *Souvenirs d'un déporté . . .* (Paris, 1802).

Walter, Gérard, *La Conjuration du neuf thermidor* (Paris, 1974).

————, *Histoire des Jacobins* (Paris, 1946).

————, *Robespierre*, 2d ed. (Paris, 1946).

————, *Robespierre*, definitive edition, 2 vols. (Paris, 1961).

Wolfe, Bertram D., *Three Who Made a Revolution* (New York, 1948).

Index